Cultural Geography in Practice

Edited by

Alison Blunt

Pyrs Gruffudd

Jon May

Miles Ogborn

David Pinder

First published in Great Britain in 2003 by
Hodder Education, part of Hachette Livre UK,
338 Euston Road, London NW1 3BH

http://www.hoddereducation.com

The advice and information in this book are believed to be true and
accurate at the date of going to press, but neither the editors nor the publisher
can accept any legal responsibility or liability for any errors or omissions.

British Library Cataloguing in Publication Data
A catalogue record for this book is available from the British Library

Library of Congress Cataloging-in-Publication Data
A catalog record for this book is available from the Library of Congress

ISBN 978 0 340 80770 5

Typeset in 10/14 Humanist Light by Tech-Set, Gateshead

If you have any comments to make about this, or any other of our
titles, please send them to educationenquiries@hodder.co.uk

Contents

List of contributors

Les Back is Reader in Sociology at Goldsmiths College, London. Previous books include *Out of Whiteness* with Vron Ware (University of Chicago Press, 2002) and *The Changing Face of Football* with Tim Crabbe and John Solomos (Berg, 2001).

Alison Blunt is a Lecturer in Geography at Queen Mary, University of London. Her research interests include geographies of home and identity, cultures of imperial travel and domesticity, and feminist and postcolonial geographies. She is author of *Travel, Gender, and Imperialism: Mary Kingsley and West Africa* (Guilford, 1994), co-author (with Jane Wills) of *Dissident Geographies: an Introduction to Radical Ideas and Practice* (Prentice Hall, 2000), co-editor (with Gillian Rose) of *Writing Women and Space: Colonial and Postcolonial Geographies* (Guilford, 1994), and co-editor (with Cheryl McEwan) of *Postcolonial Geographies* (Continuum, 2002). She is currently writing a book on Anglo-Indian women and the spatial politics of home in India, Britain and Australia.

Maria Helena Braga e Vaz da Costa was awarded a doctorate from the University of Sussex in December 2000 for a thesis entitled *Cities in Motion: Towards an Understanding of the Cinematic City* from which she has published widely. She currently teaches cultural geography in the Arts Department at the Federal University of Brazil, Rio de Janeiro (UFRN).

Mike Crang is a Lecturer in Geography at the University of Durham. He has worked on themes of qualitative methods, social memory, tourism and informational space. He wrote *Cultural Geography* (Routledge, 1998), and co-edited *Virtual Geographies* with Jon May and Phil Crang, (Routledge, 1999), *Thinking Space* with Nigel Thrift (Routledge, 2000) and *Tourism: Between Place and Performance* with Simon Coleman (Berghahn, 2002).

Gail Davies is a Lecturer in Cultural Geography at University College London. She is interested in the hybrid spaces of science, nature and the media. She is currently working on a public engagement process of exploring future options for organ transplantation, including xenotransplantation. Her previous research has looked at the contested wildlife value of brownfield sites, and the development of natural history filmmaking.

Mona Domosh is a Professor of Geography at Dartmouth College. She is the co-author (with Joni Seager) of *Putting Women in Place: Feminist Geographies Make Sense of the World* (Guilford, 2001) and author of *Invented Cities: The Creation of Landscape in Nineteenth-century New York and Boston* (Yale University Press, 1996). Her current research project investigates the connections between gender, 'race,' and commodities in the making of an American commercial empire.

Pyrs Gruffudd is Senior Lecturer in Human Geography at University of Wales at Swansea. His earlier work was on landscape and national identity in inter-war Wales but more recently he has been researching the relationship between modern architecture, planning and health. He is currently working on the idea of 'national natures,' including a project on 'Big Cat' sightings in Wales.

Tim Hall is an urban geographer based at the University of Gloucestershire. His interests include cultural representations of urban change and regeneration, and the employment of public art within urban regeneration. He is the author of *Urban Geography* (Routledge, 1998/2001) and co-editor of *The Entrepreneurial City: Geographies of Politics, Regime and Representation* (Wiley, 1998); *The City Cultures Reader* (Routledge, 2000) and *Urban Futures: Critical Commentaries on Shaping the City* (Routledge, 2003).

Susan Hanson is Landry University Professor of Geography and Director of the School of Geography at Clark University. Her research interests include feminism, daily travel-activity patterns in cities, and urban labour markets. She is currently working on a study of gender, geography and entrepreneurship. Her publications include *Gender, Work, and Space* (with Geraldine Pratt, Routledge, 1995), *Ten Geographic Ideas that Changed the World* (Rutgers University Press, 1997), and *The Geography of Urban Transportation* (Guilford, 1995, 2nd edition).

Lynda Johnston is a Senior Lecturer in the Geography Department, University of Waikato, Aotearoa/New Zealand. Her research interests include feminism and poststructuralism, gender, sexuality and embodiment, tourism and subjectivities, methodologies, constructions of geographical knowledge, and cultural geographies. She has recently co-authored a book entitled *Subjectivities, Knowledges and Feminist Geographies: the Subjects and Ethics of Social Research* (Rowman and Littlefield, 2002).

James Kneale is a Lecturer in Human Geography at University College London. His interests in cultural and historical geography include popular fiction and spaces of drink. He co-edited *Lost In Space: Geographies of Science Fiction* with Rob Kitchin (Continuum, 2002) and has published several pieces on William Gibson.

Jon May is a Lecturer in Geography at Queen Mary, University of London where he teaches social and cultural geography. He has published widely on the geographies of homelessness and is the co-editor of two previous volumes: *Virtual Geographies* with Mike and Phil Crang (Routledge, 1999) and *TimeSpace: Geographies of Temporality* with Nigel Thrift (Routledge, 2001).

Miles Ogborn is Reader in Geography at Queen Mary, University of London. He has undertaken archival work on nineteenth-century social policy, eighteenth-century London and seventeenth-century globalisation. He is the author of *Spaces of Modernity: London's Geographies, 1680–1780* (Guilford, 1998) and teaches courses on cultural geography and on global historical geography. He is currently researching the English East India Company.

Hester Parr is a Lecturer in Human Geography at the Department of Geography, University of Dundee, where she teaches social geography. She has a long-standing interest in the geographies of mental health and is currently researching mental health experiences in remote rural communities in the Scottish Highlands. More recently she has turned her attention to the virtual geographies of health and illness, with a particular focus on how self-help is configured on the Internet. She is the co-editor of *Mind and Body Spaces: Geographies of Illness, Impairment and Disability* with Ruth Butler (Routledge, 1999).

David Pinder is Lecturer in Geography at Queen Mary, University of London. His research focuses on urbanism and the cultural politics of urban space, and on social theories of modernity, space and the city. He has particular interests in the urban visions of modernist and avant-garde movements, and he is the author of *Visions of the City: Utopianism, Power and Politics in Twentieth-Century Urbanism* (Edinburgh University Press, forthcoming).

Geraldine Pratt is Professor of Geography at the University of British Columbia. Her research interests include gender, racialisation and work; multiculturalism and citizenship; and film and performance studies. Her publications include *Gender, Work, and Space* with Susan Hanson (Routledge, 1995), *Working Feminism* (Edinburgh University Press, forthcoming), and articles on film and theatrical performance in *Screen* and *ACME.*

Joan M. Schwartz is an historical geographer and now Queen's National Scholar / Associate Professor in the Department of Art, Queen's University, Kingston, where she teaches courses in the history of photography and society. From 1977 to 2003 she was a specialist in photography acquisition and research at the National Archives of Canada, Ottawa. She is co-editor (with James R. Ryan) of *Picturing Place: Photography and the Geographical Imagination* (IB Tauris, 2003). She is currently pursuing research on the role of photography in society and on the relationship between archives, national identity, and collective memory, for a book on photography in the making of early modern Canada.

Rachel Silvey is Assistant Professor in the Department of Geography, University of Colorado. Her research interests include gender and feminist geography, migration studies, social activism, critical development studies, and Indonesia. Her publications have appeared in the *Annals of the Association of American Geographers*, *Political Geography*, *Gender, Place, and Culture*, and *World Development*, among other outlets.

Acknowledgements

The editors would like to thank Liz Gooster, Lesley Riddle, Tiara Misquitta and Colin Goodlad at Hodder Arnold for their help in putting this book together. We would also like to thank all those who contributed their 'Tales of Research' to this book, giving it an extra dimension. Alison, David, Jon and Miles would like to acknowledge the students – especially on the Masters in *Cities and Cultures* at Queen Mary, University of London – with whom many of these ideas have been tried out. We would also like to thank Edward Oliver for drawing Figures 1.2 and 6.1, and for his technical expertise. Miles Ogborn's work on this project was funded by the Leverhulme Trust via a Philip Leverhulme Prize.

Tales of research

Concept boxes

List of figures

List of tables

Introduction

Cultural Geography in Practice

Alison Blunt, Pyrs Gruffudd, Jon May, Miles Ogborn and David Pinder

Take another look at the cover of this book. How might you understand the picture shown there? How might you do research in cultural geography on this source or piece of evidence, which the back cover tells you is an artwork called *West Meets East* produced by an artist called Lorraine Leeson and something called 'The Art of Change'? In fact, the cover only shows you part of *West Meets East* which combines both words and images, a photograph and what looks like embroidery (see Figure 0.1). When you know that its aim is to provide a representation of the cultural experience of young Bengali women in London you might try to understand its visual and textual signs and symbols in these terms. What we see is a woman stitching together different materials – blue denim and red silk – associated with 'West' and 'East'. The woman's henna-patterned hands and bracelets suggest the pleasures of celebrations, while the sewing machine's associations are with the sort of poorly-paid work that many Bengali women in Britain do at home or in small factories. The central picture is surrounded by words in both Bengali and English (including the word 'bilingual') denoting things which are significant in these women's lives – community, religion, music, friendship, dance, fashion – and various small embroidered images. These draw on conventions of representation from Bengali cultural traditions and from 'Western' advertising and mass media – Coca Cola, McDonalds, and a footballer in the bottom right-hand corner. Understanding these representations might mean looking at traditions of cloth production, at different conventions of art, music and material culture, at adverts (in all sorts of media), or at representations on film or in literature. For example, you might understand *West Meets East* alongside films like *Bend It Like Beckham* (Gurinder Chadha, 2002), *Mississippi Masala* (Mira Nair, 1992) and *Bhaji on the Beach* (Gurinder Chadha, 2002); novels such as Hanif Kureishi's *The Buddha of Suburbia* (1990), Zadie Smith's *White Teeth* (2000) (both of which were TV series too) and Bharati Mukherjee's *Jasmine* (1989); or in association with forms of music such as Banghra (for example, see Dwyer 1999a, 1999b).

But you can go further than just what you can see. The Internet will tell you that The Art of Change was a visual arts organisation concerned with transformations of the urban environment and its impact upon quality of life and cultural identity. It ran for ten years (1992–2002) working with communities, regeneration authorities, young people, educational institutions, artists and architects. *West Meets East* was produced in 1992 in collaboration with pupils and teachers from the Central Foundation School for Girls in Bow, East London. If you had been in the right place at the right time you could have studied the process by interviewing the participants or conducting focus groups with the pupils, you might even have been able to research its production by getting involved (what is called participant observation). Finally, *West Meets East* was presented as a 16-foot by 12-foot photo-mural in a touring exhibition. It became a piece of public art in an exhibition presented to a variety of different audiences. There are other opportunities for research here too. You might research the organisation of this exhibition, or use

Figure 0.1 West Meets East. *Reproduced with permission of Lorraine Leeson and Art of Change.*

questionnaires, interviews or newspaper reports to understand the responses it provoked in different places and from different people. This is the sort of research on audiences which can show how different people construct particular and 'local' meanings for things that they 'consume', not only artistic works like this but also supposedly global products like the Coke and Big Macs that feature in it (for the way teenage British-Punjabi television viewers in London do this see Gillespie, 1995). As this one small example shows, in practice cultural geography can involve all these types of research and more.

Cultural geography is a very broad and diverse field with a whole series of connections to other ways of understanding 'culture'. There are lots of ways of doing cultural geography and each one finds different ways of crossing the blurred borders with other fields of study. There are, for example, connections with cultural studies through interests in things such as dance music, television and food and in questions of class, gender and 'race' in spaces like the street, the night club, the living room and the kitchen. There are overlaps with the history of art, and with literary studies and film studies, in discussions of, for example, landscape painting, photographs of the city, postcolonial novels, science fiction and Westerns, and the questions concerning the representation of people and places that they raise. There are connections with anthropology and sociology in an interest in the relationships between identity, meaning and power for social groups from Bedouin women in the Negev desert to consumers in North London shopping malls. Within this complex interdisciplinary field there are both similarities and differences. Cultural geographers' attention to questions of space, place and landscape is certainly not exclusive, and is done in many different ways, but it does offer a broad focus which differs from, but can also learn from, other areas of study which attend more to particular forms of cultural production (art, literature, film or architecture), or focus directly on the formation of social groups or on cultural identities (like work by sociologists and anthropologists). As a result, there is a need to recognise that while there is much that cultural geographers can learn from the ways in which other forms of 'cultural studies' are done – using, for instance, film theory, ethnography, literary theory or iconography – these often need to be reworked to think about them in geographical ways. This book tries to begin to do that, with the expectation that in following it up in your own work you will find interesting ideas, examples and methods both within and beyond cultural geography.

What is certain is that cultural geography is becoming more and more popular. There are more and more courses put on to introduce students to it. There are more and more books devoted to explaining what it is and how it should be thought about (for example, see Anderson et al., 2002; Anderson and Gale, 1999; Cook et al., 2000; Crang, 1998; Jackson, 1989; Mitchell, 2000; Shurmer-Smith and Hannam, 1994; Shurmer-Smith, 2002). There are more and more research projects undertaken producing published work in specialist journals of cultural geography (see, for example, the papers published in journals like *Cultural Geographies* (formerly *Ecumene*), *Social and Cultural Geography* and *Environment and Planning D: Society and Space*). There are even suggestions that cultural geography is taking over other areas of human geography as economic geographers, political geographers and social geographers become interested in what questions of identity, meaning and representation might mean for them (Barnett, 1998; Crang, 1997; Peach, 2002; Sayer, 1994). Yet, despite all this there is nowhere that students can go to really find out how it is done, and how they themselves can do it. This book aims to be that place!

The book addresses three problems and proposes a simple solution:

Problem 1 There is lots of cultural geography out there, but it is very difficult to see how it is done

It is not hard to find examples of very interesting work in cultural geography. Books, chapters and journal articles can be found from reading lists, on-line searches, or just by browsing in the library. However, most of this reading matter, while presenting fascinating discussions of, for example, landscape design, imperial cartography, or ideas of nature, will tell you very little about how the work was done in practice. Most pieces of published work in cultural geography are (and to some extent have to be to be published) presented as completed, neat and tidy arguments with all the loose ends tied away and all the evidence pointing in the same direction. Where there are discussions of methodology (and often there is nothing at all to tell you how the person found the material – the maps, pictures, novels, films or people to talk to – they worked on; how they dealt with that material; and how they came to the interpretations that they did) they are often very brief, perhaps confined to a footnote, and give little away. We want to argue that you can think of these pieces of research like a tapestry. On one side is an orderly, well-composed picture. On the other side is a tangle of threads. What we usually see is the picture, the public face of the tapestry, its finished version, all neat and tidy. We want to flip up a few corners and have a look behind at the more messy process of how the tapestry was made, and how it might have turned out differently. Hopefully, doing so will encourage you that this is something that you can do too.

Problem 2 There are many discussions of some methods and sources used in cultural geography, but almost nothing on many others

We are not arguing that there are not books on methodology out there that are useful, both specifically for geographers and from other areas of cultural analysis (for geography see Clifford and Valentine,

2003; Eyles and Smith, 1988; Flowerdew and Martin, 1997; Hay, 2000; Hoggart *et al.*, 2002; Kitchin and Tate, 2000; Limb and Dwyer, 2001; Moss, 2001; Robinson, 1998. Other fields are covered in books like Karsten and Modell, 1992; Pink, 2001; Pointon, 1997; Rose, 2001; Silverman, 2001; Storey, 1996). But it is certainly the case that some methods get plenty of coverage in most of these books, and others virtually none. This is partly about the difference between quantitative and qualitative methods, although there is now very good advice out there on both (and it is also important to stress that both can be used as part of work in cultural geography, see Hanson and Pratt in Chapter 7. It is also about a rough and ready division between methods and sources associated with the social sciences (for example, interviewing, questionnaires, focus groups) and those associated with the 'humanities' (the study of history, literature, art and music, and, increasingly a turn to considering questions of practice and performance as well as a longer-standing concern with texts and representations (Rice and Valentine, 2003)). In geography the former have had a lot more attention paid to them directly than the latter. It is much easier to find advice in the methodological literature for human geography on how to do an interview than it is to find recommendations about how to read a novel, interpret a film, or understand a song (although see Rose, 1996 and 2001). What we have tried to do here is to bring all these methods together into one book, because they are all used by cultural geographers. Hopefully, this means that there will be some useful advice for everyone no matter what sort of source material they are thinking of using.

Problem 3 Most discussions of methods are dry technical discussions that give little sense of how they are really used

Most books about methodology aim to define a set of general principles and practices which people who want to use that method can apply to any research project where they think that it would be useful. These range from the identification of the precise technical procedures for undertaking various forms of statistical analysis to broad sets of issues that should be taken into consideration when conducting in-depth interviews or focus groups. This is, of course, very useful, and one of the main aims of this book is to do that too, offering some general advice and 'how to' guidance about a much broader set of methods for use in cultural geography. However, the problem with these general discussions is that it is very hard to see how they are really used. We are back to the messy side of the tapestry again. One of the main ideas behind this book is that it is only by seeing, in some detail, how methods have been actually used in real research projects that their use can really be understood. This is perhaps particularly true of the interpretative methods associated with the humanities, but we would also argue that it is true of the methods associated with the social sciences, including quantitative methods.

The simple solution

Our simple solution to these three problems is to present extended examples of 'cultural geography in practice'. This means showing in detail how particular methods have been used to answer specific questions in key areas of cultural geography. Indeed, we have adapted our title from the 'Cultural Geographies in Practice' section of the journal *Cultural Geographies* which is devoted to showing how people's practical engagement with the ideas of cultural geography works in a range of artistic, civic and policy fields (and you might again recall the image on our cover). This book aims to offer methodological advice and instruction by showing how cultural geography is actually done. Each chapter that follows combines, in its own way, three things in order to achieve this:

i An overview of an important area of cultural geography

Each chapter is organised around a key theme that is a focus of interest in cultural geography. You will recognise many of these from your courses and reading: embodiment, marginality, empire, national identity, development, work, diaspora, sexuality. Each chapter takes its theme and discusses how and why it is of interest to cultural geographers, outlining the kinds of research questions that have been addressed, and highlighting significant work in the field. To a certain extent this means that the book read as a whole offers an introduction to cultural geography as well as to its methodologies.

ii Practical instruction in a key methodology

Each chapter is also centred on a particular methodology or source. Again many of these will be familiar, and sometimes the theme and the source are the same thing (with mapping or sound for example). In terms of methods: questionnaires, interviewing, participant observation, and the combination of qualitative and quantitative methods each feature (some in more than one chapter). In terms of sources there is attention to a wide range, including archives, newspapers, fiction, the internet, photographs, advertisements, maps, film, music, television and public art. The aim in each chapter is to offer instruction on the practicalities of using these methods and sources, so that students can get a sense of what they might do with them too.

iii Cultural geography in practice

The main focus of the discussion in each chapter is a particular piece of research undertaken by the author(s). In each case the chapter sets out how that research, and its specific research question(s), fits into the debates in the area of cultural geography to which it contributes. This piece of research is also used as the way in which the practical methodological discussion is brought to life. Through a nuts and bolts discussion of the use of the method or source in the making of that piece of geographical knowledge, the chapters show how to do cultural geography. Again, you might think of the finished piece of research (which you should go away and read as well) as the neat and tidy side of the tapestry. What the chapters in this book give is a glimpse at the other side with all its tangled threads, difficult decisions and compromises.

So, each chapter aims to ground often difficult theoretical and substantive debates in cultural geography in particular examples. The chapters also aim to use those examples to introduce the practical application and interpretation of specific methods and sources. In particular, the authors all seek to show as clearly as possible how the methods and sources that they chose and the ways in which they used them helped them to provide answers to the research questions that they had set themselves.

Like all simple solutions there are, of course, problems with this approach. In particular, we are *not* suggesting that these themes (imperialism, the body, or sexuality) *only* go together with the methods and sources with which they are paired in the chapters of this book. It should be clear that we can use all sorts of methods and sources to deal with all sorts of themes. Thus, to take just one example, national identity could be investigated through photography, public art, the built environment, landscape painting, archival sources, maps, interviews or focus groups as well as through the sorts of visual images from advertising discussed by Mona Domosh in Chapter 9 (see, for example, Back, 1998; Daniels, 1993; Gruffudd, 1995; Johnson, 1995; Leitner and Kang, 1999, Matless, 1998). Indeed, we are aware that different readers will come to this book with different needs. In terms of undertaking research, some will have the theme they want to consider sorted out. They might be interested in work, or in migration or nature. They will be looking for particular sources or methods that they can use. In order to identify them these readers will have to go beyond the chapter which deals with the theme they are interested in. Others will come to the book with a strong sense of the sorts of sources or methods that they want to use. They may be interested in doing something with film, music or photography, or want to try participant observation, focus groups or a combination of quantitative and qualitative methods. While their first task is to read the chapter(s) on that source or method, they should explore the other chapters in order to spark ideas about the themes and research questions that they can direct themselves towards.

Indeed, there is a lot of overlap between the chapters in terms of the ways in which they approach questions of 'culture' in geography. While each chapter can be read on its own for its arguments about a particular area of the subject, or for its advice on specific sources or methods, there is shared common ground in terms of some of the more theoretical terminology used and the ideas that underpin much of cultural geography. We have tried to deal with this by cross-referencing between the chapters and by using **Concept boxes** to explain highlighted terms – such as discourse, the gaze, performance and deconstruction – which crop up across the book as a whole. Each box gives a short definition of the term and suggests some reading for those who want to follow it up further. There is a list of all the boxes at the beginning of the book.

The aim of the book is to assist you in this process of investigating both methods and themes, and to focus attention on the ways in which research projects come about and are undertaken, so that you can devise such projects yourself. To help this along we have incorporated what we have called **Tales of research** between the chapters. These are short accounts written by students who have done research projects in cultural geography. These projects cover a wide range of types of study and come from a diverse set of places and institutions. In each case they aim to give some flavour of the decisions that were made in constructing a research project, some of the practical issues (and difficulties) in using the methods chosen, and a summary of the results. Each one aims to be an accessible snapshot of the process of undertaking research in cultural geography. We have distributed these throughout the book but there is also a list at the beginning if you want to search them out.

More than anything else we want this book to be useful. We are excited about the possibilities of cultural geography in practice and want others to do it too. We hope that the book's combination of general advice on methods and sources, discussion of key themes, and use of particular examples will make cultural geography seem doable. Our title has two meanings of course. It is a matter of 'practice' because we want to show the active process of making cultural geography. It is also about 'practice' because it is something that you can only do by having a go, trying new things and making mistakes. We don't believe it is something that can be done 'right' (practice does not make perfect), but it is something that can only be done better with practice!

PART I

Writing cultural geography

1
Knowledge is power
Using archival research to interpret state formation

Miles Ogborn

Cultural geographies of state formation

This chapter is concerned with doing research on the common ground where cultural geography and political geography meet. It is an introduction to undertaking archival research on the cultural geographies of state formation. This research might deal with any of the things that states do or have done over the centuries: fighting wars; gathering taxes; making laws; organising welfare systems; planning cities, economies and environments; or policing, educating and imprisoning their citizens. These are clearly matters for other disciplines as well as geography, but it is significant that recent definitions of the state (which is notoriously hard to define) have stressed that it is a matter of the geographical organisation of **power**. For example, the sociologist Michael Mann (1984) has argued that the state is 'a set of centralized institutions (predominantly military, political and administrative) which exercise power over a specific territory' (Driver, 1991: 272). The historian Michael Braddick (2000: 6 and 9) also defines the state geographically as a 'coordinated and territorially bounded network of agents exercising political power', where political power is 'territorially based, functionally limited and backed by the threat of legitimate physical force'. In other words, the state is a form of the organisation of power which has specific geographical limits (its territory), pursues certain defined functions (although what they may be differs from state to state and over time), and the consequence of not doing what it says is, in the end, the state being able to enforce its rules by using violence (see also Painter, 1995 and Taylor, 1989).

Concept Box

Power

Power is a very important concept in cultural geography and in cultural studies more generally. Understanding culture in terms of relationships of power is what lies behind the argument that questions of meaning, interpretation and **identity** are political issues, and that we can talk about 'cultural politics' or 'the politics of identity'. Power is often defined in terms of one set of people exerting power over another set of people, or over space, or nature, or the landscape in order to control them and their meanings in various ways. This 'negative' definition of power is useful in that it makes it clear that there are different interests and that they can come into conflict (often over cultural issues). It also raises the question of the forms of resistance (again often cultural) which contest the exercise of power. However, we might also understand power as being 'positive'. This means that power is not just about preventing things from happening, it is also the capacity to make things happen. Here power is part of all sorts of forms of **social and cultural**

(continued overleaf)

construction. Power is involved in constituting identities (including those of the individuals or social groups who are understood to 'hold' power), social relations (such as the relationships between men and women), and cultural geographies (such as the definition of national identities, or of 'East' and 'West' in Orientalism). Most analyses of power in cultural geography combine these senses of power to make arguments about how the active cultural construction of places, spaces and landscapes are part of relationships of unequal power between social groups.

Key Reading
- Allen, J. (1999) 'Spatial assemblages of power: from domination to empowerment' in D. Massey, J. Allen and P. Sarre (eds) *Human Geography Today*. Cambridge, Polity Pres: 194–218.
- Lukes, S. (ed.) (1986) *Power*. Oxford, Blackwell.

It is also important to note here that the state is not the same thing as 'the government' or 'the nation'. There are many different elements of any state – such as the army, parliament, the civil service, the state education system – which together are called the 'state apparatus' (Clark and Dear, 1984). These institutions are more or less well coordinated in different situations, but might also come into conflict (a military coup, for example). In each situation, what institutions the state consists of and how those institutions work is also a complex question with no simple answer. It is a matter of decisions made over time by state officials, politicians, pressure groups and the public which define and redefine what the state's role should be. For example, should the state be responsible for health care or education? As a result the state is always an unfinished 'project' made up of continual attempts at reorganising its ways of working. Since 'the state' is a term that sounds too singular and static to refer to this multiple and changing situation it is often preferable to use the term 'state formation' to get at the ways in which state apparatuses operate and change (Corrigan and Sayer, 1985).

Since the state is so active and pervasive in so many arenas of life, questions about how it works and how it has worked in the past are a matter for all sorts of geographers – social, economic and historical geographers as well as political geographers. But why are these issues which should concern cultural geographers? I want to argue that questions of meaning and **identity** are essential in understanding how states work. First, it is clear that 'States… state' (Corrigan and Sayer, 1985: 3). Part of the operation of state apparatuses is the production of statements – in reports, policy documents, speeches, press releases and parliamentary debates – about the situations they are dealing with and about what they are doing. We can use the idea of **discourse** to interpret what is being said in terms of the construction and contestation of state power (for examples from geopolitics, see Ó Tuathail, 1996 and Sharp, 1999). Indeed, we need to be aware that the meanings that the state produces are not always written or spoken but can take the form of rituals (like the rules of dress in a British law court), ceremonies (like the displays of Soviet military might on May day), or monuments (like the Vietnam war memorial in Washington DC). One important way of interpreting these statements is the state's need for legitimation, for processes of state formation to be acceptable to people outside the state apparatus. Exactly who is appealed to will depend on the context – for example, taxation increases in medieval France only needed to be legitimated to a relatively small group of powerful nobles, in contemporary France they need the support of a much wider public – but it always means that one part of state formation must be the making and negotiation of meanings about the world and about itself with other social groups (Braddick, 2000). Second, states act. Processes of state formation are about attempts to shape and regulate ways of life and identities. Not only do states attempt to define things discursively, but these statements are a crucial part of policies and programmes which seek to alter people's ways of life and their identities. One simple example is the way in which statements about the undesirability and dangerousness of 'New Age Travellers' were part of the passing of the Criminal Justice and Public Order Act of 1994 which effectively outlawed a particular way of life and an identity (Halfacree, 1996 and Sibley, 1995). A more complex example would be the contemporary British state's discourses of social exclusion and welfare dependency (or, for the early nineteenth century, of the 'deserving' and 'undeserving' poor) which are part of policies of 'Welfare to Work' (or, again, of the workhouse system and the New Poor Law of 1834) with which the state attempts to reshape the lives of those without work (Driver, 1993 and Haylett, 2001). As a result, it is important to understand processes of state formation in terms of the meanings and identities that are being put into place both for those making the rules and those subject to them. It is also important to understand that resistance to state formation is also often conducted in terms of challenging the meanings that the state is trying to make and the identities and ways of life that it is trying to construct (for example, Cresswell, 1994 and Routledge, 1997).

Concept Box

Discourse

Discourse is a way of thinking about the relationship between **power**, knowledge and language. It is a concept most associated with the work of the French theorist Michel Foucault, who understood discourses as the frameworks that define the possibilities for knowledge. As such, a discourse exists as a set of 'rules' (formal or informal, acknowledged or unacknowledged) which determine the sorts of statements that can be made. These 'rules' determine what the criteria for truth are, what sorts of things can be talked about, and what sorts of things can be said about them. One of the most carefully worked through and explicitly geographical examples is Edward Said's (1978) *Orientalism* where he sets out the discourse (which he calls 'Orientalism') through which 'the West' has made statements about 'the East', defining the sorts of things that get said about 'the oriental mind', 'the oriental landscape', or 'oriental despotism', and defining itself as the opposite in the process. This raises two important points. First, that the aim of the idea of discourse is to suggest that there are many discourses, none of which simply tells the truth about the world. All of these discourses are ways in which our knowledge and language create the world as well as reflecting it (so you can only find a 'typical oriental landscape' or a 'classic oriental city' if you already have some idea of what you are looking for). The second point is that the discourse that prevails is a matter of power not simply truth. Since discourses define the ways things are understood, even whether things can be understood to exist or not, then part of any struggle for power is a struggle over language and knowledge, over discourse. So Said directly connects the discourse of Orientalism to the power relations of colonialism and imperialism which it justified and which forged the relationships between entities created in the discourse of Orientalism as either 'West' (the colonisers) or 'East' (the colonised).

Key reading
- Foucault, M. (1980) *Power/Knowledge: Selected Interviews and Other Writings, 1972–1977*. Brighton, Harvester Press. Chapter 5: 'Two Lectures', and Chapter 6: 'Truth and Power'.
- Mills, S. (1997) *Discourse*. London, Routledge.
- Said, E. (1978) *Orientalism*. New York, Vintage.

Using these sorts of ideas geographers have been concerned to understand a whole range of questions about state practices and state formation in a wide variety of different periods and places. There are questions of how states attempt to deal with the organisation of power over space (for example, Harvey, 2000 and Jones, 1999 on the medieval state; Driver, 1993, Chapter 3 and Ogborn, 1991 on the nineteenth-century state; Blomley, 1994 and Blomley, Delaney and Ford, 2001 on the geographies of law), and the ways in which states try to separate and deal with different sorts of people through the organisation of space (for example, Philo, 1989 on the 'mad'; Ogborn, 1995 and Ploszajska, 1994 on the 'criminal'; and Robinson, 1990 on 'race' in South Africa). There are questions of the role states play in the symbolic organisation of places and landscapes, which often relates state formation to processes of nation-building (for example, Johnson, 1995 on monuments; Pred, 1992 on street names; and Daniels, 1993 and Matless, 1998 on the English landscape). There are questions of state interventions in nature, and the particular interests that that supports (for example, McCannon, 1995 and Neumann, 1995; Scott, 1998 chapters 1 and 8;). Finally, there are questions of the construction and use of geographical knowledge, and the discipline of Geography itself, by and against the state in both domestic and imperial politics (for example, Clayton, 2000 part 3 on cartography; Edney, 1997; and Harley, 2001; Bell, Butlin and Heffernan, 1995 and Driver, 2001 on geography and empire; and Nash, 1996 and Sparke, 1998 on geographical knowledge as resistance). In each case the research has involved interpreting the archival sources collected by the state in question.

Reading the archive

The record of all this discursive and practical cultural activity for and against state formation is the archive. There are, of course, many different kinds of archive – they are, after all, simply collections of material kept for later 'study' – personal archives, company archives, the archives of non-governmental organisations, or archives of specific types of material: film, television, photographs or sound recordings (Ogborn, 2003). Geographers have made use of all of them (for example, Black, 1995 and 2000; Daniels, 1999; Davies, 2000; Gleeson, 2001; Ryan, 1997). However, it is the state's concern for gathering, using and storing information that has constructed the largest and most systematic collections at all levels of government, central and local. In Britain, for example, there are city and county record offices as well as the Public Record Office (PRO) in London. These hold material from across the centuries and recent material archived from working government departments.

There are three questions to ask when considering what these archival collections contain:

i What has been gathered and why?

This relates to the documents as working records. It is important to ask what records of its own activities the state needed to construct, and what records of other states, people and organisations did it want to collect. This is the main question that will interest us here, and it will be considered further below. Suffice to say that what is in the archive relates to the priorities of the state at the time (or at least the part of the state apparatus that dealt with the issue in question). This means that it may not be precisely the information that you seek to answer your questions. It is worth remembering that, despite what the conspiracy theorists might have us believe, the state does not know or record everything.

ii What has been kept and archived?

Prior to the development of a system of archives the safekeeping of past records could not be ensured. However, archiving also causes problems. This is set out nicely by J. Talboys Wheeler (1861, iii) discussing the establishment of the Public Record Office as an introduction to his reorganisation of the Madras Records under the British Empire in India:

> *Diplomatic correspondence of the utmost value had been sold for waste paper, and was subsequently*
> *purchased by the British Museum at a fabulous price. Income tax returns, which had been entrusted to the*
> *Commissioners to ensure secrecy, were found in grocers shops wrapped around soap and sugar. The very*
> *papers which a zealous official, absorbed in the current business of the day, would regard with contempt, –*
> *turned out to be the very papers which historians and antiquaries would regard with superstitious reverence.*
> *The great difficulty was to know what to keep and what to throw away.*

The price of keeping some material has been the destruction of other records. Indeed, this has become more and more of a problem because as the state's functions have expanded the amount of information in all formats that is produced has also expanded. Not all of what is produced by the state is archived, just as you might not want to preserve for posterity all your photographs, letters or e-mails. There is, therefore, a process of selection and destruction (usually called 'weeding'). What is kept and what is destroyed depends upon the priorities of the time it was done and the people doing it, and their projections of what might be wanted in the future. Much of the systems of archiving that are now current (in places like Chennai – formerly Madras – as well as Washington and London) are inherited from the nineteenth century (and men like J. Talboys Wheeler) which was when European and American states, in their imperial and domestic forms, became much more interested in the production, collection and storage of systematic information on all sorts of subjects (Hannah, 2001 and Richards, 1993).

iii What is open for consultation?
Not everything that is in the archive is available for consultation. The most common restrictions relate to information that is still regarded as current. This is kept closed for a certain period of time. For example, material deposited in the British Public Record Office is routinely closed for 30 years, but this can be extended to 50 or even 100 years in certain cases. The most well-known 100-year closure is the personal information from each census.

Taken together the answers to these questions help to define the archival material there is and what can be done with it. What I want to concentrate on here is one important aspect of the state's gathering and use of information. It is apparent, as hinted above, that changes over time in the information gathered relate to the changing nature of the state. While care needs to be exercised with long-term trajectories of state development – for example, it is not clear that the modern secular state is any more intrusive in its subjects private lives than the early modern confessional (or religious) state was (Braddick, 2000) – it is possible to understand changes in the sorts of knowledge that the state gathered in terms of the changing nature of the state apparatus. Medieval European states were most concerned with establishing the rights of feudal property ownership and the royal dues which went with them. These were recorded in documents such as Domesday book and in the pipe rolls of the Exchequer (Clanchy, 1979). The eighteenth-century English state was most concerned with its capacity to fight wars and to raise the taxes to pay for them. The information it sought concerned the values of property, volumes of trade and population levels on which fiscal and military health were based – what was known as 'political arithmetic' (Brewer, 1989; Buck, 1977 and 1982; Hoppit, 1996, and Stone, 1994). In contrast, the nineteenth-century state – faced with industrialisation, urbanisation and political claims from the working classes – concerned itself far more with social problems of poverty, crime, prostitution and health. It sought, through empirical social investigation, royal commissions and the collection of vital statistics and census data, to understand and change the nature of society itself in order to render it more productive and less unruly (Ashforth, 1990; Corrigan and Sayer, 1985; Driver, 1988; and Poovey, 1995). We can learn a lot about each state apparatus from studying its methods of gathering and using this information. As books on methodology say, information and knowledge are not just 'out there' waiting to be gathered up. State apparatuses, like other researchers, need methodologies for constructing data that they can use.

Thinking in this way aims to reanimate the archive in order to understand state formation in action as a process of knowledge construction (see Latour, 1987 who does this for scientists and engineers). More than just the record of the state's activity, the archive is part of the state's construction and use of power. It is, of course, necessary to recognise that the archive provides only a partial record. There are the issues of selection and secrecy outlined above. But, more importantly, there is the fact that the archive preserves things in certain forms. For example, the only records of meetings are usually the minutes which were kept, which are as partial as the record a photograph album makes of a family gathering; and the only record of warfare was, before film and TV (which bring their own partialities), written orders, reports and statistics which only convey what happened in certain, often sanitised, ways. There is also the official position from which the archival record is constructed which excludes the voices of some participants in favour of others (see Lepore, 1998 who makes this case in relation to warfare). Yet it is often the only record that we have of many people, institutions, events and processes and it is possible, as Jim Duncan (1999) argues, to read the archive 'against the grain' to provide evidence for subversive and resistant meanings, identities and actions.

The implication of this is that every piece of material – every document, photograph, statistical table or map – in the state's archives can be contextualised back into the process of state formation or state operation that produced it. For example, the census and civil registration of births, marriages and deaths can (and indeed must) be made to answer questions not only about the details of the population in terms of size, composition, age and sex structure, but about the nature of the state that wanted to know these details and why it wanted to know them, and not others (Hannah, 2001; Higgs, 1996; Szreter, 1991). This means understanding the nature, structure, composition and content of the archive not only for the information that is contained within it but also to understand why that information was gathered, why certain methods were used, what purpose the information was intended for, how was it used, and how that use was implemented, negotiated and resisted.

Making accuracy: mapping the taxman

The example that I want to use to demonstrate how an investigation of the state's gathering of knowledge can illuminate processes of state formation is a study of the activities of a late-seventeenth-century English official: Charles Davenant (published as Ogborn, 1998a; and with more detail in Ogborn 1998b chapter 5). The immediate context for the research was a book on modernity in eighteenth-century London within which I wanted to have a chapter on the geographies of the English state, which John Brewer (1989) had argued was a 'fiscal-military state', increasingly strong, professional and bureaucratic in terms of gathering taxes and fighting wars. Since the book was to explore these processes through newly-constructed spaces within London I began to research Greenwich Hospital (founded in 1694 for old and injured sailors) and the artillery grounds dotted around the city. However, this material remains unused in my filing cabinet since what proved to be more productive for the themes that I was interested in was the administration of excise taxation – duties gathered on the domestic production of items like soap, candles and, especially, beer, by hundreds of local officers (excisemen) coordinated into a national system. Previous research (Brewer, 1989; O'Brien and Hunt, 1993) had suggested that it was the excise which, having provided the greatest increases in taxation revenue, also provided the best example of a 'modern' state apparatus. So I had begun reading – starting with the footnotes and bibliographies provided by these previous researchers – a series of sources which I could use to look more specifically at the *geographies* of this part of state formation and the *knowledges* which made it possible. This was a set of connections which I felt had been ignored in understanding how the fiscal-military state was constructed and legitimated.

These sources were of three different sorts:

i Manuscript (i.e. handwritten) records of the Excise. These have survived rather sporadically. There are some series in the PRO at Kew, London (e.g. the correspondence between the central Excise Board and the Treasury; and records of officers moving between posts), and some isolated examples (lists of officers, tabulations of revenue gathered, and a few notebooks) in the manuscript collection in the British Library.

ii Printed pamphlets and broadsheets that argued for or against the extension of excise taxation. Some saw these as the best way to raise revenue to fight wars, others saw them as an illegitimate extension of government power.

iii Printed books which sought to teach those who worked for the excise the mathematical principles that they needed to learn if they were to do their jobs. In particular, they were concerned with how to measure – or 'gauge' – the amounts of liquid (beer, wine and spirits) in barrels so that the tax could be charged (see Figure 1.1). Most of these printed works were available in the British Library.

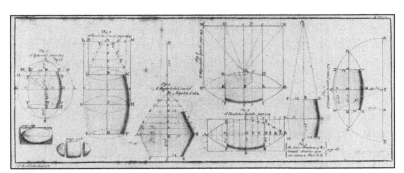

Figure 1.1 *Mathematics for excisemen. From Charles Leadbetter's* The Royal Gauger *(1739). Reproduced by permission of the British Library, 1609/4499.*

However, it was just one of these sources that seemed to hold out the promise of enabling me to connect together the knowledge required by the state (especially of accurate gauging, and whether the local officers could meet the demands of the job) and the practical geographies of state formation (the tying together of these local excisemen into an effective national system). This was a set of four diaries held in the British Library – and found by working through the footnotes to John Brewer's (1989) *The Sinews of Power* – which described in some detail the process of going around parts of the country to check on local excisemen. Each was a small, handwritten notebook, and they were catalogued under different titles: *An Account of the Management of the Officers of the West of England*, 1685 (British Library (BL) Harleian Manuscripts (Mss) 4077); *Miles Edgar on the Excise* (BL Harleian Mss 5120 and 5121); and *Management of the Excise* (BL Harleian Mss 5123). It took me some time to work out that these were written by Charles Davenant (one of the Excise Commissioners charged with overseeing the whole apparatus), and not by Miles Edgar, who it turned out was the customs inspector at the port of Rye whose name Davenant had jotted down on the flyleaf of one notebook as a reminder to himself. However, having used the evidence of one of the few personal reflections that the notebooks provided, and some corroboration via the handwriting, it became apparent that their authorship was well known (a fact that was hard to ascertain until I had worked it out for myself!). I was then able to interpret them alongside Davenant's later writings on political arithmetic and, in particular, on the benefits of excise taxation. Indeed, it is notable that in constructing an argument using these sources it made sense to begin with a discussion of Davenant's published work before moving on to an interpretation of the notebooks, even though he had written them and I had read them in the opposite order (See Ogborn 1998a and 1998b). I shall do the same here.

The argument that these sources enabled me to make was that the formation and legitimation of the English fiscal-military state was made possible by the construction of certain forms of knowledge: political arithmetic and accurate gauging. Charles Davenant's life and work as a taxman and published author connected them together, but, methodologically, they needed to be dealt with in different ways. In discussing them here I shall deal with the first more briefly since I want to pay more attention to the archival material and the state's gathering of knowledge.

Davenant's published essays – *An essay upon ways and means* (1695) and *Discourses on the public revenues* (1698) – were read as part of the discursive construction through works of political arithmetic of a legitimate fiscal-military state based on excise taxation (the essays are in Davenant, 1771). As with all political arithmetic they used the language of mathematics, and the certainty that numbers seemed to provide, to make their case and to represent the state as a 'calculable space' or an 'engine' which could be measured, understood and controlled if the right information was obtained and the right methods used. Understanding Davenant's particular arguments in support of excise taxation meant situating them in terms of the politics of the 1690s – the need to raise taxes to enable William III to fight wars against France without endangering the liberties of the English and the powers of parliament over the king – and in terms of Davenant's own position – having not been reappointed as an Excise Commissioner, he was looking for a job! These essays cannot, therefore, be read as direct statements from the state apparatus of the 1690s about state formation. Instead, they are Davenant's arguments for why the state should reintroduce the way that the excise was managed in the 1680s when he was a crucial part of the administration and when, as he proves numerically, the revenues were higher. It is, he argues, only with these management practices that revenue can be increased without endangering liberty. Therefore, reading these essays in their political and personal contexts encourages a closer look at what Davenant was doing in the 1680s and turns attention to his notebooks.

The notebooks were also to be understood in terms of how they (and the information that they contained) were part of the process of the formation and legitimation of the English fiscal-military state. Here, however, was a source that, rather than commenting on the state from 'outside', seemed to get at the very processes and procedures of state formation. The key to interpreting and analysing this source was to find out why and how the information it contained had been made, gathered and used. This clearly included the process of finding out exactly who had written it, but much of my reading of the notebooks was done without this knowledge and was concerned with the broader question of the purpose for which they had been compiled. This was more a matter of the institutional position held by the author and the detail of the procedures and practices that he was engaged in. What was the author up to?

Answers to this question were pursued through some very straightforward methodological strategies which could be applied to any archival source:

Note taking

When working on any archival source you need a record that you can work from outside the archive. In some instances archives will give you permission to photograph or photocopy sources, or to print from microfilm. However, this is often restricted to certain sorts of documents and can be very expensive. At some point you will have to make your own record of what the source contains. This may be, as in my case, with a pencil and paper (most archives ban pens for obvious reasons), or it might be with a laptop computer. It may be a process of laborious copying, it might be the selection of parts of the source (although be careful to note which part by page or folio – for manuscript – numbers), or the systematic collection of numerical or categorical data onto pre-prepared databases (electronic or paper). It all depends on the nature of the source and what you want to do with it. It should also be remembered that this is part of the interpretation and analysis. As you read and take notes you should be trying out ideas as to what the source is about and what answers it provides to your questions. In my case there were few problems once I had decided to take a very full record and had got my eye in for Davenant's handwriting. It soon became clear that the notebooks were not so much an official record as a set of personal memoranda from which official correspondence could later be compiled. They concerned a series of journeys out from and back to London on which the author was engaged in inspecting, checking up on, training and disciplining excisemen as they undertook their own duties. My notes needed to accurately record the nature of the journeys and the range of different things that Davenant did. Through them I was able to establish that he was trying to ensure that the local excisemen were able to do their jobs and that the administrative systems which linked them together would function effectively. In more abstract terms, he was concerned with state formation.

Mapping

One of the things that geographers commonly do with archival sources is to map them. Indeed, much historical geography has involved systematic mapping of material collected by the state (for example, Darby, 1977; Glasscock, 1973; Short, 1997). Like a graph this representation of the 'data' helps in the interpretation of the content and nature of the sources. In part the systematic nature of state-gathered sources makes this possible, but there are always all sorts of decisions that must be made to construct a map (for the use of Geographical Information Systems in historical geography see *www.geog.port.ac.uk/gbhgis/index.htm*). When it became clear that the notebooks recorded a set of journeys I decided that mapping them would help reveal the nature of Davenant's enterprise (e.g. see Figure 1.2 for the most extensive of his travels). This meant compiling a *full* list of places visited and the order in which they were visited (and some decisions had to be made about which were places that he had travelled out and back to from other places rather than being stops on the journey, e.g. North Petherton and Llandeilo). It also meant identifying places on the map from Davenant's notes to himself. Non-standardised seventeenth-century spelling and Davenant's (and my own) linguistic limitations meant that this was a particular problem with Welsh place names. Luckily a Welsh-speaking colleague (and contemporary health geographer!) was able to identify Davenant's phonetic attempts as particular Welsh towns. It became clear from the maps that there was, at least in the area for which Davenant was responsible, an attempt to inspect the work of every officer across a substantial part of the country. He, and the Excise Commissioners he represented, were attempting to ensure that the local excisemen were working the same way wherever they were: they were concerned with the uniformity of the state apparatus.

Figure 1.2 *Charles Davenant's travels, 15th July to 12th September 1685.*

Thematic coding

The problem with notes taken from archival sources is that they generally replicate the structure of information as it appears in the source, which is not necessarily the same as the sort of analytical structure that the researcher wants to produce in order to provide an interpretation. This is, of course, not the case if data has been gathered onto pre-prepared data sheets (either in numerical or textual form), which is most appropriate where a systematic source is being used and requires familiarity with the source to ensure that the data gathering system is appropriately designed. Using the knowledge of the source gained through notetaking, my next step was to group together references to similar practices: for example, references to standardised weights and measures, the dismissal of officers, or negotiations with local magistrates. In practice this was nothing more than rewriting quotations, memos or references from my original notes onto other sheets of paper which each had a thematic heading. I could then deal with this material theme by theme to describe what Davenant was up to. This enabled me to represent his part in the process of state formation in a systematic way. I chose to work from the smallest to the largest scale, beginning with his attention to ensuring that standardised weights and measures were used and ending with his reorganisation of the districts that excisemen covered to ensure their jobs were done properly. Taken together, I interpreted his work as part of the legitimation of this process of state formation through the accuracy of the work of the excisemen. The state's legitimacy rested on the claim that it would not take a penny more or less than it was due. However, the problem that Davenant and the Excise Commissioners faced was that they had to establish a system that could actually provide accurate measurement. That was what he was up to.

Linking sources

It is clearly very difficult to get all that you need from one source, and most projects involve a range of sources (although some may be more important than others). Indeed, other sources often provide not only additional information but also fresh perspectives on each other. One important process is to follow up leads in one source by using others. For example, from reading the printed materials (see above) I was able to identify people that Davenant visited as men who had published work on the excise. For example, Ezekial Polstead, an excise officer in Wales, had later written a comic text called *The Excise Man* (1697), and Thomas Everard, a general supervisor in the West of England, had written *Stereography Made Easy* (1684) to help excisemen make calculations. I was also able to supplement the notebooks in various ways: by pursuing some of the resistance that Davenant's activities provoked among those who paid excise duty via the archive of correpondence between the Treasury and the Excise (in the PRO); by seeing how his deliberations related to tabulations of excise revenue (e.g. BL Harleian Ms 4227 *Abstract of the Revenue of the Excise 1684–7*); and of course through reading Davenant's own later published work. Putting all these sources together gave a fuller interpretation of his activities than any single source could have provided on its own, including a sense of how others saw what he was doing, even though the notebooks remained at the heart of the interpretation.

Theorising sources

Throughout the process of archival research it is important to keep in mind the wider issues that are being dealt with while also dealing with the detailed nitty-gritty of the sources themselves. One way to do this is to read more conceptual or theoretical work alongside the original sources. The argument that I made using Davenant's notebooks and the other sources was that he was engaged in the construction, adjustment and maintenance of a state apparatus which should be understood as a 'network' which linked together people (especially the excisemen), instruments (the measuring devices that they used) and documents (the calculations that they wrote down and the notes that Davenant wrote about them). It was within this 'network' that the accuracy necessary to legitimate the gathering of increased taxes and the process of state formation could be produced and guaranteed. These ideas, and use of the term 'network' to combine intellectual, social, political and legal practices, was taken from a concurrent reading of Bruno Latour's (1987) *Science in Action* where he discusses ways of understanding the conditions under which scientists and engineers produce reliable forms of knowledge. Indeed, somewhere else in my filing cabinet are the notes which I first took on Latour's book. Each page is divided into two. On one half are my notes on chapter 6 of *Science in Action*, and on the other half are the ways in which these ideas might help me to understand Davenant and the Excise.

Writing

As always, writing is a crucial part of the process of making an argument. Decisions have to be made on how to put all the material together. There also needs to be careful attention to ensuring that there is adequate quotation from and referencing of the original sources (which most readers will be unfamiliar with and not have easy access to), so as to give a strong sense of what they contain and of how they have been interpreted. This involves some discussion of the nature and content of the sources, but also involves ensuring that the reader could, if they wanted to, trace back each reference to a specific place in the archive. Work that is based on archival sources needs itself to have something of the archive about it.

Summary and guide to further research

The main aim of this introduction to using archival sources to interpret state formation has been to encourage you to think about the archive as part of the processes that you are considering and to give you some simple ways of tackling it. State concerns with meanings, identities and knowledge as part of the construction of power and legitimacy can be explored in a huge range of different contexts, and studies that use any archival sources need to be attentive to these questions of the making, use and storage of information. In all these cases it is important to understand the context for the creation and preservation of the material that you are using and to feed that into your interpretation.

There are two possible ways into constructing a research project of the sort discussed here. The first is to identify a process, social group or set of institutions that the state has concerned itself with; a state apparatus that was or is doing something interesting; or a process of state formation that you think leads in significant directions. You then need to find out whether there are archival sources that relate to what you have identified, and whether you are able to get access to them. The second way is to find a set of archival materials – of whatever form or format you like – that interests you, and then work out how and why they were gathered. Here you need to recontextualise the archive in order to understand them as part of a process of state formation. It is, of course, perfectly possible and possibly preferable to do both, tracing processes of state formation and the archival sources for them at the same time.

In terms of finding potential archival sources there are a few easy ways of beginning (Ogborn, 2003). On foot, you can find the archives nearest you and visit them to look through the catalogues, indexes and search guides, or to talk to the archivists. In the library, you can consult books such as Janet Foster and Julia Sheppard's (2000) *British Archives* which give brief details on archival holdings and contact details. Online, you can visit archives such as the UK Public Record Office (*www.pro.gov.uk*), the French Archives Nationales (*www.archivesnationales.culture.gouv.fr*) or the holdings of the US National Archives and Records Administration (*www.nara.gov*), as well as regional and local archives. You can also visit sites which allow you to search extensive sets of archival collections using names or keywords. For example, for British Archives there is Access to Archives (A2A) at *www.a2a.pro.gov.uk* or the National Register of Archives at *www.hmc.gov.uk/nra*. Whichever way you chose you should keep in mind the politics of the archive:

> *There is no political power without control of the archive, if not of memory. Effective democratization can always be measured by this essential criterion – the participation in and access to the archive, its constitution, and its interpretation.*

> (Jacques Derrida, quoted in Kurtz, 2001 p27)

A TALE OF RESEARCH

Space as social control

The future worlds of *Nineteen Eighty-Four* and *Brave New World*

Mark Llewellyn

A dread of statistics, a fear of questionnaire surveys and a loathing of cold and wet rivers initially inspired my dissertation. This seems a curious and somewhat unglamorous place to start, but in many ways I'd worked out exactly what I *didn't* want to do for my study before I came to realise what I *did* want to do. That realisation was provoked by several lectures and practicals using qualitative sources for geographical analysis which stimulated me to think carefully about what things I enjoyed. My thoughts turned to two of my favourite novels, George Orwell's (1949) *Nineteen Eighty-Four* and Aldous Huxley's (1932) *Brave New World*, and the potential for writing geographies of their dystopian futures. Having studied English Literature at A-Level, I was not only interested in such novels, but also in the methods used to analyse and interrogate them.

The research process began by writing a review of work to date in the field of literature and geography, which also helped to shape my conceptual and theoretical approach to the novels. I considered space and power as interrelated constructs in the fictional future worlds, and as such drew on Foucault's ideas about this relationship. I also read as many of the studies and commentaries on these two famous texts as I could and I realised that although several addressed the novels' geographies as visions of the future, few commented on the connection between the actual *geographies* of the future societies envisaged and social control – the key theme of both novels, arguably. I wondered whether the actual conventions, narratives and structure of the texts reflected this desire for social control, and whether we could make sense of the books by adopting a spatial approach.

After this I made a thorough and detailed reading of these novels, making notes and comments about particular passages, or more broadly about sections of the text, that I considered to be of geographical importance in relation to social control. Having previously read these works I was able to distance myself from the plot and to become more analytical about the style of the narrative, its structure and form. At the end of this process, I was able to arrange this material into four thematic sections that formed the main chapters of my dissertation. These were 'World space and geopolitics', 'The other place' (rural/urban comparisons), 'Space in dystopia' (the small-scale spaces of control), and the 'Geographies of Mental Space'.

The second key consideration having established the thematic structure of my dissertation was to put these individual works in context. This was achieved in two ways. First, I read a series of studies of the 1930s and 1940s – ones written at the time and histories written much later – which gave me a sense of the social, political, economic and cultural circumstances in which these books were produced. These included history texts, but also biographies and commentaries on the writers themselves. Second,

I wanted to place these novels alongside Orwell and Huxley's other work. These authors were both prolific essayists and this contextualisation proved relatively easy. Importantly, this added a different perspective on the novels, because their essays highlighted different aspects not only of their writing style but also on their own lives and experiences, and how these shaped both *Nineteen Eighty-Four* and *Brave New World*.

One of the key aspects of any historical project is the analysis of 'primary' material. In this project, I didn't make much use of the archives that exist on both Orwell and Huxley to augment and develop my analysis. All of the materials I used were published, although I was in effect using the novels themselves as 'primary' sources. The principal reason for this absence of primary materials was the fact that the archives were located in London and I in Swansea, and other pressures on my time (mainly work commitments during the vacation) precluded me from spending any time travelling to and fro. I was confident that this wouldn't detract from the overall analysis and my conceptual ideas, but I was a little anxious that my study might not have that something extra that good historical projects often do – critical insights from unpublished sources.

My dissertation argued, unsurprisingly, that space was indeed fundamental to an understanding of the control of society in these dystopian futures. This spatial control was exercised at each of the four geographical scales: geopolitical, urban/rural, inter-urban, and at the individual level of the body and the mind. These 'ideological geographies' were suffused throughout the novels, and by extension throughout the imagined worlds they presented to the reader. I really enjoyed doing my dissertation, and I think the key to that enjoyment was being enthusiastic about the actual topic that I had chosen. Enthusiasm is, I believe, the key not only to an enjoyable research experience but also, perhaps more importantly, to a successful piece of work.

After graduating in geography from the University of Wales Swansea in 1998, I began a PhD on the cultural geographies of kitchens, modern flats and new towns, reflecting on the nature of their 'domestic modernities'. I obtained my PhD in 2002 and am currently Lecturer in Human Geography at the University of Wales Swansea. My current research focuses on the polyvocal narratives of planning in post-war South Wales.

2

The view from the streets

Geographies of homelessness in the British newspaper press

Jon May

In this chapter I consider ways in which cultural geography students undertaking research might usefully draw upon the newspaper press – not, as is more usually the case, as one of a number of secondary sources with which to illustrate an account, but as the primary focus of their research. The chapter is based around an account of my own research into the geographies of homelessness *constructed* by the British newspaper press. While giving a flavour of this research, my main aim is to encourage readers to think more carefully about the ways in which the press operate so as to enable a better analysis of newspaper accounts whatever their substantive focus.

However defined, homelessness is an issue of obvious social concern. Though it has been a focus of enquiry for geographers working in the United States for some time, British geographers have been slow in turning their attention to the problem (for a review of recent work on homelessness by American geographers, see Takahashi, 1996). While a small geographical literature on homelessness is now emerging in Britain – most of it by cultural geographers – little attention has been paid to the ways in which homelessness is represented, whether by the newspaper press or others (for examples of work on homelessness by British geographers see: Cloke *et al.*, 2000a; Doyle, 1999; May, 2000, 2003; on representations of homelessness by geographers, May, 2002; Phillips, 2000; and by others: Beresford, 1979; Hutson, 1992; Liddiard and Hutson, 1998).

In fact, cultural geographers have shown remarkably little interest in the newspaper press in general (though see Burgess, 1985, 1990; Dodds, 1998; Vujakovic, 1998). Where newspaper accounts have been used this has mainly been for illustrative purposes (rather than for an examination of the politics of the press more widely) and rarely with the same sophistication afforded other texts (see, for example, Cresswell, 1996; Smith, 1996). Given the role that newspapers play in shaping people's understandings of the world, and the growing body of work by geographers exploring a whole host of other visual and textual media, this is surprising (see Chapters 3, 4, 9, 10, 12 and 13; Eldridge *et al.*, 1997). The lack of a literature by geographers on the broader politics of the press also makes it difficult for students wishing to examine such a politics to know how to go about it.

For those interested in such questions, homelessness provides an excellent vehicle of enquiry. Certainly, in their accounts of homelessness, newspapers often introduce readers to a world of which they might otherwise have little or no experience, defining the essential characteristics of that world and its inhabitants for a broader public. Where readers are already familiar with the problems of homelessness, the press help them make sense of their experiences: offering explanations for the presence of those seen sleeping rough, for example, or of the recent rise in levels of homelessness of all kinds (Beresford, 1979). In my own research I am concerned with tracing the picture of homelessness presented by the British newspaper press in the belief that newspaper accounts are liable to be of considerable importance in shaping broader public attitudes to the problems of homelessness (Liddiard and Hutson, 1998). A significant part of this analysis relates to the various geographies of homelessness constructed by the press, as these in turn shape the picture of homelessness, and of homeless people, readers are presented with. In the hope that it may encourage others to engage with the politics of the newspaper press, whether as part of an exploration of homelessness or some other issue, here I explain how this research was done.

Concept Box

Social construction

Social constructionism is most easily defined as the recognition that understandings of the world are determined by the social context within which those understandings are constructed, rather than by any innate quality within the object of enquiry itself. One obvious application of such ideas is to discussions of **identity**. For example, once it is recognised that ideas of femininity and masculinity vary over time and space it becomes clear that gender is constructed rather than pre-given. Very similar arguments can be made about race, sexuality, age, or disability; or about the conceptual categories that frame other identities: 'deviance' and 'crime', or 'home' and 'homelessness', for example. To say that something is constructed is not to say it isn't 'real', of course. On the contrary, such constructions shape social action in important ways as people act in accordance to their understandings of the world. As Susan Ruddick has shown, the ways in which the problems of homelessness are constructed, for example, has real and important effects on the ways in which homeless people are treated (Ruddick, 1996). Though its roots can be traced back considerably further, social constructionism first came to prominence in the social sciences in the 1960s through the work of Peter Berger and Thomas Luckmann. In *The Social Construction of Reality* (1966) they argued that 'social knowledge becomes real and takes on causative powers when people start believing it, and allow it to enter in to their everyday … routines' (Barnes, 2000: 748). Such ideas are now commonplace in cultural geography and debate has moved on from arguments as to whether or not various concepts should be understood as 'constructed' or 'real', to an examination of the ways in which those concepts are constructed and the effects of those constructions. In their study of the social construction of religion, Berger and Luckmann placed particular emphasis upon the role of institutions in reenforcing various beliefs and understandings – focusing on the role of the church. Others have studied the role of the media, or the academy itself (Cohen and Young, 1981; Sibley, 1995) while Judith Butler (1993, 1997) focuses not on institutions but *social practices*: showing how ideas of gender are reproduced through the constant repetition of various embodied performances that both help shape, and are shaped by, understandings as to how a 'masculine' or 'feminine' body should move, sit, talk, dress and so on (see concept boxes on **Embodiment** and **Performance/Performativity**).

Key Reading

- Cohen, S. and Young, J. (eds) (1981) *The Manufacture of News: social problems, deviance and the mass media*. London, Constable.
- Cresswell, T. (2001) *The Tramp in America*. London, Reaktion. Chapter 1.
- Ruddick, S. (1996) *Young and Homeless in Hollywood: mapping social identities*. London, Routledge. Chapter 2.
- Sibley, D. (1995) *Geographies of Exclusion*. London, Routledge.

Making sense of homelessness

Before trying to make sense of the **representations** of homelessness to be found in the newspaper press it is useful to have a clearer understanding of the problems of homelessness with which the press are apparently concerned. It is also useful to have an understanding as to the basic role of the newspaper press, and some idea of how the press operates.

Whether influenced by personal experience or by the newspapers they read, when most people think of homelessness they think of people sleeping rough. In fact, rough sleeping is only one form of homelessness, with rough sleepers making up only a small proportion of the homeless population (Burrows et al, 1997). In Britain, for example, even when at its peak in the early 1990s London's rough sleeping population never rose above 3000 people, with most estimates putting the current number of people sleeping rough in central London at about 300. Compared to the 15,000 or so people living in night shelters and hostels across the capital this is very low (Pleace and Quilgars, 1997).

Those sleeping rough or staying in night shelters and hostels form part of what is usually referred to as the 'single homeless population' (so-called because most are indeed single) experiencing some form of 'visible homelessness'. The single homeless population also includes the 'hidden homeless' – people staying unwillingly with friends and family, for example, or living in some other kind of insecure accommodation such as squats. Gaining an accurate picture of the hidden homeless population is more difficult, but a recent estimate puts the number of people living in squats in London alone at about 11,000 (Pleace and Quilgars, 1997). Finally, in addition to the single homeless population there are those accepted by a local authority as 'statutorily homeless'. As the name implies, the statutory homeless population consists of people with a statutory right to social housing – mainly families with dependent children. With some 114,000 households (or 285,000 people) accepted as statutorily homeless by local authorities across England in 2000–2001, the statutory homeless population is considerably larger than the single homeless population and dwarfs the number of people sleeping rough (DTLR, 2002).

Establishing the geography of all of this is difficult, with accurate figures on the single homeless population only available for London. But it is clear that the problems of homelessness are at least as bad if not worse outside of London as in the capital. For example, best estimates put the number of people currently sleeping rough in towns and cities across the UK outside of London at some two to three hundred people, with many thousands more staying in night shelters and hostels (Cloke et al., 2002). Levels of statutory homelessness are also high (with 84,720 households accepted as homeless by English local authorities, outside of London, between 2000 and 2001) while the fastest rise in levels of both statutory and single homelessness over recent years has in fact occurred not in London but in rural areas, where problems of hidden homelessness are especially acute (Cloke et al., 2000b).

... and the newspaper press

A popular view of the newspaper press is that it acts as a forum for public debate, offering people a picture of things they may have no direct experience of (for example, homelessness) and explanations for those things, so that they may come to an opinion as to their meaning and importance. In fact, even a cursory glance at the day's news shows that this is not the case. Just as newspapers tend to carry a very limited range of stories, so too the interpretation of events offered by different newspapers (give or take some limited party political differences) are often very similar. Hall et al. refer to this as the 'limits to debate' that define day-to-day newspaper coverage, suggesting that far from fostering public debate the purpose of such coverage is actually to secure a consensual picture of the world where no such consensus exists (S. Hall et al., 1978).

Accepting this to be broadly true, more recent work on the newspaper press has sought to explain in more detail how and why such a consensus might emerge. Eschewing simplistic explanations that would have the press acting as a vehicle of propaganda for powerful (but unspecified) elites, such work has focused on what Allan calls the 'politics of news work' – attempting to reveal the ways in which the practices of news workers themselves give rise to a particular framing of the social world (Allan, 1999; c.f. Herman and Chomsky, 1988).

In my own research I have found an examination of two areas of news work to be especially useful. The first of these refers to the operation of what Tuchman (1978) calls the 'news net', the second to the role of what Galtung and Ruge (1981) refer to as 'new values'. The news net is most easily defined as the means by which reporters are dispersed to 'find the news'. As Tuchman notes, though advances in communication technologies might appear to remove any constraints upon the spatial reach of the news net, because of the potentially huge array of events that might be classified as 'news' (and the increasingly tight production schedules under which journalists work) the news net's reach is actually quite restricted and its coverage far from uniform. As a result, journalists tend therefore to focus their attentions on certain localities. These tend in turn to be ones in which they might expect to find issues of particular interest to their readers (those which show a high degree of 'fit' with a newspaper's news values, a notion explored below) and source agencies that they may quickly and easily draw upon for information.

'News values' are best understood as the 'rules' or 'codes' that render a particular event 'newsworthy'. The closer that an issue or event equates to these values the more likely it is to be selected as 'news'. At the same time, those same news values are liable to be accentuated in the subsequent (re)presentation of those events so as to lend further weight to their privileged position as an 'event-as-news'. In previous analyses of representations of homelessness in the newspaper press, seven such news values have been identified as of particular importance (Hutson, 1992).

First, it is clear that the press value *conflict* – allowing a newspaper to present more than one side to a story and render the impression at least of a 'balanced' report – while in their final accounts journalists tend to emphasise *contrast*: between rich and poor, the familiar and unfamiliar, housed and homeless, for example. Second, the press are drawn to events that can be shown to be *relevant to the lives of readers* and that may be understood by readers as relating to 'people like us'. Third, they are drawn to events they may *personalise* (so as to be able to explore an issue through 'real peoples' experiences on the ground' rather than focusing upon abstract structures or processes) and to those they may *simplify*: such that in an attempt to render their explanations easily understood they often draw on *stereotypes*. Fourth, newspapers favour stories that are *consonant*: easily recognised by journalists and readers alike as to 'what kind of story' they might be, and one reason that similar stories appear time and time again. Fifth, journalists are of course also drawn to stories that are *timely,* and ideally *novel*, out of the ordinary or unexpected: often leading to what Hopper has called a search for the 'grotesque' and a tendency to emphasise the unusual rather than the representative (Hopper, 1991; Soothill and Walby, 1991). Sixth, the press favour issues and events relating to *elite persons* (such as celebrities, politicians or royalty), whilst finally they favour *negativity*: as 'bad news' usually conforms to more of the above values than does 'good news'.

A number of such values are usually apparent in newspaper accounts. Different newspapers will also obviously emphasise different values in different kinds of stories. For example, whilst tabloid newspapers show a greater tendency towards the personalisation of stories than do the broadsheet press, they also often portray a certain ambiguity in their portrayal and explanation of events (Dahlgren and Sparks, 1992). Given such ambiguity, individual stories may display news values which apparently contradict one another, while the generic values outlined above may, on occasion, take rather different forms to those expected.

Getting started

Armed with a basic understanding of how the press operates, the first step in any analysis of the newspaper press is to decide which newspapers one is going to work with. Depending upon the issue under investigation, it may be appropriate to look at newspapers from different ends of the political spectrum. In Britain, for example, the national press tends to divide along fairly clear party political lines. Amongst the broadsheets, whilst *The Times* maintains a position slightly to the right of centre, both the *Guardian* and *Independent* are clearer in their support of New Labour with the *Telegraph* supporting the Conservative Party. Amongst the tabloids, the London *Evening Standard*'s position is best described as populist (shifting its party political allegiances in line with the assumed values of its readers), the *Mirror* (and more recently, the *Sun*) explicitly support New Labour, with each of the others (the *Daily Star*, *Daily Mail* and *Daily Express*) more obvious in their support for the Conservative Party. It is also important to think through whether one wishes to work with the tabloid or broadsheet press. While the tabloids tend to carry very different kinds of stories, they are also aimed at a very different (and much larger) audience. Finally, it is necessary to determine the timescale one is working with.

Having done this, the next step is to build some kind of archive of stories. If working with broadsheet newspapers this is relatively easy. Most British broadsheets now provide free on-line access to editions reaching back to 1999. Most sites also include a simple search function, enabling one to search back issues according to crude content descriptors (for example, homelessness) though one needs to be aware that these tend to pick up only those stories in which the chosen category is the main focus of a piece. If wishing to go back further, or working with tabloid newspapers, the British Library Newspaper Archive in Colindale, North London, is also free of charge and contains microfiche copies of all national newspapers reaching back to their first publication. Whilst more comprehensive than on-line archives, searching through the archives at Colindale is extremely time consuming (necessitating that one searches perhaps thousands of pages of microfiche to identify just a few dozen stories) and, if copying stories for later analysis, expensive.

An attractive alternative is therefore to try and gain access to organisations that might have already constructed an archive of newspaper material relevant to one's research. In my case I was able to use the newspaper archive at Shelter, who employ a commercial clippings service to select and archive all the stories relating to housing and homelessness across a huge range of papers (including all of the major national dailies and weeklies). This was especially useful to me because I wished to compare coverage across a broad time period (to see how it changed throughout the 1990s) and to analyse coverage in both tabloid and broadsheet newspapers of different political persuasions. Working with pre-selected material, however, meant I had to check to see whether the archive on which I was drawing indeed included all of the stories relating to homelessness in the national newspaper press through this period. I did this quite simply by checking the stories I found at Shelter against stories I had found myself in one tabloid newspaper at Colindale and working on-line with more recent editions of a broadsheet paper.

If working with more recent editions of the broadsheet press, or able to use an existing archive, it may well be possible to try and analyse all the stories relating to the issue under investigation in your chosen timeframe (as I did). Otherwise it is necessary to employ some kind of sampling procedure (random, stratified, systematic or cluster sampling, for example) searching a selection of editions for stories (see Krippendorf, 1980). The danger of proceeding without a clear sampling procedure is that you will be unable to say how representative such stories are of that newspaper's wider coverage.

Having selected the stories one is going to work with (your sample population) the next step is to decide on a method of analysis. The most common technique in the analysis of newspaper texts, and the one I chose, is *content analysis* – defined by Rose as: 'counting the frequency of certain [themes or codes] in a clearly defined sample [of texts] and then analysing those frequencies' (Rose, 2001: 56). At root, content analysis is therefore a way of quantifying a set of themes identified within a text or selection of texts by the analyst, in the belief that the relative frequency of such themes provides an indication of the importance liable to be granted those themes by a reader. Such quantification can take different forms, with analysts sometimes seeking to offer a simple picture of the number of stories within a chosen sample population given over to a particular theme (the approach I adopted), quantifying the number of *column inches* given over to that theme, or counting the number of times particular words or phrases are used in those stories.

More used to working within a qualitative approach, such quantification often makes cultural geographers nervous. Certainly it is true that content analysis may actually offer little indication of how a newspaper's coverage is liable to be made sense of by readers (though this is a charge that can be levelled at other forms of analysis too) and runs the risk of lifting the themes it identifies out of context so that they lose their meaning. On its own the number of times a particular story runs, or the number of column inches given over to it, may also tell us little about the relative importance afforded an issue by a newspaper: a better indication of which may be whether a story is on the front, back or middle pages, or carries a photograph, for example. But the great advantage of content analysis is that it allows the analyst to work with relatively large data sets, thus enabling one to build a representative picture of the basic structure of reporting around one's chosen issue which can be supplemented with a more detailed analyses of a small selection of typical stories later on.

If working with content analysis the stories chosen for analysis must first be coded. These codes may be either *descriptive* or *interpretative* (I decided to work with both) with the exact nature of the codes falling under each depending upon one's focus of enquiry. As the phrase suggests, *descriptive* codes seek to describe the basic content of a text. In my case these referred to both the main focus of each story (whether primarily concerned with people sleeping rough, those staying in night shelters and hostels or bed and breakfast hotels, for example) and the story's geographical context (the name, if available, of the town or city in which the story was set or at least some indication as to whether set in an urban or rural context). *Interpretative* codes, on the other hand, link much more directly to the theoretical concerns of the analyst. Because one of my concerns was the more general stance different newspapers took towards the problems of homelessness, I also therefore coded each story according to whether it was simply publicising an issue (for example, a rise in the number of people sleeping rough), politicising that issue (seeking to set the reasons for that rise within a broader, and more critical, perspective) or offering a largely negative portrayal of homeless people (explaining rough sleeping in accordance with the failings of an individual, for example) (see Penner and Penner, 1994).

Either type of code may also be nested so as to add complexity to the coding procedure. For example, under my descriptive codes I added a further set of categories noting whether a story was mainly concerned with the single homeless population, statutory homelessness, visible homelessness or hidden homelessness. Whatever codes one uses, the most important thing is that they fulfil four basic criteria, being: exhaustive (covering every aspect of the text or texts under consideration); exclusive (not overlapping); unambiguous (such that one's choice might be replicated by another researcher analysing the same text(s)); and enlightening (breaking down the text so as to provide for a better sense of how it works) (Rose, 2001).

Because working across a number of newspapers over a broad timescale (and hence potentially generating a huge number of stories to analyse) rather than making copies of every story and coding this material later, I completed this coding in the archive: only photocopying those stories I felt would warrant further attention later. The actual coding procedure was very simple. With a new sheet of paper for each, I recorded a basic summary of each story, together with its headline, the newspaper in which it was found, and the date of publication. Each sheet also had a number of check-boxes marked with the codes described above, enabling me to move quickly through a large number of stories. The final product of my time in the archive was therefore a relatively small number of photocopied stories, and a much larger pile of coding sheets ready for entry into a database for later analysis (though those with a lap top computer could of course enter this material into a database in the archive).

Defining and mapping homelessness

Once entered into the database, building a picture of the representations of homelessness found in the British newspaper press was relatively straightforward. For example, searching the database for the descriptive codes outlined above I was quickly and easily able to reveal the proportion of stories concerned with problems of rough sleeping rather than other forms of homelessness. Using my interpretative codes I was also able to trace differences in the tone assumed when reporting on the problems of homelessness by different papers (or by the same newspaper when reporting on different forms of homelessness), whilst using my summary information I was able to chart both the general extent and timing of coverage.

Perhaps the most obvious, but also the most striking, aspect of this coverage was the extent to which, when reporting on the problems of homelessness, newspapers focus on problems of rough sleeping. Hence, of the 1550 stories on homelessness carried by the major British dailies and weekend newspapers between January 1990 and December 1999, for example, fully 61 per cent were concerned with rough sleeping, with just 14 per cent given over to an examination of the much more extensive problem of statutory homelessness. In some newspapers the balance of coverage was even more uneven, with 80 per cent of stories in the *Daily Express*, for example, focused on rough sleepers.

In light of such figures, it is clear that for the British newspaper press homelessness is largely defined in terms of absolute rooflessness. Indeed, for the readers of some newspapers it would be very difficult to appreciate that homelessness ever takes other forms. This focus can largely be explained with reference to the news values outlined in the opening section of the chapter. While newspapers are liable to assume that rough sleeping is the form of homelessness with which their readers will be most familiar, it also enables journalists to play up various contrasts in their accounts: between the person sleeping rough and the passer-by, for example, or between homeless people and readers themselves. A focus on rough sleeping also enables journalists to personalise a story, exploring the otherwise complex problem of homelessness through the experiences of an individual rough sleeper – often leading tabloid newspapers especially to 'explain' homelessness in terms of a range of stereotypes concerning a person's descent into homelessness because of problems of alcohol or drug abuse, for example. Journalists also often (quite wrongly) portray life on the streets as 'exciting', while rough sleeping is of course the ultimate 'bad news' story.

As a geographer, though, I was especially interested in the various locations in which newspapers set their accounts of homelessness, and what the resultant geographies might tell us about the broader picture of homelessness constructed by the newspaper press. The basic contours of this geography could also be traced through a simple content analysis and proved to be revealing. Not least, of the 1127 stories given a specific location, less than 5 per cent explored problems of homelessness in Britain's rural areas. Against this, fully 76 per cent were set in London, with the remaining 19 per cent set in other towns and cities across the country. It was also notable that of the latter a little over two-thirds (or 69 per cent) of 150 or so stories were set in just a handful of cities: namely, Oxford and Cambridge, Brighton, Bristol and Bath, Manchester and Birmingham. Though levels of homelessness rose across most towns and cities in Britain through the 1990s, and especially fast in rural areas, the impression given by the British newspaper press is therefore that the problems of homelessness are largely confined to the capital and a small number of 'homeless places'.

Such a geography is most easily explained with reference to the operation of a 'news net'. The Department of Transport, Local Government and the Regions (the government department responsible for homelessness policy in Britain) and the main homelessness charities (Centrepoint, Crisis and Shelter) all have their headquarters in London. These are the organisations that provide newspapers with the source material for their stories on homelessness – in the form of press releases. Of the other locations, it is notable that having first made an appearance in the early 1990s, each appeared with increasing frequency as the decade wore on: presumably, as journalists returned to places that they knew would provide good copy.

A number of these other locations (notably Oxford and Cambridge, Brighton and Bath) are of course also attractive because of the news values they enable journalists to mobilise. Not least, with the vast majority of coverage in the early 1990s at least exploring problems of homelessness in the capital, as journalists 'discovered' homelessness in other towns and cities so they were able to emphasise the 'novelty' of their accounts. Such discoveries were in turn rendered all the more shocking as people were found sleeping rough in the heart of 'Middle England': in university cities and wealthy spa resorts. Not surprisingly, perhaps, accounts set in these places were especially likely to carry stories on rough sleeping. In some, with headlines like 'The other side of the pier' (Guardian, 1991) or 'Homeless swell ranks of deprived in city of learning' (Independent, 1991) the contrast is simply between the person sleeping rough and the wealth of the surrounding streets. In others, the emphasis is on the threat that people sleeping rough pose to local inhabitants and more especially to the local economy (see, for example: Daily Star 'The Junkie Beggars who Hold our City to Ransom' or more simply 'Beggar Off!' 1993, 1994; c.f. Atkinson and Laurier, 1998; Mitchell, 1997).

The view from the streets

A basic content analysis enabled me to build up a picture of the broad sweep of recent homelessness coverage. However, I also wanted to explore the various settings that newspapers use in stories about homelessness in more detail – to see what those settings might tell us about the image of homelessness and of homeless people that newspapers construct. Here I turned to a small number of stories I adjudged to be typical of this broader coverage, focusing my attention on two settings in particular: those concerned with problems of rural homelessness, and those exploring the world of rough sleeping in Britain's towns and cities.

In trying to make sense of these stories I took three 'cuts' at the material. First, I read and re-read each of the stories relating to these settings a number of times so as to thoroughly familiarise myself with the material, and made a careful note of the news values evident in each piece: in an attempt to establish why each had been selected as a piece of 'news'. Second, I treated each story more like an interview transcript: searching the text for analytical themes or 'tropes' around which the journalist seemed to be structuring their account of homelessness, and constructing a series of 'etic' codes relating to those themes (see M. Crang, 1997). Finally, I paid close attention to the language used in individual pieces (both in the headlines that convey the essence of a story to a reader, and in the main body of the text itself) in an attempt to see how the language of the piece was being used to build a particular picture of homelessness and of homeless people (for a guide to the language of the press, see Branston and Stafford, 1996).

In the case of rural homelessness, I found the majority of stories in the broadsheet press at least to be given over to relatively dry accounts publicising a recent rise in homelessness in these areas, or to calls for an increased supply of affordable housing. A significant proportion of stories in the tabloid press, however, paint a more vivid picture of rural homelessness. Typical is a story run by the *Daily Star* in September 1995 under the headline 'Tramp's EIGHT years in bus shelter':

A friendly tramp faces eviction from a bus shelter where he has lived for EIGHT years. Bearded Mick has become popular with locals after snuggling up in the cosy brick building for nearly a decade. They provide food, milk and blankets and consider their jolly bagman one of the community … But Mick's days in the roadside refuge he considers just the ticket are numbered after two meanies complained to the Local Government Ombudsman.

(Daily Star 15/09/95: p13)

Such stories move around a number of classic tropes that re-enforce a typically nostalgic image of rural life: seen here in the apparent generosity of local people in contrast to a hard-hearted bureaucracy, for example (Cloke and Milbourne, 1992). They also paint a very particular picture of rural homelessness. In stories like this the rural homeless population is made up not of the younger homeless people and rough sleepers that tend to provide the focus for newspaper's accounts of homelessness in Britain's towns and cities, but a selection of eccentric and essentially harmless 'tramps' and 'hobos' (see also Crowther, 1992). In the story quoted above, for example, Mick's eccentricity is marked out both by his beard (a necessary accoutrement of any self-respecting tramp) and his choice of accommodation (as he 'snuggles up' in his 'cosy' bus shelter). The story also implies a number of other differences between (harmless) 'tramps' like Mick and other homeless people: notably, the diet of bread and milk (rather than drugs and alcohol) for example. As they work to render a picture of homeless people more in keeping with a romantic image of the English countryside, the danger of such accounts is therefore that they will in fact further re-enforce what Cloke *et al.* refer to as a wider 'de-coupling' of homelessness (in its more typical forms) and rurality (Cloke *et al.*, 2000a).

This 'fit' between homeless people and the spaces they occupy is evident in newspaper coverage relating to the problems of rough sleeping in urban areas too, though here the picture of homeless people it helps to construct is far less benign. Analysing these stories I found them to be characterised by three main tropes.

First, rough sleepers are typically presented as occupying spaces on the 'edge' of the city – symbolically if not literally. This tendency is as common in pieces sympathetic to the plight of homeless people as it is in those offering a more negative portrayal of people sleeping rough. In the former, homeless people are frequently presented as being in but not of the taken-for-granted world of readers, or as being somehow 'lost'. Hence, announcing plans for the re-development of London's Bull Ring, for example, the *Daily Telegraph* asked: 'What effect will [these plans] have on the *lost tribes* living in London's cardboard city?' (*Daily Telegraph*: 'Homeless or Hopeless?' 22/6/90). In a similar vein, in his report on the growing problem of homelessness in Brighton, Nick Davies described how 'behind the stucco of gracious Georgian buildings [there exists] a growing army of *homeless souls* urgently seek[ing] refuge' (*Guardian*: 'The Other Side of the Pier', 25/5/91). In stories offering a more negative portrayal of homeless people the tendency is to describe a world *beneath* the city, with people sleeping rough 'lurking' in alleyways and subways waiting to accost passers-by (*Daily Express*: 'Where Subway Nasties Lurk', 22/06/94). Whilst both types of piece obviously play up the *contrasts* between the 'hidden' world inhabited by homeless people and a more familiar cityscape, journalists also have a vested interest in rendering that world as unfamiliar as possible: so that they might assume the role of first 'exploring' and then 'interpreting' it for their readers (Beresford, 1979).

Second, as homeless people are portrayed as 'fitting' these environments so they also assume a certain, and often threatening, 'Otherness'. While this may seem to contradict the suggestion that journalists favour stories that may be understood by readers as relating to 'people like us', the appeal is of course that these accounts reassure readers of their own normalcy (Hopper, 1991). Once again, this tendency is as apparent in stories attempting to portray a sympathetic picture of people sleeping rough (with the story from the *Guardian* quoted above attributing a genuinely other worldly status to its subjects, for example) as in more negative portrayals – where accounts of 'shambling', 'stumbling', 'shouting' homeless people predominate. Indeed, in more negative accounts the **difference** of homeless people is taken to extremes, as they become cast not as people at all but animals. Sometimes this is done by simple suggestion – with the 'subway nasties' of the *Daily Express* sounding like a particularly irritating insect perhaps. More often it is done by a process of metaphoric transfer (with descriptions of the 'feral' existence led by people sleeping rough not unusual, for example) or as the metaphors used to describe the environment in which homeless people live are carried over so as to connect in the reader's mind with homeless people themselves (see also Cresswell, 1997). In the extract from the *Evening Standard* quoted below, for example, it is not simply that the 'animal' qualities of the two subjects John and Alex fit the nightmarish world of the 'professional rough sleeper' 'discovered' by the reporter, but that (like animals) they are to some extent a product of that environment:

> *Come with us into a vision of hell in the heart of our city … Enter the abyss; the old brewery on Stockwell Green … a modern day opium den where refugees, immigrants and homeless people from all over the world exist in conditions that would make Jack London, Charles Dickens or George Orwell blanch. Overrun by filthy addicts who live a* **feral** *existence amid their own excrement, here – two-and-a-half miles from the Palace of Westminster, with a special needs school in its shadow – exists a scene of degradation few are likely ever to witness…Here, behind a filthy sheet, is the first of dozens of* **stinking burrows**. *Slumped under a pile of half-burned sheets and plastic bags is a human being. He looks up wearily, his eyes yellow and glazed from the drugs, then slumps back to the floor, his head resting inches away from the waste of the last person to surrender themselves to this* **hovel** *…This is home to John and Alex, who could best be described as professional street sleepers.*
>
> (*Evening Standard*: 'In the heart of London, a sickening scene of squalor', 11/12/98: p. 10, emphasis added)

Whether the aim is to sympathise or vilify, the broader effect of such manoeuvres is to present homeless people as simultaneously living in the heart of the city but beyond the boundaries of (civilised) society. As a reporter from the *News of the World* put it when describing a night spent sleeping rough in central London as part of an investigation into homelessness in the capital, for example:

> *This is my first night sleeping rough on the streets of London … I am on the pavement in Shaftesbury Avenue in theatreland – the heart of our culture and civilisation. But wrapped in my sleeping bag, with my meagre possessions tied to my wrist to stop them being snatched, I am outside society and outside the law.*
>
> (*News of the World*: 'Hungry and Homeless – Our man discovers the hidden hell of living rough on streets of Britain', 26/07/98: pp. 30–31)

Finally, just as press accounts often de-humanise homeless people so too they often present homeless people not as individuals but as part of a larger whole: 'the homeless'. In describing that whole homeless people are often portrayed in ways that would seem to position them as belonging to an earlier, more primitive world – as members of various 'tribes' or 'clans', for example (*Daily Telegraph*, 1990; *Independent*, 1991). Elsewhere, military metaphors predominate, with homeless people described as an 'army' (*Guardian*, 1991). These military metaphors in particular are easily turned – so as to portray the threat such armies might pose if ever to get on the move – though the real threat is of course how close they already are: 'lurking' just beneath the reader's feet, no more than 'two-and-a-half miles from the Palace of Westminster, with a special needs school in [their] shadow' (see also, *Daily Express*: 'Beggar army lays siege to our tourists', 22/06/94).

When each of these tropes come together in a single account and are given a negative spin, as in the piece from the *Evening Standard* quoted above, the effect can be quite startling. But more generally they describe a certain tendency (or 'vocabulary of precedence') that appears in stories of rough sleeping again and again and helps to construct a generic picture of the 'world of the rough sleeper' as likely to be found in the broadsheet as tabloid press, in newspapers on the right or left of the political divide. Significantly, whilst such accounts often provide highly detailed descriptions of this world (so as to add 'realism') they are in fact quite placeless: with descriptions of the alleyways and subways, sleeping bags and squats that define the world of London's rough sleepers indistinguishable from accounts of rough sleeping in Bristol, Brighton or Bath (for a similar tendency amongst reporters to construct a generic 'inner city', see Burgess 1985).

Conclusions and suggestions for further study

In my own research I have focused on the geographies of homelessness constructed by the newspaper press because I believe these geographies are central to the picture of homelessness, and homeless people, that newspapers present to their readers. This picture is in turn important because it may shape broader public attitudes to the problems of homelessness and, by extension, any response to those problems formulated by policy makers.

Tracing these connections between newspaper representations, public attitudes and the actions of policy makers is of course extremely difficult (Liddiard and Hutson, 1998; May, 2002). But it is notable that just as newspaper accounts of homelessness are dominated by stories of people sleeping rough, so too recent government initiatives designed to tackle homelessness have focused almost exclusively on the problems of rough sleeping: with the launch of the Rough Sleeper's Initiative in June 1990, for example, and the more recent formation of the Rough Sleepers Unit. It is also striking that when distributing money under the Rough Sleepers Initiative, of the £177 million made available between 1999 and 2002 to reduce the number of people sleeping rough in England and Wales more than £145 million went to London: with just £32 million left to be divided between 'the regions' (most of it going to the handful of towns and cities identified earlier in the chapter as being especially prominent in recent press reports) (Cloke et al., 2000a).

As Cloke et al. argue, the tendency of newspapers to construct an image of homelessness as rooflessness, and as a problem mainly confined to London, poses significant difficulties for rural areas where problems of hidden homelessness are especially acute (2000a and b). But the geographies of homelessness described above may be significant in other ways too. Having constructed a decidedly negative picture of homeless people, in the early-to-mid-1990s a number of British newspapers embarked upon campaigns calling for the clearance of homeless people from the streets (*Daily Star*, 1993; *Daily Telegraph*, 1993; *The Times*, 1991). All too often such calls were heeded. Beginning in June 1990 with Operation Burlington in London's West End, for example, the Metropolitan Police launched the first of what was to be a series of campaigns aimed at ridding the streets of what they referred to as 'parasitic' and 'bogus' beggars. In August 1991 Operation Burlington was followed by Operation Taurus such that between 1991 and 1992 arrests under the powers of the Vagrancy Acts (1824) increased from 192 to 1,445 in London alone (*Independent*, 1992). Similar operations followed across the country, often focusing on exactly those cities singled out for attention in earlier press reports: Bath (in 1993 and 1994); Brighton (1993) and Bristol (1996), for example (see also Dean, 1999). This more aggressive stance towards people sleeping rough has continued under the New Labour government (Fitzpatrick et al., 2000). In the Rough Sleeper Unit's *Make a Difference Campaign*, for example, the world of the 'professional street sleeper' presented in newspaper stories and on posters clashed violently with the world of real people sleeping rough, as the government urged people not to give money to rough sleepers and beggars lest it encourage a damaging 'street lifestyle'.

For those interested in making sense of such campaigns an understanding of the wider geographies of the newspaper press is vital. But whatever the substantive focus, cultural geographers wishing to explore the politics of the newspaper press must first develop a more sophisticated understanding of the press itself. Certainly, this means paying close attention to the operation of the news net and to the role that news values play in shaping both the selection and subsequent (re)presentation of 'events-as-news', but readers should also consider a number of other issues I have not had space to elaborate on here and which might usefully form the basis of further study.

First, the account of newspaper constructions of homelessness presented here is necessarily schematic. Not least, I have said next-to-nothing about the obvious differences in the accounts of homelessness to be found in newspapers of differing political persuasions. Notwithstanding the broader 'limits to debate' that are a feature of the British newspaper press (and that are evident in the overwhelming tendency across the press as a whole to define homelessness as a problem of rough sleeping, for example) important differences in the reporting of homelessness are sometimes apparent between papers on the left and right of the political spectrum. Such differences are most apparent in the positions assumed by different newspapers in response to recent attempts to clear homeless people from the streets. Flowing from a newspaper's party political allegiances, the position that individual papers have assumed in these debates are both complex and have changed – most obviously, in line with a change of government. Similar differences are liable to emerge in the reporting of other issues (immigration, unemployment, or the environment, for example) and are also worthy of analysis.

Second, I have not said much about differences in the reporting of homelessness in the broadsheet and tabloid press. Some such differences are obvious. For example, in keeping with their traditional role as a forum for public debate, the broadsheet press carry a relatively wide range of stories on homelessness (covering both problems of rough sleeping and of statutory homelessness, for example) and pay particular attention to government policy. In contrast, the tabloid press tend to focus more on specific forms of homelessness (notably rough sleeping) and particular groups – especially, younger homeless people, but also beggars – and are more likely to base their stories around (stereotypical accounts of) the experiences of individual homeless people. Given their much wider readership the tabloid press have received surprisingly little attention from those interested in the newspaper press and certainly warrant further study (see, for example, Dahlgren and Sparks, 1992; Fiske, 1992).

Third, while my own research has been concerned with representations of homelessness in the national newspaper press, a fascinating study could be done comparing the accounts of homelessness (or some other issue) in the national and local press, or in different local newspapers. The local press is interesting because its coverage is often far more obviously shaped by assumptions as to the values of its readership than is the case with the national newspaper press (Franklin and Murphy, 1991). Significant differences are therefore liable to emerge in the coverage afforded an issue in different places. Gaining access to local newspapers is relatively easy, with many local libraries providing free access to archives already catalogued by subject.

Fourth, whilst my focus here has been on making sense of existing newspaper accounts, it would be interesting to follow the *production* of these accounts in more detail. Not least, Hall *et al.* (1978) suggest that the main reason newspapers tend to carry such similar stories, and interpret those stories in similar ways, is that they draw upon a very limited range of sources: privileging accounts provided (in the form of press releases, for example) by a small number of 'primary definers' who come in effect to determine not only which issues are worthy of being selected as 'news' but how that news might be presented. A problem with Hall *et al.*'s model is that it fails to recognise the diversity of agencies on which the newspaper press draw, not all of which share the same agenda (Schlesinger and Tumber, 1994). It also pays little attention to the way in which journalists themselves 'translate' the accounts of their primary definers – often presenting a story in ways quite different to that originally intended by the source agency (May, 2002). A fascinating project could be done tracing the ways in which a story changes from its initial press release to its eventual publication in a number of different newspapers. Many of the larger charities now archive past press releases on the world-wide-web, as do government departments. But it might also be possible to supplement an analysis of these texts with interviews with agencies workers and journalists so as to gain a much fuller understanding of the 'making of the news'.

Finally, it would be interesting to examine the ways in which newspaper accounts are made sense of by their readers – that is, to focus on the *consumption* of the news. In place of earlier models that tended to ignore the active role played by audiences in the consumption of media texts, most researchers now recognise that it is more useful to think about the way in which press accounts 'resonate' with rather than directly shape a reader's understandings of an issue: with considerable variation evident in those understandings according to a person's own experiences, political consciousness, or socio-demographic position (Negrine, 1994). At the same time, the notion of an active audience should not be over-emphasised. Research in to the role of the press in shaping public understandings of a number of social issues ranging from AIDS to zero tolerance policing by members of the Glasgow Media Group 'consistently reveals a clear correspondence between certain recurrent themes in news reporting and what is recalled, understood, and sometimes believed by audience groups' (Eldridge *et al.*, 1997: 161; Kitzinger, 1993; Kitzinger and Hunt, 1993). Warning against the more recent tendency to place ever greater *power* in the hands of the audience, Eldridge *et al.* therefore conclude that: 'Acknowledging that audiences are "active" does not mean that the media are ineffectual. Recognizing the role of "interpretation" does not invalidate the concept of "influence" ' (Eldridge *et al.*, 1997: 160).

Unless able to draw on their own experiences, it would certainly be difficult for a reader of the *Daily Express* to understand that the problems of homelessness extend beyond people sleeping on the streets or begging for change, for example. But it would be useful to gain a fuller understanding of precisely how these kinds of stories are made sense of by their readers. It would be even more interesting to consider the understandings of the one group never afforded a position of readership in the accounts analysed here or elsewhere – namely, homeless people themselves.

Further reading
Making sense of homelessness
- Burrows, R., Pleace, N., and Quilgars, D. (eds) (1997) *Homelessness and Social Policy*. London, Routledge.
- Kennett, P. and Marsh, P. (eds) (1999) *Homelessness: Exploring the New Terrain*. Bristol, Policy Press.
- Ruddick, S. (1996) *Young and Homeless in Hollywood: Mapping Social Identities*. London, Routledge.

... of the politics of the press
- Eldridge, J. (ed.) (1993) *Getting the Message: Essays from Glasgow University Media Group*. London, Routledge.
- Eldridge, J., Kitzinger, J. and Williams, K. (1997) *The Mass Media and Power in Modern Britain*. Oxford, Oxford University Press.

... and of the language of the news (and other texts)
- Allan, S. (1999) *News Culture*. Buckingham, Open University Press.
- Cohen, S. and Young, J. (eds) (1981) *The Manufacture of News: Social Problems, Deviance and the Mass Media*. London, Constable.
- Branston, G. and Stafford, R. (1996) *The Media Student's Handbook*. London, Routledge.
- Krippendorf, K. (1980) *Content Analysis: An Introduction to its Methodologies*. London, Sage.
- Rose, G. (2001) *Visual Methodologies: An Introduction to the Interpretation of Visual Materials*. London, Sage.

A TALE OF RESEARCH

The geography of Middle-earth

Mark Biles

Watching the film *The Lord of the Rings: The Fellowship of the Ring* directed by Peter Jackson (2001), inspired me to read the novel by J. R. R. Tolkien (1999). This made me think about the ways in which the geography of Middle-earth is portrayed through the medium of film and text. Having taken second year courses in cultural geography about society and space, nature and culture, I had a vague understanding of how I could use film for my dissertation. I decided, however, to focus just on the novel because I had never used fiction in my geographical studies before. At first this idea appeared quite daunting as it seemed so different from other dissertations that used focus groups, questionnaires and interviews; but at the same time, it was a refreshing opportunity to try something new. Having decided on the source of reference for my dissertation, all that was needed was an argument and a few key research themes in order to explore representations of the geography of Middle-earth in *The Fellowship of the Ring*.

I began my research by reading about the existing relationship between geography and literature to see if I could find any existing methods of research that could assist me with my research on the geography of Middle-earth. Historically, I found that many geographical studies of literature have been critiqued due to their lack of analytical rigour or application to theoretical concepts (Burgess and Gold, 1985). It was because of this that I decided that one of my research themes should be to try to find new methods of research to assist with the use of novels in geographical research.

My second research theme was to focus on the ways in which *The Fellowship of the Ring* creates a 'believable' geography of Middle-earth. This did not involve analysing the geography in the text such as the mountains or other physical geography, or, for that matter, whether or not the journey of Frodo and the Fellowship to Mordor is possible in real terms. Instead it focused on the ways in which textual inscriptions and narrative devices within the novel imply a sense of place. I was interested in how the fictional landscape in the novel is real within the fantasy world of Middle-earth, even though it does not exist in real life. My research on this theme was influenced by the work of Kneale and Kitchin (2002), who focus on the ways in which off-world narratives in science fiction create plausible geographies because they do not stray too far from the real.

Owing to the subjective nature of the novel, the fundamental problem with my literary dissertation was how I could support my own readings of the text, because there are no 'correct' answers as to what makes the geography of Middle-earth 'believable'. The feedback on my dissertation proposal suggested that I should use focus groups to investigate my assumptions of the text. But a problem that can sometimes occur with this form of research is that the group will often read for pleasure and focus on scenes of action or suspense, which are often not the parts of the novel you may want to discuss. Only discussing the parts of the novel you are interested in for research has the effect of ignoring the novel as a whole.

In my research, I was not claiming to be finding the precise meanings Tolkien intended when he wrote *The Lord of the Rings*. Instead, I was trying to suggest and persuade the readers of my dissertation that the ways in which the narrative is written conveys a 'believable' geography of Middle-earth. It was important therefore that my methods of research were rigorous and thorough to support my findings.

One method that I used to assist me in this matter was Pickles' five levels of textual analysis (Pickles, 1992) to ensure that I took meanings *from* the text rather than projected my own meanings on to it. One way in which I was able to use this method of analysis was to suggest that there is an ever-growing awareness of the invasion of the evil armies of Sauron across Middle-earth that encourages the reader to follow the map and become aware that different things are occurring in different geographical locations at the same time. Known as 'interlace', West (1975) argues that this mimics the ways in which time behaves in real life, which adds to the integrity of Middle-earth as an organic 'secondary world' because it resembles elements of reality that the reader can identify with (on 'secondary' worlds, see Chapter 3).

A second part of my methodology involved the use of the theoretical concept known as the 'Theories of the Fantastic', which, put quite crudely, suggests that the parts of the text that create 'believable' geographies are those that involve the uneasy mixing of real and unreal phenomena within the novel (Armitt, 1996). One of the many places in *The Fellowship of the Ring* where such fantastic inscriptions occur can be seen when Sam Gamgee, the down-to-earth character, is confused by his experiences in Lothlórien. So perplexed is Sam that he calls out to the rest of the Fellowship 'anyone would think that time did not count in there' (510). This fantastic inscription has the effect of questioning the ways in which time is experienced by the different beings of Middle-earth. Whilst the Fellowship rests in Lothlórien, Tolkien attempts to hold the oxymoron between mortal time and immortal time (or Elvish time) together through an uneasy mixing of real (mortal) and unreal (immortal) elements. What is most significant about this passage is that Tolkien discusses these unreal elements through an ambiguous form of dream-like narrative, as dreams are one way of accessing a greater experience of consciousness and therefore perhaps emulate an experience of immortality. Its purpose, perhaps, is to try to introduce the reader to the fantastic element of Middle-earth, and in doing so distinguish Middle-earth as the fantastic secondary world where immortality can occur (unlike in the real world). Sam for example feels as if he 'was *inside* a song' (460) and Frodo experiences heightened senses like an Elf but in a dreamy sort of way.

By giving this brief summary of the ways in which I have used textual and theoretical methods of analysis to support my research into the geography of *The Lord of the Rings*, I wish to add to the ever-expanding and diverse canon of geographical research into literature. For example, recent studies include the above-mentioned use of science fiction novels for research, whereas other studies have looked at the way in which literature reflects political and dominant social ideologies (see Cresswell, 1993 and Dennis, 2002). I hope that this will encourage other geography students to explore the use of literary novels for academic study.

I am in the final year of my geography degree at University College London. I am currently taking courses on the geographies of modernity and consumption, and a new course on the geographies of cyberspace. The latter considers the ways in which virtual environments and online virtual communities constitute new spaces in society. I am hoping to continue with these studies, either on an MSc in Virtual Environments at the Bartlett School of Graduate Studies or the MSc in Geography at UCL on Modernity, Space and Place, with a view to carrying this on to a PhD in Geography.

3
Secondary worlds
Reading novels as geographical research

James Kneale

Let's imagine that you want to do your research on a novel, one that seems to have something to do with your studies in cultural geography. You search around for geographical work of this sort and quickly come up against two problems. First, while you've collected a fair few articles, none of them seems to have much to say about questions of method. And second, does it matter that your choice of text – let's say J. R. R. Tolkien's *Lord of the Rings* – is set in a fantastic world? All works of fiction discuss fictional places, because novels are **representations** of reality rather than reality itself. But surely Tolkien's Middle-earth is somehow more fictional than Charles Dickens' London?

This chapter is an attempt to address these questions, based upon my own research into William Gibson's science fiction. I will offer some insights into working with literature as a geographer, as well as discussing the use of nonrealist or fantastic fictions which depict 'secondary worlds'.

Concept Box

Representation

This term has been understood in two main ways by geographers. The first approach refers to mimetic representation, which implies a transparent, knowable world as if a mirror could be held up to reflect reality. In contrast, the second approach suggests that representing the world is not a neutral practice. Working within this latter approach, cultural geographers have studied representation in a wide range of forms, particularly in terms of writing and visual images. An important theme in this work has been a concern with the politics of representation. Rather than view texts or images as detached from wider **discourses** and **power** relations, cultural geographers have explored the ways in which texts and images are part of wider discursive formations that are themselves inseparable from the exercise of power. Edward Said's work on 'Orientalism' (1978) has been very influential in this context. Said analysed the 'imaginative geographies' of the Middle East produced by travel writings and other texts written by Western scholars and travellers over the last two centuries. Orientalist discourses produced knowledges about colonised people and places as 'other', inferior and irrational in contrast to a powerful, rational, western 'self.' As Ania Loomba writes, *Orientalism* is 'a book not about non-Western cultures, but about the Western representation of these cultures' (1998: 43). A number of geographers have also begun to recognize the limits of thinking in terms of representation. Ideas about non-representational theory focus on **embodied** practices rather than texts, images and discourses (Thrift, 1999; Nash, 2000).

Key Reading
- Nash, C. (2000) 'Performativity in practice: some recent work in cultural geography.' *Progress in Human Geography* 24: 653–64.
- Said, E. (1978) *Orientalism*. New York, Vintage.

Defining secondary worlds

Recent work in literary theory and cultural studies, influenced by poststructuralism, has convinced many cultural geographers that representations of the world are not mimetic. This means that they do not mirror reality and must always *re*-present elements of the world. This has lead to numerous studies of 'landscapes as text' (see Barnes and Duncan, 1992; Duncan and Ley, 1993) and an interest in visual forms of representation (see part three of this book for examples). If we accept these arguments then we can differentiate between three different kinds of writing:

- writing that claims to represent the world objectively and faithfully (like journalism or a geography textbook);
- writing that represents the world in fiction, but in a realistic way (like the novels of authors such as Dickens or Balzac);
- and writing that represents a coherent world, but one that cannot claim to be realistic because it contains things that do not exist in our world (like utopian or dystopian fictions, science fiction, and so on).

The last category is the one that concerns us here. Tolkien described places like his 'Middle-earth' as 'secondary worlds' because they are deliberate distortions of the real or primary world. These secondary worlds do *not* exist. This is why the word 'utopia' means 'non-place' as well as 'good place'. But why should we be interested in this? Plenty of people have read *Lord of the Rings*, but if these places don't exist then surely topics like this are a diversion from more important geographical issues? In this chapter I will argue that these kinds of literary fictions can be useful to geographers, and I will suggest a number of ways to investigate their meanings.

Obviously all fictions create secondary worlds, but the kinds of secondary world we are interested in are re-presentations of the primary world of their authors. It is the distance between these primary and secondary worlds that is important, because this distance opens up the possibility of critical or political readings of the texts. In utopian fiction, for example, the secondary 'good place' implicitly criticises the author's primary world. The future America depicted in Edward Bellamy's *Looking Backward: 2000–1887* (1888) is a socialist paradise offered as a contrast with the United States of 1887. Dystopias like Aldous Huxley's *Brave New World* (1932), on the other hand, present a frightening secondary world extrapolated from trends that the author has discerned in his own society. Both criticise a primary world; the difference is that Bellamy suggests an alternative while Huxley provides a warning. In science fiction (SF), the secondary world can be either utopian or dystopian, though authors are usually less explicit with their judgements. And fantastic fictions can offer us a glimpse of hopes and fears usually suppressed in representations of the primary world, although these are even less obvious: is Tolkien's Middle-earth a nostalgic and conservative fantasy or a criticism of modernity's assault on the natural world (Curry, 1998)? When we study these places which don't exist, we are therefore mainly interested in the gap between the primary and secondary world. Thomas More's *Utopia* (1516) was not simply a blueprint for a better world; it was an invitation to think about the gap between his pictures of the world-as-it-was and the world-as-it-should-be. This is important because, in encouraging readers to think about the differences between their world and the fictional worlds of utopic, dystopic or non-realist fiction, these visions can spark political action.

I think this makes these new worlds valuable and interesting, and they have received some attention from geographers and those working in related disciplines – largely through the exploration of utopias.

In describing this interest it is worth making a distinction between utopian thought, practice and representation, though the three are obviously related.

- Utopian *thought*, or ideas about and yearnings for a better world, clearly has an important role in geography, from the influence of Kropotkin and Marx to the writings of more recent feminists, post-marxists, and others (Blunt and Wills, 2000). Discussions of the history and philosophy of utopia continue to be influential across the humanities (Kumar, 1986, 1991; Marin, 1984, 1993).
- Utopian *practice*, or attempts to build better societies, has also received attention – through studies of modernist planning (e.g. Gold, 1987, 1997) as well as more marginal utopian activities (Pinder, 2001a). Research on particular sites which seem to offer the possibility of social transformation have drawn upon their similarity to utopias, though some of the most influential work develops the slightly different notion of heterotopia or 'spaces of Otherness' (Cresswell, 1996; Foucault, 1986; Hetherington, 1997). As a discipline with historical connections to both large-scale planning and more radical projects, geography is itself occasionally represented as a utopian discipline.
- Finally, in the sphere of *representations* utopias and other nonrealist forms continue to interest geographers, resulting in a number of studies of non-mimetic fictions (Dodge and Kitchin, 2001; Gold, 1985, 2001; Kitchin and Kneale, 2001; Kneale and Kitchin, 2002; Wylie, 2000).

This chapter concerns the last of these forms of secondary world, and it is limited to the written word. Applying the philosophical insights of the first two kinds of research to the field of literature, it seems that the most successful secondary worlds are those which open up the possibility of change, of transformation. David Pinder suggests that feminist critics are turning away from the idea of utopia as a 'closed, fixed form or a blueprint' towards a 'more fluid, open and partial' state (1999: 286). To put it another way, utopias and dystopias are about travelling rather than arriving, about hoping or fearing for the future rather than knowing exactly what it will be like. There is little drama in perfection, which explains why many of the classic utopias seem rather dry and boring, both aesthetically (because they rigidly adhere to generic rules and formulas) and politically (because they depend on closed and rigid frameworks for a better life). Lucie Armitt notes that 'Fictional utopias can be deceptively unsatisfactory' precisely because they offer manifestos rather than dreams (2000: 15). We should therefore keep an eye out for utopias that refuse to observe these rules:

> *Novels which ask questions rather than give pat answers, recognize problems even especially if they cannot fully solve them, but remain firmly committed to the ongoing search for new horizons while recognizing that utopia will always, by definition, be elsewhere.*
>
> (Armitt, 2000: 12)

So what should we be looking for in our studies of secondary worlds? When we are assessing their value, our research questions must consider them as representations like any other, as well as providing a more detailed analysis of their nature as secondary, non-realistic, worlds. This gives us two sets of general research questions. The first, which could apply to any work of fiction, might include the following:

- Why are they represented in this way?
- What assumptions have to be accepted for these representations to be convincing?
- In particular, does reading it from a position distant to the author's position (considered chronologically, spatially or socially) encourage other kinds of readings?

Focusing on the gap between the two worlds might then get us to think about some of the following:

- How does the secondary world differ from the author's place in space and time?
- What might this contrast mean?
- How successful is it in making us think again about our own world?

Researching secondary worlds and answering these kinds of questions means reading in a careful and critical way. It also means paying attention to representations of space and place – or reading *as a geographer*. My discussion of how you might do this will start by thinking about researching literature, move on to talk about analysing geographical representations, and then consider what might be different about secondary worlds. Throughout the chapter my examples will be drawn from my own research on William Gibson's science fiction novels and short stories (by the way, I should warn you that what follows contains spoilers, meaning that it discusses what happens in these fictions). Though I have drawn upon other methods for producing and analysing material on or by this author (Kneale, 2001; Kitchin and Kneale, 2001), here I concentrate on a textual analysis of his published novels and short stories.

I chose Gibson to investigate because several interesting things came together around his work at the end of the 1980s. 'Cyberpunk', the subgenre of SF that Gibson made famous with the publication of his first novel *Neuromancer* in 1984, was being hailed as an important way into discussions of the value of postmodernism by heavyweight cultural critics like Fredric Jameson (1991). At the same time Gibson was becoming highly influential in a world seemingly obsessed with virtual reality, the Internet, and other aspects of what became known as 'cyberculture' (Dery, 1992). Here was an author who was describing a near-future world that was a distorted version of our own, with such success that academics, SF fans, software designers, musicians and others were all discussing him. It helped that I'd really enjoyed reading *Neuromancer*, and it seemed only natural to choose Gibson as my focus for a study of the spaces of 'postmodern SF'. More specifically, I chose those works set in the same fictional world, the 'Sprawl fictions' (his first three novels, *Neuromancer*, (1984), *Count Zero* (1986), and *Mona Lisa Overdrive* (1988), plus a few short stories). The choice of the issues to study in more detail was also fairly straightforward. I was particularly interested in two kinds of place within Gibson's fictions: cyberspace (an early exploration of virtual reality and the Internet) and his urban landscapes. These spaces had also attracted a fair amount of critical interest, most of it fairly negative. I'll come back to these later, but they did help me to generate some of my initial research questions; from the beginning I wondered what we could learn from Gibson's secondary world. Did cyberspace, for example, offer us the chance to think in positive ways about the emerging virtual geographies of the Internet? How should we react to the divided and violent urban landscapes he depicted? And was it all 'postmodern' or was this a red herring?

Working with literature

When I started working on this topic I was mystified about how I could actually *analyse* literature. There's no reason why qualitative research like this should be less methodical than quantitative work, but this kind of analysis still seems to be seen as something intuitive and highly subjective. In an effort to convince you that there is a method of sorts here the following discussion represents rather general recommendations and discussions, dealing firstly with questions of 'gathering data' and secondly with analysis. It's also a good idea to familiarise yourself with some of the key ideas of literary criticism (which isn't as scary as it sounds). Ashley (1997) provides brief but useful readings from influential works of criticism and supplies examples of interpretations based upon these ideas; you might also want to look at Stuart Aitken's discussion of analysing different kinds of texts (1997).

Considering fiction as research material

The first step involves selecting the material you will be working with. Choose carefully – you will have to read this material over and over again! In terms of the amount of material you will need, use your initial research questions to work out what you should include. I was interested in the world that Gibson had used as the setting for his first three novels and some of his short stories, so they naturally became my main 'sources'. Once you've got this settled, you can start reading in earnest (though you should have already read your texts, at least briefly – or how would you know that you wanted to use them?). You will also probably want to read other textual material – pieces of criticism, interviews with the author, and so on.

In terms of 'gathering your data' the method consists of reading your texts very carefully, over and over again, until you're completely familiar with them. There's more to this than just knowing your material, though. Paraphrasing Roland Barthes (1990), the first time we read a book we concentrate on the narrative but with subsequent readings the urge to find out what happens next is gone and we pay more attention to description. So re-reading should allow you to stop and think, or to go off at tangents that the story doesn't appear to allow for on first reading.

It's impossible to consider analysis as something which comes after this stage of the research because you will come to your texts with preconceived ideas about what they mean, and as you read new interpretations will occur to you. This is perfectly normal, just make sure you write them all down. From this point onwards you will end up running back and forth between these ideas and the texts until you feel ready to write up your final argument. I started off convinced that the key to Gibson's work was postmodernism and ended up worrying about voodoo and lofts.

Interpreting fiction

So how do geographers interpret fiction? Not very well, according to Marc Brosseau:

> Most geographers have seen the novel as a dead object... that yields its information in an almost transparent fashion. Novels have been considered as geographical texts which can be combed for 'relevant' spatial elements in order to evaluate how good a geographer the novelist is... most geographers use literature to verify or confirm their own research hypotheses rather than to examine the way in which a novel generates its own geography.
>
> (1995: 89–90)

There are three variations of this problem (see Brosseau, 1994 and Sharp, 2000 for more detailed critiques):

1 Descriptions of place, space or landscape are taken as straightforward and objective representations of the real world. This treats literature as if it was a perfect copy of reality, contrary to the critique of mimesis discussed earlier;

2 While the critic recognises that texts do not contain objective facts of this kind, she assumes that the author's descriptions of subjective experiences of place *can* be objectively 'retrieved' from the text. This is also based upon a belief in a kind of mimesis;

3 Alternatively, the critic believes that the textual landscape can be read as an expression of a powerful cultural ideology ('the bourgeois mentality', 'patriarchy', 'Orientalism', etc) and that it can be made to display this through critical analysis.

I'm afraid that I don't find these ways of working with literature very convincing, because I don't feel that they really get to grips with the nature of the text itself. I have three suggestions for working with literary texts, which I will introduce and then illustrate.

1 *Keep thinking about the narrative.* You shouldn't just comb the text for the little 'bits' that take your fancy (Nigel Thrift referred to this as 'stamp-collecting' (1978)). These 'bits' are part of the narrative, which may be told in strict chronological order or via 'flashbacks' and other ways of changing the order in which events are related. The place of a chunk of text within the narrative affects how we read it.

2 *Don't be too sure of your conclusions.* Searching for isolated 'bits' also suggests that you already knew what you were looking for before you read the text. This is what happens when a critic wishes to demonstrate that the text is an 'expression' of something else (for example, an Orientalist *discourse*), and it makes analysing the text redundant. Obviously you will have ideas about what the novel means, but doing research involves paying attention to context and being prepared to change your mind. I think texts are actually often rather messy and incoherent, meaning contradictory things. This makes finding the key to the whole story highly unlikely. The method of hermeneutics presents a useful alternative because it tries to base its interpretations on the text itself, and not on something external to it (see Pickles, 1992).

3 *Concentrate on the text, not the author.* While authors are important, poststructuralist criticism plays down their influence in favour of the reader. First, you shouldn't assume that what a text means to you is what the author intended it to mean; trying to establish this is a difficult and possibly pointless task. Second, while it may seem possible to get around this problem by drawing on contextual material of various kinds (biographies, interviews with the author, histories of distinct 'schools' of writers, other interpretations and reviews, etc.) try to avoid interpreting the fictional text as a simple outcome of a 'factual' text. Even autobiographies are still only texts, as fictional as novels are; why rely on one text to anchor your understanding of another? Contextual material should be read *alongside* your fictions (see Daniels and Rycroft (1993) for an example of how to compare biographical and fictional texts without making one simply a 'translation' of the other).

However, this doesn't mean we have to throw out notions of textual politics and **power**. It is sometimes thought that hermeneutics, like other ways of approaching a text, encourages researchers to ignore issues relating to the politics of representation. I want to stress that taking the method seriously doesn't. In fact I think these issues are often better addressed when we are more careful with our interpretations. Considering the meanings of Gibson's urban landscapes will hopefully illustrate each of these points.

First, for example, we could read through Gibson and copy down all his descriptions of urban settings ('stamp-collecting'), but what would they mean? *Neuromancer*'s first and final chapters are partially set in 'Night City', a sleazy part of Chiba (Japan). The novel begins with the novel's anti-hero, Case, reaching his lowest point. At the conclusion of the novel, having achieved a certain amount of success, Case returns to Night City. However, he no longer belongs there; it doesn't mean the same thing to him, and therefore isn't the same place. As a bartender tells him 'Night City is not a place one returns to' (314), underlining the fact that Case has 'escaped' from his previous precarious existence. Taken out of the context of the narrative, however, Night City is just a run-down urban location.

Second, if you already know what you're looking for before you start, collecting these locations doesn't really prove anything. For example, Andrew Ross (1991) suggested that the fascination Gibson and other cyberpunk writers felt for the inner city was not a positive exploration of cultural **difference** but a kind of imagined re-colonisation of these 'mean streets'. According to Ross's interpretation, Gibson offered the reader the same excitement that was being enjoyed by white middle-class gentrifiers (see Smith, 1996). Interpretations like this rely on – and I would argue are in fact entirely shaped by – ideas that are drawn from sources of information outside the text. The logical extension of this argument is that literature (or cultural production in general) cannot actively shape the world, it can only be shaped by more important social processes – whereas I would argue that there is a complicated two-way relationship between the two.

Third, avoid the temptation to cut through all this confusion by appealing to the author. In published interviews Gibson has always insisted that his work is dystopian or satirical, warning readers about developments that he sees latent in our world. In fact he went on to draw on Mike Davis's book *City of Quartz* (1990) for his novel *Virtual Light*, which Davis then (1992) acclaimed as a perceptive glimpse into the future (see Kitchin and Kneale, 2001). This doesn't mean we have to read his work in this way: clearly Andrew Ross didn't, and many other critics have suggested that Gibson seems to be looking forward to seeing his fictions become reality. If he is consistently 'misread', does it make his intended meaning less important? This is an important question, because it affects the cultural politics of these representations.

I'd also like to add another suggestion: *think about the type of fiction you're researching.* Does it belong to a genre (detective fiction, science fiction, romantic fiction, etc)? Genres possess particular kinds of conventions that may affect the narrative, and skilled readers will be looking for them. It really matters if the detective doesn't solve the mystery, or if the sundered lovers aren't reunited by the end of the story; the meaning of the text will be changed. If you ignore these features, you might as well be reading a shopping list or pathology report. Obviously it has been *written* as a particular kind of fiction. I'll discuss some of the conventions of science fiction towards the end of the chapter, but for now it would probably be useful if you could see how I read Gibson's texts as a geographer.

Reading geographically

I've said that reading as a *method* involves taking the text seriously, recognising that it is organised in a particular way for important reasons. I do think it's possible to read geographically, but if we want to avoid making the mistakes I've outlined above, then we need to stop only paying attention to those passages which describe a place or setting in some detail. Of course I didn't know this when I first started and I did what most geographers have done: trawl through the texts looking for descriptions of place and space. After reading all the criticisms of this approach I reread the texts, convinced that there are two kinds of geography in Gibson's Sprawl fictions, and that they play different parts in the creation of the story.

Detailed descriptions

The first kind concerns relatively detailed descriptions of spaces or places of the sort we associate with nineteenth-century realist authors like Dickens or Balzac. This is what attracts the 'stamp collectors'. Here's an example, Gibson's description of a New York loft in *Neuromancer*:

> *Overhead, sunlight filtered through the soot-stained grid of a skylight. One half-meter square of glass had been replaced with chipboard, a fat gray cable emerging to dangle within a few centimetres of the floor… The room was large. He sat up. The room was empty, aside from the wide pink bedslab… Blank walls, no windows, a single white-painted steel firedoor. The walls were coated with countless layers of white latex paint. Factory space. He knew this kind of room, this kind of building… He was home.*
>
> (1984: 58)

This initially unpromising passage is interesting for two reasons. First, Gibson doesn't often go in for these extended descriptions of place. Second, this space is pretty ordinary: it's largely empty and very little happens in it while the protagonist, Case, is staying there. So why does Gibson waste words on it? If we were 'stamp collecting', we might suggest that this loft would have been a very trendy place when Gibson was writing, and that he included it to make his future setting seem very up-to-the-minute and believable. However, this would tell us nothing else about either the loft or the novel, because it doesn't read this piece alongside other elements of the novel or ask how the description has been *written*. We need to turn to the next kind of geography, which actually does consider the text as more than just a list of chunks of this kind.

Kinetic descriptions

The second kind of geographical description is quite different. I had noticed that many critics and readers mentioned the *pace* of Gibson's writing – things happen quickly, the characters are always on the move – and Marc Brosseau's paper on Dos Passos's *Manhattan Transfer* (1995) gave me some ideas about this aspect of Gibson's writing. Brosseau suggests that rather than looking at what he calls 'the geography *in* the text' (like the description of the loft) we need to be sensitive to 'the geography *of* the text'. Dos Passos's novel depicts the spaces of New York through what Brosseau calls 'kinetic description', representing the movements of characters through fragmentation and motion. One of these descriptive techniques, the collage, reproduces the 'spatial and temporal succession of the elements of the urban landscape' (100) and Gibson is particularly fond of it:

> She was moving through a crowded street, past stalls vending discount software, prices feltpenned on sheets of plastic, fragments of music from countless speakers. Smells of urine, free monomers, perfume, patties of frying krill.
>
> (1984: 71)

> Sally leading her past the columns of St Paul's, walking, not talking. Kumiko, in a disjointed trance of shame, registering random information: the white shearling that lined Sally's leather coat, the oily rainbow sheen of a pigeon's feathers as it waddled out of their way, red buses like a giant's toys in the Transport Museum, Sally warming her hands around a foam cup of steaming tea.
>
> (1988: 78)

These lists and collages may still be 'bits' of the novel but they describe movement through space rather than static locations or places. They represent the *experience of being in space*, so that 'reading the text becomes like walking on the sidewalk itself, not watching someone else do so' (Crang, 1998: 57). This is why the excerpts above contain descriptions of senses other than the visual: sounds, smells, and the suggestion of touch (warmth and the textures of shearling and pigeon feathers). As they move the characters encounter 'fragments of smells' and 'random information', just as real walkers receive a jumble of sensory impressions as they walk through the city. More importantly for Brosseau, the rhythm of the text also suggests constant movement because it lists one thing after another (this is more obvious if you read these passages aloud). If they were composed of short, clipped, sentences they would be more suggestive of a walker who keeps stopping to admire the view. Because of this *the form or shape of the text actually plays a part in communicating this geographical experience* – something the stamp collectors would miss because all they are interested in is the geographical information contained in the text.

For Gibson, then, geography is less to do with static views (the first kind of description) and more often something that is experienced at the level of *narrative* (the second kind of description). As the characters move through space, the narrative moves on. In the second excerpt above, for example, Sally and Kumiko move west through London, from the City to Covent Garden, and while we get very little in the way of description we do get a sensation of movement and a route through the city. This is the geography *of* the text, attempting to represent 'corporeal subjects moving through material landscapes' (Duncan and Gregory, 1999: 5).

But *why* is the second kind of geography (the kinetic description) much more important in Gibson's 'Sprawl fictions' than the first (the detailed description)? I think it's a consequence of the kinds of plots Gibson employs, which move so rapidly towards their conclusions that there isn't any time for long descriptions. Case and the other characters are constantly on the move, travelling through Japan, New York, Istanbul, two different orbital habitats, and cyberspace in the course of *Neuromancer*. Why do we get to read so much detail about the loft? Because the loft is described in some detail but nothing happens there, it helps to emphasise the events which take place *elsewhere*. This is particularly true while Case is using cyberspace while in the loft because he is simultaneously nowhere special (the loft) and in the thick of the action (riots, cyberspatial breaking-and-entering, and so on).

Hopefully this shows you something of the way my three suggestions can help you deal with textual geographies. I have tried to go beyond the collection of those 'bits' of the Sprawl fictions that seemed geographical, and I've tried to think about the place of geographical descriptions within the text. Because I've tried not to make prior assumptions about what these descriptions mean and paid close attention to the way the stories are put together I also hope I haven't simply read them as expressions of something else. Rather than suggest that Gibson's world illustrates some kind of postmodern 'speeding-up' of daily life, for example, I've tried to think of this notion of pace in terms of his narrative structure.

However, you might remember my fourth suggestion: that you bear in mind that fictions take different forms. So far I have said very little about how Gibson's texts work as non-mimetic fictions, and how this complicates their depiction of secondary worlds.

Interpreting secondary worlds

Does it matter that these are not only fictional worlds, but unreal ones too? I think it does. This is partly because though the standard way to interpret a book or film is to compare the world it represents with 'reality', poststructuralism has made us very wary of this kind of argument. Judging the 'fit' with reality is a pointless exercise, even if you're working with factual descriptions. It's obviously even more pointless to ask whether a secondary world like Middle-earth is 'realistic', which is why critics tend to read them as coded references for something else. In this kind of analysis secondary worlds are simply an expression of something deeper. A common example of this is the supposition that 1950s US flying saucer movies are *really* (and purely) about Cold War fears of the 'Red menace'. Tolkien, cross with these sorts of attempts to unravel his work, wrote that 'to ask if the Orcs "are" Communists is to me as sensible as asking if Communists are Orcs' (cited in Curry, 1998: 72). However, we can do more than just measure the distance between the author's world and their secondary creations. I said above that the successful utopia tries to ask questions rather than answer them, and the same is true for all non-realist fiction. What I find fascinating is that this can be seen in the text itself, in the way the story is written. And this is why I remain convinced that the method I use – paying very close attention to the text – is the best way to approach literature.

To give you an example of why this is the case, consider the opening sentence of Gibson's *Mona Lisa Overdrive*:

> *The ghost was her father's parting gift, presented by a black-clad secretary in a departure lounge at Narita.*
>
> (1988:7)

Everything in this sentence is described as if it really happened; we can imagine black-clad secretaries and departure lounges, even if we don't know that Narita is Tokyo's International Airport. But a reader expecting realism or even science fiction, might be surprised to read that second word: 'ghost'. In fact, the Sprawl fictions are full of ghosts. In Gibson's second novel, *Count Zero* (1986), the utterly rational universe of cyberspace contains what appear to be supernatural entities, described in only the vaguest of ways (see Kneale, 1999). *Mona Lisa Overdrive* mentions other inanimate intelligences apart from the ghost introduced in the sentence above. Of course, a reader familiar with Gibson would know that he is interested in the possibility of digital simulations of consciousness. The ghost Kumiko's father gives her is actually an artificial intelligence that can manifest itself as a hologram only she can see and hear. Some of the other 'ghosts' are recordings of people's consciousness, made so that they could 'live' on after their death, in some form anyway. So they're not really ghosts in the sense we normally think of them. Science fiction usually explains its non-realist elements away with some sort of scientific-sounding 'explanation', and Gibson's ghosts are no different. But they are still quite a strange idea, and he doesn't entirely clear away all of their mystery.

Why does this interest me so much? Well, it's one way in which the type of fiction affects the reading experience, the narrative, and the meaning of the text. All kinds of implausible and impossible things happen in non-realist fiction – people return from the dead, travel to other suns, and so on – and these events take textual form. For example, when readers encounter new words (like 'cyberspace' or 'Cthulhu') they recognise that they refer to things that do not exist. Non-realist fiction pushes the language of representation to its limits: it tells the reader that impossible things, like ghosts, *are real*. This happens in every fictional story, because all literature is consciously fabricated by its author, but it is more obvious in non-realist fiction. This is why these kinds of texts possess an appeal for critics, because they demonstrate the impossibility of mimesis. They all also possess the ability to make their reader stop and think about this, and I want to illustrate this here by briefly discussing the idea of *hesitancy*.

Non-mimetic fictions sometimes make it hard for the reader to know what is happening (by talking about ghosts, for example) (Todorov, 1973). This is especially important for ghost or horror stories because this uncertainty produces fear; the reader is left confused and anxious – or perhaps annoyed – because this isn't fully explained. If the text is unclear, the reader hesitates between rival interpretations, so that in our case you might hesitate between thinking that the ghost is a supernatural entity and guessing that it has some kind of scientific-sounding explanation. In *Count Zero* the main characters spend most of the novel trying to decide which of these explanations is the correct one, and the reader has no choice but to hesitate along with them. We can think of this hesitation as a consequence of moving between primary and secondary worlds, from things we can imagine and know to be real (airport lounges) to ones we can't and don't (ghosts). For critics interested in psychoanalysis these kinds of hesitations are expressions of the workings of the unconscious, the equivalent of the so-called 'Freudian slip'. Freud's own interpretations of fantastic fiction have inspired critics to read non-realist texts as symptomatic of these fears and desires (e.g. Aitken, 2002; Armitt, 1996; Jackson, 1981), though it's not essential to adopt a psychoanalytical framework for interpretation.

So as a geographer studying secondary worlds in literature I was particularly interested in these points where the text was suddenly unable to describe what was going on. More specifically, I was interested in the ways that this complicated the representation of space and place in these new worlds. This encouraged me to think about the distance between primary and secondary worlds, and hence the cultural politics of Gibson's representations.

Geographies of secondary worlds

So how *do* we cope with the fact that these 'secondary worlds' are described in non-realist ways?

In general, non-mimetic fictions play around with established conventions for representing space and time. Rosemary Jackson provides a useful set of examples of what she calls the 'topography of the modern fantastic' (1981: 42–8), most of which involve problems of vision, of disorientation, and ambiguity. These are all spatial metaphors for the hesitation discussed above. Sometimes there are no reference points for the reader because the space described is strangely empty or immaterial (like cyberspace). Protagonists get lost in labyrinths, mazes, or in forests; fog, mist, or darkness sometimes clouds their vision. This is also why fantastic fictions are full of invisible things, or things only half-glimpsed and half-understood. If the narrator or character is uncertain as to where they are, then the reader is unable to work out what is going on. Similar effects can also be achieved by mirrors, because not only do they reflect and distort the world we take for granted, but in doing so they seem to create another world that we may enter 'through the looking-glass'. It's an excellent metaphor for the secondary worlds that these fictions produce.

Here's an example, a fantastical encounter in cyberspace from Gibson's *Count Zero*:

> And something **leaned in**, vastness unutterable, from beyond the most distant edge of anything he'd ever known or imagined, and touched him.
>
> (1986: 32, emphasis in original)

This 'something', which is vast in an 'unutterable' way, is one of Gibson's ghosts; the character who experiences this doesn't know what is happening – and neither does the reader who reads it. Most importantly it comes from somewhere beyond the known world of cyberspace, somewhere *unknowable* and *unimaginable*…

My research provided numerous examples of this kind of textual uncertainty. I found it interesting that cyberspace had overtones of the supernatural, despite being designed by powerful corporations as a highly rational and ordered grid or matrix. I also noted those occasions where Case finds himself 'lost' in this virtual world, or where his senses are confused and he becomes disorientated. Near the conclusion of *Neuromancer*, for example, the disembodied Case finds himself on a convincing virtual beach, in a kind of 'pocket world' cut off from the rest of cyberspace. Two things mark it out as a fantastic space: firstly if you walk far enough along it you find yourself back where you started, and secondly it also seems to be inhabited by a dead woman. As I show in greater detail elsewhere (Kneale, 1999), Gibson's cyberspace turns out to be much more than just an extrapolation of our world. In the 'real' world, Case and the others also spend some time wandering through the labyrinth of the Villa Straylight, described as 'a body grown in upon itself, a Gothic folly', and an 'endless series of chambers linked by passages' (*Neuromancer*, 206). The Villa is a classic labyrinth, a disorientating space that hides the central mystery of the story. In all of these ways *Neuromancer* describes fantastic topographies: places that could not exist, moments of uncertainty.

So much for noting the ways in which *Neuromancer* ceases to be 'realistic'; what do they mean? We can interpret these moments of uncertainty in several ways. We could read these moments of ambiguity as signs that Gibson is reaching the limits of what can be represented in print. We could then develop this into a discussion of the nature of representation and a critique of mimesis. We can relate this to the geographies *of* the text, because there is a link with kinetic description; Case's senses become confused in cyberspace when he moves too quickly and loses his bearings. We could also consider these narrative, geographical and non-realist elements together and point out that in *Neuromancer* both cyberspace and the Villa Straylight represent uncanny labyrinths through which our heroes wander in an attempt to bring the story to a conclusion and make it all make sense. In some ways the book is like a detective story (which is often noted) and a fantastic quest narrative (which isn't). All of these interpretations are concerned with mysteries and the attempt to resolve them, and it's important to note that not all of them are clearly resolved.

It's this ambiguity which makes it hard for readers to decide whether Gibson's representations are optimistic or pessimistic. Gibson's cyberspace is usually read as a highly ordered space, organised in a strictly structured grid or matrix which represents a space of authority and control, what Andrew Ross called 'the heady cartographic fantasy of the powerful' (1991:148). It therefore seems to offer little to those readers who might be looking for a space of utopian possibilities. Once we consider the many points at which the text produces hesitancy in the reader, however, it becomes impossible to be so sure about whether cyberspace is a space of freedom or a space of control. These possibilities seem to exist in a state of tension with each other, making it a highly ambiguous space. The same could be said for Gibson's other geographical representations (think about the differing interpretations of Gibson's urban landscapes offered by Mike Davis and Andrew Ross outlined above).

This returns us to our original set of research questions: thinking about secondary worlds in a critical way should allow us to creatively rework them. There's a similarity between researching secondary worlds and writing them: both should 'ask questions rather than give pat answers', to restate Armitt's point about utopias. Read carefully, Gibson asks quite a few questions about cyberspace and the city, as well as making the reader think again about the representation of space in literature. Often, though, I think many critical interpretations underplay this complexity because they have ignored (or missed) those parts of the text that do not fit their arguments. To do the text justice often means acknowledging that it doesn't just mean one thing.

Conclusion and suggestions for further research

The best analyses of literature are often a pleasure to read because they're highly creative and they communicate something of the enjoyment of fiction. Unfortunately this chapter has been a little more serious than that. You probably started reading it with the hope that it would be both instructive and inspiring, and instead I've given you a long list of dos and don'ts. I've been at pains to stress that there is a method to the analysis of representations of space in literature, one that goes beyond the collection of geographical-looking titbits or the confirmation of preconceived suppositions. I've also emphasised that the representation of space in non-mimetic literature is different to the way it is achieved in realist fiction and non-fictional forms. I hope I haven't been too didactic, and that you're still keen to try out some of these ideas. If you are, here are a number of suggestions for your research.

You might want to start with a well-known author or text, simply because you will probably find more in the way of contextual or critical material to help your analysis. Tolkien's *Lord of the Rings* or *The Hobbit* would make interesting choices, simply because the world he created is so vast and so popular. More ambitiously, you might explore a specific place across a range of texts. This could be a place which does exist (like Mars, which has been represented in science fiction for almost as long as the genre has existed), or one which doesn't (the hollow Earth). Or you might be interested in *generic* places that are central to particular kinds of non-realist fictions, like the haunted house in ghost or Gothic stories. Or you could look at historical developments in the representation of unreal places: how have utopias changed in the last hundred years, for example?

Finally, one of the ways that I tried to make the most of Gibson's ambiguous texts was by asking readers what they made of them. Allowing them to discuss their interpretations in small groups showed me just how easy it is for readers to get different meanings from the same text, as well as offering tantalising hints about how they arrived at them. This can be very productive, though it does involve using another methodology (see Kneale, 2001) and combining the material gathered by the different methods can be difficult. In addition, it doesn't make the ambiguities of texts like these disappear – quite the opposite!

I hope I've demonstrated that these kinds of fictions can be interesting, enjoyable and important resources for geographical work; and I hope reading them *as a geographer* brings a new dimension to your interpretations.

Further reading

On geography and literature:
- Brosseau, M. (1994) 'Geography's literature', *Progress in Human Geography* 18: 333–53.
- Brosseau, M. (1995) 'The city in textual form: *Manhattan Transfer*'s New York', *Ecumene* 2: 89–114.
- Sharp, J. (2000) 'Towards a critical analysis of fictive geographies', *Area*, 32: 327–34.

On literary criticism:
- Ashley, B. (ed.) (1997) *Reading Popular Narrative: A Source Book*. London and Washington, Leicester University Press.

On spaces of Otherness:
- Hetherington, K. (1997) *The Badlands of Modernity*. London and New York, Routledge.

On Fantastic Fictions:
- Armitt, L. (1996). *Theorising the Fantastic*. London, Arnold.
- Jackson, R. (1981). *Fantasy: The Literature of Subversion*. London and New York, Routledge.

On Geography and nonrealist fiction:
- Kneale, J. and Kitchin, R. (2002) 'Lost in space' in Kitchin, R, and Kneale, J (eds) *Lost in Space: Geographies of Science Fiction*, London and New York, Continuum: 1–16.

A TALE OF RESEARCH

Tolkien

A Re-enchantment of Nature

Jennifer Morrissey

Given the current hype surrounding the blockbuster movies of *The Lord of the Rings*, choosing Tolkien's trilogy as the focus of my dissertation seemed a bit like jumping on the popular culture bandwagon! My choice, however, was not driven by the release of the film (which happened to be coincidental) but by an avid interest in fantasy fiction and the superlative qualities of Tolkien's books. However, on its own this would not have been sufficient reason for accepting my proposal. I had to ensure that I could give a distinctly geographical dimension to my ideas.

While reading the books it was clear to me that there were a number of themes that would be interesting to explore as a geographer. I believed that there was a particular environmental message in the text that went beyond the pages of the book. My first encounter, outside the text, with these ideas was in an argument presented by Curry (1998). He argued that a 're-enchantment of nature' is taking place in contemporary society and one way that this is manifested is in popular culture texts such as *The Lord of the Rings*.

In order to further explore Curry's argument I decided to delve into other academic literature and found that he was not alone. Other scholars such as Pepper (1996) discussed this period of change in the human relationship with nature that is viewed as a characteristic of the period of post-modernity. The first part of my fieldwork involved exploring the various ideas in the text and reading critical commentaries in three main fields: human relationships with nature; the use of fiction in geography; and the role of the mass media in negotiating environmental knowledges. However I also wanted to find out what readers thought about Tolkien's trilogy. How does a 're-enchantment of nature' manifest itself in everyday thinking and ideology? I wanted to explore the encoding and decoding of the text by the author, critics and readers, and to study how their different ideas were reproduced in discourses about nature, the environment and technology. I particularly wanted to explore how people read the text in geographical ways.

Geographers have long used texts as part of exploring the geographical imagination (including Brosseau 1994, Kneale and Kitchin 2002), but there have been fewer methodological discussions about how to analyse texts. I chose to use focus groups as the forum to discuss nature as it is presented by Tolkien. The focus groups were, for the most part, very productive and enjoyable. I highly recommend their use for exploring texts in both fun and thorough ways. There was a lot of discussion, although this sometimes reared off course as the intricacies of Middle-earth were debated!

I met with four different groups, which were put together through a snowballing of contacts and comprised of three to seven participants. The number of participants varied, largely due to chance (for example the ability to arrange a time that suited everyone, or someone bringing along a friend unexpectedly; see Kneale 2001). Three of the groups involved participants aged between 16 and 30, and the final group was made up of three women over 40 who had first read the trilogy in the 1960s. Every participant had read the trilogy at least once, with some having read it more than ten times!

Throughout my research, I used pseudonyms to ensure the anonymity of all participants, and I gained permission to tape and then transcribe the discussion.

At the beginning of each session I asked participants to fill in short questionnaires to create reader profiles. The rest of each session was structured by a set of prompts and questions that I had devised, which were adapted according to the different responses and how well a group interacted together. After each session I carried out an auto-critique. This involved re-playing the tape, looking at my notes and recalling my feelings (through the use of memory and my research diary) to see how I could improve things for the next group. This also gave me an opportunity to think about how different groups were responding, and how something may or may not impact with the next group (depending on group structure, e.g. age, sex, etc.).

I transcribed all of the group discussions. I also added the tone of voice used by participants to show, for example, when they were excited or annoyed; and how participants interacted, such as interrupting or laughing together. After transcribing the discussions, I went through the systematic process of coding and analysing the transcripts (see Bedford and Burgess, 2001, Kneale, 2001, Longhurst, 2001). I read through each transcript initially a minimum of three times looking for 'similarities and differences in terms of topics that were discussed…searching for networks, regularities and patterns in the data' (Longhurst, 2001: 138). For this I used large mind maps as an aid. In order to confirm themes I thought were emerging from my data I also conducted key word search of my transcripts, searching for words such as 'community', 'nature',' home', 'Ents' and 'good.' This was to see if my tentative conclusions were feasible.

At a later stage of the research, I also conducted self-directed interviews (SDI's) by email in order to triangulate my findings and to try to reach more people. This was largely facilitated by members of the formal groups volunteering friends for participation. I also emailed all group participants to try and verify the focus group discussions. The structure of the SDI was based on the list of prompts and questions asked in the focus groups to ensure continuity.

The use of these self-directed interviews meant that people responded more directly to my questions than they often did in the group sessions. However I did feel that interviews in this form meant that at times I 'led the witness,' although I was aware that as a researcher I 'must try not to ask questions that impose an answer' (Burgess in Valentine, 1997: 120). Unlike interviews that involve direct dialogue and conversation, I felt that it was difficult to avoid 'leading the witness' in self-directed interviews.

I also kept a research diary, which assisted my more informal data collection. I recorded unplanned encounters, which often ended up being valuable discussions with interested friends who would offer their ideas and talk about their experiences in an impromptu way. The varied components of my fieldwork meant that it did not become stagnant and uninteresting. Each different approach raised new ideas or helped me to consider old ones from a different angle.

Many of the topics I raised in the final write-up were drawn from the way that participants talked about their relationship with place, their own 'local' places and the local places of the text. In my dissertation, place came to be associated with both the geography of the text (including the way that the novel is written, its different literary mechanisms, for example the characters, the history, the maps, and the sense of community in those places) and the geographical ideas in the text – how these ideas about place related to ideas about environment and nature. For example, the rising up of the Ents was interpreted, by readers and cultural commentators alike, as the symbolic rising up of nature against modernity.

The relationship between author, reader and text is cemented, in this instance, by looking at the links readers make between the primary world (this world), and the secondary (fantasy) world. For example, in the cases of particularly beautiful or 'natural' places participants suggested that this might influence how they saw their own, primary earth. As one respondent to my email interview put it, 'Rivendell was the most beautiful place in the book and perhaps this does encourage me to appreciate any natural beauty in my own world.'

This example corresponds to Curry's (1998) proposal that by reading the books, and identifying with the places within them, a (re)connection takes place with our own world. It is interesting to explore how people 'talk about their environment in the context of their attachment to local place' (Macnaghten and Urry 1998: 103). Here this may be considered to be the 'local' places of the text as well as each participant's own local places.

Adopting a text as a cultural icon can be a way of understanding how a group makes sense of their common experience. For example, many of my participants told me that what had most inspired them in the text was courage and, in particular, the courage to go and carry out the quest, just as the Fellowship did. This indicated to me that a reconnection with nature is one that people lust after but one that, perhaps, they are frightened of chasing because it is counter to the hegemonic (modern) view. The courage they are inspired by, and admire, is – according to one respondent – a 'celebration of ordinariness doing extraordinary things.' As well as courage, readers were also encouraged by the 'support of the company,' which I view as suggestive of a desire for a strengthened community and fellowship to achieve environmental goals that are sometimes transgressive.

My main conclusion is that *The Lord of the Rings* inspires action in a very powerful and moving way, by invoking wisdom as well as knowledge. The subtleties of the text and its inspiration for readers perhaps indicates a new path for environmental lessons to be learnt, through the courage to be transgressive and fighting to protect our planet. Tolkien gives us an opportunity to 'see,' to demonstrate that the quest is our own now, and to choose what part we will play, which can perhaps be best illustrated by Lady Galadriel's mirror in the first book. Galadriel offers Frodo the chance to look into her mirror which gives him the chance to see 'things that were, things that are, the things that yet may be' (Tolkien, 1993: 469). As geographers we can use *Lord of the Rings* like a mirror, an opportunity to see the possibilities of our actions or inactions on our world. As a text it also provides us with a resource to see how people mediate their social world and as a way to explore the human relationship with nature. From this we can offer advice on how to tackle political and social malaise with the environment and offer new ways to explore nature in a dis-enchanted world.

I know that in my dissertation I did not exhaust, by any means, the ways in which cultural geography can utilise novels to further geographic enquiry on how environmental knowledges are learnt and how positive action may be encouraged. This is but a tip of a very large and very interesting iceberg.

I am currently in the final year of my BA in Geography at University College London and am looking forward to taking a break before embarking on a PhD. I have thoroughly enjoyed my dissertation research, although there have been times that I have not always been as positive! However, choosing a topic that I am interested in coupled with my love for literature ensured that my research never lost its sparkle. This has been the main reason why I have decided to undertake a PhD on a similar subject. I am particularly intrigued by social networks, especially those between readers and the rise in popularity of book groups, and hope to pursue my interest in this area.

4
Researching bodies in virtual space

Hester Parr

Introduction: geographies of virtual space and the question of bodies

This chapter considers the matter of 'virtual bodies' in virtual space from methodological perspectives. The discussion, although quite focused on a particular case study concerning the **embodiment** of health and illness information on the Internet, highlights key theoretical issues surrounding bodies and virtual space as well as shedding light on methods of social research on the Internet. The chapter begins with a short discussion of the geographical significance of virtuality and proceeds with a step-by-step introduction to the conceptual and methodological bases underlining a research project which investigated the social significance of website information and the communality experienced by members of particular 'chatrooms'. The chapter concludes by offering further guides and advice for geographers who want to employ qualitative research methods on the Internet.

Researchers from across the social sciences have, in recent years, become extremely interested in what is known as 'virtual space'; the territories accessible to people through the use of computerised technologies. Everything from examples and concepts of cyborgs, cyberbodies, cyberpunks, virtual reality and new net languages have been considered by academics who have been clearly excited by the possibilities they see held within various 'utopian, dystopian and heterotopian' world visions (Featherstone and Burrows, 1995: 1). The rise of the use of computers in everyday life, especially in the Western world, has prompted an explosion of theoretical and empirical investigations in disciplines such as sociology, cultural studies and human geography that seek to understand the social and cultural dimensions to technological change. A wide range of substantive issues have formed the basis of these investigations but many of them consider, in various ways, the possibilities for the expansion and reconfiguration of human capabilities, subjectivities and knowledges.

Geographical issues and questions have been central to much of the research about the interrelationships between humans and virtual technologies and between the humans that use these technologies. For example, there are now widely circulated ideas about how accessing virtual space can lead some computer users to form meaningful experiences of 'community' which operate in certain places (chatrooms or multi-users-domains: MUDS). As Rheingold has argued, virtual space is 'one of the informal public places whereby people can rebuild certain aspects of community that were lost when the malt shop became the mall' (1994: 25–6). Here virtual space is understood as enabling new forms of social relationships and operating as a kind of 'public space', whereby people meet and share interests, experiences and encounters. As the geographer Kitchin reports (1998), often such discussions construct virtual space as a kind of utopia whereby social identities can be assumed and discarded at will, and where, as a consequence, familiar social prejudices surrounding gender, race and disabilities (for example) can be 'left behind' in 'real public space', hence:

> cyberspace ... [can be] a disembodying experience with transcendental and liberatory effects.
>
> (Kitchin, 1998a, p79)

Here the key to the 'different' social relationships which characterise the new public spaces of virtual worlds seems to be the ability of people to 'reinvent' themselves and transcend those aspects of themselves that other people form powerful (and often negative) ideas about. In this case, when thinking about gender, race and disability, it seems to be physical bodily markers which people have the ability to transcend. Again as Kitchin highlights, these arguments are ones which propose 'in cyberspace ... your body is irrelevant and invisible ...' (ibid: 80). It is hence within these very radical ideas about a new social basis for human relationships where controversial geographical questions about **embodiment** come to the fore.

Geographers have been increasingly fascinated with the body as a scale of analysis for some time now. As Cream claimed, the body 'is currently in vogue' (1995: 32) in the social sciences. Following cues from feminist and postmodern thinkers, the body, which was previously a fixed, taken-for-granted biological space unworthy of much cultural critique, was 'rediscovered' by geographers who have begun to **deconstruct** this site as one 'etched, inscribed and written on' (Longhurst, 1997: 488) by powerful social norms. In other words, bodies are often understood as geographies which, much like places, are 'made' by various moral, social and medical **discourses**. This attention to the body as a social and cultural geography has prompted lots of important research around questions of race, sex and sexuality, gender, disability and illness, nationhood and **performativity** (Bell and Valentine 1995; Butler and Parr, 1999; Duncan, 1996; Fincher and Jacobs, 1998; Nash, 2000). At the same time as geographers have begun to understand bodies as sites which are *socially* **constructed** in various ways, there is also a move to rethink approaches to biological bodies and not to dismiss or gloss over biological human form as Longhurst as argued:

> Social constructionists sometimes depict bodies as though they were little more than surfaces etched with social messages ... one of the downsides to social constructionism is that it can render the body incorporeal, fleshless, fluidless, little more than linguistic territory. The materiality of bodies becomes reduced to systems of signification.
>
> (2001: 23)

So amongst geographers who discuss body-spaces, there seems to be some tensions about how bodies can be understood, as both sites which are inscribed and made by social discourses and also as fleshy entities whose materialities should not be ignored (see also Hall, 2000). These tensions are ones that are very relevant when thinking through bodies in virtual space. However, none of the above writers have explicitly considered bodies in relation to virtual space and yet it is in this location where there seems to be a tangible threat of the body ceasing to matter – both materially and conceptually. It is in such a theoretical and empirical context that this chapter is written, then, as a methodological commentary on a piece of recent research which discussed questions of embodiment in virtual space with specific reference to matters of health and illness (see Parr, 2002).

Researching embodiment in virtual worlds

Before going any further it is perhaps necessary to briefly outline the basic elements of the research project which I am discussing in this chapter. In summary, this piece of work looked at the content of medical and health information websites and chatrooms to construct an argument about the ways in which lay society can be seen to be becoming increasingly 'medicalised' partly because of their interactions with the specialist medical knowledges available in virtual space. Using two different empirical sources of evidence, I first deconstructed examples of medical information websites on the Internet, with a view to discussing how such knowledge helped to construct bodies both abstractly in virtual space and physically in real space (with an emphasis on how the dualism of virtual-real became broken down). Second, I looked at a particular 'disease category', in this case multiple sclerosis, or 'MS', through designated Internet chatrooms in order to understand at a more in-depth level how people who seek medical information in virtual space discuss, experience and encounter their ill bodies in communal virtual spaces. The following sections elaborate this project.

The beauty of social and cultural research questions is that sometimes it is possible to stumble over them accidentally in the course of everyday life! This is the case, of course, because our experience of everyday life is the taken-for-granted 'stuff' which social and cultural geographers are always interested in understanding in more depth. I accidentally stumbled across the idea for writing about virtual bodies in the course of my other work on geographies of mental health. I was regularly accessing the Internet to find out about the mental health issues and networks when I kept coming across diagnostic tests for psychological disorders which computer users could complete for an instantaneous indication as to whether or not they were likely to have a serious mental health problem. Although I found the tests slightly ridiculous, it did make me think about the other ways in which the Internet was somehow implicated in people understanding themselves, their minds and bodies through a diagnostic and medical lens. Once on this track I quickly realised that the Internet was saturated with on-line medical tests, discussion forums, specialist advice, symptomologies, etc., which computer users could easily access. Although the 'empirical material' was the first means through which I began to think about the possibility of Internet research on virtual bodies, this does not always have to be the case, and often it is conceptual ideas that lead us into thinking about empirical possibilities. In this case, however, my next step was to think about how and why I could conceptually justify researching these issues.

The conceptual basis for the research project

In recent years, medical geography, an intellectual field I have been interested in, has been 'reinventing' itself in various ways through examining the ways in which medical geographers understand and deconstruct the sub-discipline in relation to 'place', 'space' and 'the medical' (Dorn and Laws, 1994; Kearns, 1993). Here a strong critique of medical geography argued that despite the fact that this sub-discipline was centrally focused on questions of death, illness, disease and health care, the one space that linked all these research endeavours, 'the body', was curiously ignored for many years:

> It is ironic that medical geography which draws its raison d'être from a profession that is preoccupied with exploring the differences between normal and abnormal bodies, is itself so resistant to treating the body as a problematical concept.
>
> (Dorn and Laws, 1994: 109)

This lacuna, however, has been addressed through more recent work that has concentrated on illness experiences, social understandings of the ill body and healthy corporealities (Butler and Parr, 1999; Dyck, 1999; Hall, 2000; Moss, 1999; Moss and Dyck, 1999). Some important aspects of this work have considered how powerful socio-medical inscriptions seek to shape the understanding and experiences of the bodies of those diagnosed with bio-medical disorders. Geographers have been interested to deconstruct these bodily experiences, but in ways which seek to interrogate 'the social and cognitive authority of Western scientific medicine' (Dyck, 1999: 122). Thinking about these themes in relation to the materials I had seen on the Internet was interesting as it allowed me to think about how bodies become subject to powerful bio-diagnostic resources in various ways (not just through doctor-patient relationships). It was also useful to think through such ideas with respect to other materials I had encountered in social and cultural geography which discussed the self-disciplining of body space. Here, Foucauldian analysis which highlights how bodies are worked on by their owners in order to achieve 'historically specific norms about how the space of the body should be produced' (Valentine, 1999: 330) provided pointers about how medicalised interactions in virtual space might have effects on and implications for lived embodiment. Using conceptual insights which discussed how powerful social and medical ideas served to 'inscript' body space, then, and combining them with ideas about how body spaces are often produced through self-discipline and surveillance seemed appropriate theoretical hooks to help me articulate what I understood to be important new dimensions to how 'lay' people were medically interpreting and (potentially) acting on their bodies.

This dual focus also allowed me to connect up with other theoretical tensions in terms of how geographers were predominantly discussing 'body-space'. By trying to understand how bodies were constructed through medicalised discourse in virtual space, I was paying attention to how ideas about bodies were being virtually shaped. At the same time I wanted to understand how such discourses had material effects on fleshy bodies through embodied actions, but also how material biological experiences of the ill body were being translated and encountered on the Internet, in ways which might counter expert medical discursive constructions (hence also acknowledging Longhurst's arguments which are cited above). By paying attention to the discursive and the messy ill body experience on the Internet the intention was to centralise questions of the body in relation to virtual space and counter the criticism that this was a geography where the corporeal was irrelevant. My second major task was then to think through what were the most appropriate arguments in relation to the most appropriate selections of web-based materials, a process I discuss further below.

Methods in virtual worlds

Virtual space is a daunting geography of information, resources, networks, relationships, images, texts, voices, encounters and other possibilities. To use the Internet as a source material in geographical research needs a focused approach if one is not to be overwhelmed by the wealth of virtual pathways one could follow. Depending on the focus of the study, preliminary decisions have to be taken about navigating this medium, although it is also realistic to accept that navigating the web is sometimes seemingly beyond our control as we are swept through series of bewildering links, routes and networks. The latter description also summarises the types of encounter many computer users have on the Internet, and so allowing ourselves as researchers to be 'overwhelmed' by this geography is perhaps an important methodological strategy in itself. For the case study outlined above there were several methodological approaches which were employed and which perhaps give a sense of how it is possible to begin to harness different types of source material for geographical research in virtual space.

Selecting medical texts in virtual space

The materials I worked with in order to develop and demonstrate my more conceptual thinking (discussed above) included informational or interactive websites and chatrooms. The first part of the discussion will consider the research methods adopted in using websites as part of a geographical case study and the second part of the discussion will consider the methods entailed in accessing chatrooms.

There were several ways in which websites were selected for use in relation to the arguments presented above. Primarily I was making an argument about the increasing medicalisation of Western society through the use of the Internet and so I chose to highlight and interpret websites which I understood to contain medical or medicalised information. This was a practice which entailed decision-making on several different levels. Mostly I was looking for websites that combined a medicalised language with demonstrations of expert knowledge and pathways to a diagnostic framing of malfunctioning bodies for the 'lay' computer user. There was a plethora of such sites and it was rapidly clear that different kinds of interpretation were appropriate for different kinds of websites. A first step was an initial attempt to categorise sites in terms of target audience, types of knowledge available, evidence of different kinds of bodily advice, levels of user interaction, diagnostic pathways, criteria or symptomologies and discussion between computer users. Although analytical categories which are pre-supposed can always be flawed and inaccurate, it does give a useful starting point when faced with a mass of information and these categories can always be re-worked as immersion in virtual space takes place.

On the basis of my initial categorisations I firstly selected sites which I understood to be part of professional medical networks, but to which lay users still had access. A basic analysis of language use in these websites helped to confirm that it was appropriate to consider them as 'expert informational spaces', to use a brief example from one such site:

> Most pelvic inflammatory disease (PID) is managed in primary care. Laparoscopic diagnosis is impractical in most cases and diagnosis is notoriously difficult. The interval between PID and tubal damage can be as little as a week and therefore prompt diagnosis and treatment is important.
>
> (Extract from anonymised medical web-site)

Here the body is clearly constructed through medical terminologies, encouraging a medical visioning of the deviancy of the body with clear pathways for diagnosis and treatment (presumably to be administered in a medical-institutional geography). In such examples, the subjective experience of the fleshy body is practically non-existent (unless framed as classificatory symptomologies), and bodies become abstracted as typical and atypical diagnostic spaces. Such sites were fascinating textual spaces and helped to develop my thinking about how an abstract human body was virtually constructed and expertly mapped (as 'ill', 'healthy', 'potentially ill') through such authoritative geographies (and here it was also possible to link these materials with writing on bodily inscription and discourses).

Negotiating textual analysis in unfamiliar language territories is challenging, as there is a need to interpret the language used into 'lay understandings' for oneself while at the same time also forming a critique of the effects and intentions of such expert language exchange (see also methodological commentaries on qualitative and textual analysis: Aitken, 1997 and Crang, 1997). Although interpreting medical websites is a specific case study, there are other ways in which virtual research might come across unfamiliar language use when researching specific group's/communities net discourses. A good strategy for dealing with this is to immerse yourself in several sites and spend time getting acquainted with the 'expert talk' you have access to, before deciding which sites, phrases and information to analyse.

Choosing to access and attempting to interpret medicalised language use in professional networks in virtual space helped me to answer some of my research questions highlighted above concerning discursive constructions of body-spaces, but it still left me with some unanswered questions relating to how such sites enabled linkages with, effects and impacts upon material fleshy bodies in 'real space'. It was clear from my textual analysis that while some medical websites effectively mapped the body in terms of biological 'forms and deformations' (Foucault, 1973: 136) only in an abstract sense, in some sites there were clear attempts to translate this knowledgable mapping into lay messages intended for reformulated bodily actions amongst computer users. Here then it became necessary to select websites that contained interactive diagnostic technologies or clear guidelines and advice for the already diagnosed or potentially ill user. The shifting and sorting of materials in relation to these needs revealed a wealth of technological aids to interpreting the fleshy bodily form from 'body mass calculators' which quantify (un)healthy body weight, to questionnaires about various bodily sensations (interpreted as 'symptoms'), to moving images which demonstrated how to search the flesh for cancerous lumps (see also Figure 4.1 below). The websites with clear diagnostic pathways were selected for more 'textual deconstruction' while the sites which included bodily images were also analysed for clues about how they could be visually interpreted as a) 'spaces of representation' or b) 'representational spaces' (after Lefebvre, 1991). In this context, these terms refer respectively to a) spaces (of the body) which are produced by officially sanctioned bio-discourses which ascribe authoritative meaning through web information and b) spaces (of the body) which are more related to the experience of everyday life and which are **represented** by the owners of bodies on the web (see opposite).

Typing the word 'body' into search engines and surfing for visual bodily images as source materials on the Internet is a curious process as one stumbles across the various ways the body is encountered in virtual space, including in terms of sex and sexuality (clearly constructed as a 'morally dangerous' if not an 'unlawful' encounter in modern discourse about virtual space and therefore presenting a problem for researchers). However, more relevant for this study were medicalised bodily images where the flesh of the material body was photographed but was also pictorially constructed in ways intended to aid in lay diagnostic procedures.

In interpreting such virtual body images it is necessary to draw on techniques which encourage specific 'visual methodologies' (Rose, 2001), including critical thinking about the technical composition of such images, the **gaze** of the image-maker and the gaze of the Internet user (and how this can be manipulated by 3-D technologies, moving pictures, focusing and enlarging capabilities). Very briefly, it is possible to outline what such methods might entail. In thinking critically about Figure 4.1 for example (one of a series), it can be noted that bodily flesh is very evident in the form of a photograph, the fleshy body is not obscured by diagnostic diagrams which represent a disembodied breast and procedures of examination. Textual explanations and directions accompany the photograph making sure that the Internet users are clear about the medically correct form and location of the tactile intervention that should be achieved, and so emphasising the image as 'useful' and possible to 'implement' on 'real' bodies. So thinking about the technical composition of the image may include noting the type and quality of the image, and how there might be combinations of texts and visuals in a certain explanatory

How to do a Breast Self-Exam

Top ▲

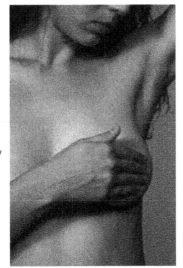

The best time to examine your breasts is during the week after your period. That's when your breasts will be softest and least tender, and a lump will be easiest to find.

Although you might feel uncomfortable and afraid the first few times you examine your breasts, the more you get to know the individual characteristics of your breasts--where there are bands of tissue, where the breast attaches to the chest-- the more comfortable the exam will become. You'll also find it easier to detect lumps, hard knots, skin thickening, or nipple discharge.

Here's a three-step technique for self-exam, courtesy of The Susan G. Komen Breast Cancer Foundation:

1. In the shower: Raise one arm and place your hand on the back of your

Figure 4.1 Visual representation of the fleshy body and ways to search for cancerous lumps (copyright: The Foundation for Better Health Care, New York).

assemblage. Moving to consider the gaze of the image maker, the visual stills of the breast and the hand are centralised in the image, but it can also be noted that part of the face of the women model has been included, helping to convey that the self-examiner is young and that these diagnostic procedures apply to women of all ages. Thinking then about the 'framing' of images on the web is revealing. In other similar photographic images on the web, doctors hands (signified by the cuffs of a traditional white coat) are included the frame, as if to convey the medical authority of the procedures represented. Dissecting this image and others for clues about how it/they might be argued to represent or resist medical authority was a key theme in the research undertaken then. As Gilman (1988) has noted, there is a long history of medical imaging in diagnostic text-books and other expert writings which encourage very particular medicalised visual readings of the deviant bodily form. One of Gilman's key points is that, historically, illness and disease have been represented in medical images (usually in drawings and paintings, although more latterly in photography) by signs of 'ugliness', and 'strangeness', that have in part been constructed by the makers of the images. In more modern representations of illness and disease (as in Figure 4.1), conventionally beautiful people are photographed in relation to warnings about disease risk (particularly in public health education material) so as to subvert older notions that beauty always equals health. Thinking through how social constructions such as beauty, strangeness and ugliness can be evidenced in web-images therefore helps in a critical reading of visual medical representation.

The technological capabilities of some computers/sites/users enable similar web images as Figure 4.1 to be manipulated, and hence help to make the reading of Internet visuals unique. Moving photographs, diagrams and on-line videos can be accessed and negotiated according to the needs and desires of the Internet user. For example, noting how 3-D imaging or diagrammatic representations of breasts allow mobile viewing of the image or frame in ways which aid self-diagnostic procedures are especially interesting to think through. Here, deconstructing how bodies can be virtually explored in multi-dimensional ways in order to enable people to literally 'see the body differently' in ways which serve to techno-medically 'make' the body in the gaze of the Internet user might be a fruitful line of enquiry. Hence, in my research project, through the use of the above methods (which represent only briefly some of the ways in which visual web images may be used and critiqued), it was possible to think about how virtual technologies can be argued to exacerbate the **power** of a medical gaze that encourages both an expert and lay objectification of fleshy bodies into potentially diseased spaces. In summary, Figure 4.1, and images like this on the web, can be argued to increase the potential for bodily surveillance and discipline in real space. The (un)healthy body which is constructed through expert talk and image-making perhaps becomes less abstract and discursive as corporeal understandings and practices have the potential to bleed between the screen and the lay computer users' bodies, partly because of the multiple ways in which these visual images convey the potential for disease detection.

As noted above, in reading and deconstructing body images in virtual space, it is also perhaps useful to understand them as both spaces of representation and representational spaces (after Lefebvre, 1991). Although the image above is clearly a space of representation as a clinically constructed diagnostic tool, in other places on the Internet it is possible to find body images that can be understood as more representational spaces. An undergraduate geography student at Dundee recently completed a project which looked at the virtual networks that exist between people with anorexia on the Internet and she came across a series of challenging images which were circulated between anorexic virtual surfers. These photographs proudly displayed the owners' thin bodies in a deliberate defiance of medical discourses about healthy body-weights that they were encountering in other spaces. Critically reading fleshy body images in virtual space, then, holds interesting potential for thinking about relations of power and resistance amongst other things.

There are clear advantages to using the methods I have outlined above – the textual and visual interpretation of websites provides rich source materials for the application of deconstructive qualitative analytic techniques. In this case, such methods aided in the construction of an argument about how bodies are spaces of inscription and discursive construction in virtual worlds but also helped in the development of critical perspectives on how such inscriptions might begin to impact upon and interact with the fleshy body-spaces of computer users. However, the major drawbacks of the methods mentioned so far is that they allow the researcher little access to the computer users who are implicated in the processes and knowledges outlined. So far the understanding of how and if computer users' bodies become medicalised as an effect of habitation in virtual worlds is limited as these methods do not help to 'uncover' emotional, corporeal and social interactions with net technologies. This, then, was my second major challenge and it is to such concerns that the chapter now turns.

Researching people, fleshy bodies, conversations and communities on the net

Using conventional qualitative methods (conversational analysis, interviewing and ethnography) in Internet research is a relatively new area of interest for social scientists (Hine, 2000; Miller and Slater, 2000; see also special issue 6 (1999) of *Cybersociology: www.cybersociology.com*), and has hardly been addressed within the geography literature. Despite the current lack of debate, there are rich possibilities for online qualitative research as well as some interesting limitations, some of which are discussed below.

The Internet as a public space of informational exchange, conversation and social connection clearly lends itself to geographical research that is interested in how bodies are cohesive material entities which enable the formation of virtual 'corporeal communities'. As mentioned above, the presence of on-line chatrooms which were orientated around particular disease categories provided a rich source of qualitative data which shed light upon research questions about how and if material bodies and illness were the focus of social interaction. I began this phase of the research by accessing various chatrooms associated with one disease category: MS (MS was chosen as it is an unpredictable illness with confusing physical effects and also has been a focus for geographical investigation in the past: see Dyck, 1995). Although there were clear opportunities for conducting on-line interviewing, I chose to use a different approach to researching people and their conversations, through the accessing of chatroom archives: spaces which hold collections of past conversations between users. This decision was taken initially as I was unsure of what questions might be relevant to the chatroom users, and I supposed that immersing myself in past narratives as well as live chatroom sites as a 'virtual lurker' might help me build some picture of what exchanges routinely occurred in such spaces without the known presence of a researcher. Virtual space is one of the few mediums which allow you to analyse past conversations. Chatrooms often include links to past conversations (although these are usually catalogued and themed, and so clearly already subject to analytical construction), as these are seen as useful for new users who wish to orientate themselves to the virtual community in question. This holds a particular purpose in illness-related chatrooms as an important resource for newly diagnosed people to have access to narratives and accumulated bodily knowledges of other users who have been debating the disease in question for some time.

Reading, sifting and analysing past conversations which the researcher has had no input in shaping is a problematic activity. In some ways it could be considered to be ethically suspect, except for the fact that these chatrooms are often considered to be accessible public spaces by the people that construct them and participate within them. This practice can also be seen as limiting as the research questions of the researcher cannot be directly answered as any measure of inter-subjectivity between researcher and researched is lost. However, at the same time, chatroom archives are clearly a substantial and rich resource that also helps to overcome problems of access to everyday conversation amongst a particular group under investigation. Accessing conversational archives is clearly different from 'listening in' to live chatroom exchanges, a practice I also engaged in. Here it is possible to argue that accessing live conversational space is ethnographic, as I was anonymously hanging out in public spaces listening to other people's conversations. Although, again, there are ethical questions associated with this strategy, in the case of virtual public space the online users realise that their conversations can be witnessed by silent others and the chatrooms I accessed did not require users to declare that they had MS. Although the research strategy undertaken for this project was problematic, then, it did reveal much about the medicalised dimensions to social interactions on the Internet between MS chatroom users. In this case the virtual lurking and archive analysis revealed rich conversational exchanges around the ill body which connected with and shaped my conceptual themes (associated with medicalised bodily knowledge, acting on the ill body, embodying medical and health advice and resisting medical expert authority). However, because I was not engaged in direct interviewing, this process took a long time, as I had to search through several years of archived chatroom exchange in order to gather appropriate materials.

The selection process used in gathering material involved coding and categorising the conversations I had access to in relation to my conceptual concerns about medicalisation, bodily knowledges and actions and corporeal communities. There were several 'layers' of coding which comprised what others might term 'emic' and 'etic' constructs (Crang, 1997: 189), which related, respectively, to the common terms, ideas and views of chatroom participants (crudely, 'insider views') and the meaningful theoretical dimensions I attributed to these (crudely, 'outsider views'). Here it is important to note that coding and categorising conversations often reveal new conceptual concerns, and do not just always fit neatly into a priori theoretical themes.

To use some small examples to demonstrate how effective analysis of conversational archives can be, one of my central research questions was whether chatrooms could be understood as medical(ised) communities which increased very specific forms of bodily knowledge. Many of the chatroom exchanges focused upon the experience, diagnosis and treatment of the ill body and can be argued to demonstrate how the Internet facilitates the presence of the material body in virtual space in particular ways, as these extracts demonstrate:

> 'I've been having symptoms of MS off and on for over one year. _Tingling, numbness, weakness in legs and eye twitching._ My testing is normal?? How long did you have symptoms and _how long did the diagnosis take?_
> (Extract from MS chatroom, November 10th, 1999)

> I have been diagnosed with MS since September. (We knew sooner, but we had to wait for the Dr. to admit it.) _Last night my right leg seized up into a bent position which finally straightened and then this morning when I stood up to get out of bed, I promptly fell, my left leg refusing to work._ I have never had this type of symptom before. Now later this morning, I am walking with the help of a cane, but _my left leg continues to feel weak and strangely heavy._ I did do some walking yesterday but nothing that was overly strenuous. _My question is, should I consider this an exacerbation or must I wait the 24hrs? What might it be? My Dr. is very unhelpful about these things._
> (Extract from MS chatroom archives, December 15th, 1999)

Here I would seek to code, categorise and analytically interpret these kinds of statements in relation to themes of medical hegemony, resistance, communality and physical embodied practice in order to build an argument about how the materiality of the body is central to the purpose of disease-orientated chatrooms and thus virtual space. In the above extracts the material malfunctioning body is given shape (note the level of detail about movement, pain and sensations underlined above), but crucially ill Internet users, rather than medical doctors (who are 'unhelpful') are asked for advice about this, demonstrating to some extent, an implied resistance to medical authority. These sorts of extracts can suggest that perhaps more 'organic' bodily knowledges are sought by Internet users, ones free from the medical hegemony that such people might experience in real medical-institutional spaces, and there is certainly conversational evidence that supports this claim. However, when looking at many responses to such bodily queries, it is clear that ill Internet users have extraordinary levels of medical knowledge, which they then circulate to others, thus increasing the notion that the Internet somehow facilities an ever more specialised medical gaze amongst lay people:

Cheryl, I too have experienced all the symptoms you mention, but am waiting for a definitive diagnosis. While I am not a doctor, I have researched a great deal to identify possible causes of my symptoms. Your actual question was about SED rate. SED rate is the rate of speed with which your blood flows when drawn. The rate of speed is important, and a high SED rate could be indicative of Vascularitis. The symptoms of Vascularitis are nearly the same as MS and the two diseases are often confused. Although Vascularitis is more common in the elderly, it has been known to occur when in your 30s and 40s. There are three types of Vascularitis which basically means an inflammation of the main arteries. In particular, if interested, research the main arteries in the head (above the ear). By the way, some Vascularitis symptoms are more prevalent if you are a smoker. Definitive diagnosis involves a biopsy of the suspected artery. A certain cell will be present if Vascularitis is the cause. Common treatment is a steroid based drug. I hope I have answered your question. I check in periodically, so if you have any additional questions, please let me know.

(Extract from MS chatroom, May 25th, 1999)

The above extract demonstrates the very medicalised knowledge which can be accumulated and circulated between lay Internet users. The underlined sections above indicate which sentences might be identified as contributing to some of the themes already mentioned. For example, in this case the theme of increasing medical knowledge/hegemony via virtual space can be explored in relation to the statements made above about medical research. The conveyed level of detail about the disease discussed and the suggestions for treatment indicates that the Internet user in question is demonstrating quite a sophisticated medicalised understanding not only of MS, but also other bio-medical disease categories as a result of Internet research. In my project I was interested in whether such accumulations of knowledge via virtual space represented a process which enabled people with MS to be further empowered in everyday bodily practice and medicalised interactions. This meant seeking out statements and conversations relating to how people translated virtually acquired knowledges in their daily lives, as is reported here by McKee (1999: 13):

I had already heard of Nabilone and wanted to try it, but my GP wouldn't let me have it. When I discovered this research paper, I printed out a copy and gave it to him. I told him these were really positive results and wasn't it worth a try? It worked! I was prescribed treatment.... if you've got the knowledge, it gives you the confidence to ask for what you want.

(Clayton cited in McKee, 1999: 13)

Indeed, in my work many users discussed the usefulness of educational Internet interactions in their own illness management strategies as well as in terms of gaining a sense of emotional communality through the sharing of illness experience, as is highlighted below:

The best thing you can do is <u>educate yourself</u> and become an <u>advocate for yourself</u>

(Extract from MS chatroom, November 7th, 1999)

Sharon   *Since I haven't been feeling well, my social contacts have been curtailed, <u>it's nice to have some</u>*
              <u>contact with people</u>.

EllenOP *I didn't have a computer at home and had to go to hubby's school to chat. It was a little scary at*
              night with me being the only one at the school. <u>I was so glad when he was able to bring a computer</u>
              <u>home for the summer.</u>

Rip   *I feel the same way, Sharon.*

EllenOP *Yes, it is Sharon. I think we all feel the same way there.*

Rip   *<u>It's nice to have people to talk to.</u>*

EllenOP *<u>Being able to come here was the only reason my hubby bought this computer.</u>*

Sharon   *<u>I wonder what I would do without my computer? I have had it for about three years now and I can't</u>*
              <u>imagine life without it</u>.

(Extract from MS chatroom, September 27, 1999)

Here then virtual interactions can be seen to make a difference – both to personal medical strategies and 'feelings' about the ill body in real space. However, further research is needed to understand more about the relations between virtual knowledge and embodied geographies of illness.

Although clearly a source of rich material, there are limitations to analysing past conversational texts in geographical research. In some cases it is perhaps more useful for a researcher to engage in on-line interviewing so that research questions can be *directly* answered by research subjects, instead of being constructed from wide-ranging discussions. However, engaging in the direct use of qualitative methods online also carries particular concerns, as I briefly indicate below. Thinking beyond my case study for a moment, the very nature of virtual space throws up new challenges when thinking about embodiment and methodologies. To explain, I would argue that in most qualitative research methods (such as interviewing and ethnography) embodied moments are crucial to intersubjectivity, interpretation and understanding. Clearly in research on virtual worlds this is difficult as bodily moments can only be witnessed through narratives of chatroom users, and no ethnographic observational notes can be made about the ways in which an interviewee or research subject types, walks, sits, cooks or opens doors for example. In on-line interviewing key bodily relations surrounding the gender of research subjects, the body language between interviewer and interviewee and eye contact are lost in technological space. In researching questions of ill-health, then, this can be problematic, as perhaps this means more limited understanding of (say) the spatial effects of pain in domestic space, for example, which can only be expressed in language rather than through embodied observations. However, new technologies such as web-cams may become more 'everyday' in virtual worlds and may address some of these concerns, although for many computer users these elite technological developments may not prove attractive or practical.

There are also less technological solutions to the need for bodily intersubjectivity in virtual qualitative research methods. For example, the use of existing shorthand net language symbols denoting smiling, winking and anger could perhaps be extended to translate pain, mobility difficulties and delimited spatial reach during interview situations which may go some way to overcoming the limitations or threat of 'disembodied' research relations. Here on-line researchers may have to develop their own language system with a research respondent in order that bodily moments can enter into the exchange beyond formal narrative reflection. Such imaginative strategies may be complicated and time-consuming, making access and participation more difficult. However, by choosing to interview people who regularly spend time type-talking to strangers it might be possible (more so than in 'real space') to undertake such new and exciting dimensions to qualitative research projects.

Conclusions and guide to further research

Overall this chapter has introduced some general strategies for investigating bodies and people in virtual worlds in ways which suggest that such geographies are not ones where bodies are 'irrelevant and invisible' (as reported by Kitchin, 1998: 80). It has been suggested that textual, visual and conversational analysis can reveal much about the social processes that underpin the production of virtual space as a geography of expanded human possibilities and embodied subjectivities. However, the methods presented in this chapter can be critiqued as rather 'passive' qualitative strategies and it has been also recommended that the direct use of qualitative methods online can potentially be even more productive (albeit with the acknowledgement that there are some key differences to the embodied execution of such methods). The following paragraphs elaborate ways forward for students who may be thinking of doing qualitative virtual research.

Before launching into on-line research, especially if using direct interviewing techniques, it is advisable to 'experiment' with mini-projects relating to perhaps less sensitive subjects than illness. For example, students could devise questionnaires/interviews for use in music or dance-orientated chatrooms, for example, to understand how such public spaces become culturally meaningful for their users and to understand how embodied practices in everyday life (like dancing) can be experienced and encountered virtually (see also Malbon, 1999). Another common route might be to research questions relating to **identity** and virtual space by examining (say) the building of social relationships in both Internet cafes and on the Internet, and thereby focusing on how the real-virtual relationship is configured in different spaces of consumption and also has differing consequences for various social groupings (see Wakeford, 1999).

If more socially sensitive research is undertaken, such as that on illness, there is a wealth of possibilities as well as many barriers. Using the example I have discussed above, it may be possible to extend the analysis to different biomedical disease categories to investigate whether virtuality has differing embodied implications for people with different illness experiences. However, when engaged in on-line interviewing of people who are maybe weak or vulnerable, care has to be taken with the questions asked, the nature and length of dialogue, and the relationship that can build between computer users. Despite the attractions that anonymous access to chatrooms can bring, if you are undertaking on-line interviewing, ideally you should always alert your research subjects, so they can adequately represent themselves and understand the basis for the conversational encounter.

Overall, the use of qualitative methods in virtual space offers new possibilities and definitely new challenges to the geography research student. The previously taken-for-granted assumptions about research access, intersubjectivity, ethics, embodiment and power relations are given new and different dimensions in virtual worlds and the discipline of human geography is only just beginning to realise the implications.

Further reading

- Crang, M., Crang, P. and May, J. (eds) (1999) *Virtual Geographies: Bodies, Spaces, Relations.* London, Routledge.

- Featherstone, M. and Burrows, R. (1995) *Cyberspace, Cyberbodies and Cyberpunk: Cultures of Technological Embodiment.* London, Sage.

- Hine, C. (2000) *Virtual Ethnography.* London, Sage.

- Kitchin, R. (1998a) *Cyberspace: The World in the Wires.* Chichester, Wiley.

- Parr, H. (2002) 'New body-geographies: the embodied spaces of health and illness information on the Internet' *Environment and Planning D: Society and Space* 20, 73–95.

PART II

Living cultural geography

5
Home and identity

Life stories in text and in person

Alison Blunt

This chapter is about the place of personal stories, everyday life, memories and experiences in research on home and **identity**. The term 'life stories' is deliberately broad, and encompasses the study of people in their own words, both in text (including diaries, memoirs, letters, autobiographies and travel writing) and in person (through, for example, oral history interviews, focus group discussions, reminiscence work, and ethnographic research; see also Chapter 6). Life stories are also created, collected, preserved and communicated in other ways too, as shown by collections of tapes, transcripts and videos in libraries, archives, and museums; exhibitions that include extracts from life stories in both oral and written form; theatre productions and other performances based on reminiscence work; and narratives that can be accessed on the Internet.

Many researchers use life stories to record and to understand the experiences and memories of people whose lives might otherwise remain marginalized or even invisible. But life stories can also be used to explore the everyday lives and experiences of people in positions of **power**. So, for example, although the rise of oral history in Britain was closely tied to writing the 'hidden histories' of women and the working class, other oral history projects involve interviews with political and corporate leaders, and the subjects of the first organized oral history project (based in the United States in 1948) were elite white men (Perks and Thomson, 1998).

Life stories are clearly diverse in terms of their content, form, purpose, and reception. While life stories provide rich and revealing sources for research on subjects as wide-ranging as human experience itself, I focus on how I have used life stories in the following forms to study home and identity:

1   Letters and diaries written by British women during the so-called Indian 'Mutiny' of 1857. These women were married to army officers or officials and were members of the imperial elite in India. Their writings reveal a great deal about class, gender and everyday life at a time of conflict.

2   Oral history interviews with Anglo-Indian women who attended the same school in India and migrated to Britain in the 1940s and 1950s. These interviews are part of a larger research project on this community of mixed descent in the fifty years before and after Independence.

Before discussing these examples of life stories in text and in person, I want to introduce feminist and postcolonial geographies of home and identity.

Concept Box

Identity

Identity – broadly, a sense of self that encompasses who people think they are, and how other people regard them – is a complex and contested term. Within geography, humanistic work in the 1970s sought to replace the abstract figure of 'rational economic man' with a human subject who had feelings, experiences and values. Although humanistic geographers put a good deal of humanity back into human geography, their work has been critiqued for overlooking the **power** relations that shape identity in different and unequal ways (Rose, 1995). Since the early 1980s, identity – particularly in terms of race, class, gender, and sexuality – has been a central part of cultural geography. Two ways of thinking about identity have been particularly important. The first sees identity in essentialist terms, suggesting a core and common identity shared by different groups of people. These ideas have been strategically important in identity politics that campaign on behalf of particular groups who share the same identity. So, for example, an essentialist understanding of the shared oppression of women is reflected by feminist slogans such as 'sisterhood is global.' In contrast, the second main way of thinking about identity is to do so in terms of **difference**. This approach draws attention to the multiple axes of identity and their interplay at different times and different places. Rather than see identity as pre-given and unchanging, this approach views identity as socially and discursively constructed. In a widely cited essay about her sense of identity, Minnie Bruce Pratt (1984) interprets her past and present in relation to multiple spaces of home and memory, and interrogates the interplay of her white, middle class, Jewish, and lesbian identities at particular times and in particular places in the American South (for a critical commentary, see Martin and Mohanty, 1986). This essay is a good example of the relational production of identity, whereby an understanding of the 'self' is influenced by assumptions about the 'other' (see Rose, 1995). It also shows the ways in which identities are not singular and fixed, but rather shift in their multiple constitution over time and space.

Ideas about identity are also important in methodological terms, particularly in the attempt to produce knowledge that is **situated, reflexive** and **embodied**. Researchers and the subjects of their research negotiate different identities. For example, Gill Valentine compares her own research experience on two projects: first, 'as an 'out' lesbian interviewing other lesbians as part of a research project on sexuality; and [second] as a researcher interviewing parents about different aspects of their children's lives where my sexuality was not disclosed' (2002: 120).

Key reading

- Pratt, M. B. (1984) 'Identity: skin, blood, heart'. In Burkin, E., Pratt, M. B. and Smith, B. (eds) *Yours in Struggle: Three Feminist Perspectives on Anti-Semitism and Racism*. Ithaca, Firebrand Books.
- Rose, G. (1995) 'Place and identity: a sense of place.' In Massey, D. and Jess, P. (eds) *A Place in the World?* Oxford, Oxford University Press: 87–132.
- Valentine, G. (2002) 'People like us: negotiating sameness and difference in the research process.' In Moss, P. (ed.) *Feminist Geography in Practice: Research and Methods*. Oxford, Blackwell: 116–126.

Home and identity

On scales ranging from the domestic to the diasporic, research on home has become increasingly important across the social sciences and humanities (Chapman and Hockey, 1999; Cieraad, 1999; George, 1996, 1998; Miller, 2001). Studies of home on a domestic scale include work on housing, household structure, domestic divisions of labour, paid domestic work, material cultures of home, and homelessness (for more on homelessness, see Chapter 2). On a national scale, ideas about home have been studied in relation to debates about citizenship, nationalist politics, indigeneity, and **discourses** of multiculturalism. Beyond national borders, research on diasporic and other transnational spaces includes studies of different domestic forms, multiple places of belonging, cultural geographies of home and memory, and global patterns of domestic labour. A key feature of research on home has been the ways in which it cuts across different scales, as shown by research on the bungalow and the highrise as transnational domestic forms (King, 1984; Jacobs 2002), research on the political significance of domesticity in anti-colonial nationalism (Chatterjee, 1993; Chakrabarty, 2000) and the transnational employment of domestic workers (Pratt, 1997, 1999; Yeoh and Huang, 2000). Another key theme within such research is an interest in the critical connections between home and identity, whereby ideas of home invoke a sense of place, belonging or alienation that is intimately tied to a sense of self.

An interest in home and identity within geography can be traced back to the work of a number of humanistic geographers writing in the 1970s and 1980s. Resisting the abstractions of positivist spatial science, humanistic geographers sought to foreground human experience and a sense of place. They did so by seeking to replace 'rational economic man' with a fully human subject, whose thoughts, experiences, values, emotions, agency and creativity shaped unique individuality within a wider humanity. Crucially, humanistic geographers also claimed that part of what made people human was their intense and sensual attachment to place. The home was celebrated as a site of authentic meaning, value and experience, imbued with nostalgic memories and the love of a particular place (Relph, 1976; Seamon, 1979; Tuan, 1977). But, as Gillian Rose (1993) argues, humanistic geographers failed to analyse gendered geographies of home, shaped by different and unequal relations of power, and as a place that might be dangerous, violent, alienating and unhappy rather than loving and secure. Cultural geographers have come to study more complex and contested spaces of home, often inspired by feminist and postcolonial theory. In metaphorical terms, images of home form part of a wider spatial lexicon that has become important in theorizing identity (see Pratt, 1998, for more on the use of spatial metaphors, particularly home, in theorizing identity). Such images of home are often closely tied to ideas about the politics of location and an attempt to situate both knowledge and identity. These ideas, in turn, reflect a wider concern with the *politics* of home and identity, and the ways in which geographies of home are shaped by **difference**, not only in terms of gender, but also race, class and sexuality. Feminist postcolonial research, for example, has investigated the politics of home and identity in the social reproduction of nation, empire and diaspora. Important themes include the domestication of imperial subjects, particularly as servants, housewives, and mothers; the material cultures of domesticity in the metropolis, colonies and over diasporic space; the home as a site of inclusion, exclusion and contestation; and the importance of the home, and particularly the roles of women within it, in shaping diasporic memories and identities (including Blunt, 1999; George, 1996; McClintock, 1995; Walter, 2001; Webster, 1998). Through their accounts of personal memories and everyday experiences, life stories provide a particularly rich source for studying home and identity.

Life stories in text: letters and diaries by British women in India

My doctoral research focused on imperial domesticity in British India at a time of conflict (during the Indian 'Mutiny' of 1857) and during the reconstruction of imperial rule. As part of a broader interest in the cultural geographies of imperialism and the gendered dynamics of imperial power, this research focused on 'empires in the home' (George, 1996) and the contested place of *memsahibs* in British India. As well as studying parliamentary papers, newspaper articles, and photographs, the main sources for my research were personal records of everyday life. The time period of my research (1857 to 1939) made it necessary for me to rely on two main sources:

1 Narratives written by women themselves, either while they were living in India (letters and diaries) or written – often many years later – once they had returned to Britain (memoirs; and see Gowans, 2001, for more on the repatriation of such women).

2 Life stories collected by researchers conducting oral history interviews and questionnaires, particularly in the 1970s. These sources included transcripts of interviews held at the Oriental and India Office Collections of the British Library for a radio programme and book entitled *Plain Tales from the Raj*, Allen, 1975; and 'British women in India: replies to questionnaires,' compiled by Mary Thatcher at the Centre of South Asian Studies, University of Cambridge. The British Empire and Commonwealth Museum in Bristol, which opened in 2002, also has extensive oral history collections that would have been relevant for my research (*www.empiremuseum.co.uk*).

While official records and newspaper articles helped me to contextualize the main issues and debates that framed my research, these personal sources were the most appropriate ones for the questions I wanted to answer: what did it feel like to live so far from home? What was everyday life like for British women in India? What were the power relations shaping imperial domesticity? How was home-life in India challenged by the 'mutiny' of 1857? How were 'empires in the home' reconstructed and maintained after the suppression of the 'mutiny'?

As well as analysing different sources to answer such research questions, it is also important to ask questions about the sources themselves. In the case of written narratives such as letters and diaries, these questions might include some or all of the following:

- Who was writing, and in what form?
- Why, where and when was the narrative written?
- What are the main themes addressed in the writings? (Also think about silences in the text. What themes and events are described, and which are missing?).
- Are the writings formal or more conversational in tone?
- Were the writings meant to be read – and, if so, by whom? – or to remain private? If the writings were meant to remain private, is it right to read them? (To whom were letters written? Were diaries intended as a private record, or to be read by friends, family or a wider readership?)
- Were the writings published – and, if so, when, where and by whom? (Some letters and diaries were published for private circulation, while others were published commercially, either during the author's lifetime or after their death).
- If the writings remained unpublished, who kept them, and why? If they have been deposited in an archive, when, where and why did this take place, and by whom? Do personal writings form part of a larger archival collection about an individual or their family? What can other archival sources reveal about the personal writings and their author?
- If the same writings are available in both published and unpublished form, how do they differ?
- Is there any evidence of how readers responded to the writings, either at the time they were written or in subsequent years? Are replies to letters available? Are there reviews of published writings?
- Do you need to obtain permission to quote from personal narratives that are held in archival collections?

Personal writings provide a particularly rich source for studying the lives of women. As Harriet Blodgett explains, letters and diaries have been the most common form of women's writing for centuries, 'expressing a resilient creative impulse that through serial writing could find outlet in a sanctioned form'

(Blodgett, 1991: 1). In my research, I found that by far the most compelling of the personal sources I studied were the letters and diaries written by British women, mainly because they described everyday life at the time and in the place in which it was lived. Such sources provide personal, and often intimate, accounts of the feelings as well as experiences of such women by describing their relationships with other people, their dreams of home, and the pleasures and challenges of living in India. Reading such personal narratives helped to embody my research, as I could imagine individual women, their families in India and Britain, and their everyday lives. Sometimes, alongside their writings, I could visualise some of these women particularly clearly as they were the subjects of photographs taken by Ahmed Ali Khan in Lucknow in the years just before the 'mutiny,' paintings and engravings of women during the 'mutiny,' and later photographs of imperial domesticity (Figure 5.1; Blunt, 2003a).

Figure 5.1 *Maria and Charlie Germon at Lucknow before the siege. By permission of the British Library. Photo 269/2/117b: The Lucknow Album.*

As well as illuminating individual lives so vividly, these personal narratives also tell much wider stories about femininity, domesticity and imperialism. I read such narratives in order to understand discourses of imperial domesticity and the ideas about appropriate femininity on which they relied by focusing on the roles of middle class wives and mothers and their exercise of power within the home, particularly through their management of Indian servants. My reading and interpretation of the writings were influenced by a feminist understanding of how and why everyday life, experiences and emotions are both personally and politically important (for more on feminist methodologies in geographical research, see Jones et al., 1997; WGSG, 1997; Moss, 2002). Rather than interpret identity in terms of a core and stable fixity, I was interested in its complexity, 'even within the span of the single life' (Whitlock, 2000: 3). Following Gillian Whitlock, I wanted to resist 'any sense of a transhistorical female experience, or the notion of the female **body** as the ground of a unified and consistent meaning.' To do so, 'rather than [construct] an identity and history of women, I am interested in difference and intimacy, in the relations between very different female subjects, and the leakage between what might seem to be secure gendered, national and racial identities' (Whitlock, 2000: 3). To illustrate what these ideas might mean in practice, I now turn to the monthly letters written by Frances Wells to her father in Britain and diaries written by six British women living under siege at Lucknow in 1857.

Frances Wells' letters to her father began on her voyage to India in 1853 and ended on her last day in Calcutta before beginning her return voyage five years later. These letters, together with occasional letters written by her husband to his father-in-law, and a newspaper article recording their return to Britain, are held in the archives of the Centre of South Asian Studies at the University of Cambridge (Bernars Papers; for more on locating archival sources, see Chapter 1). Frances Wells was a doctor's daughter and the young wife of Walter Wells, a doctor in the Indian Army. Her letters described her life and anxieties as a middle-class British wife and mother. In the first four years of her correspondence, Frances Wells wrote about her three-month journey to India, setting up home in different cantonments, the birth of her three children, one of whom died five days later, and the routines of daily domestic and social life. But her life was disrupted, and her correspondence ceased, for seven months in 1857 during the siege and subsequent evacuation from Lucknow. When she resumed her correspondence in December 1857, she wrote about the death of her baby son George five months before, the hardships of living under siege, and her desire to return to Britain. Unlike diaries written by a number of British women during the siege that were subsequently published, the candid letters written by Frances Wells – letters written by a loving daughter to her father, rather than letters written for a wider, more public readership – were critical of Brigadier Inglis, who led the defence of Lucknow (Figure 5.2). She wrote in December 1857 that his despatches provided 'on the whole a pretty fair account of the siege,' but also described him as:

> *a man universally detested throughout the garrison by all ranks: and his mention of the names of officers has excited great indignation: many of those whom he has praised never did a single thing the whole time and some of those that worked the hardest are omitted entirely because they were not favourites: he disliked the 48th [Regiment of the Native Infantry, to which Walter Wells belonged] and left them out entirely.*

She continued, 'My husband says he shall write a book about the siege setting forth the selfishness of human nature and well he may do so for indeed we have seen enough of it during the last six months.' Needless to say, if Walter did write such a book, it was never published.

Figure 5.2 *The Inglis family. From* Illustrated London News *28 November 1857.*

Frances Wells' letters provide a vivid insight into life for a young wife and mother in India in the 1850s. I interpreted her letters by drawing out key themes such as femininity, imperialism, class, family, social and domestic life, and growing unease in 1857. I also located her letters in the wider historical context of both India and Britain in the 1850s; thought about the ways in which Frances Wells positioned herself in relation to other British people, particularly women, in India; quoted particular examples to illustrate wider discursive themes; explored points of conflict and contradiction; and thought about the absences in her letters. In her descriptions of other people, and her relationships with them, Frances Wells' letters document her personal experiences of, and feelings about, married life, motherhood and imperial rule in the mid-nineteenth century. In 1856, for example, Frances confided her concern that her eldest son would acquire the worst traits of the British in India, as his father had: 'I am fearful lest he learns to abuse the natives as is too much the custom out here. Walter says he must be whipped if he does so, but I contend that will be quite useless if he hears his Papa do the same thing. You can have no idea in England to what extent this practice is carried out and sometimes it makes me feel quite ill' (Frances Wells to Dr Fox, 5 April 1856). This example can be read on a number of levels. Read in the context of her earlier correspondence, this letter confirms both the close relationship between Frances and her father and points of tension between herself and her husband. But, on another level, this letter also describes the exercise of imperial power in India and the 'abuse [of] the natives' on which it relied. As becomes clear, Frances is concerned about her son's behaviour towards Indians, which not only mirrors the abusive behaviour of his father but also the British in India more widely.

Here, and in other letter letters, Frances positions herself as both an insider and outsider in British India and provides a critical commentary on imperial life. In other letters, this is particularly evident in her descriptions of social life and the conduct of other women. Frances Wells perceived her Christian marriage as a sacred contract that was governed by certain rules of propriety. She was conscious, however, that her views differed from those of many of her compatriots in India. As she wrote to her father in 1855,

> I have never danced since my marriage and never intend to do so: I am universally laughed at but I do not think it consistent with the quietness and sobriety which are enjoined on married women: at the same time I do not exactly like to give this as my reason, because as almost everyone, married or not dances in this country it would seem to be setting up as better than others so I think the best thing is to stay at home and avoid all discussion on the subject.
>
> (Frances Wells to Dr Fox, 7 April 1855)

When thinking about how to represent Frances Wells and her correspondence, I knew that I wanted to keep a clear sense of the particularity of her life, as well as to interpret broader themes about imperial domesticity from her letters. I also wanted to reflect the fact that her correspondence spanned the whole period of her life in India, providing an unusually complete record that started on the day she left Britain and ended on the day she left India. As a result, I thought about the form as well as the content of my own writing. I wrote about Frances Wells' life in India, based on her letters home, in two shorter 'interludes' between longer, and more analytical, chapters about British women during the 'mutiny.' I wrote these interludes in a more descriptive and broadly chronological style and used them to introduce and contextualize wider themes of imperial domesticity and femininity by telling the story of Frances Wells' life before and after the 'mutiny'. I also used a different font in the interludes to signal their distinctive style and content.

The main source for studying the lives of British women under siege at Lucknow are six book-length diaries that describe everyday life during a conflict that threatened to overthrow British rule (Blunt, 2000a). These diaries are held at the Centre for South Asian Studies at the University of Cambridge and the Oriental and India Office Collections of the British Library. It is likely that diaries were written by other women, but that they did not survive the siege or the evacuation from Lucknow, were subsequently lost or destroyed, or remain in private collections. I studied these diaries to explore **representations** by British women themselves (and see Blunt, 2000b, for more on **representations** of and by British women at Cawnpore and Lucknow). Unlike letters, which are written episodically and usually read soon afterwards, diaries provide a more continuous and cumulative narrative of daily life that are often only intended to be read by the author. Diary narratives are diverse, as shown by extracts in published anthologies (including Blodgett, 1991 and Taylor and Taylor, 2002). As well as recording everyday life, diaries are also important sources for understanding experiences beyond the everyday, as shown by travel diaries and diaries written at times of war (see Baer, 1997; Frank, 1967; Hassam, 1990; Weiner, 1997). Diaries have been described as sanctuaries and as confessionals, providing a private, perhaps secret, narrative of thoughts and feelings, and the textual freedom to imagine life away from confinement and danger. But diaries are not necessarily private, as their authors might be conscious of the documentary value of their writings and might be recording events for a wider readership than themselves alone.

Unlike more general studies of 'mutiny' writings by women (such as Robinson, 1996 and Tuson, 1998), I concentrated on diaries written over the same period of time and in the same place to examine the differences as well as the similarities between accounts. Most of the two hundred women who lived under siege at Lucknow were married to soldiers, but 69 'ladies' were related to officers or officials (Innes, 1895). The diarists all belonged to this elite group and included the wives of the two most senior officers at Lucknow (Adelaide Case and Julia Inglis); the wives of two army doctors (Katherine Bartrum and Colina Brydon); the wife of a regimental chaplain (Katherine Harris); and the wife of a captain in the Indian Army (Maria Germon). Although the diarists were all middle class, married women, some were widowed during the siege, some had children, others did not, and some suffered the death of a child. The daily record provided by the diaries enabled me to compare descriptions of the same event by different women, and to compare the experiences of women who lived in different parts of the 33-acre Residency compound. I read the diaries in an intertextual way, both in terms of cross-referencing and comparing different accounts of the same people, events and themes, and in terms of studying supplementary writings by other authors included alongside the diary narrative (including military details from published sources, letters written by their husbands and, when Adelaide Case stopped writing her diary for a week after the death of her husband, her sister's record of events that ensured a continuous narrative). The diaries all describe five months of danger, discomfort and monotony. Despite their broad similarities in terms of form and content, I found that the diaries also revealed important differences, particularly in terms of a class hierarchy not only between middle-class and working-class women at Lucknow, but also within the middle class itself.

The diaries also differed in terms of their publication and readership. Three diaries were published soon after the 'mutiny,' one was published 33 years later, and two were published for the first time a century after they had been written (Bartrum, 1858; Case, 1858; Harris, 1858; Inglis, 1892; Germon, 1957; Brydon, 1978). The diaries of Katherine Harris, Katherine Bartrum and Adelaide Case were published in London in 1858 and reached a readership far beyond the family and friends for whom they had been initially writing. Bartrum and Case were widowed during the siege, and the publication of their diaries would have provided an important source of income. Each of these three diarists felt it necessary to explain why she had chosen to publish her personal writings. For example, although Adelaide Case had written her diary 'for the perusal of my relatives in England, and with no view whatever to publication' (Case, 1858: iii), she decided to publish it as a book to supplement official dispatches about Lucknow with her more personal account of daily life. She was keen to stress, however, that she had not rewritten her diary since the siege. As she wrote, 'I have not attempted, by subsequent additions, to produce effect, or to aim at glowing descriptions, but have given it as it was written, in the simple narrative form, which the dangers and privations of the siege alone permitted' (Case, 1858: iii–iv). Katherine Harris also described the practice of writing a diary under siege:

> I have kept a rough sort of journal during the whole siege, often written under the greatest difficulties – part of the time with a child in my arms or asleep in my lap; but I persevered, because I knew if we survived you would like to live our siege life over in imagination, and the little details would interest you; besides the comfort of talking to you.
>
> (Harris, 1858: iii)

The form and content of the diaries published in the nineteenth and twentieth centuries are similar. However, Maria Germon (1957), whose diary remained unpublished in her lifetime, was the only diarist to describe discord among women living under siege. As she wrote, 'I rebelled against [keeping watch at night] – we had quite a fight about it during the day' (64); 'I fought against sleeping in the dining room as I considered it dangerous but being the only one I was obliged to give in' (80); and 'Mrs Helford [is] very angry at being turned out of her room to give place to the baby' (77). Maria Germon's diary is an important reminder that there must have been disagreements between the women living under siege, even though most diarists either did not write about them, or edited the details out before publication.

At the start of the siege, the diaries recorded some continuity of both home life and imperial rule. But this changed dramatically after a few days when most of the diarists recorded the desertion of their Indian servants. The only exceptions to this were the accounts by Adelaide Case and Julia Inglis, whose servants worked for them throughout the siege (and who also, as the most senior ladies at Lucknow, lived in the safest quarters in the Residency compound). But, more typically, Katherine Harris recorded the desertion of her servants in mid-June:

> Our bearer [main servant], who has been with us almost ever since we came to India, and to whom James has been most kind, walked off, taking with him all his goods and chattels, and one of our punkah coolies to carry his bundle … People's servants seem to be deserting daily. We expect soon to be without attendants, and a good riddance it would be if this were a climate which admitted of one's doing without them; but if they all leave us, it will be difficult to know how we shall manage. Their impudence is beyond bounds: they are losing even the semblance of respect. I packed off my tailor yesterday: he came very late, and, on my remarking it, he gave me such an insolent answer and look, that I discharged him then and there; and he actually went off without waiting, or asking for his wages.
>
> (Harris, 1858: 46–7)

For women like Katherine Harris, imperial power was challenged most directly in a domestic sphere. For the first time, many British women had to make tea, clean, wash their clothes and sometimes cook, although the wives of British soldiers were usually employed for this purpose. Most of the daily entries in the diaries record domestic hardships, domestic divisions of labour, and new routines of domestic work. Moreover, the very act of writing a diary that charted a daily routine of domestic work also helped to impose a degree of order to life under siege.

Life stories in person: Anglo-Indian women and memories of school

While the main sources for my doctoral research were life stories in letters, diaries, memoirs and oral histories conducted by other researchers, my current research is about the present as well as the past. Because part of my research is about the memories and experiences of people alive today, I have used oral history interviews as a key part of my methodology. My research focuses on geographies of home and identity for Anglo-Indian women in the fifty years before and after Indian Independence in 1947, and spanning the community in India, Australia and Britain. Anglo-Indians form one of the largest and oldest communities of mixed descent in the world. Rather than focus on the diversity of individual homes and identities (which is an important theme in critical 'mixed race' studies), I am investigating their collective and political implications for a community of mixed descent. Descended from the children of European men and Indian women, usually born in the eighteenth and early nineteenth centuries (Hawes, 1996), Anglo-Indians are English-speaking, Christian, and culturally more European than Indian. Before Independence in 1947, the spatial politics of home for Anglo-Indians were shaped by imaginative geographies of both Europe (particularly Britain) and India as home (Blunt, 2002). Indian nationalism and policies of Indianization gave a new political urgency to Anglo-Indian ideas of home and identity. Those who did not feel at home in India established independent homelands or migrated after Independence (Blunt, in press a and b). In 1947, there were an estimated 300,000 Anglo-Indians in India and, against the advice of political leaders, one-third had emigrated by the 1970s (Younger, 1987). There have been two main migratory flows: to Britain in the late 1940s and 1950s and to Australia in the mid-1960s and 1970s. Alongside a proliferation of national associations, newsletters and websites, international reunions have been held since 1989 and represent a recent diasporic interest in fostering and celebrating an Anglo-Indian identity. My main research questions include: what does it mean to be an Anglo-Indian? How and why did Anglo-Indian homes in India reproduce British and/or Indian domesticity before Independence? What were the political implications of Anglo-Indian women identifying India and/or Britain as home before and after Independence? How and why have Anglo-Indian women felt at home in Britain and Australia since Independence?

My methodology combined historical and contemporary qualitative research in a transnational, comparative framework. Alongside the analysis of archival and other documentary sources, visual material (including fictional and documentary films, as well as photographs), and ethnographic research (at residential homes, fund raising events, and school reunions), I conducted 92 semi-structured interviews and 12 focus groups with a total of 180 Anglo-Indians. I talked to officers of Anglo-Indian associations, and, in India, members of Legislative Assemblies and two former MPs; Anglo-Indian women who attended, taught, or teach in one of seven girls' schools; Anglo-Indians who live, or lived, in key enclaves or settlements; and members of nine Anglo-Indian associations in India, Australia and Britain. While some interviews focused on the past and present status of the community, others were more personal, telling stories about growing up in India and what if felt like either to remain domiciled or to migrate to Britain or Australia.

There are many similarities, and some key differences, between oral history interviews and other (usually semi-structured) interviews (for more on interviews, see Hoggart et al., 2002). Perhaps the main difference is that oral history interviews focus on memories of the past. Oral history interviews also address memories and experiences in a personal way, and involve listening to individual stories that relate to much wider historical themes and events. Like personal sources such as letters and diaries, oral history interviews often address issues that might have been overlooked in other historical narratives. As Perks and Thomson (1998: ix; also see Thompson, 2000) explain, '[oral history] interviews have documented particular aspects of historical experience which tend to be missing from other sources, such as personal relations, domestic work or family life, and they have resonated with the subjective or personal meanings of lived experience.'

Oral history interviews were particularly appropriate for my research on Anglo-Indians for three main reasons (and, for other examples of geographical work that also draws on life stories in person, see Mackay, 2002 and Nagar, 1997). First, until recently, the history of the Anglo-Indian community has remained a largely 'hidden history,' in part because of imperial prejudice and in part because of the ambiguity of the term, which originally referred to the British in India. Anglo-Indians have European surnames, and it is often hard to identify them within archival and other documentary source material. Second, Anglo-Indian women have often been represented in stereotypical ways that focus on their appearance and assumed sensuality. I wanted to challenge this objectification by hearing about the lives of women in their own words (for more on oral history and feminist research, see Gluck and Patai, 1991). Third, after working solely in the archives for my doctoral research, I wanted to talk to people about their first-hand experience and memories. In particular, I wanted to talk to people who remembered living in British India and the implications of Independence for Anglo-Indians, and I wanted to ask about domesticity and everyday life.

A good place to find out more about oral history are the webpages of the British-based Oral History Society (http://www.oralhistory.org.uk/), which include details about what oral history entails, how to conduct interviews, how the material can be used, and provides links to other organizations in Britain and abroad. Also look at the following journals for further examples of oral history in practice: *Oral History*, which is the journal of the Oral History Society and includes papers, as well as listings of new collections and societies in Britain and beyond; *Oral History Review*, which is the American journal of the Oral History Association; and *Words and Silences: Bulletin of the International Oral History Association*. Other web-based guides to British oral history collections include the National Sound Archive at the British Library (http://www.bl.uk/collections/sound-archive/history); the Centre for Life History Research at the University of Sussex (http://www.sussex.ac.uk/Units/clhr); and the Panos Institute, whose Oral Testimony Programme collects the voices and opinions of 'the so-called beneficiaries of development' (http://www.panos.org.uk/oraltest; also see Slim and Thompson, 1993).

From the outset, my main methodological concern was how to reflect the transnational connections between Anglo-Indians. Initially, I hoped to interview members of the same families who lived in India, Britain and Australia, but most of the letters I wrote did not receive a reply, and I became increasingly aware that some families had lost touch after migrating, and that interviewing family members in different places – and often in very different socio-economic positions – would raise many difficult and sensitive issues. In the event, I studied the transnational connections between Anglo-Indians in two other ways:

1   By interviewing past and present residents of particular places in India. I concentrated on Calcutta, Lucknow and McCluskieganj. Both Calcutta and Lucknow were important historical centres for

Anglo-Indians and still have Anglo-Indian enclaves, schools and residential homes. McCluskieganj was established in 1933 as a homeland for Anglo-Indians in Bihar. At its height in the early 1940s, it was home to about 400 Anglo-Indian families, but now fewer than 20 remain.

2 By interviewing women who attended, taught or teach at particular girls' schools. Many schools attended by Anglo-Indians provide a diasporic focus for the community through associations, newsletters and reunions in Britain and Australia. I selected particular schools to reflect socio-economic differences within the Anglo-Indian community and the influences of Roman Catholicism and Anglicanism: two La Martinière schools in Calcutta and Lucknow; two Loreto Convent schools in each city (founded by an Irish order of Roman Catholic nuns), with one of each established to educate poor and orphaned Anglo-Indians; and the Dow Hill School in Kurseong, near Darjeeling, which was a government-funded school that educated Anglo-Indian girls from Calcutta and the daughters of railway workers posted throughout northern India.

For the rest of this section, I want to concentrate on the life stories of women who attended the Dow Hill School and migrated to Britain in the 1940s and 1950s (Figure 5.3). Maintaining their friendships and their memories of being at school for nine months of the year, these women belong to the Victoria and Dow Hill Association (VADHA; Victoria is a boys' school in Kurseong) and attend annual reunions in London (for more on Dow Hill School see Coelho, 1986, and for more on Anglo-Indian schools in India, see Craig, 1996). Among many Himalayan 'hill schools' that I could have studied, I selected Dow Hill for a number of reasons. First, it was founded in the late nineteenth century, so fitted the time-scale of my research very well. Second, VADHA is an active society, with annual reunions in London that are attended by up to one hundred people, and other reunions in Australia and Canada. Third, and most importantly, I met Grace Pereira, the Secretary of VADHA, and her husband Dereyck, at the very start of my research. Grace had been friends since university with one of my mother's friends, and had written her undergraduate dissertation on the Anglo-Indian community. She and Dereyck soon became good friends and are a great help and inspiration in my research (and, for a life story of home and identity in a different form, listen to the song 'Panchpuran' on Bill Jones' 2001 album of the same name. Bill – Belinda – Jones is Grace and Dereyck's niece, and, as she writes, 'The title track describes, through my Aunty's eyes, the trials of adjusting to life in a country which is not your homeland.' The title 'Panchpuran' is a Hindi word meaning 'five spices,' which 'in the song … is used to mean many different things all mixed together;' also see Back, Chapter 17, this volume).

Because racialized identities are a sensitive and personal concern, I approached interviewees and focus group members via Anglo-Indian associations and gatekeepers. Unlike research on mixed descent and people who 'pass' as white (Sollors, 1997), my research focuses on people who identify themselves as Anglo-Indian, although I also interviewed some women who attended Dow Hill who refer to themselves as 'Domiciled European'. I explained my research aims and objectives in writing and in person, and asked whether it was possible to tape and transcribe our conversation (for a helpful list of ethical guidelines for oral history research, see the website of the Oral History Society: *www.oralhistory.org.uk/ethics*). During my preliminary research, I assumed that interviewees would prefer to remain anonymous, so I assured them about confidentiality. But it soon occurred to me that I was recording life stories, but then effectively disembodying them from the people whose lives they represented. In the rest of my interviews, I asked interviewees to sign a form to indicate whether or not they could be named and whether a copy of the transcript could be made available to other users. Ninety per cent of interviewees agreed to be named and for their transcript to be made available. This

Figure 5.3 *Dow Hill girls, homeward bound, 1950. Reproduced courtesy of Grace Pereira.*

presented me with another dilemma. Should I name some interviewees, but give pseudonyms to others? The length of time that it took for my interviews to be transcribed – and the fact that I was by now back in Britain and at a distance from most of the subjects of my research – meant that I hadn't planned to circulate transcripts for checking. If I had done so, I would feel more confident in using the real names of my interviewees. In practice, I have decided to use real names if people are speaking in an official capacity, but to use pseudonyms for more personal memories and stories. It is also important to address the ethical considerations of quoting from oral history narratives that are available in libraries and on the internet. Some collections provide full and helpful guidelines (see, for example, the website of the Irish Centre for Migration Studies at University College Cork, which includes recordings of oral history interviews from three projects: 'Breaking the silence: staying at home in an emigrant society'; 'The Scattering: Irish migrants and their descendants in the wider world;' and 'Immigrant lives: eleven stories of immigrants in contemporary Ireland', and details about the ethical use of the site. *http://migration.ucc.ie/oralarchive*).

Oral history interviews can be conducted thematically or chronologically, and are often conducted over a series of interviews rather than in just one meeting. Given the focus of my research on home and identity (rather than a wider, and more general, study of Anglo-Indian history) and given the time constraints on my research in India and Australia, I adopted a thematic approach within a broadly chronological framework and usually conducted just one interview. However, the interviews – particularly with VADHA members in Britain – were often preceded and followed by meeting in various other contexts over a matter of years, particularly at annual school reunions. In preparation for my interviews with women who attended Dow Hill, I wrote down key themes and headings that I wanted to cover. These included family background, memories of school and home in India, when and why their family migrated to Britain, what it felt like to move to a new country, how they had imagined Britain while living in India, and their involvement with VADHA and other Anglo-Indian groups and activities. I usually asked questions rather than provide more open prompts (as might be more appropriate in a more narrative than thematic oral history research). So, for example, I asked 'Before Independence, how was your home different from an Indian home?' rather than saying 'Tell me about your home life before Independence'; and 'Why did your family migrate after Independence?' rather than saying 'Tell me about your family's experience of migration.' In practice, the interviews ranged much more widely than my key themes and headings, and were rich and interesting conversations that provided personal stories, memories and experiences alongside ideas and information about the community more widely, and a collective as well as personal sense of feeling at home – and not at home – in India and Britain. Most of the interviews were conducted in the homes of the interviewees, and I was usually invited for lunch first. Many of the women talked about Anglo-Indian traditions of hospitality and the distinctiveness of Anglo-Indian cuisine, and coming for lunch was an opportunity for me to enjoy both in practice, as well as in conversation.

Most of my interviews lasted for two to four hours, and some of my transcripts are over 50 pages long. I was lucky enough to have a grant that funded the costs of transcribing. Checking and coding the transcripts is an ongoing, and very lengthy, process. I decided to code them by hand rather than by using computer software (see Crang et al., 1997; Hoggart et al., 2002 and Kitchin and Tate, 2000, for more on how to use computer software to analyse qualitative data). This was partly because – drawing on my previous experience of interpreting life stories in letters and diaries – I felt that discourse analysis would enable me to interpret personal stories and memories in a more nuanced and sensitive way than computer coding would allow. I am reading, and re-reading, transcripts to identify and code themes and sub-themes, to quote extracts to illustrate certain points, and to explore points of conflict and contradiction. Just as with the diaries written by British women during the siege of Lucknow, I also draw out similarities and differences between accounts from women who attended the same school and migrated to Britain after Independence. But, rather than try to come up with a single, authoritative narrative, I read the transcripts in an intertextual way to explore different memories, meanings, experiences and interpretations (and doing so has made me think much more about memory and nostalgia; Blunt, 2003a). The way that I have chosen to analyse transcripts is broadly similar to my analysis of letters and diaries that I discussed earlier in the chapter. But there are some important, and probably obvious, differences between life stories in text and in person. Conducting oral history interviews enabled me to meet and spend time with the women whose lives I am now writing about. While I had many questions that I would have loved to ask Frances Wells and the diarists at Lucknow, I had to rely on their written accounts. In contrast, oral history interviews provided an opportunity to ask questions directly, participate in a conversation, and clarify any points that I was uncertain or confused about from the wider literature. Crucially, the women whose lives I am writing about are also able to read what I am writing. Rather than restrict my findings to an academic audience alone, I am also presenting my research to a wider Anglo-Indian audience in a variety of ways. Where I gained permission to do so, I am also preparing the transcripts from many of my interviews as an oral history archive, which I will deposit in India, Australia and Britain as part of a wider attempt to make community records and history available, both in Anglo-Indian association archives and in libraries that hold collections of imperial archives.

In my writing, I draw on, and interpret, material from my oral history interviews in an intertextual way. So, for example, in a paper on geographies of mixed descent and diaspora (Blunt, 2003b), I quote from interviews with women who attended Dow Hill in the 1930s and 1940s and migrated to Britain after Independence and after the British Nationality Act of 1948. I do so alongside an analysis of archival and documentary sources that include government records, Anglo-Indian journals, and correspondence between the Society of Genealogists in London and Anglo-Indians seeking to document their British paternal ancestry. So, for example, when I discuss the ways in which the British Nationality Act of 1948 recolonized an Anglo-Indian identity in terms of paternal ancestry that was specifically British, rather than European (as codified by the Government of India Act, 1935, and in the later Indian Constitution), I quote from an interview with a woman who attended Dow Hill in the 1930s. As she told me,

> We weren't all Anglo-British Indians. There were Dutch Indians, there were French Indians, mixtures of Dutch and Indian … Originally there would be, we'll say a Dutchman married to an Indian or living with an Indian, having a child by her, or a Frenchman ditto, so their child would be French-Indian or Dutch-Indian. … Eventually there were so many nationalities mixed up that it became a misnomer to call them Anglo-Indians. … Mixtures were marrying into other mixtures. … I can't call myself one thing or the other. I'm now international. My nationality has gone beyond the boundaries of one country or two countries.
>
> (interviewed August 1999)

Beginning with a more general discussion about the limits of the term Anglo-Indian, and then moving to a more personal sense of identity, this extract shows how collective and personal meanings can interweave in an oral history interview. Later in the paper, another example shows how the personal stories and memories within such interviews are shaped by, and also reveal a great deal about, much broader and more collective themes. In this case, an Anglo-Indian woman who attended Dow Hill in the 1940s told me that she only became aware of what it meant to be an Anglo-Indian once she left India:

> I came to England [in 1951] and was instantly aware of the difference in speech, the difference in ethos, the difference in manners, and the difference in daily running of one's life. That was what really made me realise that I was an Anglo-Indian. I hadn't thought about it before.
>
> (interviewed September 1999)

While some Anglo-Indians could 'pass' as white and British, others acknowledged their mixed descent for the first time. As the same interviewee continues:

We used to be told to wear a hat, because every shade counts. A lot of girls used to envy me and my blonde hair and blue eyes and fair skin and conversely I wanted to have black hair. ... I didn't really realise which Anglo-Indians were coloured though until I came to England and then remet them, and I thought, 'I didn't know you were so dark!' It hadn't registered, although I was aware that this went on in India.

(interviewed September 1999)

Conclusions

Life stories in text and in person provide vivid and compelling accounts of everyday life, experiences and emotions on subjects as wide-ranging as human life itself. It is important to situate such life stories within wider debates about identity, experience, memory and representation, and to interpret life stories not only in terms of their particularity, but also in terms of their connections with other life stories and broader themes. In the examples I have discussed, I interpreted letters and diaries written by British women during the Indian 'mutiny' in order to understand wider discourses of imperialism, femininity and domesticity; and I interviewed Anglo-Indian women to investigate collective as well as individual experiences of imperialism and migration. In both cases, I have found such personal encounters – both in imagination and more directly – to be the most revealing, engaging and challenging parts of my research.

I want to end by suggesting two starting points for using life stories in your own research. First, alongside critical studies of home and identity that draw on life stories in both text and in person, a number of scholars have begun to write about their own lives (including Pratt, 1984; Said, 1999; Young, 1997). A good place to begin to think about life stories in text, and about the interplay of home and identity, is to read some of these autobiographical writings (and for more on geography and autobiography, see Moss, 2001). Indeed, an anthology of autobiographical writings about racial identity is entitled *Names we call home* (Thompson and Tyagi, 1996), which suggests intimate connections between home and identity. As the editors explain, the contributors share a political understanding of 'home,' 'writing about 'home' in the fluid and expansive sense of the word – people's physical, political, and spiritual homes – and the homes where they do the work that sustains them and their communities. This way of seeing home links the public with the private and ties the emotional to the political' (xiv). Although each of the contributions to the book is a personal story, written in a variety of forms, the collection as a whole is bound by its commitment to anti-racist politics and activism. In different ways, the personal writings 'carve out the creative spaces we need to maintain antiracist stances in our work and lives' (ix), revealing multiple identities that resonate far beyond an individual subject, and exploring creative spaces of home that extend far beyond a singular, static and bounded location.

The second starting point is to think about conducting oral histories close to home, with members of your family, friends or neighbours. Think, for example, about the memories and experiences of members of your own family that tell you not only about individual histories and your shared family history, but also tell you stories that resonate with much wider historical themes and events. So, for example, you could ask your parents or grandparents about their personal experiences of school, work, war, migration, or home. You could also think about taking a distinctively geographical approach to oral history, by asking about experiences and memories of different places and asking about how particular places have changed over time. To help with this, you could look at how local history groups conduct oral history research, and think about how this research is often bound up with telling stories about particular places (see, for example, the work on 'Hidden Histories' by Eastside Community Heritage in London, which includes oral history projects documenting the lives of 'ordinary' people in East London. Projects include 'Green Street Lives', which is about one street in Newham, over the last 40 years; 'Stories from Silvertown,' which is run with Silvertown Residents Association; and 'The Teviot Estate', which is about experiences and memories of a post-war housing estate in Poplar; *www.hidden-histories.org/esch_pages*). Another fruitful area of research would be to study how oral histories have been created and communicated in different ways and through different media, including radio and television documentaries; the collection and display of oral history material in archives, museums and galleries; and theatre productions and other performances based on reminiscence work (see, for example, the work of the Age Exchange Theatre in London, which 'aims to improve the quality of life for older people by emphasising the value of their memories to old and young, through pioneering artistic, educational, and welfare activities;' *www.age-exchange.org.uk*).

Further reading

A good place to start thinking about geographies of home and identity is:
- Pratt, G., 1998, 'Geographic metaphors in feminist theory,' in *Making Worlds: Gender, Metaphor, Materiality* (eds) S. Aiken et al., Tucson: University of Arizona Press 13–30.

For a diverse collection of autobiographical writings about racial identity and ideas of home, see:
- Thompson, B. and Tyagi, S. (eds). 1996, *Names We Call Home: Autobiography of Racial Identity*. London, Routledge.

Also see:
- *Women's Studies International Forum*, 10, 1987, for a special issue on women's diary narratives.
- Whitlock, G. 2000, *The Intimate Empire: Reading Women's Autobiography*. London, Cassell.

The following books provide wide-ranging discussions of oral history in theory and in practice:
- Perks, R. and Thomson, A. (eds) 1998, *The Oral History Reader*. London, Routledge.
- Gluck, S. B. and Patai, D (eds) 1991, *Women's Words: the Feminist Practice of Oral History.* New York, Routledge.
- Thomson, P. 2000, *The Voice of the Past: Oral History.* Third edition, Oxford, Oxford University Press.

For diverse examples of oral history in practice, see papers in the journals *Oral History*, *Oral History Review*, and *Words and Silences: Bulletin of the International Oral History Association*. A special issue of *Oral History Review* (2002: 29:2), includes many short essays on 'My first experience with oral history.'

For more on feminist methodologies in human geography, see:
- Moss, P. (ed) 2002, *Feminist Geography in Practice: Research and Methods.* Oxford, Blackwell.

Acknowledgements

My doctoral research was funded by a University Graduate Fellowship at the University of British Columbia, and my research on Anglo-Indian women and the spatial politics of home has been funded by the ESRC (R000 222 826), the Royal Geographical Society (with the Institute of British Geographers), and the University of Southampton. I am grateful to all of the members of VADHA that I have interviewed, and particularly to Grace and Dereyck Pereira for all of their help with my research.

A TALE OF RESEARCH

Autobiography and cultural geography

Using personal experience to form research

Amanda Banks

In 2002 I was a graduate student at the University of Waikato, Aotearoa/New Zealand. I completed a piece of research for an Honours paper entitled Contemporary Geographical Thought. The research assignment prompted us to explore a topic that we were interested in, and to examine the ways in which theory informs research.

With this in mind, I turned to a topic that had been the source of many a frustrated discussion I had engaged in with friends and family. I wanted to explore in more depth my experiences as a single parent claiming the Domestic Purposes Benefit (DPB). The DPB is a government benefit administered by Work and Income New Zealand (WINZ) that is paid to single parents in order to assist them in raising their child/children. The majority of DPB recipients are women (*www.stats.govt.nz*).

By choosing to research issues that affect my life, I not only contribute to geographical knowledge, but also discover that my research findings lead to new ways of making sense of my surroundings. One way of utilizing personal experience is through the method of autobiographical research. The key aspect of this method involves reflexivity (Rose, 1997), whereby the researcher unpacks their own thoughts and feelings, which often reveals surprising 'taken-for-granted' attitudes. Making the researcher visible in the research means that our personal experience becomes crucial data.

I developed two main research questions to inform my research: how are women who claim the DPB in New Zealand constructed, and what are some of the ways in which women resist these social constructions? I explored (and troubled) some of the ways in which women are constructed as a 'DPB mothers' while maintaining a strong focus on the 'real' aspects or the lived effects of claiming the DPB.

Usually the theoretical perspectives that inform autobiographical research are feminism and postmodernism, and although these two perspectives have their own specific lines of thought, there are some similarities that can be drawn. Research methods that can be labeled as 'feminist' are particularly useful for making sense of the nuances of our lived lives. Harding's (1991) notion of standpoint theory is particularly relevant, as is Haraway's (1991) idea of situated knowledge. In a similar vein, postmodernism rejects the notion of metanarratives – 'big' stories that explain certain 'natural' laws in the world. It also seeks to validate every person's truth as a truth in its own right. Being able to incorporate personal experience into research means that a new realm of research possibilities previously deemed unworthy of research or inappropriate topics of study, become potential fields of analysis.

With a good sense of the theoretical framework informing my research, I then focused on how women who claim the DPB are discursively constructed. The reason for my specific research focus on women was threefold: first, they constitute the majority of claimants, second, particular forms of femininity that are informed by notions of sexuality, heteronormativity and motherhood play a key role in the discursive construction of 'DPB mother', and third because my research serves a political purpose in that I am concerned with addressing (and challenging) the inequalities that exist for women in (Western) society. Furthermore, the dominant discourses that presently surround benefit claiming in New Zealand mean that certain benefits are hierarchically privileged over others. In order to unpack such constructions, I employed a discourse analysis on two sets of texts: firstly, the information published by WINZ that is designed to assist DPB claimants, and secondly, I examined some recent national newspaper articles that dealt with DPB-related issues. It was particularly the latter that illustrated the prevailing societal attitudes of what it means to be a woman parenting alone and claiming the DPB in New Zealand.

One of the ways I incorporated personal experience into my research was by critically exploring my own thoughts about the DPB. In doing this exercise, it became obvious that the ways in which I construct 'women on the DPB' are both complex and contradictory. For example, despite my identity being constructed by others as a 'DPB mum' (this term has negative connotations in New Zealand), I harbour my own judgements about what constitutes a 'good' or 'bad' mother who receives the DPB. This analysis proved to be personally challenging as it highlighted my prejudices, thus showing how I contribute to the marginalization of an already marginalized (and sometimes ostracized) group of which I am a part. Such an exercise highlights the complex ways in which social categories are formed and reified.

Another way of doing autobiographical research is to keep a research journal. This can be written throughout the research process and used to record any thoughts, feelings or reactions along the research journey. Writing after interviewing each participant can also help to identify the general tone of the interview, and to note challenges to, or confirmation of, the research aims and questions. Such writing is 'unedited', and the strength of a 'field diary' is that it captures a particular way of thinking about an issue at a specific time. Excerpts of this personal data can then be included in the research findings. When included in the published research, this has the added advantage making the research more holistic, and it adds depth and richness to the research. Incorporating research journal entries also means that the researcher is visible in their research, which can minimize the risk of conducting disembodied research.

In trying to explore the ways in which women who claim the DPB resist the identities that are constructed for them, I identified some of the strategies I personally employ in order to resist such constructions. For example, I embrace my role as a mother, and shun the idea that I am lazy, can't get a 'real' job (one that is in the public sphere and not paid for by the government) or that I am claiming the DPB in order to avoid living a 'real' life. I have chosen this opportunity to claim the DPB for a limited time in order to raise my child and pursue tertiary study. Simply by doing this, I am challenging stereotypical notions of what it means to receive the DPB. I also foster my own sense of family which includes loved ones who do not reside in the same house as my son and I, thus challenging the very narrowly defined mainstream, heterosexist classification of 'family' and showing it up as a social construction rather than a natural given.

During the research process, I discovered that using autobiography as a method enables me to make sense of situations that are both complex and perplexing. For example, my exploration of the ways in which women who receive the DPB are discursively constructed revealed to me that some of the attitudes that I felt were 'put upon' me were no accident. It is important to note here that discursive constructions are not the same as conspiracy theories: there is no `enemy' out to get me, but rather that institutions are imbued with power and politics. Thus, by researching personal experience through the lenses of autobiographical research and discourse analysis, I learnt that there are some systems that function in such a way that advantage particular groups or individuals and disadvantage others. The empowering aspect of such research is that it enables me to strategize ways in which I might resist or subvert such constructions or use them to *my* advantage. Furthermore, I am also able to disseminate this information to other women claiming the DPB so that they can exercise a greater degree of agency in their lives.

However, as I discovered, one of the problems of autobiographical research is that sometimes my personal perspective on the world is not necessarily supported by research. This does not mean that my experience is wrong, but rather it illustrates that my desire to research particular issues may be based on misconstrued ideas, insecurities or personal prejudices. For example, in order to highlight the ways in which women who receive the DPB are constructed, I brainstormed all the possible 'labels' that these women receive. One such term that I identified as being perpetuated in popular media discourse is 'slut', which is based on the idea that women who claim the DPB are promiscuous and therefore of dubious moral character. This was not necessarily a label that I adapted for myself, but felt that it was often one that people put upon me (see Valentine, 1998, for a geography of harassment).

Part of my research also involved some analysis of texts such as newspaper articles. This brought the realization that my personal experiences as a single mother claiming the DPB was part of a wider way of thinking about women who receive benefits. In a personal sense, this enabled me to separate my own sense of identity from the discourse of 'DPB mother'.

In exploring notions of autobiographical research in cultural geography, I have attempted to highlight some of the ways in which women who claim the DPB in New Zealand are constructed. My research is by no means exhaustive, and the employment of methods such as in-depth interviewing and focus groups could be used bridge the gap between the ways in which these women are discursively constructed and the complex ways in which they construct their own identity.

At the time of my research on the Domestic Purposes Benefit (2002), I was studying towards an Honours degree in Geography at the University of Waikato, New Zealand. Since completing this research, I have completed another Honours paper, which focused on discourses of development. I am now co-authoring a paper with Robyn Longhurst, also in the Department of Geography, on how being pregnant affects and alters women's experience of public places. I will complete my Honours degree this year with another research paper in which I will explore skateboarding in Hamilton, New Zealand.

6
Gender and mobility
Critical ethnographies of migration in Indonesia

Rachel Silvey

While migration research has long engaged both qualitative and quantitative methods, recently migration researchers have paid particular attention to the uses of in-depth interviews and migrants' biographies for understanding migrants' identities and relationships to place (Graham, 1999; Halfacree and Boyle, 1993; Lawson, 1999, 2000; McKendrick, 1999; Skeldon, 1995). My research builds on these approaches, as well as on more intensive ethnographic work, which differs in several ways from research based on in-depth interviews and life history narratives (Herbert, 2000; see Chapter 5). In order to examine the distinct advantages and challenges of practicing ethnographic fieldwork, this chapter traces the research process behind the article, 'Diasporic Subjects: Gender and Mobility in South Sulawesi' (Silvey, 2000a). It outlines the rationale for the selection of the topic and ethnographic methods, describes the fieldwork process, and discusses the interplay between ethnographic experience and decisions about theoretical framing.

The research for 'Diasporic Subjects' explored the gender dimensions of low-income migration in South Sulawesi, Indonesia (Silvey, 2000a; Silvey, 2000b; see Figure 6.1). The project examined the

Figure 6.1 *Map of Indonesia, locating South Sulawesi.*

ways that the relationships between migration, morality, and gender were being transformed among migrants in an industrial processing zone on the outskirts of Ujung Pandang, South Sulawesi. It focused on the ways that both new production relations as well as migrants' own local inter-ethnic interactions shaped migrants' gender identities. Methodologically, the project was largely ethnographic in that it involved six months of residence with factory workers in their dormitories, yet it also employed demographic and historiographic methods. Thus, while the chapter focuses primarily on the role and process of ethnography in the research, it also addresses the limitations of classical ethnographic methods for understanding particular aspects of the processes affecting migrants' gender identities, and briefly outlines contemporary strategies for addressing those limitations.

While there are many different types of ethnographic approach (Hammersley and Atkinson, 1983), all ethnographies rely on participant observation. The ethnographic researcher spends extensive time involved in the everyday activities of the study group, and tacks back and forth between interacting with the group and analyzing the cultural meanings that shape their actions. In this way, ethnographic research extends beyond in-depth or open-ended interviews to examine 'what people *do* as well as what they *say*' (Herbert, 2000: 552, italics in original). Thus, as Steve Herbert (2000: 550, italics in original) writes, '[E]thnography is a uniquely useful method for uncovering the *processes* and *meanings* that undergird socio-spatial life.' From this perspective, there is clearly a place for ethnography in research aimed at understanding the 'processes and meanings' of migration (McHugh, 2000; Ogden, 2000), and the method lends itself particularly well to the questions at the heart of gender and migration studies. Ethnography can contribute to understanding questions about the cultural struggles surrounding gender relations and identities, and their relationships to place-based notions of progress and modernity (Boyle and Halfacree, 1999; Chant, 1992; Fincher, 1997; Hondagneu-Sotelo, 1996; Kofman et al., 2000; Mills, 1997; Momsen, 1999; Silvey and Lawson, 1999).

Feminist theory and the ethnographic study of migration

Long before beginning field research itself, a topic or theme of interest starts to take shape in the researcher's mind. In my case, four primary concerns pointed to gender relations and low-income people's migration as topics worthy of study in Indonesia. First, and most importantly, I was introduced to a number of pressing practical concerns among low-income migrant women during the year I lived in Indonesia prior to beginning fieldwork. These concerns ranged from women's fear of independent travel and social pressures against women's independent mobility, to the problems of sexual abuse, gender violence, and street harassment. It was these grounded observations in Indonesia that first highlighted the importance of the gender dynamics of spatial mobility, and it was this early experience of living in Indonesia, as well as my ability to speak Indonesian that underpinned my decision to examine these issues in Indonesia with ethnographic methods.

Second, women's mobility and the gender dynamics of migration were largely absent from the literature on migration at the time, and they were particularly understudied for Indonesia (but see Hetler, 1989 and Hugo, 1992). The existing research described gendered migration patterns and trends, but did little to explain the gender differences, and was not focused on understanding migrants' own cultural perspectives on gender and mobility. Thus, not only did the issues related to women's spatial mobility appear important on the ground, but also they were in need of research attention, and called for a specifically ethnographic perspective.

The third factor that led to my selection of gender and migration as a topic was the state of theory at the time. Migration theory had just begun to include attention to feminist theory (Chant, 1992), whilst feminist theory was continuing to move in exciting new directions (Ramamurthy, 2000). Because so many of the issues that faced women migrants were distinct from those that faced men, migration theory stood to benefit from an engagement with feminist theory. Specifically, feminist theorists were in the process of 'unpacking' the household, arguing that, contrary to the conceptualization of the household by migration theorists, the household is not a harmonious, resource-pooling unit (cf. Wolf, 1992). Rather, they argued, in practice, the household includes struggles over resources, differences in decision-making power, and gendered and generational hierarchies that determine both domestic and labour market roles and responsibilities (Lawson, 1998). Taking these feminist insights about the household, and applying them to the study of migration, then, opened up a range of hitherto unexamined questions about the gendered causes and consequences of migration (Willis and Yeoh, 2000). These questions drove the research behind 'Diasporic Subjects', and in this way, the selection of research questions was theory-led.

The final, fourth factor that influenced the choice of research topic was its importance in circles beyond the academy. The gender blindness of migration studies was not limited to scholarly circles. As Hugo (1992) pointed out, much social policy designed for migrants in Indonesia failed to account for the gender dimensions of the problems facing low-income migrants. The problems of migrants, and particularly women migrants, were perhaps exacerbated, and certainly not adequately addressed, by policies directed at a gender-neutral notion of a migrant. From both scholarly and policy-oriented perspectives, then, there was clearly a need for better theoretical insight and empirical data. Thus, I saw the research as important in part because of the ways that it could inform approaches to social service provision for migrants. In sum, then, I selected the topic because: i) it addressed serious social issues; ii) it was not well understood or represented in the literature; iii) it reflected the need and potential for creative theoretical cross-fertilization; and iv) social policy could potentially benefit from its findings.

However, these post-facto explanations for topic selection are only part of the entire story. The process of topic selection is rarely as neat, clean, or deliberate as it can be made to seem after the fact. Another part of the story is that much of the literature on feminist geography and migration studies seemed rather disconnected. But as I was reading the literature on migration in Indonesia, I also happened to be reading a Master's thesis by a fellow graduate student (Chalita, 1990). It was her particular spin on female-headed households that helped me to see the potential connections between migration theory and feminist theory. It is noteworthy that it was this thesis that made the connection for me, because the topic – female-headed households in Mexico – was at least nominally irrelevant to my own. If I had not been reading outside of the literature that was most directly and clearly relevant to Indonesian migration, the importance of examining **power** dynamics within households for understanding sex differentials in migration patterns and rates may not have emerged (but see also Chant, 1992; Radcliffe, 1991 and Lawson, 1998 whose research, along with that of many others since [cf. Willis and Yeoh 2000], has subsequently provided direct inspiration for my own). Powerful insights can come from unplanned, slightly tangential study. Indeed, reading widely can often provide the needed spark for a research project, and researchers would do well to stay open to the potential of serendipitous contact with unlikely sources of inspiration.

After selecting the topic, it was time to identify a methodology appropriate to the specific research questions to be investigated. Ethnographic methods seemed most appropriate because intra-household decision-making **dynamics and power relations** were topics that lent themselves to extended participant observation and in-depth interviews. The research questions about how household members make decisions about who migrates, and what migration means to women and men, were ones that required getting to know people intimately enough to understand the ways that their relationships worked and the ways that their values were manifested in their daily lives.

It would take at least several months of living with people to clarify the differences between what they said and what they actually did. My previous experience in Indonesia had taught me that an extended period of time would be necessary in order to establish rapport, and that a survey methodology, particularly if administered by a foreign researcher, would not be able to uncover reliable information about a given respondent's household dynamics. Thus, I planned to live with migrants and to try to understand the gendered processes and meanings of migration over the period of time I lived with them. In this way, I planned to draw not only on the methodological strengths of in-depth and life-history interviews, but also on the strengths of participant observation (Kearns, 2000) and ethnography (Herbert 2000). Because I was interested in gender dynamics – many of which go unrecognized by the people participating in them – participant-observation was as important as in-depth interviews. Spending a full year (six months in West Java and six months in Sulawesi) observing migrants in their everyday lives, and participating in their lives for much of this time, informed the analysis of the in-depth interviews, and shaped the interpretations of migrants' stated explanations for particular behaviour.

In addition to being the most fitting method for investigating these particular questions, my selection of ethnographic methods was influenced by feminist theory. In particular, the ideas of Sandra Harding (1991) and Donna Haraway (1988) were influential. Harding and Haraway argue against the privilege of partial perspective and for a feminist standpoint, which takes women's experience as a starting point for developing knowledge about women and gender. They point out that all perspectives are partial, and that in order to produce more objective and thorough social science knowledge about those who are subjugated, research must start from the perspectives of those who experience the subjugation. Ideas about **situated knowledge** and **reflexivity** are particularly important in this context. In my ethnographic research, I sought to understand low-income migrants' own perspectives on migration and to examine them in depth through the voices of women themselves.

Concept Box

Situated knowledge

Attempts to situate knowledge – and to produce situated knowledges – challenge the truth claims of detached, disembodied observation in favour of located, partial and **embodied** understanding. Inspired by the work of Donna Haraway, ideas about situated knowledge have their roots in feminist critiques of science, but now also critically inform research across the humanities and social sciences. Ideas about situated knowledge have been particularly important in feminist geography. Such ideas resist a masterful **gaze** from a distant vantage point, blind to its own specificity and location in its claims for objective, all-seeing authority. In Haraway's words, the 'god-trick' of such a gaze depends on its dislocation and distance not only from what is being observed, but also from where such observation is located. While recognizing that all knowledge is partial and located, attempts to situate knowledge make this partiality and location their explicit and critical focus, situating knowledge in particular contexts and articulating the positionality both of researchers and the subjects of research. As Haraway writes, 'Situated knowledges require that the object of knowledge be pictured as an actor and agent, not as a screen or a ground or a resource, never finally as slave to the master that closes off the dialectic in his unique agency and authorship of 'objective' knowledge' (1991: 198). Situated knowledges seek to disrupt the 'god-trick' of authority and impartiality that is empowered, in part, by denying its own situatedness. It does so by locating, and often embodying, the production of knowledge in terms of proximity rather than distance and **reflexivity** rather than detachment.

Key reading

- Haraway, D. (1991) *Simians, Cyborgs and Women: the Reinvention of Nature.* London, Free Association Books.
- Rose, G. (1997) 'Situating knowledges: positionality, reflexivities and other tactics.' *Progress in Human Geography* 21: 305–320.

Further theoretical work by Patricia Hill Collins (1990) and Gayatri Chakravorty Spivak (1990) reformulated these early feminist perspectives, and were important in further refining the project's methodology. Collins (1990) points out that feminist standpoint theory assumes a commonality among women that does not in fact exist, and she argues for a standpoint that takes into account other forms of **difference**, such as race, class, and ethnicity. Spivak (1990) complicates the standpoint picture further. She reminds researchers that even if we are able to uncover the voices and the standpoints of subjugated people, ultimately it is we who represent the researched. Thus, our ability to represent the subjects of our research is limited by our distinct subjective locations, and our interpretations of narrative interviews should take such limitations into account.

These arguments within feminist theory shaped several specific ways that I practiced ethnography. Because feminist research is principally concerned with power inequalities, it aims to be sensitive to the unequal relations between the researcher and the researched, and to the ways that these inequalities affect the production of knowledge. Feminist researchers seek to address, though do not presume to ever wholly *redress*, these imbalances by employing methodologies that reduce the differentials between the researcher and the researched (Wolf, 1996). This point underscored the value of personally experiencing as much of the daily lives of low-income migrants as possible. More importantly, it meant keeping questions about power, and the inequalities shaping fieldwork relationships and observations, at the center of analysis, both during and after fieldwork. Indeed, it was these concerns that ultimately shaped the interpretations in the article, 'Diasporic Subjects.' But long before post-fieldwork connections could be made between fieldwork and feminist theory, there were many other practical issues that needed to be addressed. It is these nuts and bolts of the ethnographic fieldwork process that the following section examines.

Concept Box

Reflexivity

Reflexivity refers to self-reflection at all stages of research. According to Kim England (1994: 82), reflexivity is 'self-critical sympathetic introspection and the self-conscious analytical scrutiny of the self as researcher.' The term reflexivity is often closely tied to attempts to **situate knowledge**, to recognize the positionality of researcher and the subjects of research, and to seek to overcome **power** imbalances in the research encounter. Reflexivity has always been a central part of ethnographic research, particularly through methods such as participant observation. Within geography, ideas about reflexivity have also been particularly important in feminist research. As Falconer Al-Hindi and Kawabata write, 'Thoughtful reflection on one's research practice, one's subjectivity relative to that practice, and self-criticism and change where warranted would certainly seem to improve the process and outcome of methodologies in which the researcher herself is an instrument of the research' (2002: 109). However, it has proved more difficult to present reflexive practice when writing about the research and reflexivity can remain 'limited to a solitary

(continued overleaf)

consideration of oneself' (2002: 109). More challenging is Falconer Al-Hindi and Kawabata's attempt to extend ideas about reflexivity so that researchers see themselves through the gaze of others and then 'return the look – now informed by the 'others'' **gaze** – to the other in order to learn from her' (2002: 110; also see Nast, 1998).

Key reading
- England, K. (1994) 'Getting personal: reflexivity, positionality and feminist research', *Professional Geographer* 46: 80–89.
- Falconer Al-Hindi, K. and Kawabata, H. (2002) 'Toward a more fully reflexive feminist geography'. In Moss, P. (ed) *Feminist Geography in Practice: Research and Methods*. Oxford, Blackwell: 103–115.
- Nast, H. J. (1998) 'The body as 'place': reflexivity and fieldwork in Kano, Nigeria', In Nast, H. J. and Pile, S. (eds) *Places Through the Body*. London, Routledge: 93–116.

Fieldwork on the ground

Having selected a topic and a theoretical framework, it was necessary to select field sites. Several practical concerns underlay my choice of field sites. First, I had worked in both West Java and South Sulawesi prior to fieldwork, and had designed my project to build on my familiarity with these places. Upon first arriving in Indonesia to carry out fieldwork, this prior knowledge of the region was a great benefit to the research because it meant that I already knew my way around the areas by public transportation, knew where the universities and post offices were located, and knew some local strategies for saving on basic living expenses. The second reason for selecting South Sulawesi in particular was that there was relatively little scholarship written on the region, and the gap was in need of filling. Third, the economy of South Sulawesi was developing rapidly, and women migrants' involvement in factory labor was increasing, making the region ripe for the study of changing gender and mobility processes. Finally, in contrast to much of Southeast Asia's gender relations (Ong and Peletz, 1995, though see Steedly, 1999 for an in-depth discussion of the nuances of this argument), South Sulawesi appeared from the literature to be relatively patriarchal (Chabot, 1996, though see also Millar, 1983). Examining the distinct gender relations in the region would add to broader understanding of place-specific gender and development issues.

Having selected the general region for fieldwork, I moved to Ujung Pandang and began to introduce myself to the local community members. This preliminary fieldwork included taking notes on general observations and discussion with local activists, scholars, and migrants on buses, on the street, in streetside food stalls, and in the neighbourhoods where I lived. I visited workplaces, homes, and dormitories to interview migrant factory workers, and engaged in participant observation. Because the questions were focused on migrants' meaning-making processes in relation to gender, it was not crucial that the sampling be 'representative' in the strict statistical sense. Nevertheless, I sought some comparative logic in my site and sample selection, and in South Sulawesi, the one site that had high levels of industrialization and women's in-migration was the Makassar Industrial Region (or *Kawasan Industri Makassar*, KIMA), an industrial processing zone on the periphery of Ujung Pandang (Figure 6.2).

A colleague of my research collaborator, who happened to be in the university office when I was there, was the one who introduced me to KIMA. He took it upon himself to personally support my research, and while his in-depth local knowledge proved to be a valuable asset to the project as a whole, the relationship was not easy. He behaved in a way that I considered mild sexual harassment (a gender and power issue in fieldwork that itself deserves a chapter), and every interaction with him held

Figure 6.2 *Street scene in KIMA. Photograph by author.*

for me the risk of further harassment. Nevertheless, we remained in contact throughout the project, and the problems ultimately paled in comparison to the benefits he provided to the project. While this situation turned out to be benign, sexual harassment and sexual violence are common to the fieldwork experiences of many women researchers. Ethnographic fieldwork, because of its emphasis on spatial proximity and extended interaction, can put field researchers in particular danger of such misunderstandings and abuse. Being prepared to confront such problems, and doing so immediately if they arise, is important for the both the safety and well-being of the researcher, and is necessary even if in some cases it may impede the progress of the research. In this case, I let him know directly that his behaviour was unacceptable to me and that my 'husband' would not be pleased to know of it (also see Wolf, 1996, on the presentation of one's relationships in the field).

After I resolved the harassment problem, he arranged for me to live in the factory dormitories of KIMA (Figure 6.3), introduced me to the landlord of the dormitory, the village leader (*Rukun Tetangga*), and the neighbours who would be asked to accept an intrusive foreigner living in the room next door to theirs. Because he was well acquainted with people in KIMA, the dormitory residents were willing to invite me into their lives, and this simple form of assistance proved extremely valuable in both the short and longer terms. In the short term, it eased my entry into the community. Without introductions, it would have been impossible to rent a room in the dormitory. In the longer term, the connection to the community permitted the highest possible quality participant observation on the project.

Living with migrants profoundly shaped my sense of factory workers' everyday lives, and my experiences in the dormitory have informed my interpretations and analyses following from fieldwork. The dormitory itself was constructed of plywood walls and corrugated aluminum siding. The walls were so thin that every noise in each room was audible in the adjacent rooms. Because factory workers held both day and night shifts, the noise was constant. Between four and six people slept, cooked, and lived in most of the small rooms. The sun heated up the aluminum siding, turning the building into an oven

Figure 6.3 Dormitory in KIMA. Photograph by author.

during the daylight hours, and leaving the rooms on the top floor unbearably hot until nightfall. The electricity blacked out at odd intervals, never providing a solid hour of light from the single bulb that hung in each room. The 53 residents in the building shared one water pump and one outhouse and bathing shed, and we lined up to use these facilities morning and night, each of us holding our pumped bucket of water as we waited in line to bathe.

In these conditions, daily life was more arduous and uncomfortable than it was for people living in the nearby rural areas with streams and relatively spacious living quarters, and it was more physically taxing than any other living conditions I had ever experienced. After several weeks, I became ill and most of my hair fell out. Many nights I awoke to find large cockroaches crawling on my body. Neighbours stopped by to visit and check on my health at all hours. Many days passed when I felt that the research was not progressing, and I often wondered if my discomfort, illness, and lack of privacy were wasted sacrifices. But it was through living with people in these conditions that my neighbours began to feel they could expose and explain to me their approaches to migration, factory work, and gender relations, and it was the perspectives they shared at this point that formed the basis of the article, 'Diasporic Subjects.' Actually experiencing, rather than simply observing, the exhaustion and everyday difficulties associated with living in the dormitory provided personal, experiential understanding of the implications of women's migration, urban lives, and factory work. As Steve Herbert (2000: 552) writes, 'Ethnography [as a method] is … distinguishable because it involves an engagement of the researcher's senses and emotions. To engage a group's lived experience is to engage its full sensuality – the sights, sounds, smells, tastes, and tactile sensations that bring a ways of life to life.' It was this full engagement – to the point of sharing physical weakness and illness – that solidified a deeper sense of identification with my neighbours, and it was this identification that underpinned my commitment to the argument in 'Diasporic Subjects' against the simplified categorizations at the centre of much migration research.

During the first month of fieldwork, I did not carry out directed interviews, and instead spoke with people in general terms about their lives, their migration, and their employment. This open-ended phase of the research proved to be quite valuable in refining the research questions. Indeed, as I spoke with people, it became increasingly clear that the standard definition of a 'migrant' in the literature was unnecessarily limiting. That is, almost all low-income people I met told me that they had migrated at one time or another, and that their sense of what it meant to have migrated had little or nothing to do with the formal census definition of migration (i.e., 'crossing a regional boundary and residing in the destination site for six months'). These early informal interviews with migrants pointed towards conceptualizations of mobility that called into question not only the definition of a 'migrant', but also the developmentalist underpinnings of much migration theory (Silvey and Lawson, 1999).

I reoriented the research from a sole focus on migration and gender (my original theme) toward related questions about social *identity*, inter-generational and inter-ethnic relations, and migrants' attitudes towards development processes and their jobs (i.e., issues of more importance to the people I was meeting).[1] These related issues came up in conversations in part because the interactions remained semi-structured, which allowed respondents greater power to decide the direction of the conversation. They also arose because living with factory workers in their dormitory re-oriented my sense of which questions were most important. Specifically, whereas I had begun fieldwork planning to examine the gender relations among the migrants of a specific ethnic group in each region, soon after arriving, it became clear that the interactions between migrants of distinct ethnic groups were vitally important to understanding how they defined their own gender identities. In addition, whereas I had arrived with a set of hypotheses about the ways that gender and development processes would play out among migrants, the fieldwork interactions with migrants indicated that migrants' gender identities, experiences of 'development', and migration processes were far messier than the neat boxes that gender and development theory might suggest.

During this period of participant observation, I took extensive fieldnotes. While much of what I observed seemed inconsequential at the time, I had been advised to write everything down. This advice proved invaluable. At the time of fieldwork, and even for months afterwards, much of the material in my notes did not seem particularly useful. But ultimately it was essential to the interpretation of the interviews, and has proven useful many times since, as I have returned to the notes and the interview material and worked to make the findings publishable. Over the years of returning to these fieldnotes, I have also found that an indexing system is important for effective organization of field observations.[2] A simple, alphabetical indexing system at the back of the field notebook can save hours of research time. For instance, an index category, 'Javanese gender and work norms,' would be followed with the page numbers including information on that topic. Indeed, while I observed differences in KIMA between Javanese and Buginese women's approaches to work, the theoretical significance of this difference only became clear after returning to the literature back in the US. The fieldnotes allowed me to return to these observations, and elaborate on them in 'Diasporic Subjects.'

It was through participant observation first, and not through interviews, that the differences in gender norms within and across ethnic groups revealed themselves. While people narrated coherent, fixed views of specific Bugis or Javanese gender norms, their stories did not mesh with their actions. Specifically, while people stated that it was considered shameful for Bugis women to work and that Bugis women tended to stay at home, most of the Bugis women in KIMA were working in the factories. Even after watching them for months, the shame they were widely purported to feel did not reveal itself. Paying attention to this disjuncture between their stories and their actions led me to ask further questions about the sources of their contrasting beliefs and behavior. Their responses to these additional questions, then, form the argument in 'Diasporic Subjects.'

A researcher's skill in observing and noting critical ethnographic moments improves with time and experience, both because the researcher grows more fluent in the local cultural norms and thus is less focused on her own behaviour, and because she gets better at differentiating between meaningful social patterns and random blips on the screen of daily behaviour. Further, over time, ethnographic subjects begin to pay less attention to the ethnographer, and they begin to act more as they might if she were not in their presence. One of the major challenges of ethnographic fieldwork, therefore, is remaining patient, both with oneself and with the initial discomfort of the situation. 'Diasporic Subjects' emerged out of over two years of experience living in Indonesia, six months of site-specific fieldwork, and over a decade of study focused on Indonesia. All of this background experience helped in dealing with the stresses of fieldwork, and it contributed to the quality of the observations and fieldnotes recorded.

The fieldnotes, because of their breadth and richness of detail, have been especially useful in thinking through an evolving set of research foci. My interests broadened both in the field and after returning to the library for project write-up. Specifically, it was the critical development literature (Crush, 1995; Escobar, 1995, 2001; Rahnema and Bawtree, 1997; Sachs, 1992) that encouraged me think not only about the ways that migrants responded to the pushes and pulls of development, but also how they understood the notion of development itself. In addition, the post-colonial feminist literature (cf Bulbeck, 1998 and Mohanty, 1991) pushed me to think about the question of the migrant as a paradigmatic subject of Western modernizationist thinking, and the universalized 'woman' within migration studies (when she appeared at all) as an extension of that ethnocentrism (Silvey and Lawson, 1999).

Thus, the themes that are at the centre of the piece 'Diasporic Subjects' are in part responses to this post fieldwork reading of critical theory. While I had been reading work in this vein prior to fieldwork, it was only upon returning to the literature that I made these connections between the ethnographic observations in KIMA, the narrative interview data, and the theoretical literature. While some advisors might recommend for the sake of expediency that a student stick with a particular theoretical framework, openness and flexibility are also necessary for forming creative contributions to the literature. Nevertheless, in the process of remaining open to new ways of thinking through one's data, it is helpful to rely on some systematic analytical procedures. Specifically, keeping notes on the literature in a bibliographic computer database program is very helpful, and especially so if the notes in the database also include relevant data from fieldwork and analysis of the connections between the literature and fieldwork.

The field research was explicitly oriented toward in-depth examination of migrants' experiences in their destination site, and my directed approach to sampling was appropriate for the questions at hand. However, because the study was focused on migration, questions arose which required additional methods as well. First, because I wanted to analyze the consequences of migration, it was important to have some baseline data from migrants' origin sites. Fortunately, migrants frequently invited me to travel back to their rural homes with them when they were not working. Rather than select particular origin sites to research, I accompanied the migrants who had become closer friends and key informants. Several of these women originated in villages that in later surveys were revealed to be important source areas of migrants in KIMA.

Although the project in Sulawesi was not centrally focused on migration patterns and trends, the regional migration flows were important to address in order to provide a picture of the scale of changes in women's patterns and rates of migration. These data were also important for explaining to migration scholars the broader importance of the in-depth study. Analysis of the formal Indonesian census data confirmed that rates of women's migration to South Sulawesi had increased, a foundational empirical point from which the remainder of the analysis could build. Examining additional sources, both demographic and historical, and placing the ethnographic material in the context of these other data, made 'Diasporic Subjects' better social science. By tying the findings to the broader historical, empirical, and theoretical literature, it was possible to develop a measure of theoretical abstraction. These are some strategies for ethnographers to employ as they seek to confront the criticism of ethnography that it is unscientific and too limited to allow for abstraction (Herbert, 2000).

Lastly came the write-up and the revision phases. Writing is a far smoother process with a database including bibliographic sources, fieldwork notes, excerpts from interviews, and notes on the connections between these sources. But writing usually takes more time than a researcher expects that it will. It is particularly helpful to have a trusted fellow student read and review drafts of one's work, as a fresh pair of eyes can help the researcher identify points that need revision or reinterpretation. It was the comments on an early draft of 'Diasporic Subjects' that led me to revisit the primary ethnographic data and fieldnotes, and to identify the importance to the literature of inter-ethnic relations in shaping gender norms. Seeking feedback from colleagues on one's written work leads to richer, higher quality ethnographic interpretation and better research overall.

Conclusions

Several key points can be drawn from the research process underlying the article, 'Diasporic Subjects.' First, there are multiple influences that shape a research question and many forces that affect the ultimate framing of a research project or argument. Remaining receptive to a wide range of sources can enrich a project, and allowing a project to grow can potentially lead to more interesting findings. Second, there are many unlikely and potentially fruitful connections that can be made if one stays open to the implications of one's observations, the analyses of fieldwork data, and the literature. One of the strengths of ethnographic work is the open-endedness of participant observation.[3] The ethnographer is not in the field to fit respondents into conceptual boxes, but rather to see the ways that the processes and meanings of their lives are expressed. This requires that the ethnographer be deliberately flexible in his or her approach to the fieldwork situation, and provide ample room for the subjects of the ethnography themselves to organize and manage the fieldwork encounter. Rigorous ethnography demands that some time be planned as unstructured.

Third, good ethnography requires revisiting fieldwork notes and interview material through the lenses of the theoretical literature on which a researcher is currently focused. I have emphasized the importance of theory, both in selecting one's research question, and in analyzing one's data. The fit between one's own research and the existing theoretical literature is a crucial element of research proposals and publications. Therefore, it is advisable to engage in explicit, on-going conversation, ideally in the form of notes in a bibliographic database, with the literature. All of these factors shape the sort of methodology that is possible for a given researcher to adopt at a given time, and all should be considered in the initial selection of a research question. Lastly, this case study should serve as a reminder to write down everything one observes and learns in the field. The implications of field observations and narrative interviews may only become clear years after the project has been carried out, and the wealth of their potential insight can only be elaborated with solid field evidence at hand. This is as true for critical ethnographic work as it is for any other form of research.

Future work that extends critical ethnographic research, and that examines issues of gender and migration could take a number of fruitful directions. Several themes are of particular interest in light of the cultural turn within geography. These include ethnographies that are explicitly self-reflexive, examining the power relations at work both in the fieldwork encounter and their relationships with broader fields of social differentiation. There is also a need for migration studies that take seriously the insights not only of feminist theory but also of critical social theory. Further, as understandings of economic development change, we will need research that examines the interactions between complex subjectivities and the shifting **discourses** of development. Finally, there is room for many more investigations of the politics not only of gender but also of culture more broadly, and specifically the implications of a politicized theorization of culture for questions at the heart of population and development geography.

This research was made possible by a grant from the National Science Foundation. That support is greatly appreciated.

Notes

[1] In 1998, interviews also examined people's attitudes towards women's involvement in strike activity.

[2] Many thanks to Tony Bebbington for suggesting this system, and more generally for the valuable contributions he provides to my work.

[3] This open-endedness, however, does not imply that ethnography is wholly inductive, nor does it suggest that ethnographers operate without theoretical framing (Burawoy, 1991).

Further reading

The following article locates ethnographic methods within the discipline of geography, outlines recent critiques of ethnographic methodology, and provides suggestions for addressing these critiques:

- Herbert, S. (2000) 'For ethnography,' *Progress in Human Geography* 24 550–68.

For more on gender and migration, see:

- Lawson, V. (1998) 'Hierarchical households and gendered migration in Latin America: Feminist Extensions to Migration Research', *Progress in Human Geography* 22(1): 39–53.

- Willis, K. and Yeoh, B. (eds) (2000) *Gender and Migration*. Cheltenham, Edward Elgar.

While Lawson provides an overview of the developing theoretical approach to research on gender and migration, Willis and Yeoh provide an overview of the sub-field as a whole and includes research based on a range of methodological approaches.

The following special issue on women in the field discusses the theoretical, methodological and practical gender issues tied to geographical fieldwork:

- *The Professional Geographer* 46 (1994).

For more on the critical issues that face researchers who are either involved in gender focused work, or who are concerned about gender politics in research more generally, read:

- Wolf, D. (ed.) (1996) *Feminist Dilemmas in Fieldwork*. Boulder, Westview.

The essays in this book provide both a range of compelling analyses of fieldwork experiences, as well as a series of practical and insightful resolutions to the problems that may haunt the consciences of feminist fieldworkers.

A TALE OF RESEARCH

Resistance and organizing among Polish domestic workers in New York City

Monika Szymurska

For the last two years I have studied and explored the situation of Polish immigrant women employed as domestic workers in the New York City area. I began the investigation in an undergraduate class that focused on geography, gender and work. What began as a final project for a senior class has turned into a more extensive investigation, one fulfilling the requirements of my Master's degree at Clark University in Worcester, Massachusetts.

For reasons that are both academic and personal, I set out to conduct the research in a community that I am very familiar with – the Polish-American community in New York. I came to the United States from Poland at a time of profound political and economic change in the early 1990s. The aftermath of the collapse of the Soviet Union resulted in the considerable increase in the migration from Eastern Europe to the West. While living in Poland I knew of many women who occasionally worked abroad, for months at a time, in order to contribute to the family's income back home. Domestic work became and continues to be the source of employment for many women in my family who chose to migrate. Guiding this research was my strong interest in the socio-demographic, economic and political aspects of human migration, as well as my interest in labour organizing and workers' rights. I wanted to look at migration and labour through a gendered lens, one that highlights the unique experiences and position of women. I was particularly excited about working within dynamic fields of study. Both migration studies and labour organizing are very complex, multi-layered and ever-changing areas, where there is a great need and potential for research and analysis, as well as advocacy and activism.

The limited academic discourse on women, work and migration, as well as labour organizing within an informal sector, sparked my interest to investigate the fate of women from Eastern Europe who migrate in search of employment. Although many studies have been conducted on the organization of labour in the formal economy (trades, industrial and manufacturer's unions), little analysis examines organization and resistance in the informal sector. I wanted to explore the organizing strategies of an informal labour force in the United States, a labour force that is largely composed of immigrant, female workers.

The primary questions guiding my research were:

- What forms of resistance and organizing characterize the lives of Polish domestic workers in the US?
- What factors influence their ability to organize and negotiate for better working conditions?

The methods and research strategy of the study consisted of a combination of interviews and surveys, participant observation, the use of secondary data from the US Census and other agencies.

In the interviews with domestic workers I sought to learn about the work and immigration history of each woman, her personal and professional contacts, changes in her labour activism as a result of immigration, her views on formal (unions) and informal organizing, as well as the factors she sees as impediments to organizing. I relied on the interviews with Polish domestic workers to learn about the 'informal' forms of resistance and activism that these women undertake, the way they bargain and negotiate for better working conditions with their individual employers, and the factors that influence this process of negotiation. I interviewed twenty-six women, either in person or over the phone. All of these interviews were conducted in Polish and were later translated and coded to identify common trends and themes. Because of the difficulty of identifying Polish immigrant domestic workers via any random sampling strategy, I used a snowball sample: I began by contacting people I knew and these women then introduced me to other Polish domestic workers. I tried to expand the scope of the sample by distributing surveys, in Polish, to individuals who knew other women working as domestics, to local businesses in New York's Polish neighborhoods, as well as to offices of selected immigrant organizations. Only a few surveys were returned to me. As a result, I did not statistically analyze the information from the surveys as I had initially intended.

Additional interviews were also conducted with individuals and organizations relevant to the status of immigrant Polish domestic workers. Phone interviews were conducted with representatives of various domestic workers' organizations to learn about the type of services they provide to people employed as domestics. I contacted Polish immigrant organizations in New York City to investigate whether there have been any initiatives in the Polish community to set up advocacy and support agencies for women working as domestics. I also spoke with union organizers in order to evaluate and assess the potential for formal organizing initiatives in the domestic work sector, as well as to learn about organizing immigrant workers and workers who often work in dispersed, informal settings.

Data from the US Census and other agencies provided background information about immigration patterns, the clustering of Polish immigrants within the US, and the make-up of the Polish immigrant population (gender and age, in particular). It was very difficult to obtain accurate statistics on Polish domestic workers because many are undocumented immigrants.

Organizational efforts and resistance strategies present in the lives of Polish domestic workers are often characterized by a strong reliance on individual bargaining and negotiation, often highly effective and subject to the terms of a 'personal' relationship and bond between the employer and employee. Unwritten 'contracts' and agreements also seem to control the wages, benefits, and working conditions of domestic workers. Many domestic workers I interviewed rely heavily on close social networks of friends and family for advice and support with work-related problems and concerns. The factors influencing the potential for organizing include immigration status, language proficiency, time constraints, location and geographical isolation, the fear of being fired and easily replaced, as well as a lack of solidarity and institutional support within the Polish community. My findings demonstrate the need to bridge research, policy, and grassroots organizing, as well as to promote an interdisciplinary and multi-agency approach when investigating various aspects of human migration.

Throughout the research process I became highly reflexive of my own experience as an immigrant woman. I also began to view the experiences of women I was familiar with, for whom domestic labour is a main source of income, through a gendered and more political lens. Conversations with women in my family, as well as long talks with friends and acquaintances encouraged my interest in studying this occupation and influenced the research strategy. Domestic work is a fascinating labour sector to study –

a place where personal, political, and public merge to present highly diverse and dynamic conditions. Throughout my research, the boundaries between what I consider political and personal became blurred, making this the most challenging and empowering project I have ever undertaken.

I began my research on the domestic workers' project two years ago in Susan Hanson's geography/women's studies class investigating class, gender, ethnicity and work. The class helped me to focus on a subject that was of great interest to me since coming to the USA from Poland in the early 1990s – the occupational choices for immigrant women. My mom's experience as a housekeeper in New York City for over ten years was my great inspiration. The project has turned into my Master's thesis and I am currently working to complete the research and the writing. As a result of this work, I am exploring various options to set up an agency providing services to domestic workers in the Polish community in NYC. This will involve a great deal of networking, planning and, of course, funding. I am currently working as a Housing Coordinator for a local development non-profit organization in NYC and I am looking forward to initiating a program for domestic workers – hopefully in the coming year!

7

Learning about labour

Combining qualitative and quantitative methods

Susan Hanson and Geraldine Pratt

Have you seen the postcard that shows a young man thinking, 'What was it? .... Damn! I forgot to get a job!' Think for a minute about why the message of this postcard catches your attention and may even strike you as being somewhat amusing. Forgot to get a job? A man? (It's not inconsequential, in our view, that a companion postcard shows the head of a woman, with the words, 'What was it? Damn, I forgot to have kids!' in the bubble.) Why is it so unlikely that someone would 'forget' to get a job? This would have to be a person whose bank account is magically forever replenished, whose interests keep him fully occupied outside a workplace, and – assuming that he enjoys the company of others – someone whose friends likewise forgot to get jobs, so he has some good company during the day.

The humour in this image turns precisely on the centrality of paid employment in the contemporary world, especially – still – for men. Perhaps what signals this centrality most strongly is the sheer amount of time spent at work and the income derived from it. For many of us work does more than occupy half of our waking hours; it is a key site around which women and men create meaning in their lives. And far more than just a source of livelihood, paid work is for many people the dimension of life that defines their **identity**. When you meet someone for the first time, one of the first bits of information you want to know is not whether the person has children or siblings or is a skier; it is what that person does for a living: Is she a physician or a nurse? Is he a teacher or a bricklayer?[1] When we think about the social status of ourselves and others, paid work, especially occupation, is what we usually focus on.

Indeed, as historian Alice Kessler-Harris (2001) points out, economic independence in the form of paid employment has long been seen as the essential pre-condition to women's full participation in political society; when women's employment opportunities are restricted, women are denied full citizenship. In her award-winning autobiography, *Personal History*, Katharine Graham, who eventually became publisher of the *Washington Post* and president of a large TV-magazine-newspaper conglomerate, poignantly describes the incapacitating effects of women's lack of equal access to workplaces outside the home:

> *I adopted the assumption of many of my generation [Graham was born in 1917] that women were intellectually inferior to men, that we were not capable of governing, leading, managing anything but our homes and our children. Once married, we were confined to running houses, providing a smooth atmosphere, dealing with children, supporting our husbands. Pretty soon this kind of thinking – indeed, this kind of life – took its toll: most of us became somehow inferior. We grew less able to keep up with what was happening in the world. In a group, we remained largely silent, unable to participate in conversations and discussions.*
>
> (Graham, 1997: 416–17)

The societal structures supporting this gendered separation of home and work began to be eroded in the United States in the 1960s with the passage of the 1964 Civil Rights Act. Yet, as Kessler-Harris documents, US employment legislation and social policy (such as workman's compensation and policies governing disbursement of welfare monies) throughout the twentieth century have consistently been based in the assumption that society is comprised solely of nuclear families with a male breadwinner and a female homemaker/mother.

So, forgetting to get a job means that the young man on the postcard lacks what has become a major source of individual and social **identity** in contemporary society. It also means he lacks access to a workplace, a pivotal site of social interaction and information exchange. For most people, the workplace replaces the school or university as the place where friendships are made, jokes exchanged, ideas discussed, opportunities negotiated. Educators seek to prepare students for lifelong learning, and a great deal of that lifelong learning will take place through interactions at work. An interesting indicator of how much people value social interactions – formal and informal – in the workplace is the relatively small proportion of employees who are willing to work regularly from home when given the opportunity.[2]

We do not mean to imply that a paying job is the only source of a person's identity or that the workplace is the only site of meaningful social interaction and personal growth. Many kinds of unpaid labour – including caring for children and elders, tending home and garden, bartering, and volunteering in the community – can be at least as important as paid work in shaping people's identities and their access to opportunity, as Katharine Graham's words pointedly illustrate. Feminist organisations in Canada successfully forced this recognition on the Canadian state in the early 1990s, and since 1996 the Canadian census has collected information on the number of hours that individuals spend on unpaid household work and childcare. Recognizing the importance of these other types of labour draws attention to other sites, namely the home and the community, where identities take shape. Rather than zeroing in on paid work in isolation, many of the studies in geography dealing with work have focused on the interdependencies between and among different kinds of labour – paid work, domestic work, community work, for example – and the spaces associated with them.

Because of the crucial importance of paid employment in contemporary societies and because not everyone seems to have equal access to it, many geographers have sought to understand the role of space and place in shaping people's access to paid employment opportunities. Why are unemployment rates higher in some regions than in others? Why are certain kinds of people (e.g. recent male immigrants from Pakistan) in certain cities concentrated in certain kinds of jobs (e.g. taxi driver or gas station attendant)? Although scholars first sought answers to questions like these via quantitative analysis of census data with an emphasis on paid employment only, we have increasingly come to realize that understanding patterns of paying work requires understanding, often via the inclusion of qualitative analyses, how such work is related to the rest of people's lives.

Questions about the geographies of work and about the complexities of work-life decisions have particular urgency now because of the ways in which paid employment has been changing. Three decades ago the norm was a single worker in a household, usually the male, having a secure job with one employer for most of his working life. Now, a household is likely to have more than one worker, and each one is likely to have many jobs (sometimes simultaneously) over the course of his or her working life, often in different occupations. Observers attribute these changes to the frantic pace of technological change, which continually alters the skills that employers are looking for, and to the growing competition companies now face from increased globalization, which prompts employers to cut costs by reducing the *number* of regular full-time workers and increasing the number of part-time and temporary workers.[3] As a result, there is a greater need now for experienced workers to retrain and learn new skills; workers also face greater instability and flexibility in the labour market than they did several decades ago, with shorter average job tenures and less secure employment.[4]

These changes complicate the geographies of work, especially those within households. As household members lose jobs, seek additional training, and find new jobs in locations and under terms of employment that may be quite different from their old jobs, the difficulties of coordinating their daily lives escalate. We ask you to contemplate this question: If you are a member of a multiple-earner household facing this increasing employment instability and uncertainty we've described, would it make more sense to you to locate in a large urban area or a smaller town? Which type of place do you think would offer the members of your household better job prospects? What is the logic behind your choice of place?

Changing geographies also complicate social relations around work. Although immigration from one country to another is not new, it now occurs on a massive global scale, and there is concern that immigrants, especially 'Third-World-looking' ones (Hage, 1998: 133), experience particular difficulties and barriers in labour markets of European and Anglo-American countries. Lifelong learning takes on a different and less positive meaning if it involves downward social mobility and is necessitated by a reluctance on the part of accreditation panels to recognize learning and training obtained elsewhere, or an inability to land a job in one's field without 'local' (i.e. national) experience. But immigrants are not only the victims of exclusion; Mike Davis (2000), for instance, argues that Latinos are re-energizing the union movement in the United States, bringing a new militancy, along with different cultural practices of organizing (Houston and Pulido, 2002).

Globalization also forces attention to the many ways that labour conditions 'here' are bound up with labour conditions 'there'. The fact that there are so many Filipinos working as live-in domestic workers in Canada, for instance, living in conditions that have been likened to 'modern day slavery', is understandable only within the context of the Philippine government's Labor Export Policy, itself conditioned by foreign debt and IMF policy. This policy leads one out of every ten citizens of the Philippines to work outside of their national boundaries (Morales, 2000). In the case of these overseas contract workers, the relations between home, family, and work are stretched over vast spaces, especially when parents leave their own children in the Philippines to be cared for by members of their extended families. There are, then, many different geographies to consider when trying to learn about labour in any one place.

Researching work

We explored some of these geographies in our research collaboration in Worcester, Massachusetts, and have followed others in subsequent projects that we have done separately. We trace some of this history to show how our questions have evolved through time, some coming from gaps in current research and others from surprises that emerged in our own research. We have tacked back and forth between quantitative and qualitative research methods and want to demonstrate here the strength that comes, not just from numbers, but from combining these different methods and data sources.

Worcester was the site for our collaborative study of local labour markets primarily because that is where we were living and working when we conceived of the study. In addition, women's labour market profile in Worcester closely matches that of the US, suggesting that the processes shaping gendered labour markets in our study area are probably similar to those shaping local labour markets elsewhere in the US. Located about 50 miles west of Boston, Worcester is a mid-sized metropolitan area with a population of 436,000 in 1990 (511,000 in 2000). Diverse manufacturing industries have always been important to the city's economic base, but in the past 30 or 40 years the importance of manufacturing has declined (to 21 per cent of the labour force in 1990) while the importance of services has increased (accounting for 27 per cent of employment in 1990). Among the manufacturing industries are ones that have long had a presence in Worcester – like wire, metal products, machine tools, and abrasives – as well as more recent arrivals such as computer hardware and software, plastics, optics, and medical instruments. Among Worcester's important service industries are higher education, insurance, and health care. People in Worcester tend to be more rooted to place than are people in other US urban areas. In 1990, 86 per cent of Worcester's population had been living in the metro area for at least five years, compared to an average of 80 per cent of the people in the 300 metro areas in the US.

In the Worcester project, which is summarized in Hanson and Pratt (1995), we began with a focus on spatial distance and grew increasingly attentive to the implications of the production of distinctive places within the metropolitan area. Early questions included: How do gendered relations in the home dictate certain time-space constraints and opportunities that influence the types of paid employment that women and men do? If a woman (or even a man) has primary responsibility for domestic work, what does this mean for how and where she or he searches for paid work? Finding that many women search very close to home for paid employment and in this search process relied on social networks comprised largely of women from the local neighbourhood opened a series of other research questions bound up with the existence of distinctive employment districts and gendered work cultures within the Worcester area. Does a woman search within a radically different mix of jobs depending on where she lives? Is she more likely to become a machine operator than a clerical worker because of where she lives and the kinds of jobs that are near to her home? Mapping different types of job opportunities raised other questions because we found, for example, that female-typed jobs (like clerical work) and male-typed jobs (like heavy machine operator) were clustered in different parts of the Worcester area. We wondered if this clustering pattern might be related to the extended set of socio-spatial relations shaping women's experience of gender and class.

Our subsequent research emerged out of this Worcester project in circuitous ways, allowing us to investigate geographies and forms of work that we had neglected. One such form of work is self-employment. Whereas our joint Worcester project explored how gender shapes and is shaped by wage and salary work, Susan Hanson's current project focuses on the gendered processes involved in starting and running a business. Motivated, in part, by data documenting the dramatic rise in women-owned businesses (from 5 per cent of US businesses in 1972 to 34 per cent in 1992) and in part by the high level of women's agency implied in venture creation, the study focuses on the intersection of gender, geography, and entrepreneurship. How do women and men make the transition from wage and salary work to self-employment? What role do space and place play in these processes, and how do business owners, in turn, affect the places where their businesses are located? Also, because the discourse of entrepreneurship is strongly masculine – in that entrepreneurs are seen as independent, 'self-made men' – to what degree is women's business ownership oppositional and possibly a source of change in the meaning of gender?

Again, Worcester is one site for studying these processes, but this study of entrepreneurship involves another site as well: Colorado Springs, Colorado, chosen because, in contrast to Worcester's population which is deeply rooted to place, Colorado Springs has a very high proportion of people who have not lived there very long. How are the processes of starting and running a business different – and the same – in these two places? The comparison afforded by in-depth study of two places, together with analysis of the correlates of entrepreneurship (e.g. the age and education profiles of the population) using metro-level data from the 306 metro areas in the US, expands the geographic scale of policy relevance beyond a single metro area to the national level.

Gerry Pratt's next project emerged, in part, in response to certain silences in our joint Worcester project, especially a limited focus on racial dynamics among women. A memorable reaction to one presentation of the Worcester research was when an audience member suggested that we might stop looking at employers' exploitation of women and look at our own exploitation, as white, middle-class academics, of our research subjects![5] Research on the Live-in Caregiver Program, which brings mostly Filipina women to Canada as low-cost, live-in domestic workers, directly addresses racialized class inequality among women, and stretches the geographical frame to the global scale. An attempt was made to address issues of researchers' exploitative practices by collaborating with a grass-roots organization (Pratt, 2000). Such a topic forces careful consideration of the need to combine information about different geographies, but also different types of information obtained using different methodologies. If, for example, domestic workers claim that the Canadian government fundamentally exploits third world women, might we need to look cautiously at state-provided data? On the other hand, if one aim of such research is to influence state policy, do we not need to produce the type of quantitative data governments tend to value? If these questions are highly politicized in relation to this particular research project, they nevertheless exist in relation to all topics, and our Worcester project also involved a careful integration of quantitative and qualitative methods as our questions shifted and evolved.

Integrating qualitative and quantitative methods

Through our collaborative study on Worcester as well as in our subsequent projects we have come to appreciate the complementarity between quantitative and qualitative methods. We recount a few examples here to illustrate how tacking between the two approaches allows you to follow up on surprises or puzzles that emerge, to get a sense of how generalizable certain findings are, and to better understand the causes and meanings of the patterns you see.

One part of our joint Worcester study involved personal interviews with women and men in about 650 households located throughout the Worcester area. To locate households to interview, we randomly selected census blocks from subareas of the metropolitan area[6] and then randomly selected five households per block to interview. An interviewer's first contact with a household was to deliver a letter from us outlining the purpose of the study and indicating that the interviewer would return to set up a time for the interview. Lasting on average more than an hour, the interviews were semi-structured in that the same sequence of questions was asked to each participant and most of the questions were open ended. (For more detail on how we carried out this survey, see Hanson and Pratt, 1995, Chapter 3 and the Appendix.)

We should state at the outset that we struggled toward a methodology for combining quantitative and qualitative data; only in retrospect is it a straightforward process. When we first coded the semi-structured questionnaires, we devised elaborate coding schemes in an effort to capture the nuances and complexities of individual's responses to open-ended questions. To capture the variety of responses to the question, 'How did you come to do this type of work?', we devised no fewer than 45 response categories. 'My employer trained me' was distinguished from 'I was trained to do this in the armed service' (see Table 7.1 for a complete list of codes for this question). It soon became apparent that many of these detailed categories had to be collapsed in statistical analyses aimed at finding relationships between variables. We abandoned the strategy of retaining the specificity of contextualized meaning in the quantitative analyses and returned to the semi-structured questionnaires to treat the extended quotes written down by interviewers as texts requiring and allowing qualitative analyses.

Table 7.1 *Codes developed from open-ended responses to one question*

Q5 **How did you come to do this type of work?**
1. This is the work my mother/ father did.
2. I would only consider being self-employed.
3. I was trained to do this in the service.
4. My employer trained me.
5. This job is not related to my original training/education.
6. I never really wanted to do this kind of work.
7. I needed a more dependable, secure job.
8. I always wanted to do this type of work.
9. I wanted to work in a growing sector; good opportunities in this field.
10. I needed a job.
11. I have the skills for this type of work.
12. I would only consider working for my husband.
13. Type of work another family member did.
14. I was trained to do this in high school/ college.
15. This job required no experience.
16. Decided this is a worthwhile thing to do (socially rewarding).
17. I had been ill, so could do no physical labor.
18. Wanted more pay.
19. I tried this type of work and liked it.
20. Family business (wife's).
21. I wanted to obtain certain skills.
22. It had convenient hours for childcare.
23. Not much direction for women as far as careers.
24. Parents wouldn't let me get the education to pursue ideal career.
25. Developed interest through volunteer work.
26. Got unskilled job in plant, got interested in what skilled workers were doing. Went back to school and came back as a skilled worker.
27. Wanted professional status that I could take other places.
28. Wanted flexibility (this dictated type of work).
29. Wanted to be my own boss.
30. Good field for women – field is dominated by women and we have respect in the field.
31. As a girl I was only encouraged to get training in female dominated jobs.
32. Wanted to get into white-collar work because of high rate of industrial accidents/ dirty.
33. Type of work friend did.
34. It was expected of me (to work in the family business).
35. Fell into this type of work because someone offered me a job.
36. Language problems dictated factory work.
37. My children have learning disabilities, so I'm interested in this type of work.
38. Parent/ relative suggested I do this type of work.
39. In country of origin, few professional options.
40. Work chosen because it's nearby.
41. Wanted to do something creative.
42. Took job because I wanted to get into this company; company more important than job itself.
43. The education/ skills required were affordable; preferred degree unaffordable.
44. Chose this type of work as part of healthier lifestyle.

Source: Personal interviews, Worcester, MA, 1987.

We found this interpretative strategy very useful because it allowed us to demonstrate both the complexity of and interrelations between different socio-spatial processes, and the generality of these patterns. The texts were particularly effective, for example, in unraveling the causal processes leading to the well-documented relationship – gleaned from quantitative data – between income and journey-to-work length. Many studies have found, as did we, that people with low-wage jobs have shorter commutes than do people with better-paying work. The prevailing explanation for this correlation had been, however, that people with low incomes could not *afford the costs* associated with longer work trips; that is, the assumed causal arrow was low wages → shorter work trips. Our interviews revealed a great deal more complexity than that implied in the prevailing explanation and indicated that, in fact, for many people the causal arrow should be reversed (shorter work trips → low wages).

What the interviews showed was that many women choose work close to home for a variety of reasons, including a desire to be readily available for their children in case of an emergency, the time-space constraints necessitated by a heavy domestic work load, lack of access to reliable transportation, or a reluctance to drive long distances (rooted in concern about driving in winter weather or about personal safety in the event of the car breaking down). Wanting to work close to home for whatever reason limits a person's choice of jobs to a small area, and sometimes – depending on where a person lives – all or most of the jobs in that area will be poorly paid. In addition, some employers *create* low-paying jobs in close proximity to certain groups of women (e.g. well-educated, married women), recognizing that many women want to work relatively close to home. Because these jobs are explicitly created as low-waged women's work, we can see that in this case geography contributes to the gendering of jobs. In short, the stories people told about why they work where they do revealed that when, whether out of choice or necessity, a person decides to look for work close to home, it is this decision to have a shorter work trip that can lead to poorly paid work, not the reverse, as had been assumed.

Our attempt to understand the job search process benefited enormously from tacking between qualitative and quantitative analyses. We asked people how they had found their current jobs and whether they had actively searched for them. The responses surprised us. Whereas the literature on job search, which comes mostly out of economics, describes people as actively and purposefully searching for a job by carefully weighing the pros and cons of each job possibility they come upon, the majority of people in our sample said they had not been actively searching but instead had 'fallen into' their jobs. Because we had asked the question in an open-ended way, in their responses people described the circumstances that had led them to their current jobs, and these circumstances in the case of 'falling into' a job almost always involved the person's daily travel activity pattern or conversation with friends, neighbours, and relatives. People came upon Help Wanted posters in the course of their daily travels, for example; or they may have heard about a job opening with their current employer from a high school friend who was already working there.

Because our sample was large and because sample households had been randomly selected in such a way that they were representative of the Worcester-area working-age population, we were able to generalize from the sample to that population. The finding that fully 57 per cent of women and 51 per cent of men had not been actively searching but had 'fallen into' their jobs therefore lends weight to our larger point that job search – and, indeed, the labour market – should not be understood as standing outside of, or separate from, the rest of people's daily lives. We arrived at these percentages (and the other findings about job search that involved counting) by coding responses to the open-ended questions. We were able, for example, to code whether or not a person had found a job through a personal contact, and if she had, we coded the gender of that contact and the nature of the contact's relationship to our respondent.

Quantitative analysis of these data yielded further surprises (see Table 7.2). We found that women are more likely to find out about jobs from other women than from men, and men learn about jobs from other men. The channels through which job information flows, then, are strongly gendered. The personal relationships involved are quite different for women and men, as well, with family and community contacts being more important for women than they are for men, and work-based contacts more important for men than they are for women. Male family members were particularly important in connecting women to jobs in male-dominated lines of work, which on average pay considerably more than do jobs in female-dominated occupations ($11.70 per hour vs $8.70 per hour in our Worcester study). This finding contradicted prevailing wisdom at the time, which held that relatives are generally not a good source of information about jobs that might advance one's status in the labour market.[7] And looking at the intersection of gender and type of relationship yielded the startling finding that not a single man in our sample had learned about his present job from either a work-related female contact or a community-based female contact. In this case, quantitative analysis of the open-ended interview data revealed just how deeply gendered are the conduits of job information. As we argued in the article that summarizes this part of the original Worcester project, these patterns of information flow help to explain how women and men come to be segregated into different types of work (Hanson and Pratt 1991).

Table 7.2 *Types of personal contacts used in obtaining present job**

			Women in occupations:		
	Women	**Men**	**Female-dominated**	**Gender-integrated**	**Male-dominated**
Sex of Contact					
Female	49	9	57	45	29
Male	34	70	28	36	52
Unknown	27	25	29	25	29
Origin of Contact					
Family	36	26	36	33	43
Community	24	6	29	17	19
Work	22	30	18	27	24
Friends acquaintances not specified as either work or community related	29	42	30	27	24

*Figures are percentage of each group having used each type of contact, e.g. 49 per cent of women who had received job information from a personal contact obtained that information from another woman.

Source: Personal interviews, Worcester, MA 1987. Table reprinted from Hanson and Pratt (1991) with permission of the Association of American Geographers.

In the subsequent study on entrepreneurship, Susan Hanson (2002) has found that serendipity is an important path not just to landing a job but also to business ownership, playing a role in about 44 per cent of business startups in Worcester. This finding was completely unanticipated; it does not appear in the literature, and despite our earlier discovery of serendipity's role in finding a job, there seems on the face of it to be an enormous difference between 'falling into' a job and 'falling into' owning a business!

Yet when asked in an open-ended way how they came to have their own business and when later asked when they started to think about owning a business, a large number of business owners replied that they had never intended to own a business, that 'it was an accident,' or that 'one thing just led to another.' The prevalence of serendipity as a path to business ownership goes against the dominant paradigm, which sees venture creation as the result of a careful, deliberative decision-making process. As was the case with job finding, the detailed stories people told about how they came to own their businesses highlighted the key role of place-based social networks.

Women were distinctly more likely than men to say that their business ownership had not been planned (38 per cent of the women entrepreneurs vs 13 per cent of the men in the Worcester interview sample). How can we make sense of this finding? Some might argue that the answer lies more in the gender differences in how people describe their careers, with women being more likely than men are to ascribe their successes to chance rather than to their own agency (e.g., Heilbrun, 1979). While acknowledging that this kind of gender difference may account for some of the 25-point gap noted above (38 per cent vs 13 per cent), Hanson proposes that in large measure the answer lies in setting the stories people related about serendipity against the well-known backdrop of women's labour market position, which, in general, is far inferior to that of men in terms of the conditions of work and possibilities for advancement. In comparison to men's jobs, most women's jobs pay less, have less security, and are more likely to be dead-end. If you were in such a job, and you somehow hit upon the opportunity to run your own business, what would you do? If you saw your current wage and salary job as fairly tenuous or if you have been out of the paid labour force raising children for the past 15 years, you might consider the risk of business ownership to be relatively low compared to staying with your current employer or braving a job search with no recent labour market experience.

In the entrepreneurship study, Hanson followed the in-depth personal interviews with a mailed survey to a large sample of business owners in both Worcester and Colorado Springs. She used the findings from the interviews to craft the survey questions, most of which were closed-ended – that is, the respondent either selects one among several pre-given answers or uses a scale to say how much he agrees with various statements (see Figure 7.1). Because serendipity had emerged as such a strong theme in the interviews, she asked the business owners to indicate if they completely agreed, generally agreed, generally disagreed, or completely disagreed with the statement, 'I became a business owner more by accident than by design'. The survey results, which yield only quantitative data but do so for a much larger sample (about 350 surveys vs 200 interviews in Worcester and 500 surveys vs 180 interviews in Colorado Springs), confirm the importance of serendipity, which had first been glimpsed in the interviews: 37 per cent of the respondents in the Worcester mailed survey and 35 per cent in the Colorado Springs survey agreed with this statement.

Throughout our exploration of how people find jobs and the study of how people become entrepreneurs, we drew heavily upon both the open-ended interview data (which contains the stories) and the quantitative analysis of the data we coded from this textual material. Only through the richness of the qualitative data – the stories – could we apprehend the unplanned and contingent nature of job finding and venture creation for many people and appreciate the ways in which these 'labour market' processes are embedded in people's daily space-time routines and place-based social networks. The stories were crucial, therefore, in helping us to see the processes, including the causal sequences leading to landing a particular type of job or starting a business. Only by quantitatively analyzing the coded data could we understand how prevalent these unanticipated processes are. The quantitative data help us to

Please indicate the extent to which you agree with each of the following statements. Beside each one circle the number that indicates how much you agree with the statement.

1 *completely agree*   **2** *generally agree*   **3** *generally disagree*   **4** *completely disagree*   **NA** *not applicable*

I always wanted to have my own business.	1 2 3 4 NA
The Colorado Springs (CS) area is a good place to have a business.	1 2 3 4 NA
I am thinking of closing my business here and moving it to another place outside the CS area.	1 2 3 4 NA
Opportunities in my previous job were limited for me.	1 2 3 4 NA
I wanted to have my own business so I could have more flexibility for family responsibilities.	1 2 3 4 NA
I disliked my previous job.	1 2 3 4 NA
I disliked my previous boss/management.	1 2 3 4 NA
I wanted to run my own business so I could become more involved in the community.	1 2 3 4 NA
I never really intended to have my own business.	1 2 3 4 NA
I enjoy running this business.	1 2 3 4 NA
Non-financial help from *family members* has been essential to the success of my business.	1 2 3 4 NA
Non-financial help from *friends* has been essential to the success of my business.	1 2 3 4 NA
One of my goals in starting a business was to create a good work environment for my employees.	1 2 3 4 NA
Zoning laws negatively impact my business operations.	1 2 3 4 NA
I have a lot of competition from larger firms.	1 2 3 4 NA
Owning a business is the best way to have a good income.	1 2 3 4 NA
The Internet is important to the success of my business.	1 2 3 4 NA
I have consciously limited or cut back my business for family-related reasons.	1 2 3 4 NA
I became a business owner more by accident than by design.	1 2 3 4 NA
The fact that my spouse/partner had a steady income allowed me to become self-employed.	1 2 3 4 NA

Source: Mailed survey sent to business owners in Colorado Springs, CO, autumn 2000.

Figure 7.1 *A portion of the mailed survey sent to business owners in Colorado Springs, CO, 2000..*

see the degree to which the results from one or two places might be generalizable; such data begin to put an insight gleaned from someone's fascinating story into a larger context.

Gerry Pratt's study of paid domestic work in Vancouver was largely conceived as a qualitative study, but quantitative data, specifically census data analyzed by a colleague, Dan Hiebert, has been pivotal at various stages in the research process. Possibly because this was unanticipated, and in some senses unplanned, the rich possibilities of mixed methods seem even more remarkable. Pratt's study involved in-depth interviews with small samples of various groups involved with paid domestic work: nanny agents, employers of nannies, and European nannies. The experiences of a small group of Filipino nannies were explored through participatory workshops in collaboration with an activist group at the Kalayaan Centre (Pratt, 2000).

Though the majority of resources have been expended on this qualitative research, just two tables derived from census data have been very important to the project, in precisely the ways that we have already elaborated. First, the census data has verified patterns that the qualitative data could only suggest. The interviews with parents, for instance, were divided between households living in the City of Vancouver and an outer suburban area. The interviews in the suburban area revealed an entirely different labour supply of domestic workers than exists in the City of Vancouver: almost no Filipina women but many more Canadian women, both very young and quite elderly. Because this marked difference in labour supply within the metropolitan area was so unexpected (and has such an impact on the quality and types of childcare available), it was important that it could be verified by more generalizable census data. Dan Hiebert's analysis of special runs of census data revealed that fully 35 per cent of childcare workers in Vancouver are Filipina while this is the case for only 10 per cent of childcare workers living in the outer suburbs under study (Pratt, 2002).[8] Thus census data effectively turned a 'hunch' into a 'fact', a social process that has attracted considerable attention from historians of science (e.g. Porter, 1995).

Another table of numbers produced by Dan Hiebert served the same purpose of verification and also served to open up a line of causal analysis. One of Hiebert's (1999) analyses of occupational data from the census shows that Filipinas are the most occupationally segregated of all women in Vancouver. The fact that Filipinas are largely segregated in childcare and housekeeping occupations has led Pratt to ask why it is that Filipinas are ghettoized within these occupations. Patterns of occupational segregation offer few clues about causality but they establish the existence of a pattern to be explained, a puzzle to be solved, with the help of qualitative, contextualized data (Pratt, 1999).

Finally, quantitative and qualitative data speak to different audiences and carry different types of authority. It is striking how often Dan Hiebert's statistic about the extreme degree of occupational segregation of Filipinas in Vancouver has been mobilised by Pratt's community collaborators at the Kalayaan Centre, especially when they speak to academic audiences or government representatives. But audience reaction to another 'research outcome' is equally striking. This is a play that has been written, produced, and performed by the Filipino-Canadian Youth Alliance at the Kalayaan Centre, which describes the experience of a trained nurse coming to Canada to work as a domestic worker. When the first act of this play was first performed in May 2000 at the Kalayaan Centre, the play was in draft form, the acting was mostly amateurish and wooden, and the space was 'non-theatrical' (for example, it was performed with almost no stage set in broad daylight). And yet at the end of the performance, many faces in the audience were streamed with tears. Different representations of facts move us in different ways and not all of us place our trust in numbers.

Conclusions

Quantitative and qualitative methods thus serve different, complementary purposes. Qualitative data and analyses allow us to understand causal processes in context, to investigate meanings attributed to these processes, and to see more clearly the interconnections between various spatialized parts of our lives. Quantitative analyses are equally suited to discovering surprises, especially surprising patterns, and are essential for establishing the generality of these patterns.

The questions that we have addressed represent only a fraction of the fascinating and important questions about work that require further research. There are many questions to ask about the ways that labour is intertwined with the reproduction of social differences. In our research we have said little about sexuality, for instance, even though Valentine (1993a) has written about the ways that many workplaces are profoundly heterosexist. It is worth considering how this heterosexism is itself racialised. One striking aspect of the Live-in Caregiver Program, for example, is Canadians' general acceptance that Filipina mothers may need to leave their children in the care of relatives for many years in order to care for them economically. In other words, they seem to implicitly accept that rights to heterosexual norms of family life are unevenly distributed across the globe.

Attending to the production of social **difference** through work also draws us to particular, under-researched sectors of the economy. There is relatively little geographical research on public sector employment even though, in the United States, public sector employment has been an important site of employment opportunity for women and African Americans. The voluntary sector is another important under-researched area of employment, and is especially important for immigrants who are effectively closed out of the formal labour market until they are able to establish local (often voluntary) employment experience. There are very important equity issues to be pursued in relation to such practices, if certain categories of people are required to work for extended periods without pay. In British Columbia in Canada, it is arguable that this type of inequity has even been formalized within state employment regulations, with the introduction in 2001 of the 'training' minimum wage that allows employers to pay a reduced wage for the first 500 hours of work. This practice has been justified as a means to encourage youth employment, but you might ask yourself whether individual youth should bear the costs of their own training. Beyond official practices of governments and voluntary organizations, there are vast networks of deeply exploitative undocumented labour, including child labour, periodically sensationalized by media accounts of human smuggling, of which we know relatively little.

The language of exploitation leads us to an important social category that we have not thus far discussed: that of class. There is a renewed interest in studying class-based organizing. A particularly interesting line of analysis for geographers considers the ways that the union movement in one place is being affected by organizing strategies imported from elsewhere. Mike Davis predicts that the Mexican/Central American working class in Los Angeles 'may yet reshape the American labor movement' (2000: 144). Particularly interesting is their use of an 'innovative tactical repertoire' (ibid. 149) that includes new spaces of organizing and confrontation, including public transit. The potential to move lessons learnt from organizing around one type of work to another context is also pursued by Gibson, Law and McKay (2002) in relation to Filipina domestic workers in Hong Kong. They have been interested in how organizing against exploitation as domestic workers in Hong Kong has created opportunities for women-led entrepeneurial activities in the Philippines. There is vast potential to research the myriad ways that transnational connections open opportunities for new relations of work that are often more, but sometimes less, exploitative.

Each of these research topics invite and sometimes demand different methods. One can hardly envision a survey of a representative sample of human smugglers. Our experiences suggests the benefits of blending quantitative and qualitative research whenever possible, not only because this allows you to see different things, but to substantiate hunches and convey your research findings to the widest possible audiences.

Notes

[1] Of course, the context of the meeting helps to determine which aspects of a person's identity will matter first to you, and the aspects that are deemed pertinent will vary by class and culture.

[2] In 2000 only 3 per cent of the US labour force worked at home, and this figure includes farm, domestic, and self-employed workers, as well as telecommuters (US Bureau of Census); in addition, Mokhtarian (1998) reports that, among those who do telecommute, the average frequency is about once a week.

[3] This is called increasing the numerical flexibility of the workforce.

[4] Between 1972 and 1995 in the US the annual rate of growth in temporary services employment (for agencies, not including direct-hire temps) was almost 12 per cent, compared to an annual growth rate of only 2 per cent in all non-farm employment (Segal and Sullivan, 1997).

[5] This statement overlooks the fact that many of the people – and especially many of the women – we talked with as part of the original Worcester study thanked us at the end of the interview, telling us that the experience had given them a new perspective on their lives and reflecting on the insights that the interview process had prompted them to make.

[6] The number of blocks selected from a subarea was proportional to the population in the subarea.

[7] In general, jobs in male-dominated work pay higher wages than do jobs in female-dominated occupations. In a study based on an all-male sample, Granovetter (1974) found that family members did not connect men to jobs that were significantly better than the jobs they already had. Our study showed that this finding was clearly not true for women.

[8] The census data is by no means perfect because it shows the residential location of childcare workers rather than the childcare workers' workplace location. Given the spatially circumscribed searches of the parents interviewed, however, there is likely a close relationship between home and workplace locations for the majority of childcare workers.

Further reading

For sustained discussions of the complementary use of quantitative and qualitative methods we suggest:

- Hodge, D. (ed.) (1995) 'Should women count? The role of quantitative methodology in feminist geographic research', *The Professional Geographer* 47: 426–66.

- Hoggart, K., Lees, L. and Davies, A. (2002) *Researching Human Geography*. London, Arnold.

- Maxwell, J. (1996) *Qualitative Research Design: An Interactive Approach*. Thousand Oaks, Sage.

- Ragin, C. C. (1987) *The Comparative Method: Moving Beyond Qualitative and Quantitative Strategies*. Berkeley, University of California Press.

- Ragin, C.C. (1994) *Constructing Social Research*. Thousand Oaks, California, Pine Forge.

Acknowledgements

We thank the National Science Foundation (grants SES 86-84347, SES 87-22383, and SES 90-22868) and the National Geographic Society for supporting our collaborative Worcester project. In addition, Susan Hanson thanks the Sloan Foundation and the National Science Foundation (grant SBR 9730661) for support of the gender and entrepreneurship study and The William and Flora Hewlett Foundation (grant # 2000-5633) for supporting her fellowship at the Center for Advanced Study in the Social and Behavioral Sciences, Stanford, 2001–02. Geraldine Pratt wishes to acknowledge the support of the Social Sciences and Humanities Research Council of Canada for her research with and on domestic workers.

A TALE OF RESEARCH

Essays from the field:

Science and Native American burial in Kansas

Toby Butler

Most of my undergraduate dissertation was written in the University of Kansas, USA where I was an 'exchange' student for a year. Perhaps the toughest part was getting the topic right. Other people in my class seemed to find all sorts of great things to study; an interest in rap music led one student to the study of gang culture in Kansas City; another was interviewing someone who had been wrongly convicted of murder in a local civil rights protest.

I was surprised that such good subjects could be found so close to what appeared to be a quiet university town. But I had a real problem – I had only been in Lawrence for a few weeks. I had little knowledge of what had happened there.

So I started thinking local. I visited museums, asked librarians if they could think of any interesting records that had been recently deposited in their library; I read local papers; I even cornered lecturers and asked them if they had any ideas for research that they didn't have the time or inclination to look into themselves.

I got a few suggestions, but nothing that really grabbed me. Eventually my lecturer in Native American history, Rita Napier, came up trumps. She told me about some legislation that had been passed six years before concerning the desecration of a Native American cemetery in Kansas.

The story began in the 1920s, when a farmer uncovered 136 skeletons in a field. It turned out to be a thirteenth century cemetery, one of the biggest ever found in America. The farmer had turned the graves into a tourist attraction for many years and the state archaeological service had recently come up with a plan to turn it into a multi-million dollar museum of Native American history.

Kansas still has a sizable community of Native Americans and coincidentally Lawrence contained a unique college established specifically for Native-American students. Many were horrified that the bodies of their ancestors were being exhibited in the first place. Yet legally there was nothing they could do. As one lawyer put it, 'dig up a white grave and end up in prison. Dig up an Indian grave and you will get a PhD.' After a long period of debate, the grave was covered up, the museum plans were shelved, and the state law was changed to resolve any future problems over Native-American graves.

It sounded like a fascinating story. How did the scientists react? How was compromise reached? My lecturer said she knew most of the people that had sat on the committee; Native Americans, archaeologists and anthropologists. Several of them even worked for the University. I felt exhilarated; I had a good, local topic and it seemed 'do-able'.

Rita gave me some phone numbers and I quickly lined up my first interview with one of the Native American protagonists; Dan Wildcat, an academic at Haskell Indian Junior College.

I turned up at the college as nervous as hell. My first ever oral history interview was going to be with a Native American – I couldn't quite believe it. It went surprisingly well, considering how little I knew of the topic (my first question was along the lines of: 'er, so what happened then?') My interviewee was incredibly kind and patient. He didn't just answer my questions. He suggested some other people to talk to, and before I left he went over to his filing cabinet. He took out a huge wodge of papers. 'This is everything I've got on the burial pit and the legislation. I'll put it in the college library, and you can come and look through it whenever you want.'

The papers were fantastic. I had minutes of meetings, lists of names, a video of the burial site, letters from lawyers, dozens of magazine articles and relevant academic papers. I cycled down to the library regularly and started taking notes on index cards, writing one fact or idea on each one. If I had any questions or thoughts of my own on why something might have happened I would jot it down on one of the cards, marking 'me' on it. I got the idea for the card system from a 'how to' book on writing dissertations that I found in the library, which was invaluable. I put the cards in a box, sorting them into vague categories as I went along.

That was the first of many interviews. Some were by telephone, but the best ones were face to face. I visited several academics and archaeologists in their offices. I got into the habit of asking them if they had any papers that could help me – almost without exception they gave me access to their filing cabinets. I was flabbergasted when the state archaeologist said I could look at whatever I liked – in the lunch hour I photocopied hundreds of documents at the local copy shop – I was terrified that he might change his mind.

I didn't have time to transcribe the interviews; instead I listened to them and took down just the really good quotes, particularly ones that revealed something about people's attitudes. The quotes went on cards too and slotted into my themes. Writing the dissertation was actually very easy; all I had to do was sort the cards into relevant piles which then became sub-sections of chapters.

The first draft of my dissertation was a straightforward account of what had happened. Moving it on from that – thinking about why the events happened in the way that they did – was more difficult, particularly when you are faced with a ridiculous number of conflicting interpretations and views. My lecturers helped with this. They helped by giving encouraging comments, pointing out things that weren't clear and suggesting possible angles to take. For example, one lecturer suggested that I put the local situation in Kansas in a bigger, national context. I cursed him at the time (I thought the damn thing was nearly finished!) but it worked out well. Other states had different approaches to the legal problem. I even took a trip to Washington DC to interview a museum curator who had perhaps the biggest museum collection of human remains in the world – nearly 30,000 individuals – at the Smithsonian Institution. The resulting extra chapter gave the dissertation greater significance and I am glad that I took the advice.

But lecturers can't give you all the ideas you need. In my experience the real breakthroughs came just after a good interview, or discovering a document that was an important part of the puzzle. I'd get a buzzy 'eureka' feeling when I had thought of a really good idea, or a way through it all. Get those ideas down on the 'me' cards! This is how I finally worked out what my dissertation was really going to be about: why have scientists and Native Americans got such different ideas about death? Rejigging the story with this question in mind gave the dissertation a different structure; my explanations of what had happened were interspersed with new sections exploring ideas of how bodies came to be seen as artifacts rather than ancestors. It also made the dissertation more of an argument than a description.

I was really proud of my dissertation when it was finished. It was the most satisfying thing I did in my degree – it was also the most exciting, partly because no-one had written about my topic before.

Discovering new things from people; uncovering new documents that change the whole picture; getting those eureka moments are a total thrill. And it paid off – my dissertation mark was 80, the highest mark in my year.

I studied history at the University of Wales, Aberystwyth, and spent a year of the course at the University of Kansas, USA. After graduating in 1994 I organised a major oral history community project in Aberystwyth. After two years as a tour guide at Hampton Court Palace and the Tower of London, I then worked as a journalist and editor of several magazines. After taking a part-time MA course in Public History at Ruskin College, Oxford, I am now a full-time PhD student in cultural geography at Royal Holloway, University of London. I am researching oral history and the development of London along the river Thames.

8
Surveying sexualities:
The possibilities and problems of questionnaires

Lynda T. Johnston

In this chapter I discuss the use of questionnaires as a research tool for understanding geographies of sexualities. In doing so I wish to articulate the possibilities and problems of using questionnaires for the practice of cultural geography. Sexuality has become an area of considerable interest within cultural geography. Gay, lesbian and bisexualities within geography have become a rapidly expanding body of knowledge. Furthermore, recent attention has been directed towards constructions of heterosexuality. Not surprisingly, there have been considerable changes to the ways in which geographers have studied sexualities. Research on sexuality and space has tended to move from a type of 'mapping' of sexualities, towards a more critical treatment of the constructed relationship between sexuality and space.

My research focuses on the multiplicity of sexualities and the ways in which sexuality and place are mutually constituted. Furthermore, my research is receptive of critical social theory, in particular feminist and poststructuralist theories that emphasise **difference** and (in)equalities. This work is based on the assumption that there is an integral relationship between theory and practice. I combine theoretical frameworks with methods of data collecting to suggest that it is not just the methods that enable 'queer' inquiry but also the theoretical orientation that guides the conceptual framing of research.

Robyn Longhurst states:

> *The epistemological questions raised by feminist, postmodernist, poststructuralist and postcolonialist theorists in the critical examination of the social construction of knowledges, have in the last few years, helped to bring about a growth of interest in what we do as human geographers ... and how we do it.*
>
> (Longhurst, 1996: 143 emphasis in original)

The use of questionnaires is not common in cultural geography for a number of reasons. Questionnaires are usually used to generate statistical information on a particular sample population. They are commonly associated with, and subjected to, statistical testing. Counting something – or more accurately, someone – can bring into being and essentialise identities. During the course of designing a questionnaire and writing this chapter I have juggled books and articles that purport the use of, for example, 'repertory grids' and 'semantic differentials', alongside texts based on queer and poststructural theories of **identity**. This uneasy alliance has led me to raise epistemological and ontological issues and ask: can sexual categories, such as lesbian, gay, queer, transgendered, be understood as discrete categories for the purpose of geographical analysis? In this chapter I provide an example from my research on gay pride parades and tourism and address the practicalities, problems and possibilities of questionnaire design and implementation. Throughout, I draw attention to the cultural politics of sexualities which are produced through the adoption and implementation of questionnaires.

Concept Box

Difference

Ideas about difference are important for cultural geographers who are interested in **identity**, **representation** and the politics of knowledge. Often informed by post-structuralism, psychoanalysis and/or postcolonialism, ideas about difference complicate an essentialist, unified subject by exploring different axes of **power** that shape identities in terms of, for example, class, gender, race, age and sexuality. The work of feminist geographers has been particularly important in this context. Feminist geographers have studied both the differences between women and men and the differences among them. While the former approach can lead to essentialist ideas about identity (as shown by a universal category of 'woman/women'), the latter approach highlights the more complex and diverse facets of identity that intersect with gender. The work of cultural geographers is often concerned with the spatiality of identity and difference. As Geraldine Pratt and Susan Hanson write, geography reveals 'the ways in which gendered, racialised, and classed identities are fluid and constituted in place – and therefore in different ways in different places' (1994: 6).

Ideas about difference pose important methodological questions about the ethics of research and the politics of representation. The work of many cultural geographers has been sensitive to the difficulties of representing people and places in ways that avoid rendering them as 'other' and exoticising them as 'different.' Often these challenges are articulated through ideas about being an 'insider' or an 'outsider' (or, as in a great deal of research, being positioned as *both* insider and outsider), and intersect with debates about **situated knowledge**, **reflexivity**, and positionality. Such concerns have been particularly prominent in cross-cultural research because of the need to avoid academic 'tourism' or voyeurism. Researchers 'negotiate difference' in a variety of ways and with different degrees of success (Valentine, 2002).

Key reading

- Pratt, G. and Hanson, S. (1994) 'Geography and the construction of difference,' *Gender, Place and Culture* 1: 5–30.
- Valentine, G. (2002) 'People like us: negotiating sameness and difference in the research process.' In Moss, P. (ed) *Feminist Geography in Practice: Research and Methods.* Oxford, Blackwell: 116–126.
- Weedon, C. (1999) *Feminism, Theory and the Politics of Difference.* Oxford, Blackwell.

Sexuality and space: a brief introduction

There has been a recent and rapid growth of work on the geographies of sexualities. A useful review of this work is the introduction to the edited collection *Mapping Desires: Geographies of Sexualities* (Bell and Valentine, 1995; see also Binnie and Valentine, 1999). Reviewing this research gives some insight into the ways in which certain methodologies may determine particular research outcomes. The earliest piece of sexuality and space research was one that sought to 'map' gay and lesbian spaces within North American cities. An urban sociologist, Manual Castells (1983) in *The City and the Grassroots*, examined gay guides and business directories in San Francisco. Castells represented gay male neighbourhoods and commercial districts as dots on maps. His research was based on certain assumptions, for example, what gay men and lesbians 'looked like'; and that gay men and lesbians lived distinct and separate lives from each other and from heterosexual spaces. While this research has been heavily criticised for relying on a particular way of seeing, it did bring attention to the connections between space and sexual identity.

Other studies in North America have focused on the role of gay men in urban regeneration. Larry Knopp pursues the question of sexuality in the context of the spatial dynamics of capitalism in New Orleans and Minneapolis on gay men, gentrification and urban political economy (Knopp, 1987, 1990a, 1990b). Benjamin Forest (1995) discusses the relationships between gay identity, space and place in West Hollywood.

Lesbian geographies are the focus of Sy Adler and Johanna Brenner's (1992) study that contest Castells' (1983) early assertions that lesbians are placeless, and argues that there is a quasi-underground and ephemeral 'community'. Notably, Adler and Brenner (1992) recognise their 'subjects' as not just 'lesbian', but as multiply constituted by gender, class, race and so on. These characteristics are also observed in studies of lesbian residential areas in other North American and European cities (see Ettore, 1978; Peake, 1993; Valentine, 1995; Winchester and White, 1988). Tamar Rothenberg (1995) provides a nuanced study on the Park Slope lesbian community in Brooklyn, New York. She problematises the notion of what constitutes a lesbian community by arguing that while economic factors influence the formation of lesbian communities, *symbolic* importance has also facilitated growth and development in the Park Slope area.

Many academics are now exploring the links between sexualized cultures of consumption and the production of sexualized space (Binnie, 1995a, 1995b; Mort, 1995; Munt, 1995). Lesbian and gay tourism is becoming a focus of geographers, with studies being done in places such as Amsterdam (Binnie, 1995a), South Africa (Elder, forthcoming), New Zealand and Australia (Johnston, 2001).

Some studies have highlighted the fact that everyday spaces are heterosexualized (McDowell, 1995; Valentine, 1993a). Nancy Duncan (1996) argues that lesbian and gay practices – if they are made explicit – have the potential to trouble the taken-for-granted heterosexuality of public places. The street tactics of gay men and lesbians, such as kissing in public, might be understood as 'crisis points in the normal functioning of 'everyday' experiences' (Cresswell 1996, cited in Duncan 1996: 139). Gill Valentine (1996: 152) discusses the transformative potential of pride marches, claiming that: 'pride marches also achieve much more than just visibility, they also challenge the production of everyday spaces as heterosexual.'

Very few geographers have addressed how heterosexual identities are spatially constructed and performed in space. The lack of critical attention towards heterosexuality means that geographers 'risk presenting an overly sanitised and ordered conception of sociospatial relations which excluded the central desires and disgusts which infuse all people's lives (Hubbard 2000: 192). In other words, heterosexuality remains a dominant, homogenous, yet 'invisible' category.

Recent work, sometimes called 'queer geographies' has been a response to earlier research on geographies of lesbian and gay men which adopted an uncritical conceptualisation of lesbian and gay identity. Using social theories, queer geographies challenge the notion of 'fixed' identities. A useful example is the work of David Bell, Jon Binnie, Julia Cream and Gill Valentine (1994) who adopt theoretical concepts such as **performativity** (Butler, 1990) to think about the production of both sexuality and space. This work inspires me to think critically about queer identities, parades and tourism and the ways in which certain methodologies can assist political intentions.

Practising geographies of sexualities

In 1996 I designed and implemented a questionnaire as part of my doctoral research on gay pride parades (Johnston 1998). This research theoretically and empirically examines the ways in which gay pride parades – Auckland's HERO and Sydney's Gay and Lesbian Mardi Gras (see Figure 8.1) – are socially constructed and embodied tourist environments. I draw on critical social theories, such as feminist, poststructuralist, postmodernist, and postcolonialist theories in order to offer both new challenges to, and exciting possibilities for, the construction of geographical and tourism knowledge. I am interested in the events themselves as powerful spaces where certain identities are produced and/or contested. Theoretically, I build on work by Soile Veijola and Eeva Jokinen (1994) who examine epistemological assumptions to argue that tourism studies is masculinist and tends to render watching tourists as disembodied gazers. My research is, in part, motivated by what I understand to be an absence of 'bodies' in tourism academic literature. While categories such as 'host' and 'guest' are used, there is very little attention paid to bodily specificities, such as gender, sexuality, race and ethnicity, disability and so on, and the ways in which these bodies are included or excluded (privileged or devalued) in tourism academic **discourse**. Some research, however, has started to unpack the powerful position that tourists may hold as 'gazers' on 'Others' (see, for example, Urry, 1990, 1992). My argument is that this **gaze** must be mediated through the desires of particular bodies, be they gay, lesbian, heterosexual, male, female and so on.

Figure 8.1 *Mardi Gras, Sydney, 1996. Photograph by author.*

My research is informed by multiple methods, which include questionnaires. Indeed, questionnaires are a small part of my methodology, but play a significant role in my theorising of bodies, sexuality and tourism. Gaining data on people involved in gay pride parades was achieved by conducting focus groups and individual in-depth interviews with parade participants and organisers. Participant observation at the HERO parade workshop, where paraders made and assembled their floats, was carried out for six weeks prior to the 1996 parade. I conducted participant observation at the 1996 Sydney Gay and Lesbian Mardi Gras. I also drew on media representations of parades from 1996 to 1998. Drawing on a multitude of research methods enabled me to gather diverse data from different sources. I found that some of my participants responded more openly in focus groups, others seemed to prefer individual interviews, and still others were more comfortable chatting to me whilst making pom pom balls for the HERO Marching Boys' parade entry. Using a variety of methods allowed me to be flexible and responsive towards the people I studied. For example, I planned to conduct a focus group with the HERO Marching Boys, but their tight training schedule and the large number of people involved meant that only impromptu individual interviews were possible. Using multiple methods has analysis implications. Miles and Huberman (1994) suggest three components of data analysis: data reduction, data displays and conclusion drawing and verification. I found this framework useful, as it enabled me to group together disparate data units (interviews, media texts, questionnaires and so on).

Gaining information from people watching the parades was my biggest methodological challenge. I wanted this data because one of my theoretical aims was to **'embody'** tourists. Furthermore, spectators are not neutral viewers, as an audience (made up of individuals, groups of friends, partners, families and so on) they occupy multiple and powerful positions in which to sexualize bodies and spaces. Audiences not only have internal differences, they differ nationally. Most of my research was based in Auckland, but I also conducted research in Sydney. The Sydney Mardi Gras Parade became an important backdrop for my understandings of the HERO Parade as it strongly influences the formation and running of the Auckland HERO Parade.

It is worth noting that HERO and the Sydney Mardi Gras are very different from parades in the 'North'. Northern hemisphere parades tend not to be structured around entertainment and difference. They are held during the day and often it is not clear where the spectators end and the paraders begin. HERO and Mardi Gras are intensely structured spatial events with clearly marked borders between paraders and tourists maintained at the roadside through the use of road markings, road barriers or barricades, parade 'officials' and police, as well as self-policing by tourists. This may be one of the reasons that the HERO Parade and the Sydney Mardi Gras are so popular amongst 'straight' tourists, because spectators are physically separated from the gay bodies on parade. The threat of sexualized transgression is, at one level, controlled. The spectators can keep their distance from the Other (Johnston, 2002).

My literature review confirms that:

> It seems that the construction of Pride marches for a straight [tourist] spectator audience is becoming a very important issue for marches in the US and, judging by some footage of Mardi Gras shown on British TV recently, in Australia too (look at who's **watching** the parade).
>
> (Bell and Valentine, 1995: 26, emphasis in original)

I therefore focused my attention on trying to understand the dynamic between spectators and paraders. My interviews had elicited responses such as:

> *Well the parade is basically put on for the straight community when it comes down to it. Like a hundred thousand people there, I don't know, 5000 would be gay? … Ah, so it's for straights and that's fine. I don't think we should have a problem with that at all. We should encourage it.*
>
> (HERO Project Director, 22 September 1995)

Another indicator of the construction of HERO for the 'straight' public is that in 1997 and 1998 the full parade was presented in 'prime-time' on national television. The HERO Parade as public 'product' is now sold to television production companies and can be purchased as a video cassette. The Sydney Mardi Gras is also televised in Australia and marketed in video cassette form. Such products are advertised as tourist souvenirs in Sydney, along with tee shirts, tea towels, key rings and so forth.

With this data informing my research I constructed a questionnaire with the aim of eliciting quantitative and qualitative data on the relationship between sexuality, parades and tourism. I wanted to find out what proportion of spectators defined themselves as heterosexual, bisexual, gay male, lesbian and so on. I also wanted to find out about their experiences of the event. Individuals experience the same event differently. My results, however, indicate a strong emphasis on sameness, which I discuss later in this chapter.

At this point I must confess to having broken many of the questionnaire 'rules'. Most researchers employing questionnaires address issues of reliability (they wish to be able to replicate the results) and validity (the questionnaire must measure what it intended to). My biggest 'error' is my sampling technique, which led to several other 'sampling errors'. I administered the questionnaire in different places (Sydney and Auckland), there was a large disparity in the number of questionnaires completed (Sydney 26, Auckland 118), and I was completely anarchic when approaching potential participants on the street (actually, some practitioners call this 'purposive/non-random sampling', see Parfitt, 1997: 97). I address these 'errors' throughout the chapter in order to highlight the ambiguous alliance between cultural geography and questionnaires.

Queering questionnaires

A research question or aim is necessary before designing a questionnaire in order to structure the nature of the data generated. One of my aims was: 'How and in what ways are gay pride parades constructed as tourist events?' The sample population was the people on the roadside watching the parades. I chose questionnaires as a method to elicit data from spectators based on temporal and spatial factors as well as the number of spectators at each event. Gaining data at parades is a difficult process. They are well suited to participant observation, but not conducive for gaining and conducting interviews. I had considered using a video recorder to conduct short, on the spot (vox pop) interviews. I have ethical and political concerns about this method. In particular, I doubt my ability to offer an explanation for my research, ask for and receive consent from each participant, then conduct a short interview with a video camera, in a very large and tightly packed crowd.

I wanted to understand spectators' motivations for attending the parades. I had spent six weeks working with, interviewing, and conducting participant observation with people involved in setting up, running and participating in the parade. Finding out the identities or subjectivities of the spectators was my research priority on the night of each parade. I wanted to know if the 'collective audience' shared certain characteristics and how this shared collectivity constructed notions of sexuality and of tourism and tourists. My pilot study at the 1995 Coming Out Day Parade had already alerted me to the difficulties of gathering data during a parade. Therefore, I decided to use a very short questionnaire.

Questionnaire design

A questionnaire should be designed with the respondent in mind. For a postal questionnaire an introductory letter can be included. I was face to face with respondents so rather than approach people with letters, I introduced myself to respondents on the street and discussed the research with them, before asking them to fill in the questionnaire form. The questionnaire was printed on university paper, with clear instructions for answering questions. Respondents were told (and read) that the filling out of the questionnaire is voluntary and that anonymity is assured (see Figure 8.2).

Each question should be clear, composed of everyday words and simple sentences, and progress in a logical order. Question wording is crucial so that they cannot be misinterpreted or misunderstood. The order of the questions will make a difference to the way people respond. I drafted a questionnaire, tested and edited it before I used it at Auckland and Sydney. Questions need to be relevant as the selection of the question type affects the type of information gained. For example, double-barrelled questions tend to confuse respondents, as this one might: 'What do you feel about the parade being on Ponsonby Road rather than Queen Street, as it was three years ago? This should be broken down into simpler questions, such as 'What do you feel about the parade?'; 'Can you recall the parade when it was held on Queen Street three years ago?'; 'How do you feel the Queen Street parade compares with the Ponsonby Road parade?'. The language I chose for my questions is based on the context in which the questionnaire was administered. A large crowd gathered together in the small space of the sidewalk for just three or four hours meant that I needed to keep the questions direct and the entire questionnaire short enough to fit on one page. Some general wording rules are detailed in Barrat and Cole (1991); Kitchin and Tate (2000); Mikkelson (1995); and Robson (1993).

There are nine basic types of questions which can be used in a questionnaire which generally are designed to seek descriptive or analytical answers. Descriptive questions tell the researcher 'what' and analytical questions tell the researcher 'why'. These are: quantity or information, category, list or multiple choice, scaling, semantic differential scaling, ranking, complex grid and table, contingency, open ended (Kitchin and Tate, 2000). In my questionnaire (see Figure 8.2), I chose three open questions in order to obtain people's feelings and experiences (questions one to three) and two closed questions in order to obtain people's age and sex (questions four and five), and three semi-open questions on occupation, ethnicity, and sexuality (questions six to eight). The semi-open questions all have options for respondents to write their answer, rather than just circling or ticking boxes. These semi-open questions elicited some surprising data, particularly the ethnicity and sexuality questions.

Most questionnaires use closed questions where the respondent is given a set number of answers, one of which they must choose to be the most representative of their views. Questions that are based on categories, for example: 'How many times have you attended a gay pride parade? First time, twice, 3–5 times, over 5 times' are useful for obtaining 'factual' information. The main advantages of closed questions are that they are usually easy to ask, answer and analyse. They also might indicate a pattern of variation in the sample. By this I mean that if I asked this question at the parades where there was a large

The University of Waikato
Te Whare Wānanga o Waikato
Private Bag 3105, Hamilton, New Zealand.
Fax (07) 856-2158. Telephone (07) 856-2889.

Department of Geography

Questionnaire for People Attending the HERO Parade

The filling in of this questionnaire is **voluntary**. Any information that you give
will be treated as **confidential**. In this questionnaire data is being collected on
the **Auckland HERO Parade as a tourist event**.

1: Do you think this is a tourist event? Yes/No? Why?

*It's Strange, Freak show (a laugh.
If youre striaght*

2: What do you think the parade does for Auckland's image?

Not alot
Good road, now its maed
Brings atmosphere

3: Why have you come to the parade tonight?

have a look.

4: Age: 0-14 ☐ 15-25 ☐ 26-35 ☐ 36-45 ☑ 46-55 ☐
56-65 ☐ 66+ ☐

5: Sex: Female ☐   Male ☑

6: Occupation (please state): *Self employed*

7: Ethnicity: ☐ New Zealand Māori   ☑ New Zealand European/Pākehā
☐ Other European   ☐ Pacific Islander
☐ Other Ethnic Group (please state):_____

8: Sexuality (please state): *hetro*

(For example: heterosexual, bisexual, gay male, lesbian, transgendered.)

often.

MANY THANKS - *Lynda Johnston*

Figure 8.2 *Questionnaire for people attending the HERO parade.*

gathering of gay men or lesbians, I might find that the bulk of the responses occur in the category 'over 5 times'. This pattern is called heaping (Bourgue and Clark, 1992). Questions which ask the respondent to rank, scale or list their feelings or thoughts can be useful. Scales can indicate respondents' negative or positive reactions. The semantic differential scale (Frankfort-Nachmias and Nachmias 1996) is a common form of ranking question. For example, I might consider asking the following question:

'Indicate on the scale below how important you think this parade is for the city:
very unimportant, fairly important, slightly important, neutral, slightly important, fairly important, very important.'

This type of question can be followed with a contingency question which enables the researcher to probe particular issues further. A contingency question, based on my research, might be:

'If you answered 'very important' to question five, how much do you think the city council should spend on this parade?:
Less than $5,000; $5,000–10,000; $10,000–$20,000; $20,000–$30,000; $30,000–$40,000, Over $40,000.'

These types of questions can create skip patterns, where a certain question is skipped depending on the respondent's answer. I agree with Kitchin and Tate (2000: 49) that 'which of these question types you choose to adopt depends upon exactly what you want to know, determined ultimately by your research problem'.

To illustrate these practicalities of question design, I critically examine my own questions. My questionnaire contains three open questions where there are no set answers. Open questions allow for spontaneous responses. They can be, however, more demanding of respondents and open questions take more time to complete than closed questions. Open questions require a specific form of analysis. I use a form of content analysis and a deconstructive textual analysis (Fairclough, 1989).

The first question of my questionnaire was: 'Do you think this is a tourist event? Yes/No? Why?' This question was designed to prompt the respondent into thinking about the parade in the context of being a major tourist attraction. My second question was: 'What do you think the parade does for Auckland's image?' This question was designed to contextualise the event within the city. The third question was: 'Why have you come to the parade tonight?' These questions were purposely broad and left room for immediate responses. My aim was to understand the diversity of people's experience and behaviour and with this in mind I did not want to limit the ways in which people responded in the questionnaire.

The parade questionnaire has five questions that relate to people's identity: age, sex, occupation, ethnicity and sexuality. These profile or personal questions are important to embody the respondents. I did not want to continue the masculinist tradition of disembodied tourist gazers, rather, I was interested in respondents' subjectivities and how that may impact on – and change – their reactions to the paraders and themselves. In my analysis I wanted to establish some connections and/or contradictions between the answers to the first three open questions and the age, sex, ethnicity, occupation and sexuality of each respondent. A tick-the-box system was used for ease of answering closed questions such as age and sex.

Constructing the closed questions proved to be the most difficult part of my questionnaire design. I hesitated at the 'sex' question and considered asking if people were male, female, transgendered? This reflection is based on whether the category of transgender should be understood as a 'sex' question or a 'sexuality' question. Earlier, I had conducted a focus group with transgendered paraders at the HERO workshop. The male to female transgendered respondents indicated that they were more at ease with being understood as heterosexual, rather than being aligned with homosexuality. Many male to female transgendered respondents wanted to be identified as women, and as seeking male partners. One respondent noted that she had more in common with heterosexuals than with homosexuals. I pause on this example because it highlights some contemporary cultural geography debates. There is a danger in the fixing of subjectivities around one component – be it sexuality or sex – as it is clear from my interviews that people who identify as transgendered understand their subjectivities to revolve around *both* sex and sexuality. Queer theorists have been debating these ideas for a number of years. On the one hand gay pride parades are part of gay rights movements which place identity politics at the core of their political intervention. On the other hand, identity categories 'tend to be instruments of regulatory regimes' (Butler, 1993: 308). My research is centred on a poststructuralist understanding of 'subjectivity as precarious, contradictory and in process, constantly being reconstituted in discourse' (Weedon, 1987: 33). I am reluctant to let go of these categories, however, as they can provide the political ground for problematising dominant discourses at gay pride parades, such as heterosexism.

This uncertainty was one of the reasons that I was uneasy about using questionnaires *at all* in my research. Questionnaires are powerful discursive constructions of normative understandings of bodies, gender, sexuality and race. In an effort to subvert normative understandings I use various categories such as: homosexual, gay, queer, lesbian, gay male, and transgender, to indicate that there is no one universal sexualized Other. Furthermore, I also provide a space for respondents to *define* their preferred identity, which elicited responses such as 'dyke', 'intending bisexual (hetero at present)' which were not pre-set categories in my questionnaire. These responses can be understood using poststructuralist theories of identity which purport subjectivities to be fluid, multiple and contingent on place.

Sampling and distribution

One hundred and eighteen questionnaires were completed during the hour and a half before the 1996 HERO parade began. I had three pairs of 'helpers' – six research assistants – distributing questionnaires as well as myself. I preferred 'pairs' to individuals for safety reasons. I felt that there was some danger in approaching people at a parade, especially if those approached were drinking alcohol and/or taking drugs. People were approached, told about my doctoral research, and then asked if they would be willing to fill in a questionnaire. This approach worked extremely well when talking to groups of people. Up to six or seven questionnaires and pencils/pens could be distributed in one group. The respondents completed the form then handed them back after two to four minutes.

This is generally regarded as an unorthodox way to administer questionnaires because of positivist understandings of 'validity' and 'reliablity' (see Kitchin and Tate, 2000 for a description of sampling methods). My sample population had assembled itself at the roadside. My sampling method was based on the assumption that I did not want to employ probability-based statistical methods. Rather I opted for non-probability-based descriptive techniques such as raw counts and proportions, which I discuss later in this chapter.

I also employed my unorthodox (or non-random) sampling method at the 1996 Sydney Mardi Gras. I adjusted my questionnaire so that it reflected questions on and about the Mardi Gras and Sydney but the concepts were the same as for the HERO questionnaire. My friend agreed to help me distribute questionnaires before the parade began. She had, however, an unsafe experience with the first man she approached. The man was under the influence of alcohol and/or drugs. We decided that she would follow me as I distributed the questionnaires. Twenty-six questionnaires were completed in the two hours before the parade began. I was overwhelmed by the huge crowd (approximately 650,000 people) in Sydney and administering questionnaires was much more difficult than at the HERO parades. To begin with, I was unfamiliar with the street layout. I used published gay guides and gay maps as a way of choosing the best research location. Once in position I could barely move because of the layers of people around me, which influenced the number and selection of respondents (only 26). This example highlights one of my sampling errors. Usually, if the selected sample is below 50, then there is a high probability that the sample population will be atypical of the target population (Parfitt, 1997). I am hesitant to 'disregard' this data, however, because I find it useful. As I have already mentioned, both parades are contingent upon each other in terms of their timing, aims, and outcomes. The differences in the data are most evident when I examine the ethnicity question (I discuss this the next section). Fundamentally, however, I believe that 'validity' and 'reliability' are methodological concepts that need to be critically examined – perhaps subverted – as they reduce data to numbers and frequency. The 26 Sydney questionnaires are 'reliable' when the questionnaire data is considered alongside other data (from interviews, media, participant observation and so on).

Analysis

There are various options for the analysis of questionnaires, some of which may be computer based. It may be necessary to code questions. For closed questions it is possible to pre-allocate codes to answers prior to the distribution of the questionnaire. The codes are usually printed on the questionnaire adjacent to each question and aligned to the right. Kitchin and Tate (2000) draw on Bourgue and Clark (1992) to advise that when designing closed and pre-coded questions the researcher should be careful to ensure that the categories offered in each question are exhaustive. If this is not the case, then an 'other' category needs to be utilised. I used this option for my ethnicity question. Respondents were asked to chose from the following categories:

'New Zealand Maori, New Zealand European/Pakeha, Other European, Pacific Islander, Other Ethnic Group (please state)_____'.

Another aspect to consider when using pre-coding for analysis is that categories offered in questions need to be mutually exclusive. The use of a consistent coding method across different questions is worth considering, especially when dealing with large numbers of questionnaires (for example, no = 1, yes = 2, don't know = 3, and so on).

My statistical analysis is 'simply' based on raw counts and proportions. I did not wish to use a statistical computer package such as MINITAB (Ryan and Joiner, 1994), or to understand the basic concepts of probability (Kitchin and Tate, 2000). I employ an analysis that is in keeping with the theoretical aims of my research.

Deconstructive discourse analysis

In this section I blur the boundaries between quantitative and qualitative data. To help understand the responses in the questionnaires I employ a type of deconstructive textual analysis. In this sense, all data that is collected during research becomes text. Discourse analysis is a specific form of text analysis which usually has set patterns. Specific linguistic features may be the focus, for example, vocabulary, grammar, punctuation, turn-taking, types of speech acts, direct and indirect expression.

Discourse analysis includes these 'mechanistic' aspects of text analysis as well as an interpretation of the interaction between text, interpretation of the text and the social context in which the text appears. Textually oriented discourse analysis (Fairclough, 1989) establishes a discursive context in that it can identify social and ideological elements rather than just semantic or linguistic elements.

The discursive context of pride parades is that they are frequently and predominantly understood as protests for equal rights, or equality. David Smith (1994: 49) argues: 'inequality can be thought of as a particular type of difference between people, about which moral questions arise. Social justice is concerned with this sort of difference.' Smith (1994) refers to a specific, socially constructed conception of normal and acceptable behaviour. Young adds:

> *When public morality is committed to principles of equal treatment and equal worth for all persons, public morality requires that judgements about the superiority or inferiority of persons be made on an individual basis according to individual competence.*
>
> (Young, 1990: 134)

In many societies there are broad commitments to equal rights and equal treatment for all persons, whatever their group identification. Young identifies this as a discursive commitment to equality. She states that:

> *racism, sexism, homophobia, ageism, and ableism ... have not disappeared with that commitment, but have gone underground, dwelling in everyday habits and cultural meanings of which people are for the most part unaware.*
>
> (Young, 1990: 124)

Overt group oppression has, in many western societies that are committed to equal rights, resurfaced as liberal humanism (Young, 1990). Liberal humanism treats each person as an individual, ostensibly ignoring differences of race, ethnicity, sex, religion, and sexuality. Structural patterns of group oppression remain and are often unidentified in the rhetoric of equality that liberalism sustains (Young, 1990). Liberal humanism means that the construction of the dominant culture as the norm remains unchanged.

Liberal humanism, or commitments to equal rights for individuals, were evident in the questionnaire responses. Many people at HERO and the Sydney Mardi Gras stated that they thought gay pride parades made Auckland and Sydney 'liberal, contemporary and tolerant' cities. First, I situate these comments within Young's (1990) theory that dominant discourses of equality and liberty create blindness to difference. Second, I argue that within the parade context, heterosexual tourists are positioned as the dominant cultural imperialist group, that is, as unified, unmarked and neutral.

'Tolerant', 'liberal' and 'open-minded'

At the HERO Parade I asked parade watchers: 'What do you think the parade does for Auckland's image?'. At the Sydney Mardi Gras I asked parade watchers the same question in relation to Sydney. Tourists, who identified themselves as heterosexual, responded with words and phrases such as 'tolerant', 'liberal' and 'open-minded'. Some of these responses are included in Table 8.1. These responses can be read as underpinned by a liberal humanist notion that society is composed of individuals who have commitments to their own autonomy, the general idea of liberty, and to the notion that this liberty constitutes the primary social good. Group difference and the lack of liberty for certain group memberships nevertheless continues to exist. Certain dominant groups are privileged and other groups have their liberty consequently compromised (Young, 1990). Insisting that all individuals are equal entails ignoring difference, which has oppressive consequences.

Table 8.1 *Discourses of Liberalism*

Auckland (from 118 questionnaires)

'General acceptance/tolerance'
'Increases tolerance and awareness'
'Open-minded city'
'Cosmopolitan, open-minded, liberal'
'Gives a party/tolerant image'
'Shows broadness of mind'
'It shows that we are more liberal than other cities, progressive and modern'
'It shows that we are open-minded and tolerant city'
'Makes us more open to everyone'
'Makes us more enlightened, open-minded'
'It tells other cities how liberal we are'
'Makes us open to all walks of life'
'Great – shows how open-minded people in Auckland are'
'Shocks people, but encourages open-mindedness'
'Positive – makes people open their minds'
'Shows that Auckland has a liberal population'
'Positive, lively, diverse, tolerant, fun'
'It makes it funnier, it seems more open-minded than other cities'
'The people of Auckland are hopefully more tolerant of others'
'Shows a tolerant attitude towards gays and sexuality'

Sydney (from 26 questionnaires)

'It definitely portrays it as a liberal (in terms of American liberals) city'
'Promotes Sydney as a friendly city and show that gays and lesbians can definitely fit into Hetro [sic] society'

> *Blindness to difference disadvantages groups whose experience, culture and socialized capacities differ from those privileged groups ... The strategy of assimilation aims to bring formerly excluded groups into the mainstream.*
>
> (Young, 1990: 164)

The ideal of a universal humanity without group differences allows privileged groups to ignore their own group specificity.

The 'heterosexual' responses of tolerance, liberalness, and open-mindedness, however, mark the bodies on parade as different and as Other from the dominant and normalized social group, heterosexual tourists. This group seem to have to constantly remind themselves to be 'tolerant' and 'open-minded' in relation to the Other.

The responses also show that there is an unstated 'us' at work here. In Table 8.1, the final comment is: 'gays and lesbians can definitely fit into Hetro [sic] society.' This comment attests to Young's (1990) notion of assimilation. The 'strategy of assimilation always implies coming to the game after it has already begun, after the rules and standards have already been set, and having to prove oneself according to which all will be measured' (Young, 1990: 164). At the HERO Parade and the Sydney Mardi Gras, heterosexual tourists can be identified as the 'game starters'. As cultural imperialists they have the rules and standards by which gays and lesbians are judged. Such judgement rests on the idea that queers have to 'fit' into heterosexual society.

The (un)marked tourist

I have been arguing that the bodies on parade become the marked Other and are deviant from the dominant imperialist group, the tourists. There were several indicators on questionnaires that highlighted heterosexuals' privileged position as 'natural' and 'normal'. One indicator may be found in the propensity of many respondents to misspell 'heterosexual'. The questionnaire had several categories of sexuality to choose from. Of those respondents claiming heterosexual status, the majority circled the heterosexual category. Of the 45 people who wrote the word, 19 (42 per cent) wrote either 'Hetro', or 'Hetrosexual'. One explanation for the misspelling of 'heterosexual' could be found in an examination of Aotearoa/New Zealand and Australian accents. Another explanation, however, is to assume that heterosexuals are not often asked to think about their sexuality, state their sexuality, or spell their category of sexuality. It could be argued that the status of heterosexuality is a taken for granted norm. There is another important methodological point to make here. This type of data and subsequent analysis would have been absent (not textually represented) if I – when administering the questionnaires – had verbally asked each question and written the responses myself. My initial reasoning for asking respondents to fill in their own questionnaire was based on an expectation that I would be able to capture more respondents in the limited time available. By asking respondents to fill in the questionnaire themselves, I was able to get groups of people in one approach. I also wanted to make the data collecting process as 'fuss free' as possible, as I had six other people working on my behalf.

The unmarked tourist appeared in Sydney also. The confusion was not so much over the spelling of heterosexual (although this happened also), but centred on the categorisation of ethnicity. In my questionnaire for the HERO Parade, I relied on categorisation for ethnic groups used in the Aotearoa/New Zealand census. In Australia, the census does not require its citizens to distinguish their ethnicity, but citizens are asked in which country they were born, and if they are Aboriginal. I left the ethnicity question open (please state). Many 'white' Australians did not understand the question. Two people, whilst reading their questionnaires asked each other: 'What's ethnicity'? The other one looked puzzled and then replied: 'Oh, she means 'authenticity'.' People who wrote 'Chinese', 'Asian (Indonesian)', Italian', or 'Indian', did not seem to be troubled by this question. 'White' people, however, wrote 'Australian', 'Aussi' or even 'New South Wales.'

Discourses of celebration

Responses that exemplified support and pride, especially from those tourists who identified as gay, disrupted the notion of the unmarked tourist. Gay tourists can be conceived of as both Self (being subsumed as part of the largely heterosexual audience) and Other (willing to identify as not heterosexual). They may also be conceived as both tourist and host. These respondents tended to embrace and celebrate the parade as part of their identity, rather than attempt to create a conceptual barrier between the paraders and the tourists. Furthermore, there did not seem to be any misunderstandings over questions, gay respondents did not make fun of the questionnaire, and no one misspelt their sexual category (for example lesbian, gay, queer, transgendered, dyke and so on). Some examples of responses to the parades are listed in Table 8.2.

Table 8.2 *Discourses of Celebration*

Auckland:

'To support it and have a look and suss out talent.'
'Promotes Auckland as a gay oriented city.'
'Improves it. Makes Auckland cosmopolitan. Shows that there are many different groups in New Zealand and they should all be represented. Many people are not Christian.'
'To be part of some thing I am and that I don't have to hide behind.'
'Because I am gay and very supportive of the community I live and work in. Living and working in this gayest suburb is very important to me.'
'Fun/diversity of inhabitants.'
'Shows that we are a multi-sexual culture! It helps to show those against us that we are 'normal', from all walks of life and not necessarily stereotypically "queer".'
'It shows that all groups make up the city.'
'To participate in the occasion, do my part to draw attention to our community, and of course, as a social event!'

Sydney:

'Well, well, well, it's a happening fantastic place to be out and proud.'
'It is an event where you can be yourself, express yourself – FREEDOM.'
'Because Mardi Gras is for queers what Xmas is for heterosexuals.'
'To celebrate what I am and to find a man. To have fun and be happy.'
'To grasp the wonderful atmosphere – to be a proud Australian – to be part of a great moment.'

I include my analysis in this chapter as an example of the ways in which questionnaires can be useful both quantitatively and qualitatively. Part of my questionnaire analysis is based on textual oriented discourse analysis because it allows me to bind theory with method. Textually oriented discourse analysis is widely used in cultural geography, in particular, for interview data, media representations and participant observations. It can, as I have illustrated, be extremely useful for questionnaires.

Conclusions

I have discussed the practicalities, possibilities and problems of using questionnaires in cultural geography. Questionnaires are useful for surveying large numbers of people, in a short period of time. I was able to gain an understanding of gay pride parade spectators – their motivations, their beliefs, their identities – by using a one page questionnaire. My discussion of the design and implementation of questionnaires at gay pride parades is ambivalent. I have posed questions about differences, for example sex and sexuality, between respondents rather than about the similarities that conventionally form the basis for categorising and counting.

Typically, geographers have employed quantification to categorise and that process of categorising has involved fixing subjectivities and context in order to stabilise categories for analysis. Early work in geography on sexualities reflects this methodology. Gays and lesbians were counted and mapped. Subjectivities are, however, difficult to 'pin down' and recently geographers have been examining the ways in which people's sexuality are entwined with other forms of subjectivity, such as gender, race and class.

My questionnaire involves some fixing and 'raw counting' of identities. My analysis, however, works to problematise these fixed identities by also employing a deconstructive textually oriented discourse analysis. I made a number of questionnaire sampling 'errors' which would usually discredit the data if positivist understandings of validity and reliability are employed. I found that the data gained from my 'errors' was extremely useful for understanding inconsistencies and contradictions around sexuality and ethnicities. Furthermore, I recognise that my choice of study, and how I study it, reflects my values and beliefs.

Combining questionnaires with interviews and participant observation can provide both the individual and the general perspective on an issue. The research project can be approached from different angles. The data and its analysis, however, need to be intimately related to the theoretical perspectives which steer the project.

The encounter between queer theory and questionnaires suggests that combined 'statistical' and textually oriented data discourse analysis can enrich cultural geography. Whether the aim is to count or to understand the discourse of questionnaires, the ultimate question to ask is 'how does the questionnaire fit the research aim'?

Further reading

Two good places to start reading about sexuality and space are:

- Bell, D. and Valentine, G. (eds) (1995) *Mapping Desire: Geographies of Sexualities*. London, Routledge.
- Blunt, A. and Wills, J. (2000) 'Sexual orientations: geographies of desire.' In *Dissident Geographies: an Introduction to Radical Ideas and Practice*. Harlow, Prentice Hall: 128–66.

Judith Butler's theories of performativity have become increasingly important for researchers who wish to uncover, subvert and transgress normative identities and spaces. For more on gender and sexuality, see:

- Butler, J. (1990) *Gender Trouble: Feminism and Subversion of Identity*, New York, Routledge.

For more on ideas about knowledge as embodied, engendered and embedded in place and space, see:

- Duncan N. (ed.) (1996) *BodySpace: Destablising Geographies of Gender and Sexuality*. London and New York, Routledge.

The following book introduces a range of qualitative and quantitative methodologies and provides step by step procedures for designing and using questionnaires:

- Kitchin, R. and Tate, N. (2000) *Conducting Research into Human Geography*. Harlow, Pearson Education Limited.

For more on questionnaire design and sampling, see:

- Parfitt, J. 1997: 'Questionnaire design and sampling', in Flowerdew, R. and D. Martin (eds) *Methods in Human Geography: A Guide for Students Doing Research Projects*. Harlow, Longman: 76–109.

PART III

Visualising cultural geography

9
Selling America

Advertising, national identity and economic empire in the late nineteenth century

Mona Domosh

It is difficult to imagine a world not filled with advertisements. The images and words of advertising are seemingly everywhere – affixed on buildings and signs, seen and heard on the radio and on television, flashing on our computer screens. Their ubiquity and apparent superficiality have made them objects of scorn by many scholars and culture critics. Advertisements, they argue, fill our minds with unimportant information, litter our landscape, and create an unending search for material wealth. Yet in order to be successful, advertising images and words must draw on motifs and themes familiar to people – otherwise they will hardly elicit reactions, let alone create the impulse to make a purchase. Advertisements are, in this sense, cultural documents, participants in the shaping and reinforcing of public culture. And as a diverse array of scholars have shown (Ewen 1976; Leach 1994; Lears 1994; Marchand 1985), analysis of advertising can tell us a lot about cultural anxieties, desires, and fears; about normative patterns of gendered, racialized and sexualized social relationships; and about the construction of identities – corporate, regional and national. In this chapter I show how to analyze advertisements in order to make sense of an issue of increasing interest to cultural geographers: the relationship between the construction of national **identity**, and the economic geographies of imperialism.

Cultural geographies of nationalism/imperialism

In the now famous words of Benedict Anderson (1991), nations are imagined communities; that is, a nation connotes a group of people who believe and imagine that they belong together even though an individual will never meet more than a tiny fraction of the other members of his/her 'community'. Understanding the politics of nations, therefore, involves much more than studying their geopolitical boundaries; it involves analyzing cultural **discourses**. People believe and imagine that they belong together because they participate in, read, and hear a common set of cultural practices. This national imagination is constantly being made and remade through words, images, music, **performance** – that is, through pageants, patriotic songs, political speeches, holiday rituals, iconic figures, memorialized landscapes. The political geography of nations then is intricately bound up with cultural practices and products.

Understanding how and why certain of these practices and products participate in the making of national identity is no simple matter, yet it is extremely important to do. As Jan Pettman argues, 'nationalism constitutes the nation as above politics, and so disguises the politics of its making. This is the extraordinary *power* of the nation as that thing which people will kill and die for' (1996: 48). In other words, feelings of national identity are what prompt people to act in powerful ways, yet the politics of nationalism – how and for what reasons it has been formed in particular ways – are disguised from common view. The most basic research questions stem from this quest to disclose and make visible the workings of nationalism. Cultural geographers and others investigate the constitution of national identity – how notions of race, class, sexuality and gender are used to set up distinctions between 'us' and 'them' hierarchically, so that 'others' outside the nation are placed lower in the ranking (McClintock 1995; Morin 1998; Nash 1994); they examine the deployment of nationalism – how national identity is reiterated daily, often in the most banal ways (Billig 1995); and they study the relationship of nationalism to landscape – how nationalism both shapes and is reinforced by particular symbolic landscapes and human-environmental practices (Gruffudd 1994; Johnson 1994; Matless 1998).

Imperialism – the imposition of one country on another – is often predicated on a form of nationalism based on 'natural' superiority. The Roman world, for example, distinguished between those 'civilized' people of the Roman nation who spoke Latin, and those living outside of Roman boundaries who spoke other languages – the 'barbarians'. Assumptions of natural superiority provided both the reasons for and legitimation of the conquest of 'barbarians' by the 'civilized' Romans. National identity in nineteenth and early twentieth-century England was based partly around notions developed from evolutionary theory that posited the English people as 'naturally' more evolved and civilized than others living outside its borders; again providing cause for and legitimation of imperial conquest. Understanding the cultural practices and products of national identity formation, therefore, is critical to analyzing imperialism – the actual military or political or economic imposition of one country over another is made possible by and legitimized with a set of cultural ideologies and practices that we call nationalism. Cultural geographers, among others, investigate the ideologies that underlay the complex social relationships between the 'conquerors' and those that are 'conquered' both in colonial settings (Blunt 1999; Kenny 1995; Mills 1999) and in the spaces at the heart of the empire (Driver and Gilbert 1998; Jacobs 1996); the relationship between national identity and imperial discourse (Heffernan 1994; Sparke 1998); and the specific cultural practices that were constitutive of, and in turn shaped by, imperialism, such as photography (Ryan 1997).

Advertising is certainly one such cultural practice. Anne McClintock (1995) has persuasively shown that in the late nineteenth century Great Britain's developing commodity culture and tactics of advertising were both made possible by imperialism, and in turn given meaning through imperial conquest. In other words, many of the commodities of late nineteenth-century industrialism – like soap, for instance – were produced out of raw materials grown in the British colonies, while the commodity itself was given meaning through its association with empire. The coincident emergence of mass advertising was a vital tool in this association, as visual and verbal images that clearly expressed the relationship between being clean and white and English were littered through the pages of popular journals, and plastered on labels that lined grocers' shelves. Advertisements, then, expressed and diffused widely ideologies of imperialism, nationalism, and racism. In late nineteenth-century Britain, as in much of the world today, ads are powerful conveyers of meaning. But how can we go about uncovering those meanings?

Interpreting advertising

I chose to examine advertisements as a primary source of information for several reasons. First and foremost, I am interested in understanding the ideological underpinnings of economic imperialism in the United States in the latter part of the nineteenth century – that is, in the discourses that made the growing internationalism of American companies both acceptable and desirable. Looking at ads allowed me to examine first-hand how companies were representing themselves to consumers, both at home and overseas. Second, the late nineteenth century witnessed the coming of age of the advertising business, and an explosion in the quantity of ads themselves, so there is no shortage of material to examine. And third, based on the work of other scholars, I knew ads were rich sources of information about the past – that is, as cultural documents their interpretations could reveal some of the contours of past ideological configurations. But I still was not certain about how to proceed and I found it very useful to clarify several organizational and theoretical issues *before* I started my analysis in earnest.

For what purpose?

Because of the ubiquitous nature of advertisements, the first critical step in using them as source materials is being very precise about the purpose of the research and which advertisements will be analyzed. Advertisements could conceivably be used, and used differently, in a wide range of research areas: business history, history of technology, cultural history, literary criticism, art history. Even with my specific goal of understanding national identity and imperialism in late nineteenth-century United States, it was still unclear to me exactly which advertisements should be of interest – all ads that draw on patriotic symbols?; all that show racialized 'others'?; ads that are very common versus those that are rare? I decided to focus my study on several case studies. To assess the changes that had occurred in national identity (partly as a result of economic expansion) in the last quarter of the nineteenth century, I decided to focus on the advertising of American companies at two major expositions – the 1876 Centennial Exposition in Philadelphia, and the 1893 World's Columbian Exposition in Chicago. To understand, in-depth, how and why American companies sold products overseas and used this international experience in their advertising at home, I chose five case studies of prominent American international companies. My plan was to examine all the advertisements that I could find for each company, and those that circulated at both Expositions.

Who and what produced them?

Even though I've argued that ads are cultural documents, reflecting broad themes and motifs, it is important to recognize the specificity of advertisements as material products. Certain groups of people under particular conditions and with specific materials produce and distribute them. Understanding the actual historical conditions (the companies that commission them, the advertising agencies, the types of media available at the time, and so on) that produced advertisements provides some basic context for interpreting their meaning. For example, in my research on American commercial expansion in the late nineteenth century, it was of the utmost importance that I recognized that technology was, at the time, just making it possible to print ads in journals instead of on trade cards (so I knew where to look for what ads, when). I also realized that reproducing photographs was not yet feasible, so images were in the form of lithographs (so I didn't confuse technological limitations with aesthetic judgments) and that, historically, styles of ads had shifted from mostly text to image with text (so I was aware that visual images were 'new'). I learned this from reading through general histories of advertising, and from becoming familiar with the historical and cultural context of the time period and place under study. This familiarity with the production, form, and distribution of advertising is a necessary precondition for interpretation.

What do they mean?

The nitty-gritty business of actually analyzing and interpreting advertisements is the most challenging, and the most exciting, part of this type of work. I have found two theoretical frameworks extremely useful as general guidelines in approaching this analysis. First, drawing on the work of social theorist Judith Butler (1993), I understand that advertisements gain their power as cultural products because they are major participants in the iterative nature of cultural meaning. What I mean is that the images and words on ads are meaningful to us because they are drawing on themes and stories, or narratives, that are familiar to most people. Ads, like most (if not all) products of culture gain meaning through their associations to other cultural acts and products; they are in this sense part of an iterative process, repeating though not exactly replicating other stories or statements. For example, the Nike advertising campaign that focuses on the phrase 'Just do it' is successful partly because it plays with a phrase common to most people, but uses it in slightly new ways. If the phrase hadn't already been in common use and hadn't drawn on an implicit link between sex and sport, the ad itself would not have resonated with its audience. Nike is able to exploit this set of associations to suggest the hip-ness of its products and by implication the hip-ness of the person wearing the products – a person who is gutsy, determined, unwavering, and passionate. Advertisements are particularly useful source materials for ascertaining broad cultural trends exactly *because* of their ubiquity – their easy circulation within culture suggests the broad appeal of the narratives from which they draw their themes, and in turn those narratives are reinforced since advertisements are themselves repeated over and over, and distributed widely.

Interpreting the meaning of ads, then, requires fairly in-depth knowledge of cultural context – of the stories and themes that circulate through culture. Yet gaining this in-depth knowledge can be particularly difficult if the researcher is distanced, either through time or space, from the culture under investigation. In my research, for example, I am confronted with words and images on ads that don't necessarily resonate with me – or if they do, I may be drawing on meanings that only make sense today, and were not commonplace in the late nineteenth century. Short of a time machine that could transport us back, we can never completely understand the full range and complexity of ideas, beliefs, values that comprised the lived world of past cultures. But we can do our best to come close. To do so, I draw on the second theoretical framework I wish to highlight the idea of 'thick description', an approach to understanding culture discussed by the anthropologist Clifford Geertz (1973) and illustrated most piquantly as an historical method by Robert Darnton (2000). Geertz argued that the role of the ethnographer was to interpret the various meanings of an action or **representation**, and that to do so required an intimate familiarity with cultural codes and meanings. He used the example of a 'wink of the eye' to make his point. How does an observer know what the wink means? Is the wink simply a rapid contraction of the eyelid, or is it part of a flirtation, or does it indicate two people are involved in some sort of conspiracy or is it meant to deceive people into believing there exists that conspiracy? A thick description of winking would interpret the action within its cultural context, an interpretation therefore that requires knowing the codes of behaviour and understanding the situation in which that behaviour occurred.

In terms of interpreting the meaning of historical advertisements, thick description requires the researcher to be thoroughly immersed in the time and place where that ad circulated in order to provide an adequate interpretation. This familiarity can only be gained through reading social and cultural histories and historical geographies of the period, and through spending time with historical documents. For example, in addition to my reading all I could find about late nineteenth-century America, I found the time-consuming process of looking through late nineteenth-century popular journals, page by page, extremely useful in gleaning a picture of broad cultural trends – what people were thinking about in terms of foreign cultures, health anxieties, fashion concerns, gender relationships, military tactics, and so on. This helped me understand the advertisements that were printed in these journals, and allowed for a more 'thick' interpretation. For example, an advertisement for a new women's corset suggested it was more fashionable, though after scanning the pages of journals I realized that the new fashions were partly a reaction to concerns over the deleterious effects of whale-boned corsets on women's bodies. This ad, therefore, was drawing on the association of the new corset not only to style, but also to cultural concerns about women's bodies. Although thick description is not a methodology in the sense of providing a 'nuts and bolts', step-by-step guide to interpreting past meanings, it does provide an overarching set of guidelines: familiarize yourself as much as possible with social and cultural context; always be aware that one's own meanings may differ from what was circulating in the past; and explore the full range of possible meanings by looking at cultural associations.

Selling civilization

Part of my project to understand the ideologies involved in late nineteenth-century American economic imperialism involves analysis of the promotional strategies and advertising schemes of the major American companies that sold their products overseas during the last quarter of the nineteenth century. As I mentioned earlier, I decided to concentrate my efforts on case studies, and selected five companies (Singer, Heinz, Colgate-Palmolive, Kodak, and McCormick) for analysis. My case studies were chosen from already compiled lists of the corporations most involved in overseas marketing (Rosenberg 1982; Wilkins 1970) based on the criteria of available archival and source material, and the degree to which the corporations were involved in advertising. I am going to concentrate here on my analysis of the advertisements of the Singer Sewing Machine Company, the earliest and largest US-based international company. In my preliminary reading I had found many examples of Singer ads, and decided to start my inquiry with a series of trade cards printed by Singer and given out at the 1893 Chicago World's Fair. These cards depicted people from other countries using the sewing machine and seemed particularly representative of Singer's advertising schemes; they were also widely distributed. To help focus my discussion here, I am going to concentrate on how I went about deciphering the meanings of one of those cards. Figure 9.1 is the front of one of these trade cards, depicting India through an image of men dressed in 'native' costume. Figure 9.2 reveals the flipside of this card, carrying a verbal description of the country underscored by the characteristic printing of The Singer Manufacturing Co. This card was similar to 35 others that formed a series.

Analyzing the text

I started my interpretation with a close analysis of the advertisement itself, looking and reading carefully. Three relatively young-looking men stand and surround one more senior man who sits in front of the Singer. The man is not actively engaged in sewing, though presumably he could be. This certainly is not a candid image, since all the men are looking out toward the viewer, as if posing. Of particular interest to me was that men, not women, were depicted here. In late nineteenth-century America, sewing and sewing machines were associated with women and the domestic sphere, so why did this image associate sewing with men? The text on the reverse side starts with a physical description of India, sounding very similar to a world regional geography textbook or gazetteer, and then moves to a description of the people and their culture. Several phrases struck me as particularly interesting: 'The aboriginal races have no literature'; 'Under British rule India is making rapid strides in modern civilization'; 'The Singer Sewing machine has been a factor in helping the people of India toward a better civilization for nearly twenty years, and thousands of them are in use'. The direct message of these

INDIA.

AN EXTENSIVE EMPIRE OF THE BRITISH CROWN, CONSISTING OF THE GREAT
SOUTHERN PENINSULA OF SOUTHERN ASIA, AND A NARROW STRIP ALONG THE
EAST SIDE OF THE BAY OF BENGAL. IT IS BOUNDED NORTH BY THE HIMA-
LAYA MOUNTAINS, WEST BY A MOUNTAIN RANGE, EAST BY PARALLEL
OFFSHOOTS FROM THE OPPOSITE EXTREMITY OF THE HIMALAYAS, AND ON
THE OTHER SIDE BY THE INDIAN OCEAN. THE SURFACE OF THE COUNTRY IS
EXTREMELY DIVERSIFIED. IT HAS THE HIGHEST MOUNTAIN PEAK (MT. EVER-
EST) IN THE WORLD, THE GANGES RIVER—WONDERFUL FOR ITS ANNUAL INUN-
DATIONS OF THE IMMENSE GANGETIC PLAIN. THERE IS GREAT DIVERSITY
OF RACE AND LANGUAGE; IN UPPER INDIA THE INHABITANTS ARE OF THE
INDO-EUROPEAN STOCK, WITH A LANGUAGE ALLIED IN THE ROOTS TO THE
SANSCRIT. THE RELIGIONS ARE MOHAMMEDANISM AND BRAHMANISM. THE
ABORIGINAL RACES HAVE NO LITERATURE. THE GOVERNING RACES ARE OF
ARABIC, BRAHMANICAL AND PERSIAN STOCK. UNDER BRITISH RULE INDIA IS
MAKING RAPID STRIDES IN MODERN CIVILIZATION. OUR PICTURE REPRESENTS
THE SINGER MANUFACTURING COMPANY'S NATIVE EMPLOYEES IN THEIR
USUAL COSTUME. THE SINGER SEWING MACHINE HAS BEEN A FACTOR IN
HELPING THE PEOPLE OF INDIA TOWARD A BETTER CIVILIZATION FOR NEARLY
TWENTY YEARS, AND THOUSANDS OF THEM ARE IN USE.

THE SINGER MANUFACTURING CO.

Figure 9.1 *Singer Manufacturing Company's trade card, India 1892. Collection of the author.*

Figure 9.2 *The flipside of the India trade card, with a descriptive 'geography' of India. Collection of the author.*

phrases is that Singer machines and British rule are helping people in India progress toward something called 'civilization', and for that reason American consumers (presumably women) should buy these machines. I didn't quite understand the connection – why would American women want to buy a product that was being used by Indian men? In addition, from my early twenty-first-century vantage point, the text struck me as particularly racist, yet the image did not seem particularly so – the men were presented as dignified and almost stately. What was going on here?

Understanding context

I realized that I needed to know more about Singer itself, about the advertising industry at the time, about common advertising motifs, about notions of gender and 'race', about constructions of American identity in relationship to outsiders, and so on. To start, I read whatever secondary sources that I could find about the company and its advertising strategies, and used that information to identify and then locate the majority of its ads. I started a file on Singer, and began a sort of chronological list of developments within the company, and what sort of advertisements it was producing when. I consulted the advertising histories that I had read previously in order to produce a framework for understanding American late nineteenth-century advertising. My goal here was to place this particular trade card within the context of Singer, and of advertising in general. I found two frameworks useful for thinking about American advertising. Jackson Lears (1994) argues that in the late nineteenth-century American 'fables of abundance' (the narratives of advertising) shifted from an emphasis on the farm and stories centring on the yeoman farmer, to the factory and the products of industry used in the home. This was, in part, due to the major shift in the American economy – from one based on agricultural production to industrial production – and due to a concomitant shift in America's sense of nationhood – from a country whose identity was based on westward expansion to one whose new identity was to be based on its position on the world stage. Richard Ohmann (1996) suggests four significant themes that linked consumers to products in the late nineteenth century: health, youth and good looks; family and home; the exaltation of the historically new (modernity), often combined with the traditional; and aspirations to the two highest social classes. I could see where the Singer card fitted into some of these scenarios: it was certainly an image and text that was drawing on 'fables' centred on the benefits and the 'abundance' of industrial products (note the last sentence of the text 'The Singer Sewing Machine has been a factor in helping the people of India toward a better civilization for nearly twenty years, and thousands of them are in use'); and it related to at least one of the four themes – the exaltation of modernity combined with tradition (the sewing machine is presented as the latest in domestic technology, yet it is pictured with men wearing their 'usual costume'). This helped me place the trade card within the general historical shift in the United States from agriculture and westward expansion, to industry and outward expansion; and it provided a way of understanding *how* the card worked, as it linked the Singer machine to modernity, yet kept important ties to the traditional.

At the same time that I was making my way through these advertising cultural and social histories, I continued to research the Singer Company. I discovered, through reading corporate histories, that there was an extensive archival record for Singer that was readily available to researchers. I had little idea what sort of information was actually in the archive, but I wanted to find out as much as possible about the company and its advertising strategies, so I planned a trip and found myself at the State Historical Society of Wisconsin (the Singer Company's records from the mid-nineteenth century until the mid-twentieth century were deposited there). The records were vast, and incredibly detailed. They included extensive correspondence, record books, boxes of ephemera, folders of maps, and so on. Amidst the chaos and excitement of it, I needed to remind myself of my research questions: understanding the ideologies of American economic expansion; figuring out in what ways ideas of gender and race participated in those ideologies; and examining the shifts in American identity that shaped and were shaped by these ideologies and processes. Would examining correspondence between executives of the company (including a person I realized was in charge of marketing) help answer these questions? Would looking at the records of overseas manufacture and sales be the most appropriate way to use my time? Should I focus on information about the company from 1892 and 1893, hoping I would find material about the trade cards? With limited time, I tried my hand at all of these tactics, in a way sampling what the archive contained. I did not answer any of my research questions *per se*, but by scanning letters and records I became more familiar with some of the people involved, with the corporate culture that was being expressed, and with, in general, the complicated processes by which the company grew overseas. Just as important, instead of focusing my analysis, the archive visit made me broaden it. I realized that in order to understand ideologies of late nineteenth-century economic expansion as expressed through advertising, I needed to understand more about the processes of that economic expansion. It wasn't that I was trying to find a more materialist basis for understanding representations (advertising), but that I needed to understand advertising within the frame of other business documents that expressed cultural meaning about American identity and its relationship to 'others' – maps the company had drawn dividing up countries into business 'districts'; book-keeping records that sorted information about foreign countries into very interesting categories; letters between Singer employees overseas. All of these provided intriguing glimpses into how American companies viewed other nations and other peoples and in what ways they would and could sell them products. My study of advertising strategies and advertisements, I realized, would be strengthened if it was presented and analyzed within the context of these other documents. And my more immediate interest in figuring out the meanings of the India trade card was piqued by the information I gathered at the archive. Singer, I found out, had been involved in overseas sales much earlier and to a much greater degree than I had previously thought, and although India was not the largest market, it was a very significant and important one. At the archives I found maps of India with hand-drawn lines indicating Singer 'districts' – regions allocated to one salesman. I scanned letters between Singer employees in India and the head office in New York. I read newsletters published by Singer and aimed at its overseas salesmen. I had a lot of information and many new questions, but I still had not made sense of the trade card itself, nor had I been able to connect the card with ideologies of American economic imperialism.

Making connections

Armed with my new information about Singer, I returned home and to my trade card. I realized that I now had enough (probably too much!) information, and that I needed to put my 'facts' together and start my own interpretation. The men depicted on the image made more sense to me; the text on the back calls them 'native employees' and I now knew that Singer employed thousands of Indian men, some who ran Singer stores in towns, and also many who went door-to-door selling the machines. The other 35 trade cards in the series were similar; most depicted men, and some women, dressed in 'native' costume using the machines, with text on the back explaining that these people were employees of the company. But I was still puzzled over my initial queries: why were (predominantly) men depicted doing activities associated with women, and how was I to interpret the apparent racism of the text? What cultural meanings were being reiterated in these cards? I returned to some of my initial readings about late nineteenth-century America, and about constructions of ideas of gender and race. Gail Bederman's *Manliness and Civilization* (1995) had been one of my inspirations for the project, but now her explanation of what constituted the discourse of civilization in late nineteenth-century America had real meaning for me. I sketched out on paper her explanation of *civilization*, the dominant discourse of late nineteenth-century America, as a narrative that placed human beings in a hierarchy, from savagery (defined as a stage of no gender specialization, indicative of the 'lowest' societies that were non-white) to barbarism (a stage characterized by some gender specialization and primitive agriculture – societies 'on their way' to being 'civilized') to civilization (white, industrialized societies, characterized by complete gender specialization). According to Bederman, middle- and upper-class Americans envisioned world geography and history in these terms, categorizing countries and peoples within this hierarchical relationship. With this as a framework, I looked again at the trade card. Depicting men using a sewing machine, I realized, was an immediate message to American consumers that India was not yet completely civilized. After all, according to the narrative of civilization, gender specialization – with women assigned to the domestic world (i.e. sewing) and men assigned to the public world – was a key indicator of the 'highest' stage of civilization. India, apparently, had not yet reached that stage, but according to the text on the trade card, it was on its way, helped partly by Singer. How was Singer doing this? First, and related to Ohmann's themes, owning and using a Singer machine was considered a 'modern' thing to do; second, using a sewing machine facilitated the production of clothing, another sign of civilization.

This message became clear to me when I contrasted the card with another 1890s advertisement for Singer (Figure 9.3), a photograph with the caption 'The Herald of Civilization – Missionary Work of the Singer Sewing Machine Company. The King of Ou (Caroline Islands) is seated before the 'Great Civilizer''. The men in this image are not even 'properly' clothed. Apparently the people of the Caroline Islands are just in the process of 'discovering' the Singer. I realized that Singer was promoting itself as the 'great civilizer' literally. If, according to Bederman's account of the discourse of civilization, human history and geography was moving inexorably forward to the stage of civilization, that movement could be helped along with the use of the Singer machine. If the people of the Caroline Islands were clearly savages, those of India were on their way to civilization – not yet completely civilized since men are sewing, but more civilized than the shirtless men of Ou. The implied message is that ownership of a Singer machine was both a sign of civilization and a means of obtaining it. By purchasing a Singer, therefore, American women consumers were participants in the process of civilization; they were using a 'modern' contrivance, they were carrying out the domestic duties assigned to women, thereby expressing their 'civilized-ness', and they were using a device that was bringing civilization to others. I realized that the key to interpreting this trade card lay in understanding the discourse of civilization, and in seeing its connections to the rest of the series (each represented a country or region where Singer had sales, and each depiction represented a particular 'stage' on the way to civilization), as well as the other ads for Singer (Singer used the association of its machines to 'civilization' in many of its other advertising schemes).

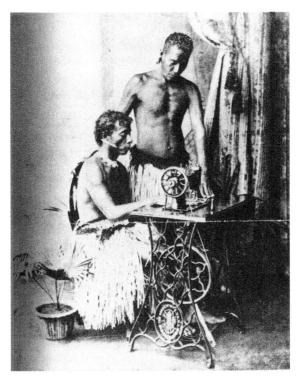

Figure 9.3 *A Singer Manufacturing Company advertisement from the 1890s with the title 'The Herald of Civilization – Missionary Work of the Singer Manufacturing Company'. From Robert Bruce Davies,* Peacefully Working to Conquer the World: Singer Sewing Machines in Foreign Markets, 1854–1920, *New York: Arno Press, 1976.*

Conclusion

Through what I have called a thick description, I was finally able to make sensible links between Singer ads and American national identity and economic imperialism. I concluded that the Singer trade cards were drawing on and reiterating meanings that ran deep in American turn-of-the-century society – that American identity as the 'civilizer' of the world provided motive and legitimation for its economic imperialism, and in turn the international success of its industrial products was itself a sign that the United States was at the top of the hierarchy of civilization. My next task, then, was to see in what ways these connections held true for my other case studies – were Heinz, Colgate-Palmolive, Kodak and McCormick also trying to sell their products by selling 'civilization'? In my research on American economic imperialism and its relationship to national identity, I was able to use advertisements as sources of information based on my theoretical assumption of ads as participants in the iterative nature of cultural meaning, and on an assumption that cultural meaning could be de-coded through the notion of thick description – finding out as much as I could about the cultural codes that provide a framework for deciphering meaning. Familiarizing myself with the advertising industry in general, and with the Singer Company provided necessary guideposts for my interpretation, but the interpretation itself stemmed from my re-reading of the discourse of 'civilization' and its role in legitimizing commercial imperialism. I found the right set of connections.

Advertisements can certainly be used to investigate many substantive research topics, particularly those that relate to the social and cultural construction of consumers and consumer and corporate identities, throughout the world, both today and in the past. And the method of thick description, broadly conceived, can be used as a method for interpreting a wide range of cultural documents – from buildings to television commercials. The most exciting research, I believe, will come from using these methods and sources to continue to break down the boundaries between cultural and economic geography. As Trevor Barnes (2002) has recently reminded us, 'One of the impulses behind the cultural turn in economic geography is to undermine dualities, and the dualism of culture and economy is one that should go.' For example, work that investigates the role of consumption, international marketing, and the making of consumer identities within the larger framework of the discourses of imperialism will add an important layer to our understanding of the gendered and racialized spaces of empire; and conversely interpreting business records, products (such as advertising), and processes as cultural documents will help us understand the deep-seated cultural ideas and frameworks that have made globalization seem both inevitable and desirable.

Further reading

The following books are particularly useful and provocative for pursuing the broad topics outlined above:

- Burke, T. (1996) *Lifebuoy Men, Lux Women: Commodification, Consumption, and Cleanliness in Modern Zimbabwe* Durham, NC, Duke University Press.
- Jacobson, M. F. (2000) *Barbarian Virtues: The United States Encounters Foreign Peoples at Home and Abroad, 1876–1917* New York, Hill and Wang.
- Laird, P.W. (1998) *Advertising Progress: American Business and the Rise of Consumer Marketing* Baltimore, The Johns Hopkins University Press.
- Merish, L. (2000) *Sentimental Materialism: Gender, Commodity Culture, and Nineteenth-Century American Literature* Durham, NC, Duke University Press.
- Reynolds, L. J. and Hunter, G. (eds) (2000) *National Imaginaries, American Identities: The Cultural Work of American Iconography* Princeton, Princeton University Press.
- Wexler, L. (2000) *Tender Violence: Domestic Visions in an Age of US Imperialism* Chapel Hill, University of North Carolina Press.

A TALE OF RESEARCH

The politics of memory in the urban landscape:

London's blue plaques

Caroline Harper

Pinpointing what it was that prompted me to investigate how blue plaques help shape public memory for my undergraduate dissertation is difficult. First, I have a certain fascination with analyzing something that is typically taken-for-granted or deemed insignificant, so as to understand its part in broader socio-cultural processes and the implications this has for society. Second, I love to explore London on foot. Consequently, following a review of literature of the existing research into monuments, statues and memorials and walks in London which brought to my attention some of the city's 1400 official and unofficial 'blue' plaques, I decided to explore the politics of memory, through an analysis of these plaques, in an effort to comprehend how past acts of commemoration shape the memories of present and future society.

Blue plaques, currently the responsibility of English Heritage, are the signs mounted on buildings where distinguished people have lived, or significant historical events taken place, that are known to the 'well-informed passer-by' (Weinreb and Hibbert, 1983: 72). Typically circular in design, with white lettering on a blue background (Figures 9.4 and 9.5), those honoured have to have been dead for at least 20 years. Numerous 'unofficial' plaque schemes also exist, usually controlled by local authorities (Sumeray, 1999). Although the requirements of these schemes do not necessary duplicate those of English Heritage, criteria do overlap considerably indicating that many of these schemes have modelled themselves on blue plaques. It is for this reason that my project referred explicitly to blue plaques, even though London's plaques vary in colour depending on the controlling authority.

Specifically, it was the interplay between memory and social identity and the effect this had on the landscape of the city that intrigued me. Conscious that memorials are 'aimed at the production of a sense of a shared past' (Azaryahu, 1996: 502), but that memory is dependent on a social group's positionality and thus not a collective term and constantly open to conflict and resistance, questions as to who and what is deemed appropriate to memorialize is open to debate (Jackson, 1989). It is therefore inevitable that certain memories are neglected, causing a 'landscape of exclusion' (Sibley, 1995: x) to develop, as certain people are denied public recognition of their interpretations of the past. Therefore, whilst the broader aim of my project investigated whose memories are commemorated in plaques and why, in doing so it was necessary to gain a thorough understanding of the process by which a plaque comes to exist. This was intended to establish who decides which parts of history are officially memorialized and, as a result, who is ignored.

I was keen that my project genuinely contributed something new towards existing research and read extensively in order to identify issues that demanded closer attention. I structured my reading according to areas typically defined as issues of socio-cultural conflict: gender, race and class and, in doing so,

Figures 9.4 and 9.5 *Blue plaques in London*

I noticed that studies investigating disputes within processes of memorialisation tend to focus on the effects on the society of the time. Even where moves have been made to examine long-term implications, such work tends to overstate the divide between 'official' (or dominant and authoritative) cultures and 'vernacular' (or subordinate) cultures. Given that recommendations for blue plaques usually come from the public, with the appropriate authority then responsible for selecting successful applications, the scheme was an ideal means of examining the *interconnections* between official and vernacular cultures in shaping public memory.

Research took a four-stranded approach and focused on specific case-studies, with the intention that these would illustrate the wider picture about plaques in London. Qualitative methods were adopted, with in-depth interviews predominant. These were supplemented by an analysis of secondary data. First, I interviewed plaque authorities. An interview with English Heritage, as the official and original plaque scheme, was crucial to the success of my project. Time constraints, however, meant it was impossible to speak to all those others who had put up a plaque and interviews were held only with the most active groups, as defined by Sumeray's *Discovering London's Plaques*, on the assumption that they had the greatest influence on whose memories are embodied in the landscape. Second, I spoke with individual members of the public and representatives from heritage groups who had proposed plaques to English Heritage and other plaque installing authorities. Adopting a snowballing technique, these contacts came from the authorities responsible for approving these nominations. Thus, and third, to avoid this second round of interviews becoming too narrow, in the sense that organizations were at liberty to provide contacts who reflected their scheme favourably, I also approached heritage groups in general. In this way I intended to put plaques into a wider heritage context, allowing their significance to be compared to, for example, monuments, statues and memorials. In a similar vein, I gathered secondary data such as cartoons, newspaper articles and television documentaries to provide an insight beyond those of heritage organizations to understand the broader significance of plaques and to establish whether they truly influence *public* memory. It was here that the internet proved invaluable. For example, knowing that the blue plaque for Jimi Hendrix had generated mixed reactions, the Internet helped me to gain a better understanding of the controversy, which led to help from the editor of *Jimpress*. Of course, conducting interviews quickly amasses lots of information, which inevitably means the time taken to analyse the data is considerable. This is daunting, particularly when it is difficult to admit that not everything you have taken the time and effort to discover is relevant to your project. I found the easiest way of deciding what I should and should not include was to return to my research questions in order to organise my analysis.

Subsequently, I concluded that the politics of memory is a highly sensitive issue, sometimes sparking intense debate. For instance, a dispute between those who felt 'rock's first blue plaque' to Jimi Hendrix lowered the value of other plaques, especially as it was erected next to one honouring George Handel, and those who considered it appropriate to commemorate such a significant rock idol, made national newspaper headlines in 1997. Broadly speaking, London's plaques present a distorted public memory, skewed towards white males, implying that those memories selected are chosen in order to convey a particular message of domination in space. Moves have been made to correct this imbalance, although sources of contention varied beyond the areas that have been typically defined as issues of socio-cultural conflict. The blue plaque to Radclyffe Hall exemplified this particularly clearly. The house owner, whilst not objecting in principle to a plaque, did not want the word 'lesbian' to appear and so it was agreed the word be omitted. Thus it is apparent that many discourses operate within the landscape, depending on the way in which different people make the world meaningful. That said, in the long term, no one ideology predominates as impressions on the landscape are constantly negotiated as 'relations of dominance and subordination are defined and contested' (Jackson, 1989: 2).

My dissertation was not by any means exhaustive and there are parts that, in hindsight, I would do differently. Despite the fact that I had collected large amounts of data, for example, I discovered black plaques, which remember notorious criminals, only a week before the deadline. Needless to say, these remained unexplored and I think demonstrates that there is no flawless approach to conducting research. It is, however, extremely satisfying to research something entirely of your own choosing and to feel that this can make a valuable contribution to cultural geography more broadly.

I graduated in Geography from Queen Mary, University of London, in 2001, and am currently applying to postgraduate courses in the United States and at University College, London. This will enable me to pursue my interest in socio-cultural geography, focusing on issues of representation within the urban landscape in relation to children and their use of space.

10

Photographs from the edge of Empire[1]

Joan M. Schwartz

'There are sent by mail this day a series of photographic views of various portions of the city.'

So read a handwritten note on the verso of a letter, dated 15 June 1857, from the Mayor of the City of Toronto to the Right Honourable Henry Labouchère, Secretary of State for the Colonies. The photographs were sent to London to accompany Toronto's formal petition to be named capital of Canada. Research has shown that this was the first use of photography by government in Canada for self-promotional purposes. The Toronto portfolio presents an opportunity to consider the relationship between photography, geography, and empire, and, at the same time, explore why and how geographers might look at photographs.[1] When returned to the contexts in which they were originally created, circulated, and viewed, the Toronto city views are revealed to be visual arguments intended to transform a physical place on the edge of empire into a symbolic space linking colonial periphery to metropolitan centre. Sent to help imperial decision-makers envisage the City of Toronto as a colonial capital, these photographs can be seen as part of a larger political process to define the official ties of Empire. In the process of interrogating these photographs and recovering these contexts, the broader conceptual issues and practical methodological considerations involved in using photographs as primary sources in practising cultural geography will be addressed.

Geography, photography, and empire

In his seminal work *Culture and Imperialis*, Edward Said (1994: 7) declared, 'Just as none of us is outside or beyond geography, none of us is completely free from the struggle over geography. That struggle is complex and interesting because it is not only about soldiers and cannons but also about ideas, about forms, about images and imaginings.' In this statement can be found the theoretical links between the theme of this chapter and the broader concerns of this volume: photography, empire, and cultural geography. In pointing to the complexity of the struggle over geography, Said also opened up studies of imperialism to new research questions and new methodological approaches. Whereas imperial history has traditionally been full of soldiers and cannons, explorers and discoveries, bloody battles and quiet rebellions, government administrations and military operations, Said reclaims the cultural dimension through which our relationships to place, and our sense of self and belonging, are shaped and nurtured, reflected and reinforced, confirmed and contested, through 'images and imaginings'. Thus, while photographs *per se* are not a key component of Said's analysis, his statement linking geography and imperialism validates and encourages the incorporation of photographic sources into mainstream research agendas in cultural geography.

The longstanding relationship between photography and empire is, as Said suggested, both complex and interesting. When first made practicable in the mid-nineteenth century, photography was not simply a new means of making pictures; it was a new mode of encountering the world. Increasingly simple and popular as the age of imperialism progressed, the new medium was employed in a variety of ways to establish imperial control, extend imperial authority, reinforce imperial **power**, survey imperial possessions, demonstrate imperial connections, and articulate imperial **identity**. It was used not only by British, but also by French and American interests – government and private, political and economic, military and intellectual – to appropriate new territory and push back geographical frontiers. Photographs were spaces where facts, in visual form, were stored and communicated, ordered and conceptualized, reconstituted and transformed by an imperial **gaze** into the myths and metaphors of place and identity. As such, they demand a place in the practice of cultural geography in general and in the study of empire in particular.

Concept Box

Gaze

Ideas about the gaze are inherently spatial, suggesting a distance between the observer and what is being observed and often involving different strategies of bounding or enframing what is seen. In an attempt to challenge a masterful gaze of detached authority (the 'master-of-all-I-survey' or the 'god-trick' that is the focus of Donna Haraway's (1991) critique of **situated knowledge**), cultural and feminist geographers increasingly seek to situate the gaze, observation, and the production of knowledge. This more critical engagement with the gaze seeks to destabilize the privileged position of the observer that works, in part, by objectifying who or what is being observed. Many feminists have challenged a masculinist and heterosexist gaze that objectifies women. Feminist work in film theory and art history – often informed by psychoanalysis – has been particularly important in embodying the gaze, spectatorship, the observer and the subject of observation. Within geography, Gillian Rose has critiqued the heterosexist masculinism of a cultural geographical gaze on landscape. She writes that 'pleasure in the landscape is often seen as a threat to the scientific gaze, and it is argued that the geographer should not allow himself to be seduced by what he sees' (1993: 72). As she continues, 'cultural geography's erotics of knowledge' (1993: 109) is enacted by a voyeuristic, distanced and disembodied gaze on the feminized landscape. In her more recent book, Rose (2001) shows how feminists and other scholars have challenged the **power** of a masculinist and heterosexist gaze in practice.

Key reading
- Rose, G. (1993) *Feminism and Geography: The Limits of Geographical Knowledge*. Cambridge, Polity.
- Rose, G. (2001) *Visual Methodologies*. London, Sage.

Existing literature on photography and empire

The existing English-language literature on the theme of empire, the British Empire in particular, is extensive and encompasses work in a variety of academic disciplines. While historians, foremost among them John MacKenzie (2001) (whose name has become synonymous with writing on British imperial cultural and environmental history), traditionally paved the way, more recently scholars with diverse interests in imperialism have responded to the challenges of postcolonial theory and the crisis of **representation**. And while studies of British imperialism predominate, European imperialism more generally has been examined in terms of current concerns for the relationship between power and knowledge. Imperialism on the North American continent has been a chequered past of Spanish, French, Russian, and British possessions, and a two-edged American policy with adherence to the Monroe Doctrine limiting European incursions on the one hand and a belief in Manifest Destiny sanctioning continental expansion on the other. William Goetzmann's (1966) *Exploration and Empire*, Mary Louise Pratt's (1992) *Imperial Eyes*, and Anne McClintock's (1995) *Imperial Leather* all raise issues of fundamental concern to geographers: territorial expansion, travel writing, and domestic space.

Drawn deeply into the imperial fray, cultural geographers have contributed to this growing corpus of writing through explorations of a range of topics relating to the geographical reach of imperial expansion and the spatial dimensions of imperial authority. Alison Blunt's work on spatial **discourses** of home and empire, and the gendered spatiality of imperial travel, has focused on British women in Africa and India. Important collections of essays edited by Morag Bell *et al.* (1995) and by Anne Godlewska and Neil Smith (1994) have examined the relationship between geography and empire using a variety of representations and touching upon a range of debates. *Imperial Cities: Landscape, display and identity*, edited by Felix Driver and David Gilbert (1999), explores the influence of imperialism on the landscapes of modern European cities.

With the visual turn in the social sciences, studies of imperialism turned to images as tools of empire and, reciprocally, instruments of colonialism. Such studies of empire bump up against academic concerns for representation across a range of academic disciplines, and the role of photography in imperialism, colonialism, and nationalism has begun to be investigated within the fields of history, geography, art history, visual anthropology, cultural studies, women's studies, and literature. Resonant with Said's stress on ideas and forms, images and imaginings, scholars have turned to these spaces and tools of empire – in particular, the home, the exhibition, the map, the travel account, and the archive. While Thomas Richards (1993), writing about the imperial archive of nineteenth-century Britain, makes no mention of photographs, it is clear that photography was enlisted as a communication tool by which to overcome the immense challenge of administering the empire through 'control at a distance'. If, as Richards claims, 'the narratives of the late nineteenth century are full of fantasies about an empire united not by force but by information', then photographs were an integral part of those narratives, offering information and conveying messages in visual form.

With a primary interest in photographic images or their makers, museum curators and photographic historians – most notably Ray Desmond, Arthur Ollman, Clark Worswick, John Falconer, and Roger Taylor – pioneered research on photography and empire through articles, monographs, and exhibition catalogues, especially on photography in British India. For example, in a monograph on Samuel Bourne, Ollman (1983: 8) boldly asserted that 'the British awareness of what was contained within the confines of the Empire was often tied closely to the photographic evidence they saw.' Since then, interest in the theme of photography and empire has developed in two quite separate professional spheres: the curatorial and the academic. Where curator scholars have often looked to theories of post-colonialism and representation after being drawn to the aesthetic qualities of the images in their care, academic researchers have more often been attracted to photographs by their primary theoretical interest in the role of (visual) representation in the power/knowledge nexus. Increasingly, however, these two spheres of scholarship are coming together in serious efforts to place aesthetic qualities in socio-historical context, achieving a rich balance between empirical and theoretical approaches, visual and textual source materials, and curatorial and academic perspectives. Nevertheless, as academic interest in the theme of photography and empire increases, exhibition catalogues constitute the single most important secondary source for study. In the most sustained academic study of photography and imperialism to date, the geographer James Ryan (1997) explores photography and the visualization of the British Empire. Focusing on travel and exploration, military campaigning, hunting and native peoples, Ryan considers the ways in which photographic practices and aesthetics expressed and articulated ideologies of British imperialism. And nowhere is the theme of British imperialism more obvious than in the efforts of the Colonial Office Visual Instruction Committee which 'developed an Empire-wide scheme of lantern-slide lectures and illustrated textbooks to instruct, first, the children of Britain about their Empire and, second, the children of the Empire about the "Mother Country" ' (Ryan 1997: 186).

Much of the literature on empire has addressed the ways in which the metropolitan centre visualized, administered, and maintained the colonial periphery. Yet not all parts of empire have commanded equal scholarly attention. Academic interest in British imperialism, for example, has concentrated primarily on British interests in India and Africa, and even in Ryan's extended examination of photography and empire, Britain's less exotic white settler colonies receive scant attention. Interest has also tended to focus on the way in which Britain visualized its empire – through a variety of written, visual, and physical representations (see, for example, Duncan and Gregory 1999; Edney 1997). Far less attention has been paid to the ways in which the colonial periphery – in particular the colonies of Canada, New Zealand, and Australia which rose to prominence and developed into modern nations within the photographic era – imagined, constructed, and articulated their notions of, and ties to, Empire (for example Greenhalgh 1988; Rydell 1984). Thus, whereas scholars have tended to investigate the impact of imperialism, not only on colonial identity but also on the face of modern Europe, their concerns for the influence of imperialism on cultural and political identity suggest a corollary in studies of imperial identity on the edge of empire: how, for example, were ties to empire constructed, expressed, and maintained?

This chapter traces the ties of empire in the other direction: from colonial periphery to metropolitan centre. It explores the photograph as a primary source in geographical inquiry through an examination of the way in which the political aspirations of the City of Toronto to be a colonial capital of the British Empire were articulated through a portfolio of photographs included with the documentation supporting Toronto's claim. The larger 'seat-of-government question' and its resolution have been explored in detail by David Knight (1991). His study examines the political, cultural, and regional tensions involved in the choice of Canada's capital through original maps, newspaper editorials, legislative debates, official papers, and private letters, but he refers only in passing to the Toronto photographs to demonstrate the 'hierarchical nature of Colonial Office decision making' (Knight 1991: 202). This research, then, extends Knight's work by adding the photographic dimension to the documentary mix, and in the process, sheds light on the use of photographic sources, as well as on the role of images and imaginings, in practising cultural geography.

The photograph in cultural geography

While doing research in the Foreign and Commonwealth Office Library in London, I came across a portfolio of 25 prints of Toronto, mounted on card and stamped on the verso, 'Armstrong, Beere & Hime, Civil Engineers, Draughtsmen and Photographists'. Here were views that had only been known through references to them in government reports, newspaper accounts, and secondary sources: a handwritten note about 'a series of photographic views of various parts of the city'; a mention that 'Messrs Armstrong, Beere & Hime are at present engaged in taking a series of Photographic views of the principal streets, public buildings &c in Toronto'; and evidence that Toronto City Council authorized payment of £60 for 'One Hundred Views of Toronto by Armstrong, Beere and Hime'. Here was a significant body of early photography which was not mentioned in the first major history of photography in Canada published in 1965, nor in the revised edition which appeared almost 15 years later. From my 'discovery' of this set of 25 prints in the Foreign and Commonwealth Office Library, I concluded that the 'one hundred views' consisted of four copies of the portfolio. An interesting research question presented itself: what could an examination of these photographs, sent to London to accompany Toronto's petition to become capital of Canada, tell me about colonial dreams and imperial realities? Furthermore, how, as a geographer, should I interrogate them, and what role were they expected to play?

Why we look at photographs and how we look at photographs is contingent upon disciplinary assumptions and priorities, and critical engagement with the photograph requires clarification of what it is we are looking for when we, as cultural geographers, study photographs. Photographs are, of course, first and foremost, visual images, and like other pictures they cannot be understood apart from their visual qualities and their adherence to prevailing pictorial conventions. Nor can they be investigated without due regard for their accuracy and selectivity. However, geographers are not primarily concerned with aesthetic quality, or pictorial status, or immanent genius, although all these factors certainly bear close attention for the ways in which they were received, and influenced perceptions of landscape and identity. Rather, we are concerned with the ways in which the photograph expressed and mediated, reflected and constituted ideas about people, place, and the relationship between them. Because research priorities in geographical inquiry are different from those of other scholarly pursuits, and because photographs acquire and generate meaning, simultaneously, in a variety of ways, analysis of photographs in cultural geography must proceed from, build upon, combine, or ignore – as appropriate – existing methods of critical engagement which examine the photograph as image, object, artefact, text, and commodity, and which study the factors that shaped the way they look. It must also address assumptions about place on the one hand, and about photographs on the other, assumptions which have undergone a profound shift as a result of the problematization of foundational beliefs about 'truth' and 'reality'. At the same time that landscape ceased to be 'anything and everything seen from the top of a hill' (Taylor, 1990: 177), the photograph lost its claims to truth and objectivity. With the postmodern turn geographical approaches to landscape interpretation changed, and with the visual turn images became heavily implicated in the processes by which space on the ground is transformed into place in the mind. As a consequence, the way in which cultural geographers view material reality through historical photographs must shift accordingly, from a search for facts to an analysis of meaning and an exploration of agency.

This chapter is not a search for the 'truth' of these images; nor is it an attempt to bring about closure of meaning. Rather, by seeking to comprehend this portfolio in terms of what it was *of*, what it was *about*, and what it was intended *to do*, it seeks the meanings that swirled around and through it in search of a clearer and fuller understanding of time and place, landscape and identity, image and reality. It returns the content of the portfolio to the historical, technological, and documentary contexts in which it was created, circulated, and viewed, to show how photographs functioned as both tools of description and devices of inscription, to reflect and constitute notions of place and identity. It looks beyond their indexicality to consider their instrumentality, being careful to distinguish between authorial intention and audience impact. It views the photographic record as the product of human choices over subject, composition, and lighting, process, format, size and style, the form and trajectory of circulation, the target audience and circumstances of viewing. In so doing, it suggests that historically specific technological and cultural parameters – pictorial conventions, public taste, and the pre-texts of viewing; prevailing geographical knowledge and imaginative geographies; notions of what was appropriate or desirable to photograph – determined what could and could not be photographed, privileged some subjects and marginalized or excluded others, and influenced the creation and preservation of the photographic record. Ultimately, it suggests that cultural geographers can profitably engage photographs as primary sources because they have been and continue to be an integral and influential part of the way we have come to know the world, situate ourselves in it, and articulate our relationship to it.

The content of the Toronto memorial portfolio

The series of photographs which accompanied the Toronto Memorial consisted of 25 albumen prints from wet collodion negatives: three multiple-plate panoramas and 13 individual prints. The photographs were most likely taken between early November 1856 when the roof of the Rossin House Hotel in Toronto was completed and the late winter of 1856–57 when a notice in the *Daily Globe* in early February announced that 'Messrs. Armstrong, Beere and Hime are at present engaged in taking a series of photographic views of the principal streets, public buildings &c in Toronto'.[2] Two of the photographs – King Street East and King Street West – are inscribed 'Winter 1856' (Figure 10.1). The three panoramas – in five, four and three parts respectively – connect to form an almost-360° view of Toronto from the top of the newly completed Rossin House Hotel (Figure 10.2), located at a major intersection in the city's central business district. In the individual prints that form these panoramas (Figures 10.3 and 10.4), houses, businesses, and factories occupy the foreground, streets lined with newly planted trees criss-cross the downtown, church spires pierce the horizon. Osgoode Hall, home of the Law Society of Upper Canada, the Normal School, Trinity College with its Church of England affiliation (Figure 10.5), and the Rossin House Hotel, described as 'the first Hotel in Toronto which could make any boast of architectural beauty',[3] were singled out for individual attention. The Exchange, the Bank of British North America (Figure 10.6), and other buildings celebrated the city's economic well-being, demonstrated its urban development, and exhibited its architectural sophistication. The identification of individual buildings declared the function of the structure; here are views representing law, government, church, and institutions of banking and higher learning. The view of the Parliament Buildings (Figure 10.7) had direct bearing upon the reference in the Toronto memorial to the fact that 'buildings amply sufficient for [Government] wants are already erected and occupied, representing an immediate saving of at least half-a-million of money, an item of no small consequence to a colony whose debt in proportion to its revenue already exceeds that of the mother country' (Knight ,1991: 217). In a three-part panorama looking directly south to Lake Ontario (see Figure 10.3), a train in the middle distance and Toronto Bay beyond suggest the water and rail links described in the memorial as key to commerce and defence.

This was not the first time that visual images had been enlisted to display the merits of Toronto's built environment to an imperial readership. Six months earlier, these same buildings had figured prominently in a four-page pictorial supplement published by the Toronto *Globe* to accompany an article entitled 'An Account of the Rise, Progress, and present Position of Toronto' (see Figure 10.8). Praised as 'well fitted for an extensive circulation in Great Britain',[4] the supplement contained more than a dozen specially prepared wood-cuts intended to demonstrate 'to our British friends, that Canada is not all in that primitive condition'.[5] At the very time that the seat-of-government issue was coming to a head, the London *Builder* of 7 March 1857 responded:

Although quite aware that those who went to Canada under the idea that they had little else than log huts to see, even in its cities and towns, were destined to find themselves rather pleasantly surprised when made conscious of their mistake, we really were not prepared to find Toronto so well worthy to be regarded as a city, and a capital, as it appears to be, if this pictorial illustration of its more important edifices be correct. Some of these are really handsome structures, and the dimensions of others are quite extraordinary for such a city.[6]

Figure 10.1 King Street West, Toronto, C.W., Winter 1856; photograph by Armstrong, Beere & Hime, courtesy of National Archives of Canada, PA-186729.

Figure 10.2 Rosssin House Hotel, Toronto, C.W., Winter 1856–57; photograph by Armstrong, Beere & Hime, courtesy of National Archives of Canada, PA-186727.

Figure 10.3 *3-part panoramic view looking south from top of the Rossin House Hotel, Toronto, C.W., 1856–57; photograph by Armstrong, Beere & Hime, courtesy of National Archives of Canada, PA-186715.*

Figure 10.4 *5-part panoramic view extending from York Street to King Street East from the top of the Rossin House Hotel, Toronto, C.W., 1856–57; photograph by Armstrong, Beere & Hime, courtesy of National Archives of Canada, PA-186733.*

Figure 10.5 *Trinity College, Toronto, C.W., 1856–57; photograph by Armstrong, Beere & Hime, courtesy of National Archives of Canada, PA-186731.*

Figure 10.6 *Bank of British North America, Toronto, C.W., 1856–57; photograph by Armstrong, Beere & Hime, courtesy of National Archives of Canada, PA-186740.*

Figure 10.7 *Parliament Buildings (front), Toronto, C.W., 1856–57; photograph by Armstrong, Beere & Hime, courtesy of National Archives of Canada, PA-186726.*

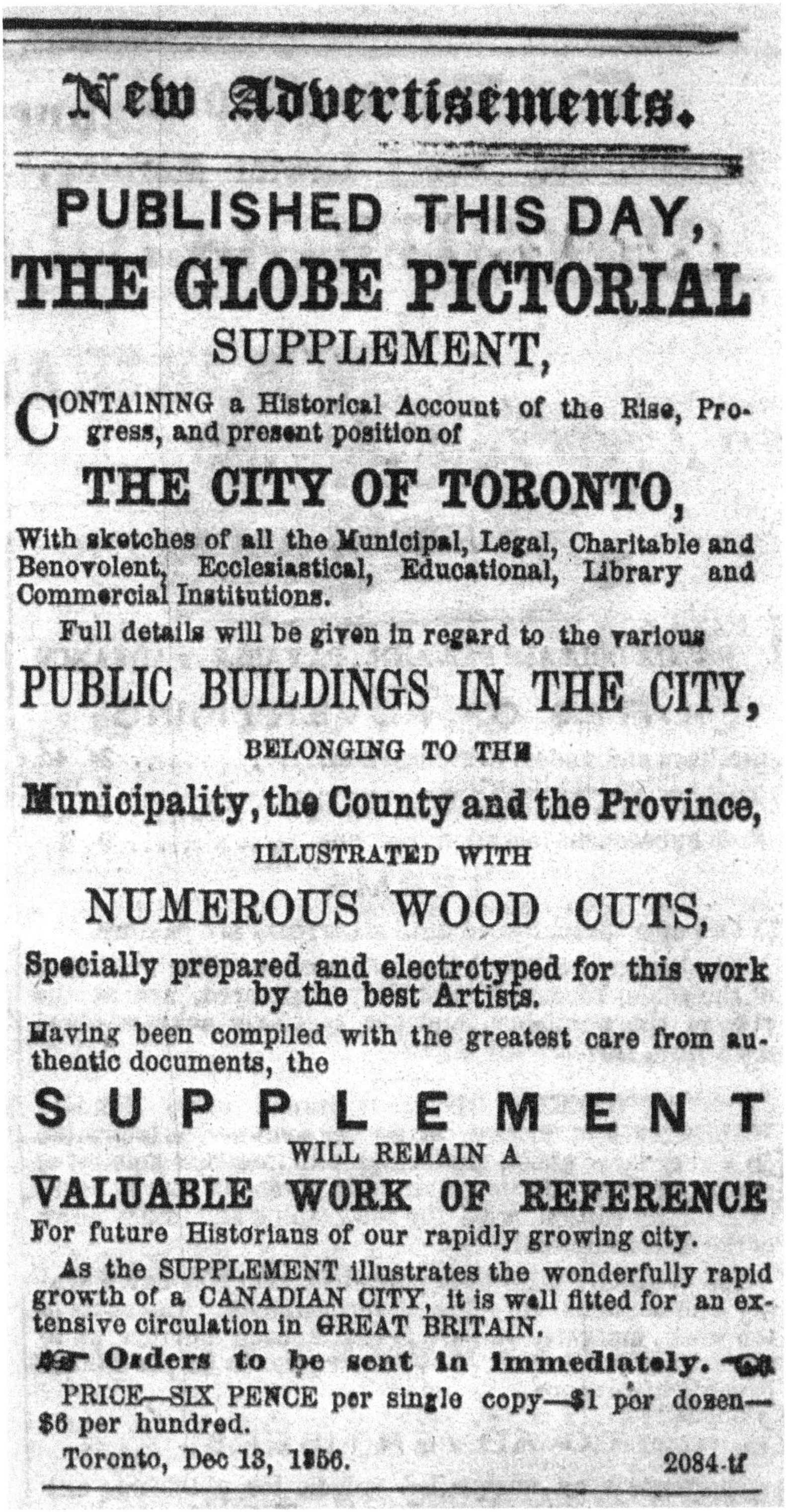

New Advertisements.

PUBLISHED THIS DAY,

THE GLOBE PICTORIAL

SUPPLEMENT,

CONTAINING a Historical Account of the Rise, Progress, and present position of

THE CITY OF TORONTO,

With sketches of all the Municipal, Legal, Charitable and Benovolent, Ecclesiastical, Educational, Library and Commercial Institutions.

Full details will be given in regard to the various

PUBLIC BUILDINGS IN THE CITY,

BELONGING TO THE

Municipality, the County and the Province,

ILLUSTRATED WITH

NUMEROUS WOOD CUTS,

Specially prepared and electrotyped for this work by the best Artists.

Having been compiled with the greatest care from authentic documents, the

S U P P L E M E N T

WILL REMAIN A

VALUABLE WORK OF REFERENCE

For future Historians of our rapidly growing city.

As the SUPPLEMENT illustrates the wonderfully rapid growth of a CANADIAN CITY, it is well fitted for an extensive circulation in GREAT BRITAIN.

☞ Orders to be sent in immediately. ☜

PRICE—SIX PENCE per single copy—$1 per dozen—$6 per hundred.

Toronto, Dec 13, 1856. 2084-tf

Figure 10.8 *Advertisement for the* Globe *'Pictorial Supplement', 13 December 1856, courtesy of National Library of Canada, NL-453.*

Unlike the woodcuts which clearly betrayed manual intervention by an artist, the Armstrong, Beere, & Hime photographs were believed to carry the authority of visual truth produced by a mechanical recording device and scientific optical-chemical transformations. Enlisted by the City for promotional purposes, Armstrong, Beere & Hime's views trumpeted the architectural merit of Toronto's public buildings and declared the city's suitability as capital of the Province of Canada.

The Toronto portfolio in historical context

Canada – the largest red expanse occupying space on that icon of the British Empire, the Imperial Federation Map of the World Showing the Extent of the British Empire in 1886 – was a product of both the Victorian and photographic eras. Indeed, modern geographical and political ideas about Canada were born at precisely the same time that photography stepped onto the world stage. Lord Durham's report, which led to the Union of the Canadas and the establishment of responsible government, was presented to the British Parliament in February 1839, only three weeks after news of Louis Jacques Mandé Daguerre's invention had been presented to the Académie des Sciences in Paris and just ten days before William Henry Fox Talbot announced his process for photogenic drawing to the Royal Institution in London. Thus, developments in British North America shared intellectual space, legislative energies, and public attention with the invention of photography and the evolution of modern geography as exploration, settlement, urbanization, and industrialization largely proceeded under the watchful eye of the camera. Photographs were part of the process of transplanting old identities and establishing new ones. Building upon the visual foundation laid by British explorer-artists and military topographers, they helped Empire to visualize colony, and colony to develop into nation. The political stage upon which the story of these photographs unfolds consisted, at the time, of Canada East (formerly Lower Canada and now the southern part of Quebec), which straddled the St. Lawrence River, and Canada West (formerly Upper Canada and now the southern part of Ontario), which extended from the Ottawa River to the shores of Lake Superior. According to the census of 1851, Canada East had a population of just over 890,000, the majority of which were French-speaking and Catholic; the population of Canada West was 952,000, the majority of which were English-speaking and Protestant. Prior to 1841, the two political units each had its own capital; however, after 1841, the two Canadas – united politically, fairly equal demographically, but deeply divided over linguistic and religious lines – became a British possession with a single legislative parliamentary system, making it necessary to designate a single seat of government.

The capital function was situated temporarily in Kingston in 1841, then moved to Montreal in 1844. But in 1849 – as a result of political unrest, an attack on the Governor-General, public demonstrations, and a disastrous fire which destroyed the Parliament buildings – a 'perambulating system' was instituted, rotating the seat of government every four years between Toronto and Quebec City. However, the system proved both expensive to operate and inefficient to administer, causing chronic political frustration and regional friction. Sir Edmund Head, the Governor-General of Canada, called it a 'constant source of heart-burning and local jealousy' (Knight, 1991: 196) and a 'stimulant to the hatred of race and the conflict of religious feeling (Knight, 1991: 250). By 1857, a stalemate was reached in the Canadian parliament over the seat-of-government question. Finally, on 24 March 1857, after years of heated debate had failed to settle the issue, a resolution was narrowly accepted by the Legislative Assembly of Canada that Her Majesty, Queen Victoria, be requested to exercise the Royal Prerogative in the selection of a permanent site for the seat of the government. The Times of London called the Queen's task of deciding between the rival claims 'one of the most interesting and poetical duties of the empire' (Knight, 1991: 197). The mayors of five cities were invited by Governor-General Sir Edmund Head to furnish Her Majesty's Secretary of State for the Colonies with a statement of their claim to be named permanent seat-of-government for the Province of Canada. Written submissions – or Memorials – were received from Quebec City, Montreal, Ottawa, Kingston, and Toronto. An uninvited petition was received from Hamilton urging the Queen to refer the question back to the people of Canada. Unsolicited memorials were also submitted from Sarnia and Belleville in support of Kingston's claim. Three of the written memorials were accompanied by a map. Only the Toronto memorial included photographs.

The Toronto portfolio in technological context

By the winter of 1856–57, when Armstrong, Beere & Hime were reported to be busy taking their views of Toronto's principal streets and public buildings, photography was a deliberate, costly, and time-consuming practice. The wet collodion process they employed required access to a darkroom in order to prepare and develop photographic negatives immediately before and after exposure in the camera. Outdoor photography required that hundreds of pounds of equipment, large quantities of chemicals and water, and heavy crates of glass plates had to be carried around, unpacked, and repacked at each location. Slow emulsions made it difficult to take photographs in low light levels; indoor photography was only possible with the use of skylights, and only later with magnesium flash powder. The stiff poses and dour expressions in studio portraits were the result of visual convention on the one hand, and practical necessity on the other, as posing stands and head clamps were used to keep sitters still; children were often only photographed when the sun was highest in order to take advantage of the shortest exposure time. Slow emulsions and long exposure times also precluded most action photography, and while 'instantaneous' photographs were possible with certain lenses and under certain conditions, for the most part, anything that would not or could not remain motionless for the duration of a several-second exposure was registered as a blur, if recorded at all; as a consequence, Armstrong, Beere & Hime's bustling thoroughfares were transformed into empty streetscenes as pedestrians and carts left only ghostly traces. In addition, their glass negatives, once prepared, had to be contact-printed. Large prints required large negatives, and large negatives necessitated the use of large, cumbersome cameras. Photographers were, thus, compelled to be efficient and deliberate in composing and exposing their negatives in order to maximize the use of each exposed plate. All these factors combined to make the act of taking a photograph a conscious, carefully considered, and pre-meditated decision to record.

Any surviving photographic record must, therefore, be assessed against the changing context of what was 'photographable' – that is, what could and could not be photographed. This requires familiarity with the chronology of cameras and processes in order to appreciate the limitations of photographic technology, assess their implications for the production of photographic images, and comprehend how size, texture, colour, format, and presentation are integral to the way photographs speak to us as evidence. What *was* photographed can then be understood in terms of human choices. Only then can we inquire how the photographic record, and erasures from it, reflect socially or culturally prescribed, preferred, and proscribed applications; how geography, gender, class, and ethnicity influenced the production and consumption of photographs; how the privileging or marginalization of subject matter can provide insights into authorial intention or market taste; how the meaning of photographs was linked to the practices of production, the means of dissemination, and the circumstances of viewing; and how written and unwritten rules governed the role of photography as a medium, the role of the photographer in society, and the role of the photograph as image or information. At yet another level, the photographs were, in themselves, an argument about modernity and progress. Paper photography in Toronto was but in its infancy in 1857 (Koltun, 1978). Made practicable at a time when vision and knowledge came to be inextricably linked, the new medium was embraced as a means of observing, describing, studying, collecting, classifying, and thereby knowing the world. Made popular at a time when mechanization was a sign of progress and light was a symbol of the Divine, the photograph boasted mechanical and optical origins, carried scientific credentials, promised exact reproducibility, and communicated visual truth. Along with steam power and the telegraph, photography was considered one of the most important discoveries of the age. Its very use by Toronto's civic officials was surely proof of their progressive outlook.

The Toronto portfolio in documentary context

Photographs do not circulate as pure images nor are they viewed in material isolation; rather, their trajectories are framed by a larger documentary universe which may consist of any or all of other photographs, other kinds of images, numbers, words, and material objects which, separately and in concert, frame the meanings they generate. The Toronto portfolio must, therefore, be understood in terms of its immediate documentary context. The Toronto memorial took the form of a letter from the Mayor of Toronto to the Secretary of State for the Colonies. The arguments set out in the Mayor's letter revolved around location, commerce, and defence. Population and distance figures were called upon to prove that Toronto was, or soon would be, 'the centre, not only of the greatest wealth, but of the greatest number of inhabitants' (Knight, 1991: 212) and claimed that 'both as regards population and territorial extent, this city occupies a more central position than any other city named as likely to be selected for the seat of Government' (Knight, 1991: 214). Average earnings per mile for railways east and west of Toronto, and Trade and Navigation Returns for goods passing through the St. Lawrence canals were cited to demonstrate the 'westward tendency of wealth'. A memorandum from John Naylor, a London actuary, analysing census figures for Upper and Lower Canada between 1825 and 1851, was submitted in support of Toronto's demographic claims. The Toronto memorial conceded that Quebec was the obvious choice *if* the decision were based solely upon military position, but suggested that 'it would be unreasonable to allow such a contingency to override the convenience of the whole country …'. It went on to cite lake and rail access to bolster Toronto's military position as best capable of defence after Quebec and in comparison with the other cities under consideration.

A map accompanied the Toronto memorial to buttress the text and demonstrate the strength of Toronto as a hub of railway activity: 'Toronto is the only point upon which several railways converge, it already being the centre of no less than four important lines', as well as the terminus for other important lines already projected, one of which would afford 'the most direct access to those regions in the great north-west … which are now exciting so much attention, not only here, but in the Imperial Parliament' (Knight, 1991: 216). With Expansionist references to the isothermal line of 41°F of mean temperature, the timber resources and agricultural potential north of Lakes Huron and Superior, the 'magnificent uplands drained by the Saskatchewan and other rivers' and the 'probable future connection' of Canada to the Red River Settlement and the Hudson's Bay territory, the Toronto Memorial not only established the position of Toronto as the optimum location for Canada's capital, but also linked Toronto geographically to the great project of bringing the North-West under Canadian and Imperial control.

The inclusion of the Toronto photographs was undoubtedly the initiative of William Armstrong (1822–1914), senior partner in the firm of Armstrong, Beere & Hime, Engineers, Draughtsmen and

Photographers.[7] A well-known watercolourist and civil engineer who emigrated from Ireland to Toronto in 1851, Armstrong was a latecomer to one of the committees that met to prepare Toronto's claim. Perhaps not coincidentally, he attended his first meeting on the same day that Toronto City Council resolved that the mayor should take 'such steps as he may deem advisable in obtaining and forwarding such further information and material as he may think likely to be of benefit and advantage in securing the permanent location of the seat of government in the City'.[8] Part of the 'further information and material' was the portfolio of photographs, no doubt proposed by the enterprising Armstrong. However, apart from the brief mention on the verso of the mayor's letter that 'There are sent this day a series of photographic views of various portions of the city', there is no reference to the photographs in the text of the Toronto memorial. Why then were the photographs sent, and what were they intended to convey?

Text: civic pride and political persuasion

Photographs are the material residue of an act of visual communication. The message they bear can only be deciphered when content is returned to context. The written arguments in the Toronto memorial were not 'illustrated' by the photographs; rather, an editorial comment published in the *Daily Colonist* in early May of that year suggests that the portfolio was a visual argument which complemented and supplemented the written submission:

> *We have been favoured by W. Armstrong, Esquire, with an opportunity of examining a series of photographic views executed by Messrs. Armstrong, Beere & Hime of the City of Toronto as seen from the top of the Rossin House. Nothing can be more curiously beautiful than these views, which form a complete panorama of the city, and would certainly if sent home, as we trust they will be, materially assist Her Majesty the Queen in estimating the actual condition and importance of her good and faithful City of Toronto. The most pleasing architectural group in these views is, perhaps, the cluster of churches and chapels situated between Adelaide and Queen Sts., west of Yonge St. The view of the Harbour is highly picturesque, and gives a good idea of its extent and capacity.[9]*

The 'good and faithful City of Toronto' was faithful to God, seen clearly in the 'cluster of churches and chapels'; to Britain and Empire, alluded to in the reference to 'home'; and to photography as a truthful medium for representing urban development and communicating the values it embodied. This faith in photography allowed the Toronto portfolio to serve as a surrogate for first-hand observation. The views, as noted in the Toronto paper, were expected 'to materially assist Her Majesty the Queen in estimating the actual condition and importance of her good and faithful City of Toronto'. Thus, it would appear, the photographs were intended to act as visual arguments: through them, distant audiences, most notably the Queen and her advisers, could 'see' what Toronto looked like. Through them, the buildings and streetscapes were expected to raise a chorus in support of Toronto's claim to become capital of Canada. The photographs were sent to communicate, to validate, and to persuade. It is in their dual role – as tools of description and devices of inscription – that these and, for that matter, all photographs merit the attention of cultural geographers.

Successful as reflections of civic pride, the Toronto photographs ultimately failed as tools of political persuasion. As 'immutable mobiles' (Latour, 1986) they failed to mobilize allies in the Colonial Office;

simply, they were, in fact, never seen by the audience for whom they were intended. The city memorials along with various other written documents were collected and published in a limited edition for use within the Colonial Office, the British Cabinet and by the Queen; however, the maps and photographs were awkward in size and/or difficult to reproduce. Technological constraints clearly caused problems for the Colonial Office: 'What should be done with the plan and the views?' Arthur Blackwood, Chief Clerk of the North American Division asked his superiors. 'The printing of them will add to the expense; but if the correspondence on the subject of the Seat of Govt. should eventually be laid before Parlt. the omission of them from the series may give rise to complaints' (Knight, 1991: 202). In posing the question, Blackwood demonstrated an awareness of the possible political consequences of ignoring the visual evidence, and therein acknowledged the relationship of the portfolio to the Toronto memorial and its potential importance in the decision-making process. However, his superiors dismissed his concerns. Their reply was unanimous and became more emphatic as the question rose through the hierarchy. On 10 July, Herman Merivale, permanent Under-Secretary for the Colonies replied 'I should say there is no reason for printing'. Three days later, Chichester Fortescue, Parliamentary Under-Secretary for the Colonies, concurred, 'I think not'. Finally, on the 16 July, The Rt. Hon. Henry Labouchere, Colonial Secretary, ended the discussion, 'Certainly not'. As a result, the memorials were published without the Toronto photographs and what had been submitted as compelling visual testimony of the city's built environment went unseen by those responsible for making the decision. Eventually – and most likely as a result of political decisions in no way related to the omission of the photographs from the publication of the memorials – Ottawa was selected capital. It was an unpopular decision which engendered further political wrangling, but, in this 'choice of evils', it was deemed 'the least objectionable place' and promoted as 'a fair compromise'.

The decision to publish the memorials without the maps and Toronto portfolio also alerts us to the fact that the meanings generated by the Toronto photographs were intimately tied to the relationship between audience and pre-photographic referents, a relationship which governed the pre-texts brought to viewing and valuing the portfolio. The citizens of Toronto would have looked with pride at the photographs of King Street and envisaged the bustle of pedestrian and cart traffic in the heart of the city's business district, where Merivale, Fortescue, and Labouchere would only have seen the sidewalks and muddy roads of a sleepy provincial town, a scene which, in fact, had been emptied of activity by the lengthy exposure required by wet collodion technology. For those familiar with the city of Toronto, here was evidence of urban development and architectural sophistication. For them, neither captions nor memorial text were required to establish the import of the photographs. Government, civic, religious, and commercial structures, easily identified by citizens, confirmed the city's identity as a civilized, economically viable, and spiritually sustained place on the edge of Empire. For such an audience, the portfolio was expected to carry a message about colonial progress and economic opportunity to the imperial centre. However, photographic meaning is not an observable property: it is neither singular nor stable. One can only speculate on the reception of these views by imperial decision-makers. With only skeletal handwritten titles, and in the absence of textual explanations in the memorial, the authorial intentions of the Toronto city fathers may not have been clear to the London lawmakers for whom they were intended. Indeed, the very indeterminacy of the portfolio's visual argument may well have contributed to the Colonial Secretary's insistence that the photographs not be reproduced.

The failure of the Armstrong, Beere & Hime views to 'mobilize allies' in the Colonial Office in no way diminishes the rhetorical power with which they were invested. Nor does it detract from their value as evidence for geographical inquiry. What it does do is force us to distinguish between intention and impact, on the one hand, and content, context, and text, on the other, when assessing the constitutive role of photographs. The Toronto photographs may be used as historical records of the outward appearance of Toronto's urban landscape. These panoramas, street scenes, and architectural views are visual descriptions of topography, architecture, and urban development. They provide empirical details – of the height, design, and material of buildings, the width of streets, the layout of the city. But photographs can only offer us a record of what could be seen, just as census records, assessment rolls, and financial statements can only provide us with information about what could be counted or measured or tabulated. But the Toronto photographs are more than just a visual record of the facade of Toronto's past. Through selection, portrayal, and ordering, the portfolio conveyed the values and beliefs of Toronto's civic promoters. In concert with the mayor's letter, the map, and the statistics, the photographs presented a social and political narrative. For the city's politicians, the media, and the citizens of Toronto, the portfolio was a strong and clear visual argument, enabled by photographic technology, founded upon the urban landscape, and expected to complement and supplement Toronto's written petition.

Lessons for practising cultural geography

What lessons can we learn from this example? Armstrong, Beere, & Hime's photographs of Toronto suggest that, if photographs record outward appearance with unparalleled realism, their optical precision does not preclude ideological intent. Whatever the analogical perfection of the individual images, the Toronto portfolio was a carefully crafted representation of reality, shaped and coloured by the national hopes and imperial aspirations of city officials and prominent citizens, silent on many aspects of urban life, silent on issues with no obvious visible manifestation in the landscape or better argued in textual or statistical or cartographic form. Our own postmodern rejection of mirror theories of reality cannot change the fact that the society which produced and consumed these images placed unwavering faith in the truthfulness of the photographic image and its ability to act as a surrogate for first-hand seeing. Critical engagement with photographs is, therefore, a cumulative exercise, a sort of layered looking. As products of technology, they must be seen against a background of photographic practice, cumbersome equipment, and refractory processes. As visual records, they must be examined as descriptions of unparalleled optical accuracy. As cultural artefacts, they must be studied as statements about the society in which they were created. As historical documents, they must be understood in relation to other documents – letters, statistical tables, maps – with which they circulated and generated meaning. For us to explore the Toronto photographs as a site where landscape meaning was negotiated, to comprehend the faith placed in them to influence political decision-making, to recover the message(s) they were intended to convey, and to understand their role in the production of geographical knowledge, we must return them to the action in which they participated, study them as art, fact, and artefact, consider the ways in which they were created, circulated, and viewed, distinguish between their authorial intent – that is, the meanings with which they were invested – and their audience impact – that is, the meanings which they generated.

The Toronto portfolio is, effectively, the visual residue of an act of communication between a municipal government and an imperial administration. The photographs as images were taken by the commercial photographic firm of Armstrong, Beere & Hime, but the portfolio as a document was authored by the city government, the committees that drafted the memorial, and the mayor who signed it. The portfolio both complemented and supplemented the mayor's letter, acting as a visual 'pre-text' for reading the written text, for picturing the prosperity of the trade and navigation figures, for visualizing the city at the centre of the map, and, ultimately, for imagining the symbolic spaces of a capital city. Its audience was Queen Victoria and her advisers. Its meaning was presumed to be fixed, obvious, and inherent; but, in fact, it was both dynamic and intertextual, contributing to and amplified by words, numbers, and lines. Compiled for the purpose of influencing the seat-of-government decision, it was integral to, not merely illustrative of, the Toronto memorial. Viewed in this way, the Toronto memorial photographs were clearly intended to assume a constitutive role conveying visual evidence of the suitability of Toronto as the permanent capital for Canada. Photographic technology allowed Toronto's urban landscape to make a visual and self-referential argument for its own transformation into the seat of government. Evocative of the city's fabric, self-image, and political aspirations, the photographs were expected to act as reliable purveyors of visual testimony, to conjure up in the mind of Colonial Office viewers a sense of being there, and, thus, to assume a constitutive role in imperial decision-making. Viewed in this way, the Toronto memorial photographs reveal themselves as active participants in an exercise to represent and, thereby, to create a landscape of colonial power, a place of national pride, and a site of imperial connection.

The Toronto portfolio offers an opportunity to consider not only *how* we look at photographs, but also *where* we look at photographs. Two copies of the Toronto portfolio are known to exist: one in the Foreign and Commonwealth Office Library, formerly the Colonial Office Library, in London and a second in the National Archives of Canada.[10] The five-part panorama and four of the individual prints now in the holdings of the National Archives of Canada were purchased in 1992 from Sotheby's, London. (The three- and four-part panoramas and the remaining prints were subsequently acquired directly from the owners who had broken up the portfolio to 'test the market'.) Their appearance, in five separate lots, on the lucrative auction market alerts us to a research issue: the influence of commercial interest and institutional discourse on scholarly inquiry. Photographs created as documents are now collected, exhibited, and studied as art. Albums and collections are broken up – with related material inevitably going to different buyers – in order to maximize prices achieved. Acquired by private collectors and thus removed from public view, or added to the holdings of art galleries or museums and thus transformed into art objects, such photographs are frequently severed from their functional origins and documentary roots, making it difficult to recover the purpose(s) for which they were created, the audience(s) for whom they intended, and the meaning(s) they were intended to convey. When collected for their aesthetic qualities rather than for their documentary evidence, historical photographs often fall outside the primary source-focus of mainstream research agendas. It is, therefore, important to cast one's research net wide across archives, libraries, museums, and galleries, both public and private, remembering that institutional practices – acquisition, description, access, exhibition – not only govern what material is held or how it is made accessible, but more importantly, who their users are based upon what they expect to find and, as a consequence, which academic fields are served.

Notes

[1] This chapter is based on ongoing research into the use of photography in the making of early modern Canada. I am grateful to Richard Huyda, former Director of the National Photography Collection at the National Archives of Canada, for sharing his interest and his research with me. My analysis here expands upon his pioneering essay, 'Photography and the Choice of Canada's capital', *History of Photography* 20: 2, 104–7.

[2] *The Globe* (Toronto), 3 February 1857, p.2, col.1.

[3] *The Globe*. 'Pictorial Supplement', 13 December 1856, p.4.

[4] *The Globe*, 13 December 1856.

[5] *The Globe*, 'Pictorial Supplement', 13 December 1856.

[6] *The Builder* (London), XV, 735, 7 March 1857, p.141, cited in Huyda (1996).

[7] Armstrong's photographs had won awards at the provincial exhibition of 1856. Beere's view of the railway disaster at the Desjardins Canal in March 1857 marked the beginning of photojournalism in Canada and received widespread attention as an engraving in the *Illustrated London News*. Hime produced his best known work in 1858 as official photographer with the Assiniboine and Saskatchewan Exploring Expedition.

[8] *Daily Colonist* (Toronto), 9 June 1857.

[9] *Daily Colonist* (Toronto), 9 May 1857.

[10] These photographs were acquired by the National Archives of Canada with the assistance of a grant from the Minister of Communications, under the terms of the Cultural Property Export and Import Act, in order to repatriate original material of national significance.

Further reading

There is a large literature available on photography and imperialism. From geography, good places to start are:

- Schwartz, J.M. and Ryan, J. R. (eds) (2003) *Picturing Place: Photography and the Geographical Imagination*. London, IB Tauris. This edited collection includes a wealth of case studies that should give you some ideas for further research of your own.

- Schwartz, J.M. (1996) 'The Geography Lesson: photographs and the construction of imaginative geographies' *Journal of Historical Geography* 22: 1, pp.16–45.

- Ryan, J.R. (1997) *Picturing Empire: Photography and the Visualization of the British Empire*. Chicago, The University of Chicago Press.

Historians of anthropology have written widely on photography and imperialism. See, for example:

- Edwards, E. (2001) *Raw Histories: Photographs, Anthropology and Museums*. Oxford, Berg.

- Edwards, E. (ed.) (1997) *Anthropology and Colonial Endeavour*, a theme issue of *History of Photography* 21: 1.

- Scherer, J.C. (ed.) (1990) *Picturing Cultures: Historical Photographs in Anthropological Inquiry*, a special issue of *Visual Anthropology* 3:2–3, pp. 235–58.

For contextual studies of direct relevance to themes in this chapter, see the following:

- Headrick, D. (1981) *Tools of Empire: Technology and European Imperialism in the Nineteenth Century*. New York, Oxford University Press.

- Moyles, R.G. and Owram, D. (1988) *Imperial Dreams and Colonial Realities: British Views of Canada, 1880–1914*. Toronto, University of Toronto Press.

- Worswick, C. and Embree, A. (1977) *The Last Empire: Photography in British India, 1855–1911*. New York, Aperture.

11
Mapping worlds
Cartography and the politics of representation

David Pinder

Political demonstrations during the war against Iraq in 1990–91 included one held outside the United States Defence Mapping Agency in St Louis. Its target was the role of maps in the conduct of warfare, and specifically the agency's involvement in producing map data for the US troops in the operating areas. Referring to this little reported event, Brian Harley notes how, regardless of different views about the morality of war, the demonstration highlighted the important ethical issues that map making can raise (1991: 9). Other commentators went further in describing the war as 'the first full-scale GIS [Geographic Information Systems] war', in which the development of computerized cartographic technologies 'definitively altered the way in which modern warfare is fought and staged and the way it is consumed by a global public transformed into video voyeurs' (Smith, 1992: 257). With US and British troops once more assembled in the region in early 2003, and having launched another war against Iraq, such connections between cartographic technologies and military **power** are again being demonstrated with force. Not only at issue is the production of maps and cartographic techniques to plan and guide military campaigns. Also significant is the day-to-day use of maps to depict the region in particular ways on news bulletins and other television programmes, scripting its geographies in ways that have material effects on how they are viewed and understood.

The involvement of maps and processes of mapping in the exertion of military power and political interests more generally is, of course, nothing new. 'Maps are synonymous with strategy,' asserts one writer in the field, 'and strategy wins wars' (Brown, 1951: 309). Despite such connections, however, the politically interested nature of maps and practices of mapping are often unexamined. Maps are still frequently viewed as factual statements that are essentially neutral, objective and above political and grubbily material concerns. The idea that they are transparent 'windows' or 'mirrors of nature', with direct correspondence with visible elements in the world, remains powerful. So too does the historical narrative whereby cartography advances through a series of stages, increasingly less hazy, towards an enlightened position founded on accuracy and comprehensiveness. Yet theoretically informed debate about the power and politics of mapping has been developing since the 1980s. This has questioned 'the illusion of cartographic objectivity' (Harley, 1989: 82), by critically analysing maps as means of **representation**. Central to this move has been recognition that maps are **socially constructed** artefacts that can be analysed in terms of the views, values and purposes they embody and promote. Similarly, practices of mapping are not universal and disinterested but – like all forms of representation – are partial and **situated knowledges**, expressing particular concerns, priorities and positions. Cartography is therefore understood along with other geographical practices as 'worldly', in the sense of being in and part of the world (see Barnes and Gregory, 1997).

It can be argued that practising cartographers have long been aware of the partial and socially constructed nature of their enterprise in terms of the human judgements and choices involved in making maps. But recent critical literature on cartography has been significant in appraising maps and mapping within a theory of representation that goes beyond issues of technical limitations or individual fallibility in an otherwise supposedly objective science of making maps, to address more fundamental questions about the political contexts and social processes through which maps are constructed, and through which they are used and have effects (see especially Harley, 1988, 1992a, 2001; Pickles, 1992; Wood, 1993; for a review, see Crampton, 2001). This approach to the social nature of maps draws on a number of different post-positivist theoretical sources and traditions. Underpinning it is a rejection of the idea that maps are innocent and that they simply reflect reality. Instead it focuses on the power and politics of maps and mapping as explored in a range of contexts. This is especially in terms of their historical connections with colonialism, capitalism and state formation where it has involved geographical studies of such issues as surveillance, law, territorial rights, spatial administration, the demarcation of borders, colonial and anti-colonial political struggles, and the construction and use of geographical knowledge and imaginations (for example Clayton, 2000; Cosgrove, 1999; Edney, 1997, 1999; Harvey, 2001; Konvitz, 1987; Massey, 1995; Sparke, 1998). Critical theoretical debates have also entered the realm of GIS through critiques and reappraisals (Pickles, 1995; Schuurman, 2000). In this way studies of cartography share concerns with the interrogation within cultural geography of other forms of representation as well as geographical knowledges and practices more generally (for example Barnes and Duncan, 1992b; Cosgrove and Daniels, 1988; and Chapters 1, 2, 3, 10, 12, 14).

In this chapter my focus is not on technical issues about the design and making of maps, the traditional basis of much cartographic literature. Rather, I address ways of studying maps and mapping in terms of the *politics of representation*. In other words, I consider how maps and practices of mapping may be analysed as active means by which meanings are produced, circulated and exerted as well as negotiated and contested. My aim is to provide some theoretical and practical guidance to this end, especially for those interested in studying cartographic issues directly. But I also want to encourage critical thinking about maps and mapping more generally for they have long been central to both the discipline and discourse of geography, and are highly significant intellectually and politically. It is therefore crucial not to take them for granted but to consider them carefully, whether this is in terms of primary sources, secondary reading, or using them in research reports and essays. To explore these issues I draw on my research on alternative forms of maps and mapping, and on the possibilities of 'subverting cartography' as a means of political resistance. In particular, I use a case from my research on urban maps produced and used by the avant-garde art and political group, the Situationist International (Pinder, 1996). Before turning to this subject, though, I introduce some initial points about studying maps as value-laden images that were central to this research.

Maps, power and politics

In June 1929 a map of the world appeared the Belgium journal *Variétés* (Figure 11.1). Produced by members of the surrealist group, it overthrew familiar shapes and orders. The map gave new prominence to the Pacific islands with Easter Island taking on vast proportions, being depicted as almost equivalent to South America. It removed the US entirely apart from a large Alaska, shown alongside Labrador and Mexico, and rendered Britain as a dot adjacent to a more substantial Ireland. The only two cities shown were Paris and Constantinople, although France and Turkey were absent. The rest of

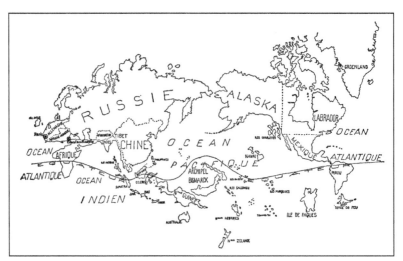

Figure 11.1 *The surrealist map of the world. From* Variétés, *1929.*

Europe was largely presented as Germany, Austria-Hungary and an immense Russia, with the latter also dominating Asia along with China, Afghanistan, Tibet and a small India. This map reflected the surrealists' artistic, cultural and political interests. Particularly apparent were their antipathy towards the logical and rational within western thought, their desire for the 'marvellous' and exotic, something they combined with an anti-imperialist stance, and their taste for scandal as they mocked norms of representation.

The surrealist map challenges the 'naturalness' of cartographic conventions and invites the viewer to imagine alternatives. By disrupting familiar orders, it poses questions about why maps take the form they do. It draws attention to the ideals that underpin all maps – surrealist and 'conventional' alike. Maps have been defined as 'a symbolized image of geographic reality, representing selected features or characteristics' (International Cartographic Association, 1995, cited in Dorling and Fairbairn, 1997: 3). Mapmaking necessarily involves choices about what to include and what to exclude, what perspective to take, what codes to employ, what mode of projection to adopt and so on. It entails processes of selection, classification, abstraction, translation and inscription. Maps are therefore social products, providing particular perspectives on the world. They also promote interests and ways of seeing. Once accepted and in circulation, they can have effects and influence how the world is understood and constituted. They may help to legitimize certain conditions and ways of seeing, for example by 'naturalising' arrangements of property rights, or by drawing boundaries to partition territories, or by inscribing place names to make 'legible' a space previously seen as disorienting by a colonizing power.

At times the political interests of maps may be obvious. Propaganda maps are labelled as such because they serve clear political ends, deliberately distorting content to convey a message and influence public opinion (Monmonier, 2001; Pickles, 1992). The persuasive intent of many other maps such as those in advertising, government reports and the media is also often readily apparent. These can all make interesting subjects for research. But in the obviousness of their politics, and in their frequent association with totalitarian regimes and in particular with examples from Nazi Germany, one of the functions of propaganda maps has been to serve as a buttress against which cartographers have defined other maps as 'scientific'. Such oppositions need challenging. It is important to recognize that *all* maps serve particular interests, even – or perhaps especially – in cases that claim to be scientific and impartial.

Even those seemingly presenting unmediated views of the world, such as those derived from satellite imaging, involve a whole range of practices and conventions in order to compose 'realistic' images that seem to connote the world as it really is. These include decisions about scanner technology, the selection of colours, the choice of projection and so on (for good examples, see Braun, 2002: 213–55; Wood, 1993: 48–69). As Brian Harley (1988: 278) argues: 'Both in the selectivity of their content and in their signs and styles of representation, maps are a way of conceiving, articulating, and structuring the human world which is biased towards, promoted by and exerts influence upon particular sets of social relations.'

How can the power and politics of maps be uncovered, given their common mask of neutrality? A starting point is to approach maps as texts and a form of language. Maps employ rhetorical devices to make statements about the world, advancing particular propositions and arguments. Interpretation therefore entails decoding that language in terms of the visible as well as hidden codes, signs, rules and conventions through which maps are constructed. It is *not* a case of trying to expose how maps are somehow 'wrong' or 'untrue'. Such a stance assumes that it is possible to produce a value-free image that leaves an external world 'undistorted'. As I have argued, that claim is untenable. More to the point for the position that I am advocating here is to analyse how claims to truth or the 'truth-effects' of maps are constituted, to address how they are part of a **discourse** of cartography through which they derive their authority and work as a form of knowledge and of power (on using discourse analysis to study visual images more widely, see Rose, 2001: 135–63). This approach was outlined most influentially by Brian Harley in a series of essays that took apart the 'naturalness' of maps and explored the presence of power as well as its effects in map knowledge. He drew on a number of theoretical sources, including Michel Foucault's studies on the connections between knowledge and power. He also wrote of '**deconstructing** the map' in terms of uncovering contradictions, silences and ambiguities that undermine its apparent coherence and objectivity, and that open up other ways of reading them. Harley was still developing his position when he died in 1991, aged 59, and it has been suggested that his work lacks 'a clear research agenda for how one might implement his theories in practice' (Crampton, 2001: 236; for stronger criticism along these lines, see Andrews, 2001: 27–31). Harley himself noted that focusing on maps as texts offers no simple set of techniques for their interpretation (1992a: 238). However, his theoretical writings offer many important insights into the analysis of maps that I have found useful in my own research and that form the basis of my discussion in the next section.

Concept Box

Deconstruction

The term 'deconstruct' is sometimes used loosely in cultural geography to refer to the process by which a critic interprets, decodes or unpacks the meaning of a text. This 'text' might be a report, novel, map, monument, landscape, television programme, film or other cultural production. In its stricter sense, however, deconstruction relates to the method developed by the contemporary French philosopher Jacques Derrida. This explores how the meanings of texts are not as stable as they often first appear, how they contain inherently contradictory elements that undermine their apparent order and coherence, and how their claims to truth therefore rest on insecure grounds. Texts do not have a single truth that can be uncovered or demystified through a proper reading, in this view, for their very construction means that they are open to different readings through which the supposedly consistent face they show to the world

(continued overleaf)

can be unravelled and exposed. In methodological terms, deconstruction most often focuses on binary oppositions – such as nature/culture, male/female or West/East – and subverts these binaries, not by reversing their hierarchical values but instead by destablizing both parts. It shows how the distinctions fail on their own grounds with each term containing within itself traces of the other. In so doing deconstruction often attends to exclusions in the text and the significance of silences, absences, repressions and what has been defined as marginal. Instead of being an operation that is applied by critics from the outside, as it were, it therefore involves attending to the instabilities that are always already within the text. Controversy has surrounded the approach with critics being disturbed by its relativism, arguing it dissolves all grounds for determining the value of competing perspectives. Other writers, however, including some postcolonial and feminist geographers, have found it politically valuable for questioning the 'naturalness' of conceptual orderings and disrupting processes through which powerful definitions of 'centres' and 'margins' become installed. It has also been central to some attempts to find new ways of writing geography as part of a wider poststructuralist project (notably in Doel, 1999).

Key reading

* Barnes, T.J. (1994) 'Probable writing: Derrida, deconstruction and the quantitative revolution in human geography.' *Environment and Planning A* 26: 1021–40.
* Norris, C. (2002) *Deconstruction: Theory and Practice*. London, Taylor and Francis.

Interpreting maps as texts

A key first step involves situating maps within their contexts. This may be understood in three ways. First is the context of authorship: for example, who made it and what were their positions and circumstances? How was the map constructed? What processes and technologies were involved? What were the map's intended uses? How does it relate to other maps such as those produced by the same authors or those of the same area, the same genre, or the same era? How does it relate to other forms of representation at the time? Second is the immediate context of the map itself. This includes questions about the book, essay, painting, film or display within which it appears as well as intertextual relations with materials beyond it. And third there is the wider social context. This includes questions about the social and political relations, institutions and practices through which a map is composed, viewed and used. Here it is not a case of viewing maps as separate entities that simply express social structure for, as has been argued, they are part of society and are active in its constitution. Instead it means exploring what Harley (2001: 44) called 'the web of interconnections, stretching both inside and beyond the map document'. Cartography has traditionally been seen as an elite practice, not least due to the costs and resources involved. Its main context is therefore frequently powerful political, social and religious settings where it can be studied as part of more general archives relating to those contexts alongside other textual and visual materials (see Chapter 1).

Another stage involves analysing map content. It is important to spend time with the maps, to study them in detail. Try to see them anew, in the sense of stepping outside familiar ways of looking in an effort to disturb the taken-for-grantedness of the materials in front of you. Describing them carefully is a useful starting point for interpretation. This can be followed by a more structured attempt to draw out key themes and to explore the ways in which the maps produce effects, including effects of truth. In studying questions of power, four aspects of map content may be highlighted (derived mainly from Harley, 1988: 287–300).

1 *Hierarchies of representation.* This involves examining cartographic signs and the ways in which their visual importance is structured. For example, what signs are used for categories of settlements and how do their sizes compare? What significance is given to religious buildings of different faiths? Why are motorways often shown more prominently than rivers or railways? Why do the signs used in some maps of apartheid South Africa render Black settlements relatively invisible compared to the White towns adjacent to them (Stickler, 1990)? What do these discriminations tell us about the values of the societies concerned and about the power of maps themselves? It is important not to take these discriminations for granted but to consider the rules and conventions, whether visible or hidden, which underpin them in particular contexts. Contemporary books on the construction and design of maps can provide a helpful resource for making sense of these hierarchies.

2 *Silences.* What is absent from maps can be as interesting a matter for research as what is present (Harley, 2001: 83–107). Political silences include deliberate omissions of elements that otherwise might be expected to be present, such as the censorship of military installations and nuclear waste dumps on grounds of 'security', or the erasure of place-names relating to indigenous groups by a colonizing force. But silences are also the product of a less conscious process of what Harley terms 'ideological filtering'. This is apparent, for example, in early urban plans that omit the alleys and courtyards of poor urban areas through their focus on grander roads, civic buildings and the like. Silences are not simply 'blank spaces' or gaps but positive statements that require interpretation.

3 *Geometries.* This refers to how maps are oriented and centred, and how they are projected. Such questions often go unasked but their importance can be quickly demonstrated when they are challenged, as shown by the surrealist map of the world, or by 'upside down' and recentred maps that alter familiar images, or by the controversy surrounding alternative projections of the world such as that presented by Arno Peters in 1974. Peters was conscious of the political stakes involved in promoting his famous equal-area world map and atlas. He wanted to contest 'normalised' views of the world associated with the Mercator projection and its revisions, and especially the way in which they exaggerated the spatial extent of land areas in the northern hemisphere and gave undue prominence to what he called 'the colonial masters of the time' at the expense of 'non-white-peopled lands' (see Crampton, 1994).

4 *Symbolism and decoration.* This is especially important for understanding the rhetoric and power of maps, according to Harley, who suggests using **iconographic** methods with their sensitivity to historical context and intertextuality in trying to go beyond the 'literal' meaning of the map to draw out its symbolic dimensions (2001: 46–48). Included here is an interest in how the decorative elements of maps such as borders, dedications, lettering, title pages and the like contribute to the political meanings of the map. For example, the theme of colonialism might be most vocally announced in the margins of a map through images of explorers, stereotypes of inhabitants, or the use of national flags, crowns and so on. Colour use is significant, depending on historically contingent conventions. Also worthy of attention is the symbolic use of maps as emblems within art works or advertisements, often as a means of conveying power over territory. Where maps are plain and apparently devoid of decoration, their realism can similarly be analysed as a form of rhetoric. In such cases, '[a]ccuracy and austerity of design are the new talismans of authority, culminating in our own age with computer mapping' (Harley, 1992a: 241).

Concept Box

Iconography

Iconography is concerned with interpreting the meaning of images and texts. As a methodology it involves situating **representations** within their historical contexts and attending closely to their composition and content. It aims to draw out the symbolic meanings of representations and to understand their significance within particular cultural settings, including what they might say about the values and norms of the society in which they were produced. Significance is placed on developing skills in reading and interpreting, and on learning about connections between cultural forms as well as historical context. The method is associated especially with the work of the art historian Erwin Panofsky. Concentrating on Renaissance art, he sought to study the signs and symbols of a painting in terms of the time and space of its composition. In his view this required gaining acquaintance with the texts with which the composer of the image was familiar, including guides produced for artists and their patrons at the time to explain the meanings of symbols and motifs. It also depended upon a certain amount of intuition. Of particular importance was going beyond the 'primary' or 'natural' subject matter of an image, where interpretation focuses on individual artistic motifs, to explore a 'deeper' level of symbolism and cultural significance that Panofsky associated with 'iconological' interpretation. Brian Harley draws a parallel with levels of meaning in a map, suggesting an equivalent primary level of individual conventional signs, and a level concerned with symbolism and ideology that understands maps in relation to the values of particular societies (Harley, 2001: 46–48). Within cultural geography, iconography has been especially important in interpreting landscapes, in built form and in visual and verbal representations through different media (Cosgrove and Daniels, 1988). Attention has focused on how landscapes embody relations of **power** and ways of seeing, and they are socially negotiated and contested.

Key reading

- Cosgrove, D. and Daniels, S. (eds) (1988) *The Iconography of Landscape*. Cambridge, Cambridge University Press.
- Daniels, S. (1993) *Fields of Vision: Landscape Imagery and National Identity in England and the United States*. Cambridge, Polity.

Mapping and political contestation: the situationists

The approach outlined above has provided the framework for my own research on maps and mapping. It has allowed me to consider the field in terms of the politics of representation, suggesting ways of examining the social construction of maps and their political significance. However, my initial research in this area came from a different direction from most of the writers cited above. Rather than focusing on the presence of power and its effects within map knowledge through studying powerful representations, the primary concern of much critical cartography literature, I became interested in 'alternative' practices that sought to subvert cartography as part of a project of political resistance. In what ways can 'official' cartographic schemes be countered and reworked? How might other subversive practices of mapping and map-making be developed based on different values, desires and needs? The immediate context for these questions was my interest in a group of political activists, artists and writers called the Situationist International (SI). I was initially drawn to the group for political and artistic reasons, being inspired by their activities and ideas, and this later led to research. The group was active in western Europe between 1957 and 1972, and it was committed to a radical critique of what it saw as the increasingly alienated social conditions of the post-war period. Influenced by earlier groups like the surrealists as well as by Marxist theory, and having an important association with among others Henri Lefebvre, who has since had a profound influence on geographical and urban thinking (Gregory, 1994; Shields, 1999), the situationists advocated political contestation and the revolutionary transformation of both space and everyday life. Many of their ideas and practices were concerned with the geographies of the city and how they might be changed, and in exploring them I became intrigued by, among other things, their interest in maps and mapping. What role did this cartographic interest play within their wider programme?

The situationists recognised the power of cartography and other discourses in influencing the ways of seeing the city. Denouncing the 'systematic falsification of basic information' that reinforces the 'great lie' imposed on urban space by dominant social interests, one member cited idealist conceptions of space 'of which the most glaring example is conventional cartography' (Kotányi, 1960: 34). But the situationists also used cartography in other ways. Their publications contain a range of real and imaginary maps among their texts on art, urbanism, contemporary politics and revolutionary organisation. They also refer to practices of 'psychogeographical mapping', something that had earlier been developed by the SI's predecessors in the Letterist International (LI), a group of activists based in Paris in the 1950s. Of particular interest to me were so-called 'psychogeographical maps' of Paris, arrestingly different cartographic representations of the city produced by Guy Debord when he was a member of the LI, shortly before he co-founded and became a leading member of the situationist group. While studying these materials, I was struck by the following passage about cartography in one of Harley's essays on maps and power:

> *The ideological arrows have tended to fly largely in one direction, from the powerful to the weaker in society. The social history of maps, unlike that of literature, art, or music, appears to have few genuinely popular, alternative, or subversive modes of expression. Maps are preeminently a language of power not of protest .... Cartography remains a teleological discourse, reifying power, reinforcing the status quo, and freezing social interaction within charted lines.*
>
> (Harley, 1988: 300–303)

Harley stressed that these observations were among 'preliminary ideas for a wider investigation', which he believed needed to be explored in specific contexts. Nevertheless, I wanted to study how situationist interventions in cartography ran counter to his arguments and how they might be seen as subversive. I saw this as significant for both intellectual and political reasons, to develop understandings of the situationists and their geographical concerns, and also to encourage critical engagements with urban mapping against a widespread tendency to renounce such practices as inherently oppressive.

In asking these questions I was aware of a variety of other forms of mapping that likewise could be used to question Harley's claim, some of which had attracted greater attention from geographers and others. Environmental and political activists, for example, commonly use cartography to promote campaigns and to get issues 'on the map'. Popular 'state of the world' atlases and 'radical GIS' are similarly based on the idea of using cartography to convey information often neglected in mainstream media, such as patterns of economic and social inequalities, the conditions of women's lives, or the threats and consequences of war (for example Seager, 1997; Smith, 1999, 2003). What is alternative about these maps is usually the subject matter rather than the cartographic form. But there are also projects that seek to reclaim cartography from 'experts' and to develop grass-roots mappings. Based on encouraging people to map localities in terms of their own concerns, these use different cartographic strategies and sometimes draw inspiration from practices from other historical periods or cultures, including those used in Aboriginal maps (for examples see Crouch and Matless, 1996; Dorling and Fairbairn, 1997: 137–55). Later work by Harley provides a further interesting case. Investigating indigenous cartographies in colonial New England, he explores the place of maps not only in the exertion of colonial power but also in resistance to it, and in cartographic exchange between Indians and Europeans (Harley, 1992b, 2001: 170–95; for developments of this theme, see Sparke, 1995, 1998). Considering this broad area helped to sensitise me to issues I was exploring, and to alert me to parallels and contrasts. In my initial take on 'subverting cartography', however, I wanted to keep the focus on the situationists (Pinder, 1996). My research was concerned with three main aspects of their interest in cartography: the group's practices of mapping; their appropriation and use of other urban maps; and their production of new psychogeographical maps of the city. In what follows I concentrate on the third of these, although I refer to elements of the others in discussing aspects of the research process.

Psychogeographical maps of the city

In 1956–57 two maps of Paris by Guy Debord were published: 'The naked city' (Figure 11.2) and 'Guide psychogéographique de Paris'. I first saw original versions of these maps at a retrospective exhibition on the Situationist International that visited Paris, London and Boston in 1989–90. At the time there was nothing substantial written about the maps. This was surprising given that, as one critic has since pointed out, reproductions of 'The naked city' in various texts were already making it 'an almost iconic image of the early years of the group' (McDonough, 2002: 241). The maps were framed and displayed alongside a range of other documents, texts, paintings, urban models, plans and slogans relating to the situationists and their associates. They were collectively presented as traces of 'the passage of a few people through a rather brief moment in time' (to use the title of the exhibition that was taken from one of Debord's films from the 1950s). It was strange to see these materials, which had been developed as weapons in an effort to change the world, in the reverential and decidedly non-revolutionary setting of an art gallery. At the very least it raised questions about how radical projects get absorbed by the kinds of art and media institutions that they once so vigorously opposed (and indeed by

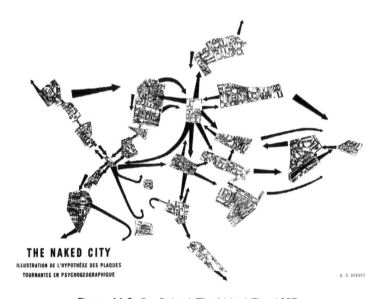

THE NAKED CITY
ILLUSTRATION DE L'HYPOTHÈSE DES PLAQUES
TOURNANTES EN PSYCHOGEOGRAPHIQUE

Figure 11.2 *Guy Debord,* The Naked City, *1957.*

academic institutions, as studies such as this one testify). It also raised the problem, which has continued to concern me, of how to engage with them today without deadening their spirit and political purpose completely, while at the same time avoiding hagiography or an approach based on preserving their 'purity'. I have not found easy answers to this. But I do know that traditions of radical geography have long given the lie to the notion that there is some fundamental divide between the academy and political struggles beyond it; they have also shown how connections between them can inspire writing and action that are themselves committed to making a difference (Blunt and Wills, 2000).

I have already noted the importance of looking carefully at maps, of spending time with them. The two maps concerned are composed out of fragments cut from existing black-and-white maps of Paris. The sections are surrounded by white space and linked by red arrows, which point towards or curve away from areas, suggesting connections, directions, movements. Some arrows also gesture beyond the edges of the maps. 'The naked city' measures 33 x 47.5cm and was originally published in May 1957, and in Asger Jorn's book *Pour la forme* (1958). It consists of 19 sections of map, which are taken from the 'Guide Taride de Paris' of 1951. 'Guide psychogéographique de Paris' is larger, measuring 60 x 74cm. It was published as a separate fold-out map slightly earlier, its pieces plundered from the bird's-eye view of the city in Blondel la Rougery's 'Plan de Paris à vol d'oiseau' of 1956. Both maps shatter the continuous space of standard cartographic representations. They take apart the geometric and ordered appearance of the original sources, subverting their illusion of reality. The broken and patchy replacements serve as a critique of orthodox surveys of the city, revealing fractures and fissures that are usually elided by such representations. What particularly interested me, however, was how the maps nevertheless serve *as maps*, in other words as representations of the city based on more than simply a rejection of conventional cartographies.

The presence of the arrows seems to convey a sense of unity and disunity at the same time, a feeling that the city is tied together but also fractured and in pieces. This spoke to the context of Paris at the time, which was undergoing the beginnings of a vast programme of reconstruction that between 1954 and 1974 would lead to almost a quarter of the surface of its built environment being demolished and rebuilt, and around half a million inhabitants being moved out from the city itself to the suburbs or beyond (see Pinder, 2000). It also chimed with writings by associated theorists such as Lefebvre, who later came to understand the 'abstract space' produced under capitalism from a Marxist perspective as being simultaneously homogeneous and fragmented, whole and broken, continuous and cracked (Lefebvre, 1991: 355–6). But rather than presenting a view of the city from on high, the maps seemed to invite the reader to take the perspective of someone moving through the city, to consider questions of urban experience and activity from a more **embodied** perspective.

To consider the context of map production further, I wanted to know whether Debord had produced other maps. I later came across an advertisement for an exhibition at the Taptoe gallery in Brussels, in February 1957, that had promised to show five 'psychogeographical maps' by Debord. Listed alongside the two already discussed were three maps more whose titles included 'Paris sous la neige' and 'The most dangerous game'. It turned out that Debord never exhibited at the Taptoe, and indeed he never seems to have produced the additional three maps. But the titles demanded consideration with their evocations of events, situations and atmospheres. 'The naked city' could be connected to the detective film of that name of 1948, set in New York (see Chapter 13). That in turn followed a book of crime photographs based in that city by Weegee in 1945 (McDonough, 2002: 245). Intertextual associations were also significant in relation to 'Guide psychogéographique de Paris', which was advertised at the Taptoe by its subtitle 'Discours sur les passions de l'amour'. The latter title proposes seeing the city in terms of a love affair, with routes through it relating to the passions of love. This time a much older map was relevant, one that the situationists reproduced in their journal in 1959 and that originally appeared produced in a book by Madeleine de Scudéry in 1654 under the title 'Carte du tendre'. The latter 'tender' map featured an imaginary land with geographical sites connected with emotions and feelings, suggesting possible routes of a love affair. The situationists never drew connections between the maps themselves. But the unexplained presence of Scudéry's map in their journal, printed within a discussion of alternative ways of thinking about the city, cast new light on my first viewing of Debord's maps. Exploring such intertextual connections may at times be a matter of intuition, at others one of common sense. As these examples suggest, though, it depends upon openness and flexibility in relation to materials, and an immersion in their details and contexts.

The titles are not the only text on the maps. Turning to further linguistic components led me to consider other terms that played a key role in interpreting the maps. Under the subtitle 'Discours sur les passions de l'amour' in the 'Guide psychogéographique', a rather cryptic line states (in literal translation): 'psychogeographical inclines of the drift and localization of unities of ambience'. What does this mean? Underlying the reference to 'localization of unities of ambience' is the idea that different parts of Paris have particular atmospheres and ambiences that can be identified through investigation. These 'unities' are represented by the segments cut from existing maps, with their spatial localization indicated by their arrangement in relation to each other. The maps feature a selection of areas from central parts of Paris. At the centre of 'The naked city' are Les Halles and Plateau Beaubourg, for example, which are presented as key hubs or 'turntables' (described on the map as *plaques tournantes*), with numerous arrows showing connections with other parts of the city (for more details on the areas represented, see Sadler, 1998: 81–92). Neither map follows standard north–south orientation, nor do they employ a formal scale. The position of segments turns out to relate not to physical distances but to what effectively separated them based on influences, connections and human experiences.

The approach is explained further by the reference in the first part of the line quoted above to 'psychogeographical inclines [*pentes*] of the drift'. The letterists and situationists developed psychogeography as a means of appraising the emotional contours of cities, the relationship between behaviour and urban geography, and how they might be transformed. It involved wanders through the streets on what they called drifts or *dérives*, and combined a playful and freeform spirit with radical politics. In using the term 'psychogeographical inclines', the map refers to the inclinations and tendencies of those drifting through the city. As people put aside their usual concerns and break with habitual constraints, so the argument went, they tend to be drawn by certain zones and encounters, repelled by others, and excluded from some altogether. The map presents aspects of the resulting 'psychogeographical relief', with a sense of determinism by social and spatial forces being lent by the use of the term *pente*, with its connotations of a physical slope. But the flows and turns of direction on the map also suggest how spaces are **performed** through movements, actions and desires. An interesting contrast can be drawn with another representation of Paris that was reproduced by the situationists in their journal. Taken from an academic study by the contemporary sociologist Chombart de Lauwe (1952), this charted the pattern of daily movements during the course of a year made by a female student living in the 16th arrondissement (Figure 11.3). Used to demonstrate constraints on movement and the prevalence of routine in showing a highly restricted set of routes based around three sites, it was described by Debord as an example of 'a modern poetry capable of provoking sharp emotional reactions' (1981 [1956]: 50).

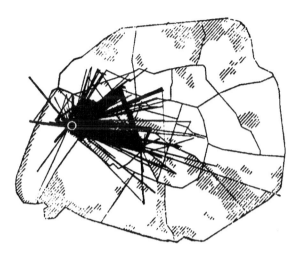

Figure 11.3 *Routes taken during one year by a female student living in the 16th arrondissement of Paris, by Paul-Henry Chombart de Lauwe. From* Internationale situationniste *1, 1958.*

My interpretation of Debord's maps therefore depended upon understanding their place within practices of psychogeography and within critiques of capitalist urbanization developed by the letterists and situationists during the 1950s and 1960s. It also required considering their intertextual relationships with other visual and textual materials as well as situating them within the geographies of Paris at the time. Essential to the process was addressing texts and other works produced by the groups, in the public domain or in archives, including the letterist newsletter *Potlatch* (since republished as *LI*, 1995), and the twelve issues of *Internationale situationniste* published between 1958 and 1969 (reprinted as *SI*, 1997). Fragmentary reports of urban *dérives* were considered alongside more sustained studies of the psychogeography of particular areas. Included among the latter was Abdelhafid Khatib's (1958) report on Les Halles, in which he carefully mapped the 'unitary ambience' of the area as well as its 'internal currents and external communications' (Figures 11.4 and 11.5). He explicitly situated his mapping project against plans at the time to redevelop the area, an action that in his view would entail a 'new blow' to working-class Paris. Also intriguing were other appropriations of maps by the groups, including experiments seemingly designed to undermine the hold of habit and to see places afresh, such as the playful attempt by one of Debord's friends to navigate through the Harz region of Germany while blindly following a map of London. An anti-war theme emerged in a further situationist cartographic project through J.V. Martin's 'thermonuclear maps'. Aiming to illustrate the effects of nuclear war on different regions of the world after the start of a Third World War, including a representation made in June 1963 of Europe four and a half hours into a nuclear conflagration, they anticipated the work of the radical geographer Bill Bunge in his *The Nuclear War Atlas* (1988), which itself had origins in protests against war in the late 1960s.

Figure 11.4 *Map showing the 'unity of ambience' of Les Halles, Paris. From Abdelfahid Khatib, 'Essai de description psychogéographique des Halles', 1958.*

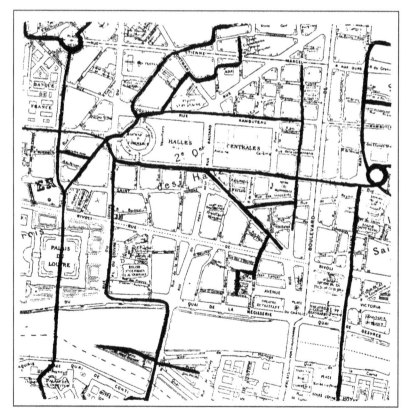

Figure 11.5 *Map showing the 'internal currents and external communications' of Les Halles. From Abdelfahid Khatib, 'Essai de description psychogéographique des Halles', 1958.*

My argument about the psychogeographical maps centred on how they counter the desocialised and disembodied nature of orthodox cartographies, and how they address interactions between people and the city. Through movements and activities in the city, particular areas are enunciated and appear on the maps as islands of urban fabric. Others are avoided or passed through without being acknowledged or registered, and so seem to vanish. In relation to the last point, it is instructive to recall Harley's stress on attending to silences in maps as constituent parts of their language. The maps thus demonstrate something of the interdependence of behaviour and urban space, and the ways in which urban spaces are constituted through social, subjective and psychological dimensions. In this way they differ from many 'community mapping' projects that seek to register and represent the views of people in particular neighbourhoods. They are perhaps closer to certain forms of humanistic cartography, which are based on daily human experience and view mapping as a method for encountering the world rather than simply mirroring it (Wood, 1978). They might also bring to mind aspects of mental maps and the 'cognitive mapping' tradition that was pioneered by Kevin Lynch in his book *The Image of the City* (1961), the legacies of which still play a significant role in many geography departments. Lynch developed a mode of mapping based on journeys through cities where he aimed to attain composite pictures of urban spaces in terms of how people image their surroundings. But among the many crucial differences was the way in which the situationist project was centred on contestation and intervention, and was underpinned by a contrasting normative vision. As Alastair Bonnett insists, psychogeography was 'expressly designed, not just to study aloofly the interaction of people and their environment, but to subvert and explore revolutionary possibilities within the urban scene' (1992: 76).

Conclusions

My aim in this chapter has been to introduce critical approaches to maps and mapping within cultural geography, and to suggest ways they might be studied within research concerned with the politics of representation. By discussing the approach taken in some of my own work, I have focused especially on the contested nature of maps and practices of mapping, and on how they might be explored as part of projects seeking social transformation. This has taken a different line from much recent research, which tends to focus on the use of maps within powerful political contexts and even to portray maps as authoritarian images that invariably support the status quo. But in seeking to open up different perspectives on these issues, I also intend my discussion to be of more general relevance for those interested in conducting research into the power and politics of mapping worlds from other perspectives. In conclusion I want to consider some specific points raised in my own research and a few general issues stemming from them.

From the discussion above it should be clear that Debord's psychogeographical maps challenge conventional cartographic practices in a number of ways. This is not least by bringing issues of the body and desire back in. Yet there is a danger in presenting the maps as 'resistant' or 'alternative'. While they may be regarded as subversive in some ways, viewed from other directions they are much less so. The paths remain undifferentiated and leave certain questions about power relations unaddressed. Whose experiences and whose movements are represented here? What about the different constraints placed on mobility by sexual violence against women, for example, or racist and homophobic attacks? By relying on lines on a static map, the representations further miss out a substantial part of what psychogeography was meant to be about, with its interest in the sensuous, emotional and fluid. It is perhaps not surprising that the letterists and situationists seem to have favoured practices of psychogeographical mapping over the more specific practice of map-making. The maps should therefore not be approached as models for cartographic practice, waiting to be plugged in to confront different social and spatial situations prevailing today (and, indeed, I slightly dread the thought of geographers and others uncritically trying to use the *dérive* as a research method, stripped of its political intent). They need to be understood in their contexts, as part of a project with particular social and political objectives.

This leads into a wider concern about the risks of setting up a simple opposition in cartography between powerful practices and those deemed resistant. Such a binary vision of cartography is implied in the quotation from Harley earlier, where he presents maps as *either* a discourse of the powerful *or* as a discourse of protest, with 'genuinely popular, alternative, or subversive modes of expression'. This opposition gives his arguments about the power of maps useful rhetorical force. But it poses difficult questions about how truly 'alternative' and 'popular' forms of expression might be known, and its either/or logic inevitably means that other possibilities and practices are neglected. Talking in terms of 'an alternative' also risks assuming a universal norm against which it is judged, and leaving the constructedness and particularity of that norm unexamined. This is something that Harley was careful to avoid but it is apparent in much Eurocentric thinking about 'other' practices of mapping. When researching these issues, it might therefore be more productive to think about the power of cartography in more entangled ways. This has indeed been the tenor of some postcolonial and feminist writings that have explored the possibilities of parodying, dismantling and displacing cartographies, and of working with different forms of mapping that 'do not replace one authoritative representation with another but with multiple names and multiple maps' (Nash, 1993: 54). It is also to some extent apparent in Debord's work, where he notes the need for a self-critical and provisional approach and implies that subversion is a continual process rather than an end state.

Despite stressing that Debord's maps should not be seen as a model for future action, I do think they raise important issues about cartographic practices and attempts to represent the city when understood in relation to the situationists' overall project. In particular, they underline some of the creative potential of maps and mapping, and the ways in which they might be reworked, reappropriated and used for diverse ends. In recent work I have been interested in relating this to earlier avant-garde traditions, especially around the surrealists, as well as more recent artistic practices that work with notions of mapping, through interest in senses beyond the visual including an attention to 'cartographies of sound' (Pinder, 2001b; see also Chapter 17). Approaching the world of maps critically and openly, and thinking creatively about practices of mapping, is of vital importance in a map-immersed society. As Harley pointed out some time ago, cartography is too important to be left to cartographers alone. Or perhaps more to the point is that cartography goes well beyond an 'official' terrain of experts, and embraces a whole range of practices through which people make sense of – and often seek to change – their environments. Having an experimental attitude to maps may include thinking about how to use them in your own texts. While there are useful guides on the more technical aspects of making maps in relation to research reports (for example, Dunn and Roberts, 1997), there is also currently wider interesting discussion about how cartographic forms can be used methodologically in innovative ways that take the power and politics of representation seriously (in relation to feminism, see Hoffman, 1997; Kwan, 2002). The need to recognize the multiple possibilities of maps and how they may be experimented with for particular ends also extends into other political and aesthetic realms. At the end of his book *The Power of Maps*, Denis Wood invokes: 'A legion of mapmakers, bewildering in their variety: *this* is the world of maps' (1993: 195).

Further reading

For influential theoretical perspectives on studying maps and cartography, see the work of Brian Harley and especially the posthumous collection of essays:

- Harley, J.B. (2001) *The New Nature of Maps: Essays in the History of Cartography*. Baltimore, The Johns Hopkins University Press.

Two good accounts of maps and mapping that adopt highly contrasting perspectives and styles, are:

- Dorling, D. and Fairbairn, D. (1997) *Mapping: Ways of Representing the World*. Harlow, Longman.

- Wood, D. with Fels, J. (1993) *The Power of Maps*. London, Routledge.

The following richly illustrated volumes present and discuss a range of interesting maps and forms of mapping:

- Barber, P. and Carlucci, A. (eds) (2002) *The Lie of the Land: The Secret Life of Maps*. London, British Library Publishing.

- Cosgrove, D. (ed.) (1999) *Mappings*. London, Reaktion Books.

- Kaiser, W.L. and Wood, D. (2001) *Seeing Through Maps: The Power of Images to Shape Our World View*. Amherst, Mass., ODT Inc.

- Turnbull, D. (1993) *Maps are Territories: Science is an Atlas*. Chicago, Chicago University Press.

For a selection of writings by the situationists translated into English, see:

- Knabb, K. (ed.) (1981) *Situationist International Anthology*. Berkeley, Bureau of Public Secrets.

A TALE OF RESEARCH

Researching sound art

Holly McLaren

Sound art is a relatively obscure aesthetic field, insecurely positioned between visual and acoustic realms. Whilst it draws upon both painterly and musical practices, it refuses to be bound by these categories and in doing so eludes concise definition; indeed, some may question the very designation of sound as a distinct artistic genre. As such, my decision to develop a research project concerning this ambiguous endeavour evolved not through an initial concern for sound art per se, but rather through the confluence of a number of interests, which led to my chance discovery of a group of public artists whose work frequently incorporates sound.

As an undergraduate, I had been particularly interested in cultural geographical scholarship concerning music, and I was keen to somehow work with sound in my postgraduate studies. I was also eager to embrace the discipline's growing interest in notions of performance and practice, an idea which directed me to consider the possibility of a project concerning musical consumption and the practice of listening. With these (rather sketchy) thoughts in mind, I decided to attend State of the Nation 2002 – a platform for new and innovative composers and performers – hoping for further inspiration. It was whilst there that I came across the public art of Greyworld, a group of artists whose work includes a number of interactive sound installations, many of which operate by translating touch and motion into sound (for more on the diverse work of Greyworld, visit www.greyworld.org). Take, for example, *Playground* – an installation of what appears to be a well-worn, but now forgotten, play area, situated in Yorkshire Sculpture Park. Using a computer programme and electronic sensors embedded in the ground, this installation transforms visitor movement into a multiplicity of ambient sounds, which vary according to weight, gait and footsize.

Intrigued by the characteristics of such artwork, and particularly by the extent to which it is performed or co-created by its 'audience', I decided to pursue the issue further. I contacted Greyworld, who kindly agreed to an interview, and followed this with a series of web searches which directed me to the public sound art of Graeme Miller and Brandon LaBelle, both of whom were willing to discuss their forthcoming projects with me. Each interview took a semi-structured format, as I was keen to gain insight into issues seen as relevant by the artists, whilst also incorporating a number of key themes which I considered particularly pertinent to cultural geographical enquiry. These included the relationship between sound art and site (and here I was particularly interested in how sound art might articulate space and place differently from purely visual art forms), the relationships between artist, artwork and audience (with an emphasis upon how sound art might destabilise traditional notions of creative authorship), and, connected to these topics, the extent to which sound art engages with contemporary debate concerning the nature and function of public art. By exploring such issues I hoped, firstly, to move geographical discussion of sound beyond the realm of music (and thereby gain further insight into the capacity of sound to modify the function and meaning of space and place); and, secondly, to extend

Playground *by Greyworld*

and enrich discussion of public art, particularly within the discipline, where discussion has focused mainly upon monuments and statuary.

Further to these objectives (and inspired by the content of my interviews), I also became increasingly interested in exploring the idea of art as a practice – something 'in-process' – rather than art as the subject of textual analysis. This idea emerged most notably through my discussion with Greyworld, whose art (more often than not) is complete only though audience participation/involvement – the human body frequently becoming an essential aesthetic focus within the work. As such, I decided it would be beneficial to engage with some of this work myself (and here Greyworld's *Playground* proved the most feasible case-study) in order to enrich my understanding of sound art as an embodied practice. I also believed that such participation would allow me greater insight into how sound art articulates and appropriates space and place.

Contemplating this approach, I realised that any consideration of sound art as practice would necessitate the employment of methodological strategies quite different from those associated with visual art forms such as landscape painting or sculpture. It also became increasingly apparent that many of the qualitative methodologies most commonly used within the discipline would be ill-suited to an investigation concerning the non textual, unfolding world of sound art. As a result, my engagement with *Playground* proceeded in ad hoc fashion, incorporating aspects from a variety of research methods.

The nature of this piece meant that my interaction with it was very much a physical act involving a considerable amount of running and jumping in response to the various sounds that randomly responded to my movements. During this time I attempted to keep mental notes of what I was doing and how I was feeling (although I later found it very difficult to articulate such sentiment in writing), in addition to observing how other visitors engaged with the piece. It was through this approach that I became increasingly aware of the ambiguities that characterised the site of *Playground*. To explicate further, my participation in this artwork drew my attention to the ways in which it promoted both spontaneous reaction as well more inhibited responses. So whilst I sometimes moved freely about the site 'in dialogue' with the piece, I often moved tentatively, aware of certain societal expectations of myself as an adult woman in public space.

In this respect, my consideration of *Playground* as an embodied practice, whilst sometimes difficult to articulate, offered a fascinating way to consider the performative aspects of identity and the ways in which space is implicated in such performance. It drew my attention to how bodily movements are regulated in everyday public spaces and also to the extent to which sound art creates a site of resistance to such regulation. Additionally, this approach enabled me to engage with the 'dynamics of situations' – or how events are shaped as they happen – a perspective which enhanced the more 'static'/traditional data gathered from the interviews. Consequently, I would suggest that thinking about sound art as embodied practice provides the opportunity to expand cultural geographical research, in terms of both subject-matter and methodological approach. Certainly, the difficulties I experienced in 'writing through' some of the improvisational aspects of my engagement with *Playground*, suggests the need for further consideration of the strategies used to communicate research within the discipline.

I studied for a BA Hons in Geography at the University of Exeter from 1997 to 2000, and then spent 2001–02 studying for an MA in Cultural Geography at Royal Holloway, University of London. My MA dissertation was entitled 'Between worlds: the ambiguous cultural geographies of public sound art.' The title was inspired by something that sound artist Brandon LaBelle said during an interview: 'Being a sound artist is an okay kind of title ... I like it because there's this ambiguity, people say "well, what's that?" and I sort of like that vagueness because I do feel that I can float between different worlds.' I am now working as a customer service advisor for Dee Valley Water.

12
Cinematic cities
Researching films as geographical texts

Maria Helena B. V. da Costa

The world on film

This chapter aims to encourage you to consider the ways in which geographers might analyse film. It uses the theoretical and methodological ideas of authors such as Aitken and Zonn (1994) to argue that films can provide 'maps of meaning' with which to navigate the world. More specifically, the chapter argues that there is much to be gained from trying to understand how the relationship between the world and the world on film (or the 'filmic world') is shaped, organised and understood. I assess this relationship through an analysis of the ways in which images of cities are constructed on film, and how these filmic images help in turn to shape our experience of the 'reality' of those cities.

The chapter is based on my own research into the representation of the (post)modern city in fictional films of various kinds. Here I draw on examples from a particular case study – the representation of New York City in Woody Allen's 1979 film *Manhattan*. In explaining how I analysed this film, I provide a theoretical and methodological framework for the analysis of films more generally that I hope will be of use for those wishing to read a filmic text from a geographical perspective.

Before trying to make sense of how films should be viewed from a 'cultural geographer's' point of view, it is useful to think through the complex relationships between film and the world it represents. For many cultural geographers (for example Cosgrove and Daniels, 1988; Duncan and Ley, 1993), to make sense of a specific space or place it is important to examine not only its material elements, but also the various ways in which that space or place has been represented. These **representations** are seen not as illustrations, as 'images standing outside [of] it', but as 'constituent' of its very meaning or meanings (Cosgrove and Daniels, 1988: 1). A very wide range of representations – painting, photography, literary works, film, and so on – can provide a potentially rich source for geographical analysis (see Chapters 3, 10 and 11). And because the essence of these representations is that they are an *interpretation* rather than a *record* of the space or place in question, we can ask questions of how these interpretations may in turn shape the ways in which these spaces and places themselves are interpreted and hence acted upon/in by a variety of people.

These representations are themselves constructed by the coming together of many different texts, and the relationships between them. This is called *intertextuality*: the idea that meaning is not simply produced in the relationship between a text and the thing it 'represents' (the 'outside world') but in the space between a variety of texts (see Barnes and Duncan, 1992). If taking inter-textuality seriously, it is clear that we can not simply use film to understand the city in the sense of 'checking' the filmic representation of that city against the 'reality': first, because the film is not simply a more or less distorted reflection of 'reality', but an inter-textual set of meanings which has to be understood in terms of the other representations of the city on which it draws; second, because we can have no sure way of saying what the city 'really' is: since this is always a matter of its various representations, and of the ways in which we respond to these in our understandings of and actions within the 'real' city. To grasp the latter, think of how difficult it is to imagine New York, Los Angeles or London without having one's imagination coloured by how these cities are represented in film and on TV.

In an important sense, then, the city on the cinema screen – what I refer to as the *cinematic city* – is a cultural representation which moulds our views of, and helps us to understand the meanings of what we might call the *concrete city* (Clarke, 1997). As Hopkins puts it:

> The cinematic landscape is not, consequently, a neutral place of entertainment or an objective documentation or mirror of the 'real', but an ideologically charged cultural creation whereby meanings of place and society are made, legitimized, contested and obscured. Intervening in the … cinematic landscape will … contribute to the more expansive task of mapping the social, spatial, and political geography of film.
>
> (Hopkins, 1994: 47)

If it is true that we **construct** the world and our attitude towards it from cultural texts (Barnes and Duncan, 1992), then the filmic text is one in which identities, wishes and desires can be powerfully visualised. Films are one of the key places where the world acquires 'life' and can be interpreted. We might even say that the physical, concrete city only becomes 'real' when it is represented, when it is *re-presented* to us through different interpretations. The representation of the city by the cinema is a fundamental part of the cultural politics of actual cities and of the lived experience of the individuals who inhabit them.

For example, the surface of the modern cityscape – its streets, skyscrapers, bridges and landmarks – has been a fixation of and a shaping influence on many different films. They have, however, been used in a range of very different contexts to put forward quite different ideas, and to present interpretations of a selection of different social and cultural conflicts. Hence, there are different projections of the future city in of science-fiction films like *Metropolis* (Fritz Lang, 1927), *Blade Runner* (Ridley Scott, 1982), *The Fifth Element* (Luc Besson, 1997) and *The Matrix* (Larry Wachowski and Andy Wachowski, 1999). There are representations of the contemporary modernist city in the films of the French director Jean-Luc Godard and Italian film-maker Michelangelo Antonioni. There are utopian versions of the modern city, such as *The Crowd* (King Vidor, 1928) or *Sunrise* (F.W. Murnau, 1927) and dystopian ones too, such as *Seven* (David Fincher, 1995) or *Minority Report* (Steven Spielberg, 2002). In each case the cultural construction of the city is grounded in imagery already established in other texts and narratives. The same city can also be represented very differently, giving it distinct meanings. Martin Scorsese's New York in *Taxi Driver* (1976) is not the same New York as the one in Spike Lee's *Do the Right Thing* (1989). Though both films are references to the same place, the way the cityscape is represented and interpreted indicates differences of 'race' and politics. They are both New York, but they are different New Yorks.

There are, or course, different sorts of films which make different claims about how they are representing the city. We can distinguish between three types: (1) those in which the *cinematic city* claims to represent the 'reality' of the city not only realistically but objectively and faithfully – for example in non-fictional genres such as documentaries; (2) those in which the *cinematic city* represents a fictional world, but one with a counterpart in the real world. That is, the film narrates fictional stories set in 'real' and recognisable cities like Detroit, e.g. *8 Mile* (Curtis Hanson, 2002); Los Angeles, e.g. *Boyz N The Hood* (John Singleton, 1991), Paris, e.g. *La Haine* (Mathieu Kossovitz, 1995); or Rio de Janeiro, e.g. *City of God* (Fernando Meirelles, 2002); and (3) those which represent a *cinematic city* which does not have a counterpart in reality (for example, *Batman*'s Gotham city (Tim Burton, 1989) or Godard's (1965) *Alphaville*). Even in this third case, however, the visual construction of this 'unreal city' or 'city of the imagination' draws upon references to existing cities and their meanings. Film-makers must inevitably take some elements from contemporary cities to construct their fictional urban realms. For this reason, even science-fiction films set in imaginary cities – or in the case of *Blade Runner*, a future Los Angeles – offer a commentary on contemporary notions of issues such as inequality, corporate **power** and social change.

My own research, and this chapter, are concerned with the second type: cinematic cities with a clear counterpart in the 'real' world. Of these I pose a set of key questions: Why is the city represented in the particular way that it is? What kind of relationship does the film try to establish between the 'concrete city' and its cinematic counterpart? What makes this relationship convincing, apart from visual resemblance? How does the film-maker draw upon other forms of representation of the same subject? What kind of interpretation or reading is encouraged by the film?

Working with film

How can this potentially creative 'dialogue' between cultural geography and film be made productive? The first step is to develop a rigorous approach to the source material. Familiarity with the 'source' or the 'data' (for example, films that you really like and have watched many times) makes it, if anything, all the more important that you step back from its apparently 'transparent' nature in order to grasp its structure and complexities. The fact that we live in a movie-saturated culture does not mean that we understand all the ways in which these images work. Film Studies is a well-established academic discipline and you should familiarise yourself with some of its literature and debates, as well as with the work of those geographers who have engaged with it (for example Agre, 1993; Aitken and Zonn, 1994; Bruno, 1987, 1997; Burgess and Gold, 1985; Clarke, 1997; Denzin, 1991; James, 1999; Lury and Massey, 1999; McArthur, 1997; Robins, 1991). You should also familiarise yourself with some of the key ideas of film criticism and analysis. Stam (2000) and Andrew (1984) provide succinct guides to film theory and criticism, and give examples of interpretations. Collins *et al.* (1993) discuss the analysis and comparison of different kinds of texts. You then need to think about the films that you want to interpret.

Researching a city through its cinematic image

Research involves the selection of material. If your intention is to do research on films, think first about the themes you intend to look at within these representations (urban space, for instance, or ideas of national **identity**). Then start to think about the films you wish to analyse. Be aware that your first choices might change during the investigation, so allow yourself some freedom to alter your approach. Once you have chosen your broad area of investigation – the theme and the film(s) – it is wise to situate the film or films you have selected within a wider body of cinematic work. This process might mean starting by watching as many films as possible directed by the same film-maker or within the same film genre, though after that you might decide to work with only one or two of the many films you have watched. You should also search for literature – especially academic, but also popular – about the films, or written by or about the filmmakers, and including any reviews, pieces of criticism or interviews with the filmmaker. With as much supporting material to hand as possible you can begin to interpret these films as 'geographical representations' in relation to your theme. For example, to understand the representation of the Los Angeles of 2017 in *Blade Runner*, it might be instructive to understand something about how that city was understood and represented at the time of that film's production in the early 1980s (see Brund, 1987; Harvey, 1989 and Soja, 1989).

In my own research, I began with an interest in representations of New York and looked for a film-maker whose work was associated with that city. Eventually, I ended up working with and on Woody Allen's films. In doing so I approached these films from a number of different angles. I want to set out seven of these here, in the hope of providing a framework that others can use when seeking to make sense of the 'geographies of film'. They concern a consideration of: the film-maker; the film's narrative structure; locations; camerawork; sound; inter-textuality; and the audience. I illustrate each with examples from my research on New York and its representation in Woody Allen's *Manhattan* (1979) (da Costa, 2000).

1 Considering the film-maker

My decision to interpret the cinematic city of New York constructed by Woody Allen had three justifications. First, Woody Allen is one of the most self-conscious contemporary American film-makers, and so he is a good example of how the film-maker influences the kind of techniques used to construct a 'vision' of the city. Second, I realised that if I was to pick one film-maker that was directly associated with the interpretation and even celebration of New York, that film-maker ought to be Woody Allen. Between 1969 and 1995 11 out of 25 of Allen's films were set in New York and explicitly comment on 'New York life'. A further seven films used the city as a backdrop (see Kruth, 1997). Third, in his films, and especially in *Manhattan*, Allen presents a distinctive view of New York and its myths of modernity, cosmopolitanism, progress, capitalism and culture. He also represents these themes in an inter-textual way, by referring to visual motifs already established by other forms of representation.

It is, therefore, important to use biographical and critical writings by and about the film-maker to understand them as an 'author' (or 'auteur' in the terminology of film criticism), and to know how they think about the process of film-making (See Chapter 3). In my case, I was convinced by what Woody Allen himself said about his films: notably, that they can best be understood as an attempt to present a particular version of New York. In interview, for example, he has often stated how strongly he identifies himself with New York – in his way of thinking, feeling and creating – and that his films are a reflection of the enormous influence of the place on him:

> What I feel about New York is hard to say in a few words. It's really the rhythm of the city. You feel it the moment you walk down the street. There's hundreds of good restaurants, thousands of brilliant paintings, you see all the old movies, all the new ones. … It has to do with nerves, with the blood that runs through the city. It's dangerous, noisy. It's not peaceful or easy and because of it you feel more alive. It's more in keeping with what human beings are meant to feel about the world. …There's more conflict than anywhere else'.
>
> (Woody Allen quoted in McCann, 1990, p.36)

Woody Allen, I found out, is one of those film-makers who draw upon their particular self-involvement with the place they wish to depict in order to give cinematic expression to the city's way of life – to represent its tensions and tempos, its patterns and social relationships, its morals and mannerisms. Thus, looking at Allen's films and assessing the way he perceives and represents the city of New York allowed me to understand that many of the particularities of his cinematic city rest in his own individual vision and experience of that city.

It is clear that Allen's own image of New York is a romantic one. In *Manhattan* the New York we are shown is a world where well-off people worry about being safe and adventurous, witty and fashionable, unemotional and enthusiastic all at the same time. In many ways this is a nostalgic vision – a homage to a way of living in the city now long past that Allen appears to want to recapture. Yet, even as he gives the city a nostalgic gloss, Allen lends this picture a 'realistic' edge by setting *Manhattan* in modern day New York – such that we appear to have a film about the contemporary city. He achieves this, in part, by making constant reference to the 'real' public spaces of the city – showing the audience familiar spaces and places, the very apartments that are part of the city, and the very streets and parks where he himself, as well as (some members of) the audience, frequently walk – and in part through moving between the contemporary concerns of his characters and older views of the city (with clips from old movies, old photographs and old music).

As a result, it is perhaps now difficult to 'see' New York through anything other than the nostalgic lens of Allen's vision, though this is not to say that other 'views' aren't possible or that members of the audience might find it easier to identify with these rather than Allen's (assuming not all members of the audience to be as wealthy as Allen's characters tend to be, for example). Since every film-maker takes a distinctive approach to the work they do we can find many different versions of *cinematic* New York and in this regard it is useful to compare the very particular representation of New York that Woody Allen presents to that of Martin Scorsese (in *Taxi Driver* (1976), *Mean Streets* (1973), or *Goodfellas* (1990)), for example, who represents a more dangerous, dark, mean and socially polarised vision of the city.

While it is important to consider film in terms of the film-maker, it is also important to remember that any film is set in a wider web of cultural meanings that extend beyond the director's intentions. It is therefore vital not to overestimate the film-maker's view at the expense of other elements which also play a part in the process of constructing meaning.

2 Considering the film's structure

Once you have chosen the film(s) you wish to analyse you need to watch them over and over again. This means that it is important to pick films that you can get easy access to on video or DVD. While watching you should take notes. Make sure you date these so that you can see how your interpretations of the film(s) change. Although I worked with a number of Woody Allen's films, I decided to start with *Manhattan* mainly because of its suggestive title. Sometimes the simple option is best! In what follows, I want to offer some things that you should look out for in these repeated viewings.

The first step is to grasp the basic narrative structure of the film – ask yourself what actually happens and what the film might be said to be *about*? Though you will need to present an interpretation of the film that is more than just a summary of the story, you also need to convey a strong sense of the film's themes and narrative structure in your final account. *Manhattan* is about a love triangle between Isaac (played by Woody Allen himself), a writer of television comedy who quits his job in order to have time to write a 'serious' book, Tracy (Mariel Hemingway), a beautiful and sensitive 17-year-old who spends most of her time in the film trying to convince Isaac that he is not too old for her, and Mary (Diane Keaton), a 'neurotic' woman who is involved with a married man who is Isaac's best friend Yale (Michael Murphy). *Manhattan* is, therefore, essentially about relationships between men and women as well as the nature of friendship. It portrays not only how relationships form, fade and dissolve, but also the moral implications, responsibilities and potential fulfilment they involve.

You might also ask yourself how the film begins, how the themes, characters and locations are introduced, and how the film ends. *Manhattan* opens with a three-minute black-and-white montage sequence of New York's cityscape accompanied by the swelling rhythms of George Gershwin's *Rhapsody in Blue*. First we see the skyline, then individual buildings, and then the streets and the passers-by, crowded streets simmering under a summer sun and snow-covered parks, Delancey Street at high noon, Park Avenue at dawn, Broadway, Wall Street at dusk, construction men drilling a street, schoolchildren running home, joggers in Central Park, the Plaza Hotel, the 59th Street Bridge, fireworks over Central Park, and so on. The wonderful flow of street scenes in this opening montage brings the city alive and gives it a sense of power and excitement. During this sequence we simultaneously hear Isaac's voice-over (in Allen's recognisable accent) and Gershwin's music. At this point Isaac is trying to start his 'serious' book and he is struggling to find an appropriate narrative voice, and a vision of New York, for the opening of his first chapter. The distinctive content and tones of Isaac's variety of openings for his book also suggest the different moods and meanings attached to Manhattan. First, there is the voice of the experienced city dweller for whom an out-of-proportion romantic New York existed 'in black and white and pulsated to the great tunes of George Gershwin'. Then there is the self-described 'romantic' for whom 'New York meant beautiful women and street-smart guys who seemed to know all the angles'. Then we hear the worries about 'the decay of contemporary culture', the demise of 'individual integrity' that was destroying 'the town of his dreams' and the angry cry against 'drugs, loud music, TV, crime, garbage'. In describing the city, the main character and narrator in Isaac's book projects his own moods and conceptions of himself onto the setting. Each group of city images that are shown on the screen are accompanied by one of Isaac's 'word-pictures'. The final attempt is a description of the idealised position taken in relation to the city not only by Isaac's character in the book, or Isaac himself in the film, but also, perhaps, by Woody Allen himself: 'He was as … tough and romantic as the city he loved. … New York was his town. And it always would be'. The image on the screen represents what Isaac wants to explain in writing but does not know how to put into words that are not clichés. Allen seems to be saying that the image on the screen – the diversity of Manhattan's cityscape – is the only proper way to represent the city, not the 'incomplete' written or spoken word.

The opening sequence can also be read as deliberately ambiguous (Girgus, 1993). Although it seems that Isaac has 'found' his beginning, the actual result can be interpreted as exactly the opposite (McCann, 1990). Isaac's final 'draft' ('He was as … tough and romantic as the city he loved') is the only one that does *not* sum up one of *Manhattan's* several themes. Throughout the film we realise that Isaac is in fact emotionally confused over his relationship with modern Manhattan. He cannot abide its 'fake values', the pretentiousness and narcissism of its intellectual elite, its banal television shows. Yet even his friends know that 'He can't function anywhere other than New York'. Indeed, this is actually what the film is about. It is about both people and places having no single fixed identity – all of these versions of the city and its inhabitants, are true, both good and bad – and the difficulties of negotiating a way between them.

The end of *Manhattan* follows the same narrative pattern of connecting the image of the city with the characters' feelings and relationships. Settled on the couch of his apartment, Isaac meditates about the plot of his book and about people in Manhattan. He reaches the conclusion that his story should be optimistic. He asks himself why life is worth living and he starts listing his favourite things. Among a list that includes Groucho Marx, Swedish movies, Flaubert's *Sentimental Education*, and Cezanne's 'apples and pears', he discovers Tracy's face. When he cannot reach her by phone he begins his long run across town to her apartment. Isaac's exciting and climactic race through Manhattan is shown as a long take of him running on the streets of Manhattan passing people, parks and cars, with more Gershwin music (*Strike up the Band*) in the background. Arriving at Tracy's building he sees her in the lobby. She is on her way to London where she will study for six months. After trying to convince Tracy to stay, Isaac, to his disappointment, hears Tracy tell him that if they really love each other then six months will be nothing and that he has to have more faith in people. Finally, a magnificent skyline of Manhattan is shown again on the screen, at first cast almost in silhouette by an early-morning sun, then by sunset and, finally, at night with its buildings and bridges illuminated with thousands of lights, while *Rhapsody in Blue* is playing once again. As night falls on the city, so the story ends.

What is apparent in all of this, of course – and as already hinted in the previous section – is that despite the claims that the opening and closing of the film make to representing the city as a whole, the focus of *Manhattan* is very clearly upon the intimate relationships and anxieties of a small and relatively privileged section of the city's population. It concerns the ways in which they relate to each other as lovers and friends, and the relationships they have to the city. Understanding the particularity of this cinematic city involves looking more closely at *where* the action is set, and at those parts of the city we see on the screen.

3 Considering the locations

An obvious issue for cultural geographers is the locations shown on film and, again, they should feature in the notes you take. The first stage is to list what happens where. Are certain individuals consistently placed in certain spaces, for instance? Do particular sorts of action happen in particular sorts of location? Overall, you should think about the meaning of the locations used. Since all places carry certain sorts of meanings, how are these meanings used in the film to give particular sorts of significance to characters or events within the narrative (Cresswell, 1996)? In terms of representations of the city, how does the selection of particular sets of locations over others involve the presentation of a particular version, or 'vision', of the city on film?

For example, *Manhattan* certainly offers a particular view of the city through its use of certain locations in New York. Based on the understanding that New York is the centre of cosmopolitanism, culture and civility for a certain set of people, this film shows the very essence of New York's cosmopolitan cultural life and the places frequented by white upper-class New Yorkers. Characters are always walking around parks, museums, art galleries; they are always on their way to the movies and shows; and they are frequently eating in very stylish restaurants or shopping in the most fashionable stores. Consequently, places such as the Museum of Modern Art, the Guggenheim Museum, the Lincoln Center, the Hayden Planetarium, as well as restaurants and shops such as Zabar's, Dean and De Luca's, Elaine's and Bloomingdale's, all come together to display the public spaces which are the 'essence' of white, upper-class New York. Again, the contrast might be drawn between this version of the city and representations of New York that focus on the suburbs (e.g. *Meet The Parents* (Jay Roach, 2000), or, on TV, *The Sopranos*) or those that are situated in the financial heart of the city (e.g. *Wall*

Street (Oliver Stone, 1987)) or in the ghetto (e.g. *Do The Right Thing*, or, for a different era, *West Side Story* (Robert Wise/Jerome Robbins, 1961)). In each case, however, the characters and the action draw meaning from the places in which the film depicts them, and those places (or locations) gain new layers of meaning from the characters and their interaction. What this makes clear, however, is that this is not only a matter of where the action is set – the locations – but also how they are filmed.

4 Considering camerawork

The camerawork is one of the technical elements responsible for how we see the images on the screen. This is an important and fundamental aspect of the 'language' of film that you can only really learn through studying the relevant literature. You should teach yourself to look out for different camera positions and movements, and the results that emerge from the composition of different moving and still images. The use of tracking shots, close-ups, travellings, and so on, is informed by the kind of film narrative that film-makers wish to construct. They shape the kind of cinematic city we are presented with. Thus, the content of the visions of the city on film is directly related to the aesthetics and the composition of the images that appear on the screen, and not just dependent upon the story that is told, or how the characters interact. In the case of *Manhattan* it is possible to outline what such 'techniques' might indicate or signify.

There are simple visual techniques which help set the context for the narrative. For example, in *Manhattan* there is a pattern of showing images of the New York skyline at dusk and at dawn, or Central Park on a sunny afternoon or on a stormy Sunday morning, to place the action within a temporal context. Moreover, images of the same place under different conditions serve to move the narrative to a different time. There are also ways of filming that shape the meaning of what is seen. Think, for example, about the way that the use of a hand-held camera – in realist TV fictions like *NYPD Blue* or *The Office* – with its shaky framing and the moving of characters in and out of focus, is used to suggest a documentary 'reality'. Ways of *shooting* can also be used to shape the meaning of the city. In *Manhattan* images of the city are normally shot close to ground level and with medium close-ups and long shots of characters wandering about in the city – permitting a highlighted view of buildings and the wider cityscape. Allen hardly ever uses close-up shots, preferring tricky long-distance views where people struggle for position with others and the on-going life of the city. In these and other ways Woody Allen creates a continuous sense of movement and dynamism within the city.

Camerawork techniques can also be used to suggest ways in which the characters should be interpreted. In *Manhattan* the connection between the city and its inhabitants is, in part, secured by the contrast between the unusual construction of interior sequences – in which the characters are always framed, or rather enclosed, between vertical and horizontal 'lines', implying a claustrophobic sense of being trapped inside – and the use of long shots to emphasise the freedom implied in the exterior scenes when the characters walk in the streets of the city.

The *framing* of particular shots (which can be understood in similar ways to still photographs, see Chapter 10) can also shape the meanings presented of location, characters and narrative. One example is the sequence which begins with Mary (Diane Keaton) and Isaac (Woody Allen) walking at night in the dark wet streets of Manhattan after leaving the Museum of Modern Art where they had met. This pleasant walk reaches a climax when they are finally shown with their backs to the camera sitting on a bench looking out at the 59th Street Bridge (Queensboro Bridge) shot from underneath, and taking a larger part of the screen (Figure 12.2). Isaac comments on how beautiful the sight is, especially 'when the lights start to come up'. He says: 'This is really a great city. I don't care what anybody says. It's just … really a knockout, you know?' The framing of the shot, with the dramatically illuminated bridge arching over the river and occupying the centre of the frame creates a strong sense of balance and symmetry with Isaac and Mary at the lower right of the screen. This image suggests a new emotional bond between the characters and offers the promise of romance, of a relationship (even if momentary) to fill in the gaps of discontentment and loneliness they share. However, just as the bridge itself arches off into a distant fog and haze, so one can also envision a subtext evoking a relationship that ultimately is going nowhere (Girgus, 1993). This is only one of many examples that shows how in *Manhattan* the cityscape is part of the action. In the extended encounters with New York streets and the framed views of the skyline the city emerges from the shadowed backdrop to take on a narrative role.

5 Considering sound

One of the most obvious differences between film and other forms of representation – literature, painting, photography – is that it combines moving images, dialogue and music (see Chapter 17). Dialogue, music and other sounds help the film narrative to develop and to establish the mood of characters and places. It is, therefore, important to deal with film as a soundscape (Smith, 1994). In practical terms, it is normally relatively easy to find a published copy of a film's screenplay. However, if a screenplay turns out to be difficult to find in libraries, bookshops or on the internet then the *British Film Institute* (BFI) or the *American Film Institute* (AFI) can offer advice. With the screenplay to hand you can check production or direction references to the locations or comments in the dialogue. In relation to the musical score, the main question is: Why did the film-maker choose those specific pieces or types of music rather than other ones? This is a matter of trying to understand what meanings the music brings to the other elements of the film.

In *Manhattan* Woody Allen shows us how music (and other sorts of sound) can be used and controlled to make the narrative work. The dazzling opening to the film (see above) works through the combination of a dramatic cinematic display of magnificent images of New York combined with Gershwin's 'Rhapsody in Blue' and the conflicting voices of Isaac's voice-over. The visual and musical strength literally overwhelms the voices. Instead of concentrating on Isaac's voice-over, Allen highlights the montage of the city scenes and the music that engulfs it. In this way Allen calls attention to the power of the image in representing the place. For him it is the *image* and the *music* of the city, not words, which capture the essence of the place, and in this case that 'essence' is, as I have shown, a quite particular and nostalgic vision of New York. Throughout the film Gershwin's songs take us to 'another time' – the cosmopolitan New York of the first half of the twentieth century. They also explain the characters and their relationships in present time. When Isaac is with 'neurotic' and vulnerable Mary, we hear 'Embraceable You' and 'Someone To Watch Over Me'. When he is with Tracy – who, in many ways, is more of an equal – the tunes are 'He Loves and She Loves' and 'Love Is Here To Stay'. The last tune we hear just before Isaac hesitantly faces Tracy in the last scene is 'But Not For Me'. In *Manhattan*, the music, when we know what we are listening to, adds another dimension to Woody Allen's nostalgic and romantic portrait of the city.

6 Considering inter-textuality

Working with films means paying attention to inter-textuality. Film texts are influenced both by other films and by other types of text, so knowledge of these is important in the interpretation of a film. You will not be able to spot all the references that are made. Some will be very consciously done on the part of the film-maker, others will be a matter of a common set of ways of representing a place, mood or type of character. *Manhattan* has many references to different ways in which New York has been represented – other films, music, and photography. It can be regarded as a particular recollection, memory, or revival of 'past New York'. The film appears to pay special attention to a certain imagery (dark night, empty streets, the rain) that has elements in common with the *film noir* tradition of 1940s and 1950s Hollywood (e.g. *Naked City* (Jules Dassin, 1947) or *The Sweet Smell of Success* (Alexander Mackendrick, 1957)); whilst the romantic Gershwin melodies recall the glamour of other movies from that period that used New York as a setting for sophisticated romances and musicals (like *Dinner at Eight* (George Cukor, 1933) and *42nd Street* (Lloyd Bacon, 1933)). The city imagery can also be easily connected to the pictures of the city produced by the famous early twentieth-century photographer Alfred Stieglitz. There is no doubt that Allen's representation of New York is based more on the spirit evoked by an idea of the city's landmarks, panoramic skyline, earlier photographs, old movies, jazz, and George Gershwin's music rather than the everyday details of contemporary city life. Within Allen's framework, the city 'panoramas' are presented more as an 'atmosphere', a set of values, a frame of mind rather than the city of steel, concrete, glass, movement, and clamorous noise. Allen is obviously dealing with a sense of a 'lost city' by exploring the relationship between living in the contemporary city and memories of the past. In this way *Manhattan* reflects a concern for what is absent, missing, what has come to exist only in memory:

> [T]hat's how I remember it from when I was small. Maybe it's a reminiscence from old photographs, films, books and all that. But that's how I remember New York. I always heard the Gershwin music with it, too.
>
> (Allen in McCann, 1990: p.20)

7 Considering the audience

Different people can have different interpretations of the same film, and although researching audiences has not formed a part of my own work, it is necessary to point out its potential importance. The academic literature contains numerous contemporary discussions of spectatorship such as *Cinema and Spectatorship* by Judith Mayne (1993) or *Interpreting Films: Studies in the Historical Reception of American Cinema* by Janet Steiger (1992). Films are received and interpreted in a variety of settings – the public space of the cinema or the private space of the home, for example – and by individuals or groups. This raises questions about the additional layers of meaning that the film thereby acquires, and about the processes by which cultural constructions like cinematic cities are understood in relation to different people's lives. You could approach audiences in at least two ways, first, by investigating reviews and comments in newspapers, magazines and on the increasing numbers of websites devoted to film, secondly, by questioning audiences and viewers directly on their interpretations of film. Questionnaires, focus groups and interviews all offer valuable methods for understanding these questions of interpretation (see Chapters 6, 7 and 8).

Conclusions and suggestions for further research

Overall, this chapter has introduced a general strategy for investigating film as a source for cultural geography, and looked at urban space on film more particularly. I have argued that cinematic representations are structured in particular ways – by the film-maker, through narrative, in the choice of locations, by different techniques of camerawork, with the use of sound, through inter-texuality, and by the audience – and that they can shape our perceptions, imaginations and memories of all sorts of spaces, places and landscapes and the constant processes through which those geographies are reshaped or rearranged. The central argument is that the images presented in films can be read as interventions into specific sets of ideas and anxieties about society, culture, politics and economics. It is a matter of picking a theme – empire, class, national identity, industrial restructuring – and understanding how it is represented on film through the particular forms and processes that that medium makes possible (Natter and Jones, 1993).

Whilst my own research has been concerned with Woody Allen's 'vision' of Manhattan, a fascinating study could be done, as I have hinted above, comparing the different representations of the same urban space within the works of different film-makers. Compare, for instance the versions of New York presented by, white, Jewish, intellectual Woody Allen, and black, radical and hard-hitting Spike Lee. Other studies might address the representations of space within particular film genres. Genres such as *film noir* have been studied in this way, showing their connections with particular cities (such as Los Angeles, see Davis, 1990) and with particular forms of masculinity (Krutnik, 1991). The same might be done for romantic comedies or superhero movies. The possibilities are endless and film offers new directions and exciting challenges to cultural geographers.

Further reading

For geographical writings on film (and, in particular the city on film) see:
- Aitken, S. C. and Zonn, L. E. (eds) (1994) *Place, Power, Situation and Spectacle: A Geography of Film.* Lanham, Rowman & Littlefield Publishers.
- Clarke, D. B. (ed.) (1997) *The Cinematic City.* London, Routledge.
- Shiel, M. and Fitzmaurice, T. (eds) (2001) *Cinema and the City: Film and Urban Societies in a Global Context.* Oxford, Blackwell.
- Shiel, M. and Fitzmaurice, T. (eds) (2003) *Screening the City.* London, Verso.

For introductions to film studies, see:
- Andrew, D. (1984) *Concepts in Film Theory.* Oxford, Oxford University Press.
- Stam, R. (2000) *Film Theory: An Introduction.* Oxford, Blackwell Publishers.

For work on audiences see:
- Mayne, J. (1993) *Cinema and Spectatorship.* London, Routledge.
- Steiger, J. (1992) *Interpreting Films: Studies in the Historical Reception of American Cinema.* New Jersey, Princeton University Press.

13
Researching the networks of natural history television

Gail Davies

Introducing the nature of the small screen

Did you see *The Blue Planet*? It was on British television in the autumn of 2001 and has since appeared on television in other parts of the world. I have to admit I enjoyed it. Having previously done research on natural history film-making, I usually find these programmes hard to watch. It's too much like work. However, this series on oceanic wildlife was pure escapism and an example of this televisual genre at its best. Stunning underwater photography, amazing unknown creatures and a suitably ambient soundtrack seduced me into a world of pure nature beneath the waves.

This series was on the drawing board when I left the BBC's Natural History Unit in Bristol in the autumn of 1995. I had just finished researching how this television unit had created a distinctive vision of nature on television that had endured for 50 years. From its origins in the 1950s, the unit has built a reputation for what is called 'blue-chip' natural history film-making. These are programmes of animal behaviours and habitats showing 'nature in the raw' – a nature without people and a nature in which the separation of culture and nature, humans and animals is, for the main, absolute. Yet accomplishing this vision of pristine nature is a complex choreography between the practices of scientific research, filming techniques and television values. The stunning seascapes of *The Blue Planet* raised a series of questions about the mixing together of human labour, technology, and animal lives through which they were forged. For example, how had they overcome the technical difficulties in filming? It had clearly taken a while to achieve. What was the resulting balance between location filming and aquarium set ups? Which research institutes had they worked with and how had these collaborators benefited? Were the media now funding the scientists? The subject of money raised questions of how much the series cost, how much was met by the UK licence fee and how much by international co-producers. Did the involvement of these commercial broadcasters influence the style and content of filming? The programme makers had not tried to address environmental issues in the main series on BBC1, but made two separate programmes about marine conservation for BBC2. What did this say about the balance between entertainment and education on prime-time television? More personally, who out of the people I talked to in 1995 had been involved in this programme? How had it helped their careers? Clearly, other ideas and people had been sidelined by the Unit's focus on this oceanic epic; other stories of animal lives and places would remain untold.

The programmes constructed a vicarious experience of nature that was both intimate and pure, yet supporting these visions of the natural world was a complex web of interrelations, collaborations and exclusions. My first aim in this chapter is to explore why, as a geographer, I was interested in reconnecting the separation of humans and nature in the processes of making natural history films. I am not alone in this interest. Over the last ten years or so geographers have been challenging some of the dualisms that pervade their discipline. Dualisms are ways of thinking about the world, that carve it up into two separate spheres – for example, the division of the content and methods of human and physical geography. Taking inspiration variously from the work of French engineer Bruno Latour, English sociologist John Law, and American feminist scholar Donna Haraway, a growing number of geographers are exploring non-dualistic thinking about nature and culture (Castree and Braun 2001; Murdoch, 1997a; Whatmore, 1999a). In this way of thinking what is defined as 'natural' or 'cultural' is seen as a historically and culturally contingent practice of boundary-making between the mixed up realms of 'nature' and 'culture'. How nature is represented or visualised, who claims to speak for nature, is an important part of this boundary making process. Traditionally, the natural sciences are privileged to speak for nature, the human sciences for culture, yet this is also challenged. Rather, different ways of knowing about the world are viewed as differently **situated knowledges**, emerging from separate locations and practices. The differential **power** of **discourses** to speak for nature emerges through their ability to act over space (Clark and Murdoch, 1997; Thrift, Driver, and Livingstone, 1995). Often this is expressed through the metaphor of networks or assemblages, and the term 'actor network theory' is a useful – if not entirely accurate – shorthand for this approach (Hetherington and Law, 2000). A successful network is one able to organise more allies or actors, and their locations, to its way of defining the world, in ways that endure through time and are able to act over space. Our taken-for-granted separation of nature and culture emerges from these interconnected networks of **representational** practices.

This way of viewing dominant discourses of nature as emerging from successful networks or assemblages has appealed to geographers. There are a growing number of lucid introductions to this way of thinking and its implications for geographical research (Castree and Macmillan, 2001; Murdoch, 1997a; Murdoch, 1997b). The idea of a network seems inherently geographical, and has been used by geographers to research the relationship between nature, culture, technology, and space in a number of ways. Networks have been used to trace the hybrid 'nature-cultures' created by environmental policies and other practices. Whatmore and Thorne (2000) explore the real and virtual spaces created for elephants and other wildlife through international biodiversity conventions, breeding programmes and eco-tourist experiences. Burgess, Clark and Harrison (2000) use a similar approach to illustrate how nature is represented and mobilised by the different actors – conservationists, farmers and local people – involved in a wildlife enhancement scheme in South-East England. The current form of the river Cole emerges out of the restoration processes traced using actor network theory in the work of Eden, Tunstall and Tapsell (2000). Actor network theory has also been used to problematise the practices and politics of representation: Bingham (1996) uses actor network theory to explore the role of new communications technologies in creating networks of representational practices, challenging assumptions that the new technologies of cyberspace determine new forms of social organisation; and Holloway (1998) uses an actor network theory approach to explore the chains of production and consumption in the texts of the radical environmental movements. Actor network theory treats representations as precariously stabilised orderings that jostle for space with other ways of ordering the world.

Actor network theory suggests you follow the actors in order to identify the manner in which they build their world, whether social or natural, and to trace how effects emerge. This approach applied to natural history filmmaking explores the mixing up of nature and technology, scientific practices and television values from which the powerful images of wilderness emerge. The account of natural history filmmaking that emerges from this approach includes not only social meanings or social actors, but also the institutional forms, technologies, animals and environments so important throughout its history. It also promises a way of opening up questions about the politics of doing natural history filmmaking in ways a semiotic analysis does not. Wildlife filmmakers themselves acknowledge a tension between their purified images of nature, and the complex contexts from which these images emerge. As established filmmaker Mills (1997) puts it '[the wildlife filmmaker] makes his [sic] living out of nature; nature is disappearing. If he says too much about that, he loses his audience. If he does not he loses his subject'. By recovering the complex history of the development of natural history filmmaking I sought to recover more points at which to take responsibility for the outcomes of natural history filmmaking and their processes of construction. As Murdoch (1997b: 335) counters, change is better effected from within, for only 'once we understand how size and power are manufactured then we can understand how they can be transformed. But we will only fully recognize the potential for change if we stay within the networks.'

In this chapter I explore the practical implications of trying to follow the creation of natural history films from within the network by recounting some of my own research experiences with the BBC's Natural History Unit. Much geographical literature on actor network theory has been more explicit about its theoretical value than on its methodological application and so the second aim of this chapter is thus to reflect on the methodological issues and practical problems that emerge from following the multiplicity of human, technical and animal worlds that are organised together to allow purity to emerge. In the language of actor network theory natural history films are purified outcomes that compartmentalise a messy and complex world of representational practice. The technological developments, scientific collaborations, BBC employees, and oceanic wildlife in *The Blue Planet* provide just some of the raw materials from which the visions of wilderness on our screen have been forged. Practising actor network theory suggests you follow the history of connections from which these contemporary visions of nature emerge, and to trace through how it might have been otherwise. My account is divided into five sections. First, I explore issues of defining and getting access to the network – where does the network start and where should the researcher begin? In the second section I return to actor network theory to address in more detail some of the methodological issues and practical problems that emerged. In the third section I explore further what I understood by the call to follow the actors, and in the fourth section I explore the implications of this for studying the nonhuman actors that make up the network. In the fifth and final section I return again to the politics of actor network theory, exploring the political opportunities opened up through research which creates narratives that trace how networks are built and how powerful representations emerge.

Studying television networks in action

Where to begin?

Starting any piece of empirical research is daunting, but starting an investigation informed by actor network theory, which eschews *a priori* categories, can seem particularly overwhelming. Where does the network begin or end? Who or what are the significant actors? Whose are the stories to be told? This vision of the world as a multiplicity of connections between diverse materials does not present easy points of departure. However, this lack of boundaries does offer renewed importance to the localised level of the case study, the point from which everyday orderings achieve broader significance. The focus on a case study makes the empirical mapping of network dynamics manageable and provides a starting point. As Latour (1998: 10) puts it, 'storytellers […] are constantly defining actors that surround them – what they want, what causes them, and the ways in which they can be weakened or linked together. These storytellers attribute causes, date events, endow entities with qualities, classify actors. The analyst does not need to know more than they; (s)he has only to begin at a point, by recording what each actor says of the other.'

My initial access to the world of natural history film-making was through a wildlife film-makers conference in rural Shropshire. For three days I joined a community of young and more experienced filmmakers, in seminars, workshops and debates. We talked about breaking into the industry, getting films commissioned, filmmaking in different locations, and the ethics of filming animals. The conference happened early in my research and the experience was formative. The conference revealed just how many actors – scientists, camera operators, researchers, producers, commissioners, audience ratings, camera equipment, animals, environments and more – were mobilised in making a natural history film. Filmmaking debates showed how these networks framed the capacities of individuals and institutions to make the sorts of films they wanted. Central to this network was the historical legacy and current position of the BBC's Natural History Unit located in Bristol, Southwest England. The Natural History Unit had blackboxed definitions of quality in natural history filmmaking, forming a dominant node in the circulations of people, technologies, money and animals through the world of natural history filmmaking in the UK. As one eminent filmmaker put it to me 'This is the home, where it all started, and this is still the place where we are pushing the barriers'. I decided that opening up this British institution in the world of natural history filmmaking was to be the case study, the point from which to explore the durability of these purified visions of nature.

These first investigations were descriptive, concerned with identifying the important actors, events, institutions and qualities making up and animating the network. The conference allowed me to eavesdrop in the process of filmmaking before representations were blackboxed. There are other ways of identifying points from which to open up representations in the making. Much of the material I gathered from hanging around awkwardly at workshops is now archived on the internet, through conference programmes, proceedings and on-line discussions. Programmes frequently have associated web content, with the opportunity to question programme producers, or participate in audience discussions. Trawling through old copies of *The Radio Times* or similar publications, in this case *The BBC Wildlife Magazine* (Figure 13.1), reveals the names of producers, production units and places associated with particular genres of programme making. Specialist publications, such as *Ariel, Broadcast* and *Image Technology*, allow you to get a handle on how the commissioning process works, and on the technologies of filmmaking. Participant observation is possible through the short work experience placements at the BBC or as an unpaid runner for independent companies.

Having identified where it makes sense to start, there are still practical issues about how to gain access. My route into the BBC's Natural History Unit is the archetypal account of gaining access to the media. I trawled prior contacts from university; I followed up personal connections, and found I knew two people in the unit. In seeking the most supportive starting point I approached the unit's librarian and, making the most of these personal links, I set up a meeting. I networked and was lucky. Initial communication was built up over several meetings where we talked about the extent of their archives and possibility of my access. Although I was clear that my interest in the past was as context for the present, I think my overall focus on the historical contexts of natural history filmmaking helped as it possibly seemed less challenging to the unit.

Figure 13.1 *Researching the worlds of natural history through the BBC Wildlife Magazine.*

It was not the only possible access point, but the library turned out to be a good place to start. This was an important site for the Natural History Unit, although much of what I observed now takes place on-line. It was the information centre where programme ideas and animal behaviour were researched, audience figures accounted, programme scripts archived, sales made and films stored. It allowed me to research programme production, to view films, and to read media cuttings. The library was also a comfortable place to be as a researcher. It provided some indispensable allies, a desk at which to sit and an archive of material from which to work. I could hang around, listen, and observe in a way that would have been uncomfortable in the pressure of a programme production office. Once people were used to having me around I obtained a temporary staff pass, giving me freedom to move around the buildings. I introduced myself to the head of the unit, and was in turn introduced at a unit meeting, giving me the opportunity to extend conversations to other unit members. It took me a long time and a number of different strategies to gain this level of access. In the end I was in contact with the unit for nearly two years, spending about eight months intensively working there. This was longer than many contract researchers, who began asking my advice about getting access to the media. Even so, when I left there were still some people I had never managed to talk to, some meetings I couldn't access and some filming locations I couldn't reach.

Representation in television practice

On first encounter the ideas of actor network theory are counter intuitive. You are being asked to let go of familiar categories of explanation, and view the world anew. In place of previously learnt concepts such as technology, nature and culture, you are encouraged to immerse yourself in a world composed only of more or less networked things, with attributes that are contingent upon the way that they are linked to others. Nothing can be assumed from the outset. The researcher is to be agnostic, entering the field without preconceptions; and symmetrical, in treating all entities encountered in the same way. Since nothing is assumed from the outset it is difficult to issue a handbook to this new world. Bruno Latour's 1987 book *Science in Action* forms the nearest thing that actor network theory has to a field guide, and he offers few props for this expedition: 'equipment is [...] light because it means simply leaving aside all the prejudices about what distinguishes the context in which knowledge is embedded and this knowledge itself' (Latour 1987: 6). The multiple contexts in which actor network theory can be applied means there will be many potential questions of methodology and various problems of practice.

Here I focus on my application of actor network theory to study wildlife programmes. So what does this vision of the world offer for understanding visual representations? In cultural geography the analysis of visual representations has traditionally drawn on **semiotics** to study how meaning is communicated, reading visual representations as texts. Semiotics is primarily concerned with language; it treats language as a system of interrelated signs, analyzing it as a set of overlapping grids, each with a history and momentum of their own. Applications of semiotics to natural history films explore how the internal coherence of the film text is achieved through juxtaposition of image and speech (Silverstone, 1986), or critique the symbolic values encoded into language systems, such as the gendered narratives of wildlife programmes (Crowther, 1997). Actor network theory both draws inspiration from and criticises this kind of analysis.

Concept Box

Semiotics

Semiotics is the study of signs (also known as 'semiology'). Its premise is that the meanings of cultural materials can be understood through the analysis of signs and how they function as elements within a 'language'. The approach has sometimes been presented as scientific in the sense that it aims to get behind the mystifications of dominant ideologies and reveal how they work to legitimate interests of **power**. Semiotics employs a range of analytical terms and procedures in its attempts to provide a rigorous means of taking apart images and texts. Much of its inspiration is derived from the linguistic theory of Ferdinand de Saussure, who argued that the meaning of words is derived from the structures of language (the rules of grammar and meaning underlying what is written or said) rather than the objects to which the words refer. He made a basic analytical distinction in understanding signs – understood as everything that can be taken as a substitute for something else – as being composed of a signifier (a word such as 'cat') and a signified (the object to which the word refers). But he stressed there was no necessary relation between them. That people accept what the word 'cat' refers to is a matter of convention. Meaning comes instead from the relationship between signs within a wider system, and in particular from the differences between them, rather than from the object in the world to which the signifier refers. Developing from this position, critics have analysed how signs work to generate meaning in a range of different media including advertisements, photographs, television programmes and film. Within cultural geography it has included discussions of landscape, architecture and the built environment (for example Duncan and Duncan, 1992; Gottdiener, 1986, 1995). Such work often seeks to research the conventional codes through which meanings are made and interpreted so as to address wider social ideologies (what from different perspectives are sometimes called 'dominant codes', 'referent systems' or 'mythologies').

Key reading
- Barthes, R. (1973) *Mythologies*. Trans. A. Lavers. London, Paladin.
- Rose, G. (2001) *Visual Methodologies: An Introduction to the Interpretation of Visual Images*. London, Sage: Chapter 4.

In one sense actor network theory may be viewed as the extension of the semiotic method, shifting emphasis from language to other sign systems. As Madeleine Akrich and Bruno Latour (1992: 259) put it 'semiotics is the study of order building or path building and may be applied to settings, machines, bodies and programming languages as well as texts.' Rather than concentrating on the creation of meaning within texts, network analysis focuses on how networks create the conditions of existence for things. In this view the ordering of nature in natural history films is not only generated through the languages and narratives of their texts (that is, the actual contents of the programmes themselves), but also through the places, technologies, institutions and actors mobilised in the ways they are made.

However, Latour goes on to critique semiotics. He suggests semiotic analyses of the way media texts create meaning have had the effect of making it difficult to talk about anything outside of language. This is particularly problematic for studies of how science claims to represent the world, and is also pertinent to documentary filmmaking. Latour suggests that semiotics has made it difficult to talk of how representations have origins and effects outside of language, and how both human spokespersons and natural agents may be actively involved in the way representations are created. Latour is critical of academic analyses that follow only the purified categories that emerge from representational practices, rather than the diverse range of materials and fragile achievements of the actors involved in producing representations. As he explains:

> *Take some small business owner hesitatingly going after a few shares, some conqueror trembling with fever,*
> *some poor scientist tinkering in his lab, a lonely engineer piecing together a few more or less favourable*
> *relations of force, some stuttering and fearful politicians; turn the critics loose on them, and what do you get?*
> *Capitalism, imperialism, science, technology, and domination. In the first scenario, the actors were trembling;*
> *in the second they are not. The actors in the first scenario could be defeated; in the second they no longer can.*
> *In the first scenario, the actors were still quite close to the modest work of fragile and modifiable mediations;*
> *now they are purified, and they are all equally formidable.*
>
> (Latour, 1993: 125–6)

Actor network theory then aims to uncover the history of decisions, competitions, and uncertainties that underlie the unproblematic present of powerful representations. Rather than focusing attention on stabilised texts, it seeks to follow the construction of networks of practice, to show how they are made and the range of their effects.

A number of principles for 'doing actor network theory' follow from this approach (see also Murdoch, 1997b; Castree and Macmillan, 2001):

- First, actor network theory incorporates a wider range of agents than are usually found in sociological analysis. Networks are composed of heterogeneous actors: humans, technologies, and nature, all of which are attributed some form of agency within the network.
- Second, what ties the actors in networks together is the process of translation, enrolment or modes of ordering; the language used varies in different accounts. The notion of translation attempts to get at how some actors gain the right to speak for others and how they impose particular definitions and roles upon these others. For linkages to be successful, actors must share interests, either through mutually redefined goals or by actors 'colonising' the worlds of others. Translation has linguistic connotations; the network speaks for others, but in its own language.

- Translation also has a geometric implication. Callon (1986) suggests that translations take place through what he terms a geography of 'obligatory points of passage'. These are the nodes of the network, the points at which shared understandings are reached. In the history of developing networks certain assumptions are 'blackboxed', the jumble of actions from which certain qualities emerge are locked away and no longer considered. They become accepted points in the topologies through which other actors must pass to be enrolled. In this way the network gains the ability to speak for others distant in time and space.

- Finally, the power of a network emerges from these associations. Power is not related to how much power one person in the network has, but to the number of actors involved in the composition of the network. As Murdoch (1995: 748) explains 'those who are powerful are not those who hold power, but those able to enrol, convince, enlist others on terms which allow the initial actors to "represent" others.'

Following the actors

At the outset, actor network theory asks you to put aside preconceptions about the actors, entities and power effects the world is composed of. The first steps are to identify the starting points and significant actors from the view of those inhabiting these worlds. However, it is worth remembering that certain points are easier to access than others, access has to be constantly renegotiated and some actors are easier to follow than others. During the processes of doing fieldwork, age, gender and prior experience can all reassert differences. The field itself is constituted through power and not all power effects can be levelled at the outset. Questions of where to start and how to get access are not asked just once, but constantly recur. In this section I explore these in the context of interviewing the human actors, and then in the following section these again emerge in following the things that animate the network.

My research in the BBC Natural History Unit's library allowed me to construct a trajectory of natural history filmmaking. It charted the development of a small experimental unit in the 1950s, to a large television department in the 1990s charged with the majority of the wildlife output on the BBC. The association of camera operators, television executives, programme producers and scientific research stations formed the architecture of a network of connections, engineered around a shared understanding of what makes a good programme about wildlife; a dominant genre for representing animals on television. However, this mapping of network modes is not enough. This is where case studies using actor-network theory risk ending up. The black box of representation is opened up and replaced with a diagrammatic network of translations. My own attempts to map these networks for the unit fill pages of notebooks. However, for description to transform into explanation, it is essential to consider the traffic through this network; to follow the performative elements that allow it to hold together and become durable. The fact I was never able to resolve an exhaustive diagram of the unit's networks is telling. The network's existence depends upon the circulation of the actors through it, and upon the constant transformation of actors over time. It is not enough just to follow the actors in building a network, but also 'to follow the transformations that the actors convened in the stories are undergoing' (Latour 1988: 10). Networks are always in action.

The first way I sought to trace these transformations was to ask people to account for their changing perspectives through individual in-depth interviews. I sought out interviews with members associated with the unit, those in positions of responsibility, and those suggested to me from informal conversations with people in the library, canteen or corridor. These interviews asked about the contemporary issues in wildlife filmmaking, and sought reflections upon their history. They revealed a variety of ways of talking about the commissioning and filming processes and expectations of the audience within the Natural History Unit. Clear contrasts between different histories, roles and filmmaking styles emerged. There was not a single way of doing natural history television; rather a complex interlocking **performance** of researcher, producer, director and television manager from which the networks of natural history filmmaking emerged. To explore these different ways of doing natural history filmmaking in more detail I sought the views of members of the unit throughout its hierarchy. To recruit more interviewees, I circulated a brief questionnaire to the whole unit. This had just three open-ended questions. I asked people to reflect upon the programmes, people and technologies influential in the history of the unit, those important to the public, and those influential to them personally. These were followed by my asking if people would be happy to expand their answers and experiences in a confidential interview. After several trips around the building and a few circular e-mails, around 30 interviews were set up. Completing each interview required considerable determination and a thick skin, as I constantly rescheduled meetings to fit around filming.

All interviews followed a similar structure, organised around a series of interlocking personal, programme and institutional stories. I asked people's stories about their careers: how they had become involved in natural history filmmaking, their aspirations, their changing jobs, their hopes for the future. Other questions focused on their experience of the process of making programmes: where programme ideas came from, how programmes were commissioned, how animal behaviour was researched, where animals were filmed and directed, and how films were evaluated through audience measures, programme sales and departmental feedback. These accounts cut across and complemented each other, as people with different experience accounted for their different perspectives. Finally, I asked people to reflect on the institutional position of the BBC's Natural History Unit, its history, its current challenges and their own position within this institutional context. The interviews were held in the workplace, during lunch or after work; in people's offices, in the BBC bar, even in the car park. They became a forum for people to contribute their perspective to the circulation of ideas within the unit. These were ideas that they might discuss with their colleagues, but were now articulating to a partial outsider. Sometimes there were specific agendas people were keen to circulate back to the unit; other times this private forum within the public world of work provided an opportunity to raise issues they felt uncomfortable within in a more public situation. Other people were clearly just happy to communicate their ideas, talk about their skills, and to help someone else in their career.

These accounts from the individuals involved in filmmaking trace a process of personal acculturation and the institutional accumulation of resources, skills and contacts which members negotiate in order to produce natural history films. Researchers, producers, directors and television executives all play different roles in the performance of the network. Between them they enable different sites of the network to link together, from the point of filming to the point of sale. These multiple orderings or translations enable the Natural History Unit to 'act at a distance' through holding together the diverse spaces and materials of natural history. The researcher secures the collaboration of scientist and access to the right animal behaviour at a convenient time and place. The producer mediates between stories from science and the demands of the media, framing film footage into sequences suitable for broadcast. Television executives manage the circulation of materials and money through networks, monitoring performance and measuring value. These multiple orderings coexist and enable the network to cohere across such diverse spaces as the scientific institute and the television executives' office. They also involve the transformation of the individual actors, as programme researcher Gareth explains:

> *When you start work you're doing research and you just go to the library and you're looking up papers and you're phoning scientists and you're employed as a biologist to start with. That's why so many people in this unit are actually biologists with zoology degrees or PhDs, because initially you're not employed as a film-maker, you're employed as a biologist. But as time goes on you get more and more film experiences and forget all about your biology that you learnt. And it all becomes a bit of a sort of haze from the past. And you then become a film-maker. And you get to the stage where you're making the programmes. And you're employing someone to do the research for you and find out what the latest information on snakes or whatever is.*

The challenges of making natural history films have changed over time, and with them the relative importance attributed to different roles in the unit (Davies, 2000a). Yet the personal transformations of expertise from researcher to producer, and producer to manager also illustrate something of how the durability of the network is achieved. As Jenny, also a researcher, suggests, 'I suppose the people who move up are the people who fit in with the people at the top. So maybe it never changes. I hope not, I hope it doesn't, I hope it's not like that. But I imagine it's maybe how it is.' The transformations of individual actors involved in natural history filmmaking not only animate and perform the network, but also indicate the exclusions, the ways that values and priorities get passed on, differences extinguished and networks endure.

The third estate of things

The durability of networks is also maintained through what Latour (1993) calls the 'third estate of things'. The diverse range of materials that go towards programme making – the cameras, film-stock, animals, audience figures, and so on – make it possible for the networks to extend over space and endure through time. Such materials can be transported from one location to another without changing form, and form an essential part of networks. As Law (1994: 24, emphasis in original) suggests, 'left to their own devices *human actions and words do not spread very far* [...] Other materials such as texts and technologies, surely form a crucial part of any ordering.' A network approach also demands a consideration of the texts, technologies, instruments, animals and environments, used to support claims to represent others through the practices of filmmaking. If following human actors can be difficult, following nonhuman actors is perhaps more of a challenge. Clearly you cannot conduct a semi-structured interview with a film camera or an animal, so what does this part of the methodology actually involve?

The material aspects of natural history filmmaking emerge in practice. The individual narratives about filmmaking practice are revealing, but there is no avoiding the fact that when you go out filming your time is spent lugging large pieces of equipment across fields, trying not to scare the wildlife. The day is only over when you have completed the shoot, and you have captured the animals on film. The exposed film-stock is then taken back to the unit, edited, spliced, speeded up or slowed down, and transferred to computers to form the final programme. Broadcast requires a national network of transmitters reaching out to countless aerials and television sets, some of which are adorned with set-top boxes sending back information on how many people are watching. International distribution may follow in multiple formats on cable, digital, video and CD-ROM. The importance of these technologies emerged strongly during a brief period of participant observation with a magazine format programme on British wildlife. I spent two weeks watching and participating in the work of filming. It was physically tiring in a way the interviews, for all their stresses, were not. My days in the unit were spent phone bashing, sending out videos, tracking down music CDs, and shadowing long sessions in front of editing suites. Days on location started early, ended late, and involved a lot of travelling. There were few people on location, often just a researcher, the camera operator, and myself. But there was a lot to carry, even on the small shoots I attended. As one person suggested, film making is Britain's last heavy industry! There was also a constant negotiation with elements of nature, with the terrain, the changing light levels, the weather, bodily inconveniences such as hunger and sunburn, and, of course, the animals. My contribution to debates on the ethics of baiting animals for programme making was to spend an afternoon scooping up newly emerging mayfly to feed to trout being filmed underwater. These initially random observations became formalised in field notes around three types of nonhuman agents – the camera technologies involved in capturing animals on film, the audience ratings and other indicators of programme success, and the animals themselves. Finding animals, filming animals and tracking audiences are the three key challenges for natural history filmmakers. A great deal of work goes into developing new technologies for trying to overcome these uncertain points in the networks.

Once sensitised to the role of the animate nonhuman, the importance of these entities is evident throughout the spaces of natural history filmmaking. The accounts people give of their filmmaking practice reveal numerous negotiations with active agents, both animal and technological. However, the meanings of these technologies only emerge in the context of the network. For example, the first naturalist filmmakers had to actively secure the authority and trustworthiness of the camera as a reliable witness of nature, in a field previously dominated by pen and ink drawings and field guides (Davies, 2000b). More recently, developments in film stock or film technology do not self evidently result in 'better films'. The technology has to be embedded in a set of new relationships. Skilled camera operators have to work the technology. Producers seek to redefine notions of quality in filmmaking. Researchers are required to find animal stories to showcase the latest devices. Executives need to market the films. Animals must perform in front of these expensive new cameras. Investment in technology means money can no longer be spent on hanging around waiting for the animals. They are increasingly habituated or enclosed in studios. Once introduced into networks of filmmaking such devices harden new socio-technical and natural assemblages around them, redefining goals, extending the reach of the film-making and changing the scope of their visions of nature. Such technologies elevate expectations forged between programme producers, television executives and audiences over what makes a good natural history film. The new technologies have effects throughout the networks. The high cost of camera techniques makes it difficult for new filmmakers to enter the industry. It is difficult for a British unit to make films other than those sold to an international market for which they will get American co-production money. And it makes life difficult for individuals who are not comfortable with either the aesthetics or ethics of this resultant vision of wildlife. As one producer asserts:

> It's a little bit like the development of warfare. You know, once somebody has got a nuclear weapon then the ethical considerations begin to get overshadowed by the practical considerations, hang on if we are going to able to survive, sod the ethics, we need to match their weapons. And that's actually a good analogy because that's really what happens every time there is a change in technology or attitude, you're raising the kind of weapons arsenal, and then the opposition says, Well, okay we may not really like this particular weapon that you have got, but we have got to match it.

Animals, too, have agency within these networks. The quest for traces of animals and environments on film is, after all, the centre of all this activity. The locations of filming across the globe reveal patterns of animals habituated to the noise of people, traffic and filming – there are camera crews permanently located in the National Parks of East Africa – and the actions of animals alter in response. Seeking to mitigate this intrusion into their lives, lions in the Serengeti increasingly hunt at night, unwatched by the flurry of tourists and camera crews; at least until technologies in low light filming encroach on this refuge. The opportunity to work with animals is also the reason many people enter wildlife filmmaking in the first place. Yet their experiences of working with animals are often uncomfortable, trying to balance ethical considerations and the competitive demands for 'the shot'. Even environments themselves are embedded in complex networks of other representations – in science, tourism, drama, news and politics – which transform their ability to carry the narratives of wilderness natural history filmmaking demands. *The Blue Planet*, and its retreat to the wildlife under the surface of the ocean, reflects not only the opening of a new technological opportunity, but also recognition that few other environments remain accessible to these visions of pure nature.

These nonhuman actors do imbue the networks with stability and durability; but occasionally tensions arise from holding all elements of the network together. The actors in the network, both human and non-human, act upon one another. This is not the simple determinism found in much media research, but starts to reveal the politics involved in holding together all the places, animals and technologies involved in the processes of natural history filmmaking. In the final section I explore the narratives and politics emerging from the networks of natural history filmmaking.

Telling stories and constructing networks

The practice of building networks is always fragile, and networks are never fully achieved. They are held by processes of ordering, rather than structures that are given in the order of things. It is therefore through careful description of how order is *generated* and *performed* that explanation and interpretation emerges. John Law (1994: 18) puts it like this: '[Actor network theory] tends to tell stories, stories that have to do with the processes of ordering that generate effects such as technologies, stories about how actor networks elaborate themselves, and stories which erode the analytical status of the distinction between the macro and micro-social'. These stories of ordering show how technologies emerge, how organisations persist, and how localised practices form the basis of a world heterogeneously engineered from the diverse networks.

Yet there are different ways of approaching this description of ordering. In the literature of actor network theory there is a tension between telling strong narratives of centralised control and multiple stories about the diverse practices underlying fragile achievements. In the 1980s, much actor network theory research was about how things were drawn together, difference extinguished and order achieved. The results were linear narratives about how an organisation, technology or scientific discovery was able to re-engineer society around it. But recently actor network theory's own encounter with certain kinds of post-structuralist thought and non-representational theory has multiplied these ways of interpreting the creation and maintenance of order (Hetherington and Law, 2000). In place of the neat stories of network building, recent studies reveal the complexities, inconsistencies and ambiguities involved in the creation of networks, the multiple identities involved in the performance of networks, and the failure of networks to cohere. They attend to the patchwork of accounts that contest chronological narratives and indicate where alternative narratives might emerge.

Making sense of research findings using actor network theory involves following many established procedures of qualitative research; transcription of interviews, tidying up of field notes, initial coding using categories emerging from actors' own accounts, with particular emphasis on how associations are formed between actors. My coding emerged into four broad categories. These were specific to natural history filmmaking, but they may have broader application through their links to the main principles of actor network theory.

* The classification and attribution of properties to the actors involved in the history of filmmaking; including all actors whether defined as institutional, technological, or human.
* The way different 'modes of ordering' of natural history filmmaking organised these actors around them, from the performances of the researcher, producer to television executive.
* The way broader categories, such as definitions of nature, understandings of science, and ideas about programme quality, emerged from these networks.
* And finally, the exclusions and ambiguities indicated above created by these ordering processes.

These relationships were mapped, often quite literally, by cutting and pasting quantities of transcribed material and field notes onto large sheets of paper (Figure 13.2), enabling me to create composite pictures of the circulation of ideas and material around the unit.

Structuring and writing up this dynamic and contested history is complex. As previously suggested there is a politics to the way these histories are written up. By describing how order emerges from processes of translation, these narratives risk repeating the stories only of powerful networks. Accounts emerging from actor network theory have been criticised for being overly descriptive, for obscuring difference and for leaving the academic 'with no political voice, no place from which to stand and claim that our knowledge claims are more valuable than others' (Singleton 1993: 17). However, this view is countered by other proponents. Mol and Mesman (1996: 436) argue the reverse, that by emphasising narratives in which different orderings co-exist, they suggest '[actor network theory] generates *new axes of difference*. It creates new political categories. And these do not meet in some centre from which the world is ruled. For there is, in this politics, no unique parliament where one needs to be represented; no single place for speaking up or being heard. Instead of being concentrated in a privileged *location*, this politics is everywhere.' In this view all activities are political and all actors in the network have political voices. Politics lies equally with the academic researcher attempting to explain the dominance of a particular genre of natural history filmmaking, in the ethical dilemmas of the researcher working with animals, in the television executives' office and the negotiations over the future of natural history filmmaking. My attempts to construct narratives of natural history filmmaking have taken various forms (Davies, 1999; 2000a; 2000b; 2000c). These are largely organised historically, but in all cases they attempt not merely to affirm the pre-eminent position of the Natural History Unit, but to account for this durability in ways that traces the construction of the network, its weak points and its strongholds, its expansions as well as the points of tension and contraction. The elements linking these stories of natural history filmmaking are the images of animals on our screens, weaving through nature and culture, (re)making the modern myths of wilderness and our relationships with animals. Responsibility for their fate lies with all actors involved in the networks of natural history films.

Conclusions

There are several reasons why you may have come to this chapter as part of your research into practising cultural geography. Perhaps it was through an interest in the analysis of visual representations,

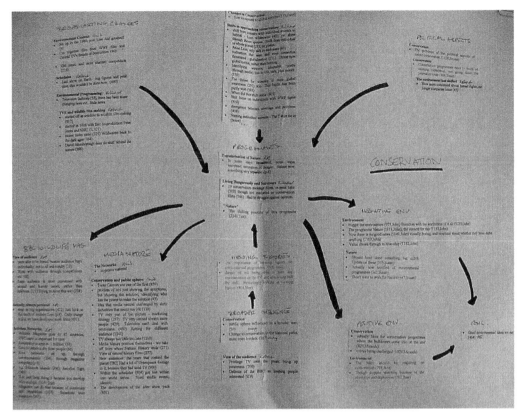

Figure 13.2 *Making sense of research findings.*

in which case this chapter presents something of a critique of textual analyses of the visual that distance themselves from the technologies and referents of their texts, exploring ordering only within language. That is why I have said relatively little about the contents of the actual programmes themselves. Rather, this chapter has argued for the extension of the register of semiotics to all manner of message bearers whether textual, technological, institutional, or natural. Maybe you are primarily interested in the study of television. In this case many of the arguments here have a precedent in the work of Raymond Williams, who stressed the complexity of the development of television communications and its linkages with other technological, ideological and aesthetic forms. As he put it 'the invention of television was no single event or series of events. It depended on a complex of inventions and developments in electricity, telegraphy, photography and motion pictures, and radio' (Williams, 1990: 14). This kind of network approach to television networks is therefore not new, but actor network theory has reinvigorated this tradition.

It might be you were interested in learning more about the new ways in which cultural geographers have attempted to approach the historically contingent boundary-making practices between nature and culture, and the complex configurations of animals and human lives. Here I hope to have contributed something to the growing literature on social nature, through exploring some of the practicalities that emerge from trying to follow through non-dualistic forms of thinking about nature and culture, human and non-human actors. Finally, you may have got here from an interest in how you might apply actor network theory in practice. In this case this chapter is not a simple call to try and enrol you into this way of looking at the world. There is much that is powerful in the critique actor network theory offers to the politics of purity, and much that is liberating in its vision of a world made up of multiple, messy and complex relations between natural, cultural and technological actors. However, I also hope I have indicated something of the multiple ways of doing actor network theory, the choices involved in their application, and the way these connect to other methodological debates in geography over the politics involved in doing research, the politics of representing networks and recovering new places from which to re-imagine future natures.

Just as there are multiple points of entry into this chapter, there are also many diverse ways of taking these ideas forward in future research. A similar approach could be used to trace the emergence of organisations which appear positioned at the centre of significant regimes of approaching nature; for example, through exploring the way aquaria, natural history museums and botanic gardens organise the plants, animals, places and technologies around them. In exploring further the contemporary visions of natural history filmmaking, there is scope for complicating this narrative of centring by the BBC's Natural History Unit, through exploring the practices of other national or local contexts of filmmaking. Mitman (1999) has traced this history for the United States, but India, Japan and many European countries are just a few of the countries with very different visions of natural history filmmaking. It would also be possible to trace the implications of the emergence of new genres mixing together traditional narratives of natural history filmmaking with new technological forms such as animatronics. Series like *Walking with Dinosaurs*, which apply the stories of natural history films to long extinct species, offer both radically new, and deeply conservative, visions of past natures and past places. The technologies from which these networks are forged would also repay further attention. Tracing the networks of technologies, like the Steady Cam or audience research statistic, offer a fascinating departure point for exploring the geographies through which networks are able to speak for others distant in time and space. Finally, actor network theory offers a fundamental challenge to assumptions underpinning contemporary political views about nature. By opening up networks of practices, actor network theory offers a political voice to challenge these new mobilisations of purified nature.

Further reading

For more on nature, culture and networks, see:

- Murdoch, J. (1997a) 'Inhuman/nonhuman/human: actor-network theory and the prospects for a nondualistic and symmetrical perspective on nature and society', *Environment and Planning D: Society and Space*, 15(6): 731–56.

- Murdoch, J. (1997b) 'Towards a geography of heterogeneous associations', *Progress in Human Geography* 21(3): 321–37.

- Whatmore, S. (1999a) 'Culture-nature,' in Cloke, P. *et al.* (eds) *Introducing Human Geographies*. London, Arnold: 4–11.

- Whatmore, S. (1999b) 'Hybrid Geographies', in Massey, D. *et al.* (eds) *Human Geography Today*. Cambridge, Polity: 22–40.

The following are helpful for more on the methodology and actor network theory:

- Castree, N. and Macmillan, T. (2001) 'Dissolving dualisms: actor-networks and the reimagination of nature,' in N. Castree and B. Braun (eds) *Social Nature: Theory, Practice and Politics*. Oxford, Blackwell Publishers: 208–24.

- Kendall, G. and Wickham, G. (1998) *Using Foucault's Methods*. London, Sage.
- Law, J. (1994) *Organizing Modernity*. Oxford, Blackwell.

On the networks of natural history filmmaking, read:
- Davies, G. (1999) 'Exploiting the archive: and the animals came in two by two, 16mm, CD-ROM and BetaSp', *Area* 31(1): 49–58.
- Davies, G. (2000a) 'Narrating the Natural History Unit: institutional orderings and spatial strategies', *Geoforum* 31(4): 539–51.
- Mitman, G. (1999) *Reel Nature*. Cambridge, MA, Harvard University Press.

PART IV

Performing cultural geography

14
Art and urban change
Public art in urban regeneration

Tim Hall

Art, the city and regeneration

The centres of major cities in the capitalist west have for some time been the focus of attention from central and local governments, practitioners, the media and academics. Much of this attention has concerned the problems afflicting these spaces and cities more generally – deindustrialisation, unemployment, the legacy of bad post-war planning and urban blight – and possible solutions to them. City centres have been seen as commodities crucial to the solution of a range of urban problems. As a consequence these spaces have been the recipients of huge urban regeneration funds. An almost ubiquitous response to these problems has been the reshaping and redesign of city centres to make them more attractive to both local citizens and outside capital of various forms.

The creation of these new urban landscapes is inevitably hung around the provision of major city centre facilities, for example, convention centres, hotels, commercial office developments or leisure, retail and sports developments. One of the most prominent and controversial components of the redesign of prominent central city spaces and one that has been the subject of a number of significant and contrasting critical literatures is public art (Petherbridge, 1987; Moody, 1990; Policy Studies Institute, 1994; Roberts and Marsh, 1995; Selwood, 1995; Miles, 1997). The study of the landscapes of post-industrial city centres has emerged as a major strand of both urban and cultural geography in recent years. Public art has been the subject of research from within these and a number of other cognate disciplines. My own research has involved investigating the various roles of public art in the regeneration of post-industrial British cities. Much of this chapter will consider this, through a review of some of my own work. In addition, it will highlight some directions to researching public art in this and other contexts.

There is great variety both in the urban regeneration programmes that public art has been incorporated within, and in public art practice itself. However, in terms of urban regeneration projects we can broadly recognise two distinct types of public art. The first is that employed in 'flagship' or spectacular regeneration projects, which are typically prominent works of public art by nationally or internationally renowned artists. By contrast the second involves neighbourhood regeneration projects that are often, but not exclusively, publicly funded, usually located away from central city locations, and having a greater emphasis on community development and participatory arts (Matarasso, 1997; Dwelly, 2001). This chapter is concerned primarily with the former.

Virtually all public art works found within major city centre projects of urban regeneration are examples of what has been called 'institutional' public art. Namely, it is art that endorses 'official' views of the city, those of local authorities and commercial developers, for example, and celebrates the spaces produced by these interests. However, a radical alternative strand of public art practice has emerged that has been termed 'new genre' public art (see Deutsche, 1991a; Lacy, 1993, 1995; Wainwright, 1997). New genre public art is an art of change and intervention and is concerned with the promotion of social and ecological healing. Typically its stance is directly opposed to that of institutional public art. Rather than seeking to beautify the city, as much institutional public art aspires to do, new genre public art seeks to disrupt prevailing conceptions of the city, highlighting contradictions, processes of uneven development and the marginalisation and exclusion of certain groups within the city, such as the homeless and women. Malcolm Miles says of new genre public art that it 'is process-based, frequently ephemeral, often related to local rather than global narratives, and politicised' (1997: 164). For example, Suzanne Lacy, in her new genre project *Full Circle*, located in Chicago, sought to make visible hidden histories of women in Chicago as well as providing an antidote to the exclusivity of masculinist commemoration in the city's landscape. The project sought to achieve this through the installation of 100 rock monuments on the sidewalks of the city's central area (Lacy, 1993: 29). Although this chapter is not concerned with new genre public art directly, much important critical discussion of public art and the city has been concerned with new genre projects and will be referred to in subsequent discussion.

Critical literatures of public art

Unsurprisingly, this very prominent renaissance of public art has not gone unnoticed by a whole range of writers, critics and researchers. Critical writing on public art and urban regeneration has emanated from a number of perspectives including those of artists, arts advocates, cultural theorists, and urban and cultural geographers. Artists and arts advocates have been predominantly concerned with examining the processes of public art production. They have been concerned, for example, with the influence of the contexts of public art production (commissions, briefs, site, consultation and various other local constraints) on the public art works produced (Jones, 1992). This literature, some positive, some more critical, reflects the concern of writers from this perspective for quality in the production of public art works. By contrast much critical research and theoretical literature has emanated from a cultural studies or cultural geography perspective. This writing has reflected the approaches and concerns dominant in these disciplines since the mid-1980s. Prominent have been a concern for the politics of **representation** and, associated with this, a variety of **deconstructive**, interpretative approaches. Typical examples have seen geographers and others writing within this vein 'read', 'unpack' or 'deconstruct' the meanings of a variety of cultural texts such as landscape paintings, films, television programmes or maps, as well as architecture and the built environment (see for example, Cosgrove and Daniels, 1988; Shields, 1991; Barnes and Duncan, 1992; Bender, 1993; Duncan and Ley, 1993; Clarke, 1997; and Chapters 2, 3, 9, 10, 11, 12, 13 and 15). These concerns and approaches have informed writing on public art that has stemmed from this perspective.

One way in which the critical writings on public art differ is in the site of meaning that they chose to focus on. 'Sites of meaning' refer to the different aspects of a text, be it visual, written or part of the landscape, at which meanings are made (Rose, 2001: 18). Gillian Rose points out that much of the theoretical dispute between writers on visual culture stems from which site of meaning each sees as most important. The same is true of much disagreement amongst writers and critics of public art, although it might only rarely be articulated in these terms. Some writers regard the site of the production of the text, for example, as the most important determinant of the meaning(s) of that text. This is largely true for writing on public art by artists and arts advocates discussed above.

Another aspect that differentiates writing on public art is the context within which writers have situated their analysis. Broadly speaking there are four such contexts, although some writers have been concerned with a mixture of contexts. These are: technological, professional, art-historical and social (see also Rose 2001: 16–17). The same piece of public art might be discussed in very different ways according to the context, or contexts, these discussions address. It is possible, for example, to discuss the technological processes that were involved in the production of a work of public art, and these might have profound impacts on what it is possible to produce. Similarly writers could choose to discuss the professional art practices of its production, again these might also have an important impact on what is eventually produced. Equally, other writers might regard other contexts as more significant. For example, they might be concerned with situating a piece of public art within the body of work of an individual artist, a broader art movement or within art history more generally: they might seek to address its art-historical context. These three contexts are those predominantly addressed by various critics writing from arts practitioner, arts advocate, art critic or art historian perspectives. From the point of view of critical social scientists or cultural theorists this writing might be regarded as parochial in that it fails to address the final context, the social. Having said that, this is not to dismiss these literatures as they are entirely appropriate for the audience for whom they are written. The term social context here is used as a short hand that refers, as Gillian Rose recognises, to 'the range of economic, social and political relations, institutions and practices' (2001: 17) – to this we might also add cultural – that surround and either affect, or are affected by, in this case, public art.

One critique that focuses on public art works themselves as a site of meaning and that examines the social context of public art is associated with the writings of the cultural theorist Rosalyn Deutsche (1991a, 1991b). Deutsche sees the provision of public art in the city as one of a range of disciplines along with architecture, planning and urban design that are responsible for the production of urban space. Deutsche argues, drawing on Marxist analysis, that urban space is both a reflection of the inequitable forces of capital and active in perpetuation of these forces. In being responsible for the production of urban space, architecture, planning, urban design and public art are implicated in these processes. Deutsche refers to these disciplines, as they are enacted in the cities of the West, as 'technocratic' (1991a: 49), namely, they are concerned, not with disrupting, exposing or intervening in prevailing processes of urbanisation, but rather working within them and solving problems and producing 'better' cities. In the case of public art this involves, according to its advocates, the provision of amenities, humanizing and beautifying urban space, addressing community needs or creating a sense of place (Deutsche, 1991a: 49; Hall and Robertson, 2001). However, Deutsche argues that in working within a set of processes that perpetuate the inequitable consequences of capital accumulation, such aspirations are ultimately delusional. Only those practices that seek to disrupt, expose or critically intervene in these processes can hope to achieve what Deutsche calls 'alternative space', the imagination of genuinely better, just urban futures. Deutsche and others have cited the potential of critical (new genre) public art, rather than institutional public art, to achieve this (Deutsche, 1991a, 1991b; Lacy, 1993, 1995). Indeed, in beautifying urban space, for example, institutional public art has been accused of being complicit in obscuring the inequitable roots and consequences of urbanisation. Deutsche contrasts this institutional public art with art that takes a much more critical stance on the process of urbanisation. Most well known is her discussion of the artist Martha Rosler's (1989) New York exhibition entitled 'If you lived here …' (Deutsche, 1991a). Although gallery based art, and hence not 'public' according to some definitions, Deutsche argues its publicness derives from its avowed intention to intervene and provide a critical perspective on the process of urbanisation, specifically on the on-going processes of urban redevelopment and gentrification in New York City. Rosler took the view, expressed through her photographs, that such development was socially exclusive and created or exacerbated conditions of abjection for economically marginalized populations within the city, especially the homeless. In revealing the consequences of development in material terms, Rosler makes visible the hidden histories and consequences of the production of space for exchange. New genre public art such as Rosler's has been described as 'public art of a critical postmodernism [that] has sought to lay bare the concealed meanings and social consequences accompanying the production of urban space' (Ley and Mills, 1993: 268). The intentions of such art then stand in stark contrast to those of institutional public art.

Definitions of public art

Much debate and disagreement has also surrounded the definition of public art. While it is not the intention of this chapter to get bogged down in such arguments, a few points are worth briefly reviewing. While some debates have been concerned with drawing boundaries around public art (questions like 'do artefacts such as street furniture or architectural decoration constitute public art?', for example) more interesting and instructive are those debates concerned with whether public art should be defined by the spaces it occupies or by the processes through which it is produced. The most widely accepted and employed definition of public art is something along the lines of 'any visual arts practice commissioned for sites of open public access' (Eaton, 1990: 71). This clearly follows the post-war institutional view of public art as art beyond or outside of the gallery. However, in the context of the increasingly privatised, exclusive post-modern city such a definition is a little problematic. Others have regarded public art as that produced through a process of public engagement, involvement and participation. This description, while ideologically more appealing, is no less problematic as it both excludes much of what is commonly regarded as public art (civic monuments and sculptures, for example) and it privileges a view of the meanings of cultural texts as lying in their production. Such a view is clearly partial (Rose, 2001). What these debates highlight is that public art lacks a clear definition or delineation. In approaching public art as a potential research subject, it is worth being as inclusive as possible, at least in the first instance, and accepting that all art beyond the gallery (and indeed some gallery based art that engages directly with matters of social and spatial change) might be open to being considered 'public' art.

Rosalyn Deutsche throws some light on this issue in her recognition of the public sphere as a social rather than physical space. Deutsche views art as being public in three ways. These are: first, where it addresses a public, for example by raising issues of relevance or interest to a public; second, by becoming significant in the everyday lives of a public; or finally, by intervening, for example by offering a critique of the processes of urban change and development.

> The ideas that art cannot assume the preexistence of a public but must help produce one and that the public sphere is more a social form than a physical space nullify, to a considerable extent, accepted divisions between public and non-public art. Potentially, any exhibition venue is a public sphere and, conversely, the location of artworks outside privately owned galleries, in parks and plazas or, simply, outdoors, hardly guarantees that they will address a public.
>
> (Deutsche, 1991b: 167)

In Deutsche's view, then, many of the most prominent examples of what is commonly regarded as public art are not public at all. While the settings of such works might be, at least notionally, public space, the works themselves are more the products of artistic egos or mere aesthetic enhancement or decoration than attempts at engaging with issues of relevance to a public. While an important attempt to problematise some taken-for-granted definitions of public art, Deutsche's view does not take account of the diverse ways that the city's publics engage with urban spaces and the art therein, no matter how egotistical or exclusive such artworks might be. Deutsche's definition of public stems, primarily, from the intentions of the artist. If these are not concerned with achieving a public engagement of some kind, then the logic of Deutsche's argument suggests that such art is not 'public' art. However, an alternative definition might start with the actual engagements that take place between art and a public and accept that these engagements, regardless of the intentions of the producers of art, define art as public. Clearly, this is not a perfect definition as all gallery-based art would be susceptible to definition as 'public' where there is some public engagement. However, in being less exclusive than Deutsche's definition it makes room to acknowledge the significance of public experiences of art, rather than focusing exclusively on the symbolic meanings of artworks themselves or the intentions of those responsible for the production of art as has been the tendency in much writing to date.

Public art and images of industry in post-industrial Birmingham

My own research has primarily focused on the regeneration of the centre of Birmingham and the central position that public art has assumed within this. The former industrial metropolis of Birmingham in the English Midlands has undertaken extensive regeneration of its central areas since the mid-1980s in an attempt to capture inward investment and rejuvenate what was a flagging economy (Hubbard 1996; Loftman and Nevin 1998). These efforts have been centred on the redevelopment of the Broad Street corridor stretching out of the city centre as a business tourist attraction. This has involved the construction of a £180 million American style convention centre (the International Convention Centre Birmingham, or ICC), which opened in 1991 (Figure 14.1). Also significant have been the development of a national indoor sports arena, the renovation of a nearby canal basin for leisure use and the complete redesign of a major civic square, Centenary Square. As part of this extensive redevelopment a large number of new public art works were commissioned to be placed in prominent civic spaces, especially in and around the ICC. Birmingham City Council's investment in public art was one of the heaviest by a public authority in the UK and exemplified the extent to which public art had become central to the refurbishment of British cities by the 1990s. Although the idea of incorporating public art into the city's new urban spaces was initially promoted from outside the City Council by local arts advocates, the authority enthusiastically embraced it (Sargent, 1996).

Public art associated with the development of the ICC included the design and paving of Centenary Square by the artist Tess Jarey, who worked closely with the city's landscape design team on all aspects of the square's design. In addition, four new pieces of public art were commissioned for Centenary Square along with four for the ICC and one adjacent to its canalside entrance.

My research has been concerned with three aspects of the public art programmes in Birmingham's refurbished civic spaces. First is the promotional role public art has played in the selling of the city. Second is the role of public art in legitimising the particular trajectory of development initiated in Birmingham since the late 1980s. And third is the implanting of images of industry into the post-industrial landscape of urban regeneration (Hall, 1995a, 1995b, 1997a, 1997b). I want to reflect on the approach

Figure 14.1 *The International Convention Centre, Birmingham. Photograph by the author.*

adopted to the final of these issues and, in doing so, illustrate some of the approaches and choices available to researchers using public art as a source, but also some of the limitations of the approaches that have been adopted. The main subject of this enquiry has been a detailed study of the most prominent piece of new public art in the city, Raymond Mason's statue *Forward*. Costing £275 000, *Forward* was the largest single commission by a provincial UK city for a work of public art at the time of its unveiling in 1991 (Weideger, 1991: 14) (Figure 14.2). The statue is located towards the centre of Centenary Square in a prominent position in front of the ICC and is orientated towards the front face of the ICC. It is constructed out of fibre-glass and coloured a soft yellow with brown and pale red highlighting. It is a tableau, four metres wide and a little over nine metres long, depicting a stream of people emerging from an industrial scene. Towards the front of the statue the figures become bigger and more clearly differentiated. The statue includes a dense **iconography** of Birmingham's history and especially the role of industry within this. References to industry also cropped up in two of the other artworks in the square, David Pattern's *Monument to John Baskerville – Industry and Genius*, and Tom Lomax's fountain *Spirit of Enterprise*.

What I was attempting to do in this work was to deconstruct, unpack or unravel the symbolic meanings of public art works (see for example Hall, 1997a, 1997b) and to relate the narratives and myths promoted through the symbolism of public art to social, economic and/or cultural changes occurring in their local, and, on occasions, global urban contexts. My approach drew on a persuasive strand of urban studies literature, which emerged in the late 1980s and early 1990s, arguing that culture was being implicated in the process of uneven urban development as a kind of 'carnival mask' to create the impression of affluence, vibrancy, conviviality, change and regeneration, while at the same time masking the increasingly fractured and polarised social and economic realities that characterised life for the majority of urban dwellers (Harvey, 1987, 1989a, 1989b). This critique has been applied to the landscapes of regenerated central city spaces and the disciplines of architecture, planning, urban design

Figure 14.2 Forward *by Raymond Mason. Photograph by the author.*

and public art that have produced them (Knox, 1993; Hubbard, 1996; Miles, 1997, 1998) as well as to the representation of regenerated spaces and cities through promotional materials and the media (Holcomb 1993, 1994; Thomas 1994; Kenny 1995b; Short and Kim 1998). Such urban landscapes and their representations have been read as texts, into which have been written elite visions of the city.

While much of this literature involves the deconstruction of images or texts such as urban landscapes, Patricia Phillips, in a highly influential essay entitled 'The public art machine' (1988 [2000]), also highlights the importance of the contexts within which such texts are produced. Phillips's concern was with the critical 'blandness' of much contemporary institutional public art, something that she attributes to the complex procedures through which public art is produced, to its relationship to sponsorship by corporate capital, and to certain fears about its reception. She argued that the 'machinery' of public art production has tended to preclude the production of challenging, critical interventions in the public realm. Public art production typically involves the negotiation of a complex bureaucracy of briefs, competitions and other selection procedures, health, safety and insurance constraints and selection committees that may comprise of commissioners, curators, other artists, local authority officers, representatives from public art agencies, administrators and local community representatives. These bureaucracies, Phillips argues, are constrained by fears of hostile public and media reactions and the desire to appeal to as wide a range as possible of the diverse publics who inevitably use public spaces. The outcomes of these processes, then, tend to be unprovocative art, offering neither critical reflection on its setting nor artistic risk. Phillips points out that public art's relationship to commercial patronage, through mechanisms such as percent-for-art, further constrains its critical possibilities. The most prominent examples of public art recently have been associated with spectacular public or private sector urban regeneration and development schemes (Goodey, 1994; Hall, 1995a; Miles, 1997, 1998). This reliance of public art on sponsorship and its location in the 'colonised' spaces of post-modern cities have again precluded it offering any critical, disruptive intervention in the urban scene. Phillips therefore argues that public art has become one of the mechanisms by which commercial capital, by taking on the cultural caché and legitimacy offered by art, is able to inscribe difference and exclusion into the urban landscape. Public art, in this context, becomes a way of lending these commercial spaces auras of distinction and exclusivity and a notional identity as public, democratic spaces.

Phillips and others since have concluded that public art, in its most prominent manifestation, is complicit in, rather than critical of, the perpetuation of exclusive, uneven urban development (Phillips, 1988 [2000]; Miles, 1997, 1998). Thus it has been argued that public art typically presents selective versions of history, or myths of harmony, offering another layer in the composition of images of the regenerated city. This is of significance, not just because the image (how cities are represented) is out of step with reality (how cities are experienced) but because there is a very real relationship between the former and the latter. Image and appearance are important parts of the way that cities are understood and acted upon and hence they are embedded in the material reproduction of urban space. Therefore, public art can be seen as one of the dominant images of the city and it can be read within the context of the reproduction of social justice and injustice in the post-modern city.

The starting point of my enquiry was the impression, at the time of the statue's unveiling, that *Forward* was anything but unprovocative. It certainly provoked a huge critical response within the city, much of it fuelled by the local media. Whilst some of this controversy concerned the value-for-money argument, much of it was concerned with an apparent incongruity. On the one hand, the city was being promoted as 'post-industrial' rather than industrial, international rather than provincial. Yet, on the other hand, a number of public art works in the city's most prominent new civic space presented images of local industrial history. The production of new city spaces and images did not appear to be as seamless in this case as the literature suggested it should. The literature on the reinvention of city images through post-industrial urban regeneration all seemed to suggest that cities in the 1990s were assiduously trying to *conceal* their industrial pasts rather than putting them on display (Eyles and Peace, 1990; Watson, 1991; Holcomb, 1993, 1994). What the literature I was reading seemed to say and what I could observe on the ground did not seem to tally.

The iconographies of industry in *Forward*

The imagery of Mason's statue was central to the research, so the choice of the statue itself as the primary site of meaning was straightforward. At the heart of the research process was an attempt to deconstruct the symbolic meaning of the industrial iconography of the statue. The first stage of this process involved a detailed observation and recording of the industrial elements in the statue, noting issues such as what aspects of industry they depicted and how they did so, their position and prominence within the statue. This involved extensive field notes and photography of the statue. However, this was not just a descriptive exercise.

The question of meaning, rather than merely appearance, is addressed by relating these observations to a number of contexts within which the statue sits and by investigating the nature of these contexts. In this case I paid attention primarily to four contexts. First was the career trajectory of Raymond Mason, in particular his concerns for industrial and working class subjects. The sources for this were publications about Raymond Mason's career (Farrington and Silber, 1989; Edwards, 1994) and a number of published or freely available interviews with him about his work and its subjects. Mason's work has largely been concerned with urban culture, particularly working-class culture. It has displayed a concern for the unplanned, the eclectic and the artisan. Mason has frequently argued that these represent the most genuine form of urban culture, and has juxtaposed his work against the threats posed to such cultures by processes of modernisation. In a personal correspondence Raymond Mason once described his work to me as a 'homage to the humble'. Mason's sculpture of the fruit and vegetable market in Les Halles, Paris, for example, was a direct response to the loss of the market to redevelopment and reflects an enduring concern for the loss of organic urban cultures and their environments. He said of the sculpture:

> It [the sculpture] was my homage to the departure of the Paris Les Halles market. The title is The Departure of the Fruit and Vegetables from the Heart of Paris, meaning not only the centre but also the actual heart, the love of Parisians. Not only of the departure of the fruit and vegetables, but also the people who sold them. They were the last images of the Middle Ages and faces like that we will never see again. These people who lived, these cold and rainy nights, that's gone and with it has gone the last image of nature in the city, in Paris at least. So this sculpture was done for that reason.
>
> (Interview with Raymond Mason in Farrington and Silber, 1989: 33)

A desire to memorialise working class culture in his home city was a key motivation for Mason accepting the commission to produce the statue in Birmingham.

> They tore the heart out of Birmingham ... When I was asked to do a monument I said yes – I if could evoke the city they had taken down ... When I think about it ... all of my work has been devoted to my own class ... The possibility of evoking the Birmingham working man was irresistible.
>
> (Mason quoted in Weideger, 1991: 14)

The presence of the working class and industrial iconography of the statue can, therefore, be easily explained with reference to some central concerns of Mason's career. However, their incorporation into a project of urban regeneration is less easily explained. I explored this through examination of three remaining contexts: first, the programme of urban regeneration and place promotion within Birmingham; second, the city's public art commissioning strategy that had the stated aims of being integral to the regeneration of the city while exploring and expressing facets of the city's multiple identity and diverse character (Lovell 1988: 1); and third, historical identities of the city that were derived from its economic life. Exploring these multiple sites of meaning meant that a variety of research methods had to be utilised. These included semi-structured interviews with representatives from the local authority, the Public Art Commissions Agency and the ICC. They also involved archival research on the background to both the urban regeneration strategies in the city and the public art commissioning strategy, something that entailed studying official reports, strategies, briefs and minutes of meetings. In addition they consisted of reviewing coverage of the public art programme in the local and national press (cf. Chapter 2) and reading social histories and reports of industrial and economic change in the city. Broadly, I interrogated these sources with the intention of uncovering further explanations for the presence of the statue's apparently incongruous references to industry when viewed within the urban regeneration programme. This involved, for example, directly or indirectly questioning interviewees or searching archives for evidence of the motivations or intentions behind the commissioning and production of the statue or public art works in the city more generally. The historical material was examined with a view to reconstructing a broad economic history of the city and especially the historical links between industry and the identity or culture of the city and region.

The next stage of the research, having established the nature of the contexts that the statue was situated within, was to attempt to view the statue from within each of these contexts and to consider the extent to which the statue was able to accommodate the very different readings that stemmed from these contexts. On the one hand the statue was clearly intended to be viewed as part of a major urban regeneration project, an attempt to refashion the image and identity of the city and influence its economic development over the coming years. On the other hand, it fitted into a tradition of British civic commemoration that venerates local histories, traditions and experiences and national values. In this latter context it represented a prominent articulation of civic and regional character and history. These two contexts produced two audiences who were likely to view the statue in very different ways and according to two very different sets of expectations. The answer to the apparent incongruity in the statue's exploration of local industrial histories lay in the contrast between these two contexts. Rather than seeing industry as polluting, mechanical and redundant, as it overwhelmingly was by many people during the 1980s and 1990s, Raymond Mason associated it in the statue squarely with a positive set of values revolving around notions of craftsmanship and individual endeavour, a set of values likely to appeal to both local and outside audiences. This was apparent from the idealised treatment of industrial and working class subjects within the statue and was supported directly by what he had said in interviews. For example, as Mason said in an interview published at the time of the statue's unveiling:

> For one precise moment in history Birmingham was unique … It founded a tradition of fine craftsmanship and fine machinery. That shouldn't be forgotten … It would be a great pity to forget what was a great moment in the human saga of fine work.
>
> (In Weideger, 1991: 14)

In summary then, the images of industry within the statue initially appeared to be highly incongruous in the context of the post-industrial regeneration of the city of Birmingham. However, the statue is both produced and consumed within a number of other contexts as well. Readings of the statue, and of public art generally, should clearly pay attention to these multiple contexts.

There is no natural, straightforward or singular route to making key choices and arriving at a seemingly coherent research framework. Similarly, despite the importance of prior planning, the process through which these choices are made is often iterative and messy. A starting point is to look at examples of literature that report researchers' attempts to investigate cognate subjects. Is it possible to define the research questions that have guided these research projects? What sites of meaning and contexts do these researchers consider and what contexts do they situate their investigations within? Finally, how do they go about doing their research? What methods do they employ? Reviewing examples of relevant literature will enable you to distil key elements from the research process and to consider applying them.

However, having said this it is important not to follow slavishly the processes adopted by others. What you might observe on the ground might be very different from what the literature appears to be saying. Indeed, this might provide the very originality that really successful projects need. Other sources of originality might include unusual or innovative combinations of questions, research choices and methods, or seeking to address issues that others appear to have overlooked. In approaching the subject of your research there is no substitute for good local knowledge. Get to know a potential subject of research, visit the site, photograph it, observe it, observe how people use its spaces, read about it, for example, in the local press or the local library. Use the knowledge that you acquire to interrogate the academic literature you have read. Again, the relationship between acquiring knowledge of the site of your research and constructing a framework to guide your research may be messy and iterative, but, ideally, it will be mutually reinforcing.

Something missing? Investigating public art's audiences

Gillian Rose (2001) in her review of the sites of meaning in visual materials outlined a third site of meaning, in addition to those of production and text, that of the audience. Investigations of the audiences of visual texts recognise the importance of the consumption or construction of meaning by audiences. They raise questions about studies that focus on other sites of meaning by recognising that there is no necessary correspondence between the intended meanings of the author(s) or producer(s) of texts and those constructed by audiences. Investigations of audiences are very well developed in disciplines such as cultural and media studies. However, a concern with audiences is less well developed in urban geography. Studies of architecture, urban landscapes and spaces have focused far more on the production and text than they have on audience. Critical writing on public art has tended to follow the approaches and concerns prominent in the disciplines within which it is produced. Hence there has been little, if any, serious attempt to investigate the audiences of public art, or the significance of public art to the everyday lives of urban publics. Certainly there was little in my own research that was able to capture the responses of audiences of the public art programmes developed in Birmingham during the 1990s despite evidence from, for example, exchanges of letters and opinions in the local press and on local radio that it was a controversial topic and one that provoked a complex range of responses from the public. Later reflection on this suggested that my own work had largely mirrored a much broader limitation of studies of the post-industrial urban landscape in missing the crucial and complex audience dimension.

This raises questions about the limitations of a wide body of writing on public art. The wealth of sophisticated theoretical writing about the production of public art and the symbolic meanings of public artworks stands in stark contrast to the dearth of writing about its audiences. Neither the intentions of the producers of public art, nor its iconographies, necessarily correspond to the meanings derived from the incorporation of public art and its spaces into the everyday lives of the publics. While understandings of the growth, production and intended meanings of public art are undoubtedly very good, understanding of its reading by its diverse audiences is much less well developed. One simple yet important question emerges from this. To what extent do the sophisticated readings of public art offered by cultural theorists, cultural and urban geographers, correspond to those meanings constructed by its audiences? The difficulty in answering this question adequately suggests that there is a partiality in previous writing on public art and that relatively untapped avenues of investigation exist.

There have been calls recently, within urban geography and cognate disciplines, to move away from an overriding concern with representation and interpretation and an associated focus on the sites of production and text. For example, Nigel Thrift (2000a) has called for geographers and other social scientists to develop 'non-representational theory' or 'theories of practice'. Thrift's own work on the multiple meanings attached to the acts of shopping and its environments offers an example of such an approach (see Miller, *et al.* 1998). Such studies have overturned earlier overly **semiotic** readings of apparently instrumental shopping environments, involving semi-scientific deconstructions of the meanings of mall design and layout, which were unable to admit or recognise the importance that users had on the construction of the meanings of space (Gottdiener, 1986).

Clearly, an exciting and timely research agenda for public art would be one that sought to include the audience, or audiences, as a site of meaning. This would both be in line with emergent concerns within urban and cultural geography and would address an obvious omission in previous studies of public art. There are a number of precedents in geographical and other studies of urban landscapes and spaces that suggest that the methodological tool-kit exists, supported by a respected body of critical theory, to uncover meanings constructed by the publics who engage with public art.

There is evidence that geographers are beginning to take on board calls to include audiences in their research. For example, Loretta Lees has argued this with regard to architecture in a way that might be applied broadly to studies of the urban landscape.

> Architecture is about more than just representation. Both as a practice and a product it is **performative**, in the sense that it involves on-going social practices through which space is continually shaped and inhabited. Indeed, as the urban historian Dolores Hayden argues, the use and occupancy of the built environment is as important as its form and figuration .... [A]ttention to the **embodied** practices through which architecture is lived requires some new approaches, just as it opens up some new concerns, for a critical geography of architecture.
>
> (Lees, 2001: 53)

Concept Box

Performance/Performativity

The recent interest shown by cultural geographers in questions of performance and performativity is closely related to the growing interest in the embodied nature of social experience and identity (see **embodiment** and **identity**); with theories of performance providing a framework through which to try and make sense of the various bodily actions that constitute identity and characterise our social interactions. Three main approaches to performance can be traced in contemporary cultural geography, each of which relies on a rather different understanding of identity. For those following Erving Goffman, social interactions can best be analysed by treating them as a piece of theatre; with different settings requiring that we don a different 'mask' and perform a different role (the 'student', 'teacher', 'straight man', 'lesbian' and so on). As Goffman has shown, whilst such roles often follow particular 'scripts' (broadly accepted ways of acting 'appropriate' to that role and setting) the notion of a mask suggests the existence of a pre-existing identity lying beneath or behind (and giving direction to) the role being played at any particular moment (see, for example, Crang, 1994; Valentine, 1993b). In contrast, those inspired by the work of Judith Butler (1993, 1997) adopt an 'anti-foundationalist' position; suggesting that rather than pre-given, it is the 'doing' of this 'script' that gives rise to identity in the first place. For Butler, identities emerge from a process of 'citation'; as we act in accordance to/act out discursive norms that always and already define the meaning of masculine or feminine, gay or straight etc. Such a model implies rather less individual freedom than does Goffman's and this is one reason that Butler prefers the notion of 'performativity' rather than 'performance'. But, for Butler, these norms are themselves the product of these constantly repeated performances. The 'script' and the 'act' thus shape each other, whilst because our actions always 'cite' rather than simply copy these discursive norms there remains the possibility of 'mistranslations' and 'improvisations' that take the script in new directions. For those working within a third body of work, loosely coalescing under the title of 'non-representational theory', it is these improvisations that are the key to understanding the concept of performance; defined by Nigel Thrift as a way of 'theorizing the day-to-day improvisations which are the means by which the now is produced' (Thrift, 2000b: 577). For those adopting this approach, the performances that define our day-to-day interactions are rarely scripted in any obvious sense. Rather we need to recognise that many (if not the majority) of our actions are 'pre-cognitive', or spontaneous; that is, we often act and relate to the environment and others without thinking. One of the tasks of non-representational theory is therefore to provide ways of representing (through the words we use in books and papers) that which in an important sense is 'beyond **representation**': a bodily action or sensual experience. Whether or not our interactions with others are really so spontaneous (and the notion of improvisation implies some kind of pre-existing script after all) or whether it is possible to represent the non-representational is a matter of continuing debate (see, for example, Nash, 2000).

Key reading

- Gregson, N. and Rose, G. (2000) 'Taking Butler elsewhere: performativities, spatialities and subjectivities', *Environment and Planning: Society and space* 18: 433–52
- Nash, C. (2000) 'Performativity in practice: some recent work in cultural geography', *Progress in Human Geography* 24: 653–64
- Valentine, G. (1993) 'Negotiating and managing multiple sexual identities: lesbian time-space strategies', *Transactions of the Institute of British Geographers* 18: 237–48

Lees (2001) employed the techniques of ethnographic observation in her study of the architectural geography of Vancouver's new Public Library Building. She was concerned with uncovering the symbolic meanings of space constructed by different groups of the library's users. Her aim was to capture the ways that meanings are performative, embodied and continually sedimented through the daily ongoing spatial practices of users. Observation of people as they use spaces captures the performative elements of meaning construction. Lees presented a series of ethnographic vignettes that revealed the ways that users of the library's spaces appropriated them in diverse ways for their own purposes. She revealed layers of the site's meaning that are not susceptible to capture either by studies of the form and design of the space itself nor its production.

In addition Jacqueline Burgess et al. (1988) have highlighted the potential of interview-based techniques to uncover meanings and responses to landscapes. Burgess and her co-researchers used in-depth small-group interviews in their study of the symbolic meanings and values people attach to urban open-spaces. They complemented this by using photographs of different physical settings to prompt qualitative reflections from their interviewees. The findings of their study in South London revealed a hidden richness in the human responses to even apparently mundane open spaces that challenged taken-for-granted assumptions that had previously underpinned the provision and management of open spaces in the city. They say of their work:

Our primary objective has been to develop a methodology which is sensitive to the language, concepts and beliefs of people whose views about open spaces are rarely heard. Through empirical qualitative research we hoped to explore the ways in which individuals and groups read urban landscapes and interpret their symbolic meaning.

(Burgess et al., 1988: 457)

There is nothing to suggest that such techniques are not appropriate to uncovering the readings of public art and its landscapes and spaces by the individuals and groups who encounter them.

Summary

Public art has become an increasingly prominent and controversial element of the landscapes and spaces of many cities. In its various forms it is both able to legitimise and criticise prevailing trajectories of urbanisation. It is an increasingly debated subject across a range of disciplines. This debate has tended to reflect approaches that have focused overwhelmingly on the production of public art and on the symbolic meanings of public art works. However, it seems timely now, given the shifting emphasis in urban and cultural geography, that studies of public art might also seek to include the audience as a site of meaning. The four questions outlined below have framed much research to date that has used public art as its source. Each could be further enlivened in future research if the audiences for whom the works are intended and the publics who engage with them could be incorporated into the research.

- What promotional roles does public art play within urban regeneration?
- In what ways do the symbolic meanings of public artworks legitimise on-going processes of uneven urban development?
- In what ways is public art implicated in the reproduction of cultural identities at a variety of scales?
- In what ways are non-institutional forms of public art able to critically highlight processes of urbanisation?

Further reading

The most comprehensive and accessible guide to public art and its literatures, one that is broad in its sweep and contains many examples and illustrations, is:

- Miles, M. (1997) *Art, Space and the City*. London, Routledge.

A good guide to the area of new genre public art is:

- Lacy, S. (ed.) (1995) *Mapping the Terrain: New Genre Public Art*. Seattle, Bay Press.

Although largely written predominantly from the perspective of arts advocacy rather than critical social science, the regular discussions of public art projects and debates in journals such as *Public Art Review* and *Artists Newsletter* will prove an invaluable source of ideas. There is also a huge amount of information, albeit of varying quality, about public art on the internet. A good starting point is the Public Art Research Archive maintained by Sheffield Hallam University:
www.shu.ac.uk/services/lc/slidecol/ pubart.shtml.

It is useful to situate the study of public art within wider debates in social and cultural studies. Regular reviews of journals such as *Environment and Planning D: Society and Space*, *Cultural Geographies*, *European Journal of Cultural Studies*, *International Journal of Cultural Studies* and *Social and Cultural Geography* will prove useful in this regard.

A grounding in visual research techniques is essential to the task of unpacking the symbolic meanings of public art. The best recent guide to this area is:

- Rose, G. (2001) *Visual Methodologies: An Introduction to the Analysis of Visual Materials*. London, Sage.

Wider debates about studying symbolic landscapes are also relevant to the study of the semantically loaded landscapes of public art. A timely collection of essays on the subject is:

- Robertson, I. and Richard, P. (2002) *Studying Landscapes: Cultural and Symbolic Landscapes in the Western European Tradition*. London, Arnold.

A TALE OF RESEARCH

Performing identities

Studying a gay community theatre group

Christopher Shippen

The question of sexuality and space has become significant in contemporary human geography and recent advances in the ways in which identity politics are theorised has had substantial impact in the field of cultural geography as a whole (Binnie and Valentine, 1999). My dissertation aimed to follow this debate by exploring the ways in which a gay theatre company in London worked to produce 'queer' space by spatially disturbing the everyday urban politics of the city. Combining my own interests in gay culture with current debates in geography around performativity, and especially of aesthetics and visual culture in the urban experience, I considered that studying this group would make an interesting piece of research in urban cultural geography and geographies of sexuality.

Personal and academic interests drove this research. First, I wanted to examine 'gay' culture and arts practices in the city by deconstructing the work of a fringe community theatre group; second, I became interested in conceptual debates about the sociality of community arts groups, especially around questions of identity and community; and third, I wanted to think about how this cultural and social arrangement provided a political architecture for this contested urban geography. So rather than looking at the 'spaces of gay community theatre' as spaces of gay culture, I wanted to show how 'queer space' as enacted by collective identity and sociability was 'performed', and in this case celebrated.

I was particularly influenced by developments in social and cultural geography around ideas about performativity. I first came across the concept through geographical studies of sexuality (see, for example, Bell et al. (1994)) that, following Judith Butler (1990), used the concept to describe social identities and identifications. In cultural geography, the notion that the 'everyday' is performed in material and embodied ways has also become an attractive argument (see Nash, 2000; Thrift and Dewsbury, 2000). Of course, this discussion has run parallel with work already happening in the humanities in the study of performance art and, by synthesising the two dialectics, I wanted to conflate ideas of an arts-based cultural performativity and a community-based social performativity upon which to base my methodology. I wanted to think about the spaces of the group as discursively produced, and to represent the ways in which this reflexive discourse was materially and corporeally reproduced.

Hence my epistemology was grounded in a phenomenological/poststructuralist paradigm, which called for interpretations that developed readings of individual experiences and also of broader notions of cultural capital and cultural practice. I felt that studying the work of the group necessitated an understanding of how those practices were performed, as well as their discursive foundations. In the context of this study, where the sociality and performativity of group members was my foremost concern, I thought it necessary to locate the research in a joint hermeneutic and critical approach.

Gaining access to the group was one of the first difficulties I encountered. I met a group member socially and asked if he thought the company would be interested in taking part in the research. He was unsure, but not discouraging, and said that he would ask the group if they would be interested. They were, at first, suspicious but intrigued by what I was doing: with a limited awareness of contemporary human geography, they were surprised that I wanted to study their group. I was then invited to a meeting where we discussed what I wanted to do. I conducted a series of interviews with eight 'actors' in the community arts building where the group was primarily based. I chose to use informal, conversational interviews to try to gain a rich understanding of the meanings and interpretations that individuals had attached to the experience of being in the group, and to consider those questions of identity and positionality of group members.

I also conducted some observational research. I sat in on two workshops and joined an audience in one public performance. This observational research method conflicted with some of the queer sensibilities of the project. Acting as a detached, passive (although not neutral) observer is at odds with the politics of what I tried to do in my research. I chose not to be a participant for numerous reasons, but mainly because I had no intention of staying as a group member when the research was finished, and I agreed with group members that this would not have been appropriate.

This does not mean however that I did not get a strong feeling for the work of the group and the ways that it operated. But it did place me in a very particular position of power to the group, which we negotiated on a continual basis. Alongside this, there were of course ethical issues involved in studying a gay community group, particularly over questions of disclosure and confidentiality, and I was acutely aware that my first loyalty had to be to the subjects of my research. I was attentive to the fact that my research was not, at the time, going to help the group in any way and that it was essentially exploitative, even if I was telling *their* story. There were times when I found that I had to be open to the group about this: they were doing me the favour, so it was imperative that I conducted my research responsibly and transparently. Setting up this dialectic helped. Letting people know about my concerns made them feel easier and more comfortable about the research. I also think it allowed group members to be more open in interviews, and made the research experience more enjoyable.

The diverse set of ideas that formed the basis of the project revealed a kaleidoscopic, although not exhaustive, set of conclusions. I found that 'performers' were continually practising their skills and abilities as actors and individuals (shaping not only the cultural product being produced, but also the sociality and 'community' of the group). The acquisition and acquiring of such skills and competencies took place in the context of group identifications and gay identities and in actors' own imaginative constructions of the self. There are social and material 'spacings' to this relationship. The creation of a 'queer space' makes social identities obvious to others; and obviously presents a spatial challenge to heterosexism and homophobia. But there is a much more intimate and bodily scale of spatiality that actors used in both social and theatrical performance, in which bodily movements, closeness and touch were important. In terms of the discourse of cultural practice, the group was jointly concerned with representing 'the experience of being gay' through a 'theatrical vocabulary' that expressed this experience to a public audience, and also with a notion that the plays they produced sought to challenge homophobic attitudes and behaviours.

My research made me very aware of how actors in the group felt about their work. The group was driven by a clearly social motive, but also a passion to 'act up' and promote a political ambition to challenge society. The liberatory nature of their work was the impetus that compelled me in the research, and is now forming an entry into a larger postgraduate research project with broader empirical, conceptual and methodological scope in which I attempt to explore queer urban arts practices as cultural geographies of gay liberation.

I completed a BA in Human Geography at Queen Mary, University of London, in 2002. My dissertation was entitled 'Making gay space and identity: the performativity and sociality of a gay community theatre group.' I have now joined the Graduate School at Queen Mary, and I am presently developing the focus of my doctoral research interests into the relationships between sexuality, the city, and the politics of gay culture.

15
Building sites

Cultural geographies of architecture and place-making

Pyrs Gruffudd

I've always been quietly jealous of some physical geographers. Whilst I don't underestimate the significant amount of theorising and abstract conceptualisation that goes into their work, there's an appealing immediacy about going out into the field, looking at a landform and trying to work out why it is where it is, and why it looks like it does. There's even a methodological parallel there with some kinds of historical geography, in that many of the events or processes that caused objects to be where and how they are are no longer around. As Alan Baker (1997: 232) put it, in a memorable analogy, 'Historical geographers arrive upon the scene of an "accident" (for example, the Industrial Revolution or the planting of a hedgerow) after it has happened and their task is akin to that of a detective whose job is to reconstruct what happened and to present a substantiated and convincing account to a court. Historical geographers cannot observe the past directly; they instead have to rely on the indirect testimony of witnesses.' In many ways, I've felt that the closest we get to this kind of immediate relationship to what we research is in our response, as geographers, to place, and particularly to the built environment. Of course, there are profounder and less personal reasons for studying the power of the built environment, and the attacks of 11 September 2001 on New York City and Washington DC demonstrated the symbolic presence -- for friend and foe alike -- of buildings and cityscapes.

Geographers have long been concerned with the cultural meanings of individual buildings, streets and cities. There has been a long and rich tradition in North America, for instance, of interpreting 'everyday' landscapes (Meinig, 1979; Wilson and Groth 2003). While for much of the twentieth century these concentrated on the supposedly 'authentic' folk landscapes of rural areas, more recently – and most notably in the work of J.B. Jackson (for example 1984) – there has been a shift to the landscapes of modernity. Indeed, just how to do this kind of work on the relationship between culture and landscape has occasioned a lively set of important theoretical debates in cultural geography (see Duncan 1980; Price and Lewis 1993; Cosgrove 1993; Mitchell 2000). More radically, many human geographers have extended our interpretation of the built landscape from the functional to the symbolic, paying particular attention to the material or social dimensions of culture. In a famous essay, David Harvey (1979) decoded the basilica of Sacré-Coeur in Paris. He began by poetically evoking the image of the building perched above the city, its domes and bell towers glimpsed from the dense network of streets below or standing out spectacularly at the end of vistas and avenues. Harvey subsequently unfolded the story of the building as a reactionary response to the Paris Commune, its turbulent past echoed in its use as political symbol in the 1970s. A few years later Denis Cosgrove (1984) argued that all landscapes had to be interpreted in relation to the social formation that underlay their production; only then could their 'true' symbolism be determined (although in a later edition [1998] he modified some of these

Marxist rigidities). Examining the cities and towns of Renaissance Italy, and the layout of Washington DC, for instance, Cosgrove interpreted buildings not only as practical outcomes of material requirements of trade, agriculture, military strategy and so forth but also as symbolically meaningful declarations of **power**, belief and intent.

In reading the sites of buildings, therefore, the question has been to what extent we can, as Mona Domosh (1989: 347) put it 'determine the links between a particular landscape artifact, its socio-economic and aesthetic contexts, and the actors who directly produced and/or created that artifact?' In an 'explosion' of work geographers have interpreted what Lees (2001: 55) calls the 'political **semiotics**' of the built environment through studies of sites like war memorials (e.g. Heffernan, 1995; Johnson, 1995), imperial and other capital cities (e.g. Duncan, 1990; Tauxe, 1996; Driver and Gilbert, 1999; Whelan, 2002) and iconic public and private buildings (e.g. Black, 2000). Lees argues, however, that much of this work has been negligent in focusing too much on the *production* of space but not enough on its *consumption* – that is, 'the ways that the built environment is shaped and given meaning through the active and embodied practices by which it is produced, appropriated and inhabited' (Lees, 2001: 56). Her own work examines the public's engagement with a new public library in Vancouver, setting ethnographic studies of the users of this space alongside the narrative of its construction, and in so doing refusing to privilege the form of the building over its function and use in ways which the architects may not have foreseen or intended. There are relatively few examples of this kind of work in cultural geography to date, though in his study of the 'modern' home in 1930s Britain Mark Llewellyn (2001) draws on oral histories, as well as more conventional architectural sources. There have, however, been other studies that consider the ways in which ordinary people 'animate' the built environment, most notably through processions and protest (e.g. Harrison, 1988; Barber, 2002).

In what follows I attempt to explain how I have tried to engage with some of these themes in my own work, using two sites as examples – the 'Italianate' village of Portmeirion in North Wales, and the Gorilla House and Penguin Pool at London Zoo. They are both, ostensibly, buildings (or sets of buildings) constructed for pleasure or edification rather than for work, economy or governance, but they raise very different questions and demand slightly different approaches. Before this, however, I'd like to set out some principles for 'reading' the architecture of the built environment.

Reading buildings

As this book makes clear, geographers need to be careful when straying far from the methodologies that our discipline considers its own, and work on architecture is no exception. I have found the following set of questions useful in trying to uncover the important questions, whilst avoiding errors of interpretation.

What? As I suggest above, it's often the immediacy of the built environment that makes it so powerful – be that an individual building or an entire townscape. But there's a danger of allowing the facade to overwhelm any kind of functional understanding, so begin by describing what's actually there, in concrete terms. Think in terms of size, shape, location, site, orientation and function, for example. Buildings have always had a close relationship with technology; skyscrapers, for instance, were facilitated by improvements in the design of elevators and fire-fighting systems, as well as constructional techniques (Domosh 1989). And even if you're studying an individual building you need to consider it in relation to its neighbours. Having done this you should have a clearer sense of what elements of the built environment to include in your interpretation.

When? You will need to develop an historical understanding of what was built when. Although the designs of a building may have one date, the final product, as it were, may not have appeared for several years. Larger buildings (let alone districts) may have taken several years to complete and buildings are frequently added to, modified and even demolished. All of this needs to be related to the broader historical context of the place where the building is located. The political and economic circumstances – at a variety of levels – can have a very direct effect on what is built, for whom, where and when. In a practical sense this can mean paying attention to the culture of development and planning of the time (what kinds of buildings were getting planning permission?); more broadly it can mean viewing buildings as expressions of intangible concepts like 'civic pride' and 'national identity'. You can only really find out about these contextual issues through reading widely, both in geography and in related disciplines like history, planning, and architecture.

Style? Architecture has its own language and vocabulary. Styles have emerged in different historical periods and acquired meanings along the way. These meanings have frequently persisted into the modern era and will usually be drawn upon quite knowingly by architects and clients. The rigid and symmetrical geometry of classical architecture – with columns, porticos and so forth – tends to represent enduring values, rationality and order. This has made it attractive to a disparate and even contradictory range of cultures and movements including the founders of the new American Republic (Cosgrove, 1988), the Nazis (Taylor, 1974) and financial institutions (Black, 2000). The restrained and even clinical simplicity of modern architecture, on the other hand, tends to symbolise a different sort of rationality – a scientific and democratic faith in universal 'progress' (see Gold, 1997; Gruffudd, 2001). Post-modernism, on the other hand, frequently preaches the divorce of style from meaning in architecture, and this eclecticism and playfully selective 'quoting' poses different problems for interpretation (see Lees, 2001).

Who? As with any text (and here I am suggesting that buildings can be understood as texts that we read for meanings), it is important to understand a building in the context of its architect's other work. This is relatively straightforward in the case of important public or private buildings, where the architect may be well-known, but more difficult in the case of humbler domestic, commercial or mass building. For the former, seek out the numerous architectural biographies and monographs published by bodies like, in Britain, the Royal Institute of British Architects (RIBA). You should bear in mind that architects often work in teams or practices and so it may be difficult to discern the influence of one individual. But the kinds of questions to ask are: how typical of the architect's work is the building you are studying?; how important is the building in any assessment of that architect's work?; can you discern the influence of the client, or a greater than usual sensitivity to context? Taking all of this into account, can the building be read as a 'statement' addressing wider issues of social context? Like any text, however, it cannot simply be reduced to the intentions of the author/architect (see also Chapters 3 and 12).

Layers of meaning? As elements of place, it is worth considering buildings as components of a 'progressive sense of place' (Massey 1993). Architecture is made up of flows of materials and of money, but also flows of ideas and creativity. This connects a building to a series of debates – some local, some national and even global – and a good interpretation will seek to draw out these connections. In any historical research it is also important to bear in mind that buildings may make new connections and thus acquire new meanings as the years pass. They may become 'iconic' – that is, particularly emblematic of a period or movement and promoted, preserved or resisted as such. Sites may, equally, become divorced from their original intention. And to return to Lees (2001), we need to take account of the ways in which buildings are inhabited, occupied and **performed** by their users or publics. Whilst your study of a building may, of necessity, take an historical snapshot of a particular moment, it's worth bearing in mind that buildings are not frozen in time.

Portmeirion: the place and its meaning

My first example concerns a place that I actually worked on for my own undergraduate dissertation (*many* years ago) and subsequently for my PhD and for publication (Gruffudd 1995a). What I write here, therefore, is the result of trial and error over several years and is naturally closer to the published version than that now well-thumbed dissertation. The place is the village of Portmeirion on the coast of North Wales (see Figure 15.1). I'd actually intended to do a dissertation on accessibility and transport in rural mid-Wales but decided I wanted to do something more cultural, and I had a sympathetic lecturer (Denis Cosgrove) to thank for suggesting I look at Portmeirion and jotting down on a scrap of paper a couple of references he thought might be useful. My immediate reaction to the place was a sense of the bizarre. Here was an eclectic (though usually referred to as 'Italianate') village of domes, colour-washed cottages, piazzas and gardens inspired by a sailing trip along the Italian coast and built on a beautiful

Figure 15.1 *Portmeirion from the south with the mountains of Snowdonia in the background (from Williams-Ellis, 1980). Reproduced by permisssion of The Hotel Portmeirion.*

wooded promontory in North Wales, of all places. Even more remarkable it transpired that, far from being the centuries-old place it appeared, it had been built as a hotel and holiday village from 1925 onwards and was still evolving during the 1970s. This sense of the surreal was only heightened by the fact that the place was perhaps best known as the set for the cult 1960s TV drama *The Prisoner* (in which the hero is frequently chased by a large inflatable ball!).

When I began to dig deeper by reading what little published material there was on Portmeirion, some of it collected on my first visit there, I discovered that the architect and owner of the place, Clough Williams-Ellis, was no less colourful. Born into a well-to-do family, he had turned his back on a formal architectural training and had set up his own practice catering mainly to friends and society acquaintances (Williams-Ellis 1980). He was only moderately successful, I found, and did not rate much of a mention in books on British twentieth-century architecture, other than as architect of Portmeirion. Nonetheless, Portmeirion was widely known, though it tended to be treated as a twentieth-century folly or erratic rather than anything more significant. Williams-Ellis's trenchant views on town and country planning were also widely known, though also not widely acclaimed. He had published extensively in the inter-war period (1924, 1928, 1937) on the lack of effective state control of urban and rural development and on the demise of aesthetic sensibility and had also become involved in the emerging conservation movement. His colourful writing style, however, seemed to mark him out as a polemicist rather than planner.

I decided to try and explain and contextualise the building of Portmeirion – to remain true, therefore, to that first immediate sense of place. Beyond that, though, I wanted to consider whether Williams-Ellis merited more attention than he'd hitherto been given and to see whether Portmeirion could be read as part of a wider social and political commentary (were he and Portmeirion ever more than just eccentrics?). I tracked down and gained access to Williams-Ellis's archive at the National Library of Wales in Aberystwyth where letters, drafts of speeches and boxes of press cuttings and 'reviews' from the professional press gave some insight into his creative process and responses to it (though sadly, in one of those twists of fate familiar to many historical researchers, most materials from the period I was interested in had been destroyed in two large fires at his home). I also went to study some of his drawings at the RIBA in London. I began with a close analysis of the village itself, detailing what exactly was there and eventually qualifying the label 'Italianate', as I found a more eclectic truth. This part of the work also included trying to grasp what had been built and when, given that the site had been developed over the course of some 50 years. I also considered the placing of the buildings in relation to the site and in relation, also, to the locality. This latter point meant becoming familiar with Williams-Ellis's other commissions in the area and with his role as a significant local landlord. Alongside this work, I read as many contemporary accounts of the place as I could find, mainly by trawling through the architectural press and popular magazines (though I was helped by Williams-Ellis's assiduous collection of press cuttings and their preservation in his archive).

Williams-Ellis (1932, 1976) had actually published what amounted to a manifesto for the village on a number of occasions. He wanted to awaken in visitors a sense of pleasure in architecture; to demonstrate that a beautiful natural site could be developed without ruining it; and to show that a concern for the environment need not imply poor economic management. A key feature of the first element of the manifesto was the eclecticism of the village and the playful use of colour and decoration. Much of this could only be fully appreciated at the site itself, though contemporary photographs (albeit in black and white) helped. Once I knew what to look for, the village started to become layered in meaning. Far from simply being Italianate, it was a pastiche of styles and references, guided in part by the fact that many elements were simply salvaged from demolished buildings throughout Britain. (Tempting though it was to see in this some kind of precursor to post-modernism, I resisted!). I could then use these material lessons in aesthetics to make sense of Williams-Ellis's published writings and, beyond that, to the manifestos of the conservation movement of which he was an influential part. In particular, I could connect with his published remarks that the Welsh lacked a visual appreciation of landscape. Given that he was writing at a time when Welsh cultural and political consciousness was on the rise, I kept an eye open for references to this debate and was rewarded with some fiery debates in the press of the day, and subsequently with some useful academic critiques of this idea (Lord, 1992).

The second aim behind the development of Portmeirion connected the village even more explicitly to debates about town and country planning. Williams-Ellis was but one of several writers commenting on the lack of sensitivity to topography and natural context in inter-war Britain, but he was one of the most impassioned. In the frontispiece to his *England and the Octopus* (1928) he foreshadowed the swamping of the countryside by a tide of industrial and urban sprawl (See Figure 15.2). But at

1914. MR. WILLIAM SMITH ANSWERS THE CALL TO PRESERVE
HIS NATIVE SOIL INVIOLATE.

1919. MR. WILLIAM SMITH COMES BACK AGAIN TO SEE HOW
WELL HE HAS DONE IT.

Figure 15.2 *'Mr William Smith …'. The frontispiece of William-Ellis's* England the Octopus *(1928). First appeared in* Punch *magazine and reproduced by permission of* Punch.

Portmeirion he had the opportunity of demonstrating what sound design principles might actually look like. Although the village appears to have grown accidentally or haphazardly there have always been consistent principles underlying the development: 'a clustering here, a dominant feature there, a connecting line, an axial vista, an interlude of gardens, lawn or woodland, the emphasizing of natural height, the opening of a sea or mountain view, the enclosing of space' (Williams-Ellis, 1976: 26). One of the village's most generous critics was *Country Life* magazine's architectural writer Christopher Hussey, a respected writer also on Picturesque aesthetics. He praised the village's ambiguous tension between an apparent randomness and an ordered plan: 'The acropolis buildings, which group together so felicitously, are disposed according to the method advocated long ago by the apostles of the picturesque: they follow the contours and the stratification of the rock, and house has been added to house as and where requirements suggested' (Hussey, 1930: 502). A belief in planned order, of which Portmeirion was a practical example, ran through all of Williams-Ellis's work. While it would be easy to interpret the conservation movement of the time as being anti-development, therefore, Portmeirion highlighted that it was *guided* development that was the ideal. Alex Potts has highlighted what he calls the 'ideal modernity' of inter-war representations of rural Britain: 'A picture of the perfect countryside and village could act as the ideal image of what a modern Britain emerging from the unsightly ravages of Victorianism might become' (Potts, 1989: 163; see also Matless, 1998). Portmeirion, I began to think, was one such 'perfect village'.

Issues of order and control also lay behind the third aim – that of proving that a concern for environment need not mean economic mismanagement. At Portmeirion financial security was achieved as the village and its hotel rapidly became an exclusive haunt for the rich and famous, run on ordered and enlightened principles, with access for the day-trippers who were supposedly most in need of aesthetic education strictly limited. It would be easy, therefore, to see the village as the latest in a long line of elitist, aristocratic escapes from a harsher reality outside the walls. But on reading his books and articles – and also noting *where* they were published – it became apparent that Williams-Ellis's concerns about governance were much more thoughtful, and that this had implications for how I should read Portmeirion. Williams-Ellis was a committed Socialist and argued that only through effective state control could a planned countryside be achieved (Williams-Ellis, 1929a). He attacked the vulgarities and lack of ethics of big business and ultimately advocated land nationalization. He would be inspired by the scale and vision of Soviet planning during a visit in 1931, and already in 1929 cast envious eyes abroad:

> We are petitioning to be governed; we ask for control, for discipline. We have tried freedom and, under present conditions, we see that it leads to waste, inefficiency, and chaos. Also we have turned envious eyes on other countries where the idea of individual liberty is better tempered by common-sense and a greater regard for joint and common liberties that private greed or folly may by no means disregard.
>
> (Williams-Ellis, 1929b)

Seen in this context, Portmeirion – which had hitherto seemed eccentric and haphazard – was an expression of regulation by a plan and planner, and a metaphor for orderly national development raising issues of guidance, authority and control.

The danger of being attracted to the immediacy of building and place is that description can take over from analysis, and explaining how the village came to be there can supplant asking what it means. Although considering that it was important not to lose sight of the unique character of the place, I decided that Portmeirion – and, indeed, Clough Williams-Ellis – was more significant than most commentators had allowed. At one level it challenged some historiographical ideas about the relationship between tradition and modernity in the middle of the twentieth century. That allowed me, therefore, to connect this example to a much wider debate about British geography and culture. But, theoretically, I had been trying to make sense of the role of this kind of place in informing social change. That eventually came through the idea of 'utopia' and a distinction drawn by the famous American writer Lewis Mumford, letters from whom I had read in Williams-Ellis's archive. Mumford (quoted in Porter and Luckermann, 1976: 200) contrasted the utopia of escape – a fantasy landscape or substitute for the external world – and the utopia of reconstruction – where 'the facts of the everyday world are brought together and assorted and sifted, and a new sort of reality is projected back again upon the external world'. In this scheme of things, despite appearing to be the former, Portmeirion could certainly be considered to be an example of the latter. In coming to that conclusion I was combining an interpretation of what I had found on the site with what I had found in the archives and in published accounts.

Zoo modernism

My second example concerns the modern enclosures built for animals at London Zoo in the 1930s (Gruffudd, 2000). I had been working on the relationship between health and modern architecture, focusing in particular on two landmark health centres in London (Gruffudd, 2001). One of these, at Finsbury, was designed by the radical architectural co-operative Tecton, led in this instance by Berthold Lubetkin. It was easy enough to understand why a group of young, socialist architects would want to be involved with the design and building of a health centre for one of the most deprived and overcrowded parts of London. As Gold (2001: 78) notes of Britain in the 1930s, many modern architects 'subscribed to a package of progressive views, particularly belief in rational philosophy and the socially-redeeming virtues of science and technology'. But it was less obvious why the same architect, Lubetkin, would have sought or accepted a commission to build a Gorilla House and Penguin Pool for London Zoo. Notwithstanding the fact that these striking enclosures, and especially the Penguin Pool (Figure 15.3), became some of the best-known and well-liked examples of modern architecture in Britain, I wondered whether there might have been any kind of functional or ideological connection between the Finsbury Health Centre (and similar health-related buildings) opened in 1938 and the zoo structures built a few years earlier. In asking this, I was also interested in Kay Anderson's argument that:

> *Zoos ultimately tell us stories about boundary-making activities on the part of humans. In the most general terms, Western metropolitan zoos are spaces where humans engage in cultural self-definition against a variably constructed and opposed nature. With animals as the medium, they inscribe a cultural sense of distance from that loosely defined realm that has come to be called 'nature'.*
>
> (Anderson, 1995: 276)

So at one level I thought that these zoo structures might tell me something about the practice of modern architecture in 1930s Britain, but at another level might reveal something about the perceived boundaries between humans and animals or 'culture' and 'nature'. I wanted, therefore, to try and understand the buildings in themselves – to see how they carried out and expressed their function – and that meant examining drawings, photographs and descriptive accounts. It also meant visiting London

Figure 15.3 *The Penguin Pool at London Zoo. Source:* Architects' Journal, *14th June 1934, p. 858. Reproduced by permission of the* Architects' Journal.

Zoo to see these buildings in context – the Penguin Pool still dramatic, though slightly shabby at the time; the Gorilla House tucked away and seemingly forgotten. I also wanted to understand the relationship of these buildings to Lubetkin's other designs and so I sought to build up a contextual knowledge of his development as an architect through published accounts. Again, I tracked down and gained access to Lubetkin's archival collection and architectural drawings at the RIBA. At their library I also carried out a thorough trawl of the professional journals of the time for material relating to these buildings: critical reviews, correspondence, photo essays, cartoons, and so forth. All the while I read various theoretical and historical interpretations of modernism.

I was both fortunate and slightly worried by the fact that there existed a very large and very good book on Lubetkin (Allan, 1992) – a not uncommon factor for anyone working on architectural history to have to deal with. I was fortunate in that I was able to develop sound background knowledge of Lubetkin's personal history and professional and technical development, as well as access to a detailed listing of his work. But I was worried to begin with because I feared it might be difficult to say anything that hadn't already been said. However, the framing of the questions I was asking within a specifically geographical context afforded me, I hoped, some academic and critical leverage.

I discovered that Lubetkin had written on the principles of zoo design in a manner which I thought related to some of Kay Anderson's 1995 ideas. He noted that there were two possible approaches to zoo building:

> The first, which may be called the 'naturalistic' method, is typified in the Hamburg and Paris zoos where an attempt is made, as far as possible, to reproduce the natural habitat of each animal; the second approach, which, for want of a better word, we may call the 'geometric', consists of designing architectural settings for the animals in such a way as to present them dramatically to the public, in an atmosphere comparable to that of a circus.

> (Quoted in Allan, 1992: 199)

At first glance this quotation clearly does not denote the breaking down of barriers between culture and nature, in any obvious sense. If anything it implies the objectification of nature for human entertainment. But closer reading suggested that Lubetkin's understanding of animals extended beyond the superficial. He argued that it was the architect's task to try to understand the animals in their essence – taxonomically, as it were – and to then coax them through design to display their distinctive characteristics and personalities. The same detailed scientific research, survey and application that underlay his housing and health designs, therefore, also underlay Lubetkin's zoo designs. Intensive research findings were incorporated into functional aspects of the buildings. It transpired that gorillas were especially prone to catching human diseases like flu and colds. They were also sensitive to bad weather. In the Gorilla House design of 1933 Lubetkin, therefore, rejected the idea of attempting to create a fake jungle habitat in favour of a concrete cylinder with a cage frontage that could be closed off by sliding screens during bad weather. The structure could be closed entirely during the winter. With powerful lamps to simulate sunshine and an air circulation system to purify and humidify the air, one architectural journal noted that 'the best place in London for a breath of fresh air will be the Gorilla House!' (*Architectural Design and Construction*, 1933: 317). The same journal seemed jokingly to suggest that this, perhaps, meant a refashioned relationship between animal and human: '... the chief gorilla having heard the weather forecast will instruct the head keeper to take the necessary steps to preserve an equable climate in his commodious cage. He – the gorilla, not the keeper – is a delicate subject, liable to catch cold and particularly prone to influenza' (1933: 317).

The Penguin Pool was composed of an elliptical concrete shell housing two interlocking ramps sloping down gradually into the water. Some suggested that the white concrete and the blue water was intended as an image of Antarctica though Allan (1987) counters that it was merely 'a visual metaphor for it'. The pool also was designed with the animals specifically in mind. Nesting areas were incorporated into the structure and a variety of surfaces were used to tackle the animals' boredom. Initial studies suggested that the birds were, indeed, more active than they were in other zoos. More significantly, this was a building designed to allow the birds to express their contrasting characters. In the water – viewed from above and through windows into the water – the penguins were naturally quick and graceful. On the ramps, however, there would be a comic contrast:

> *Penguins have an attractive and faintly ridiculous quality: their shape and black and white colouring produce an almost human effect, enhancing the grotesque awkwardness of their movements on land.... The two cantilevered ramps have a theatrical quality and provide a suitable stage for the waddling gait of the penguins, who are shown to be able to hop as well as waddle by the stepped ramps. The pond, in fact, explains the characteristics of the penguins and 'produces' them effectively to the public.*
>
> (*Architects' Journal*, 1934: 857).

The Pool was eventually listed as one of the most significant buildings of its time, and has become one of the best known modern artefacts in Britain.

Lubetkin's close scrutiny of animal behaviour and character, and the popularity and critical acclaim for these buildings led to several other commissions in London and also a complete remodelling of Dudley Zoo in the English Midlands. I felt happy, therefore, that his work was both innovative and important enough to be saying something significant about the relationship between nature and culture, as represented in zoos.

But the problem remained of how to potentially connect these structures with those health designs and how, therefore, to evaluate any significance for these designs beyond the boundaries of the zoo. I tried to assess whether there were, first of all, functional links between the zoo buildings and the later health centre designs. It appeared that some of the air purification systems from the zoo were utilized in the health centres, and even that a system for feeding the animals safely was modified to create a template for lockers in the health centre changing rooms. More generally, there was an opinion expressed in certain quarters in the 1930s that the zoo buildings were, in fact, experiments in the healthy nurturing of organisms more generally. The animals at the zoo, therefore, were a microcosm of society, illuminating principles that could be applied to human nurture through modern architecture and planning. One strand of research that convinced me of this was the influence of the Zoological Society's secretary, the eminent biologist Julian Huxley. Huxley and Lubetkin were both members of the Architects and Technicians Organisation, founded in 1935 to bring together detailed scientific research and a radical social conscience. In addition to being an evolutionary scientist (and thus himself interested in the nurture of organisms), Huxley wrote extensively on planning, architecture and health, was closely involved with another famous modern health centre in Peckham in London, and was a campaigner for the social (and frequently socialist) function of science. In a pair of photographs in his 1934 book *Scientific Research and Social Needs*, Huxley contrasted the oppressive, dark and squalid slums of the British inner city with the gleaming, sunlit Gorilla House at his own London Zoo. The message seemed to be clear enough: to escape from the physical degeneration of the slums society needed to adopt the scientific mindset that had created the Gorilla House.

The evolutionary irony of the relative conditions of humans and animals was not lost on contemporary observers. Whilst trawling through architectural journals (and often there is no alternative but to trawl) I found an article (*Architects' Journal*, 1933) called 'The descent of man'. This, too, used paired photographs for effect (Figure 15.4). On the top, a gorilla silhouetted against the sunlight in the clean functionalism of the Gorilla House at London Zoo; on the bottom, a dark, squalid and infested tenement. Here on the page was an anti-evolutionary descent from animal hygiene into human neglect. This was reinforced by a series of quotations from descriptions of the Gorilla House and from Medical Officers of Health reports, respectively, further highlighting the contrast:

> The new Gorilla House … shows the thoughtful care devoted to this housing problem. Gorillas are liable to the diseases of man [sic], and are, therefore, protected in winter by movable glass screens.
>
> *Here the place is infected by rats and cockroaches, family in bad health – suffering with chests. Two children have died of diphtheria.*
>
> The windows are provided with blinds which can darken the cage, so that the tropical conditions, natural to gorillas, of twelve hours darkness and twelve hours light may be reproduced.
>
> *Bedroom in which the family sleep is practically pitch dark even in the daytime.*
>
> In the centre of the floor of the winter cage there is a small basin and fountain, operated by a brass knob in the floor, manipulated by the gorillas.
>
> *A very bad feature of this property is the water and lavatory accommodation – one tap between six houses and one w.c. between three.*
>
> (*Architects' Journal*, 1933: 834)

Figure 15.4 *'The Descent of Man': the* Architects' Journal
on the relative conditions for people and gorillas.
Source: Architects' Journal, *22nd June 1933, p. 834.*
Reproduced by permission of the Architects' Journal.

The irony is that while human society had failed to provide the working classes with decent, healthy houses 'mere' animals were being nurtured by the careful application of science. But read alongside Lubetkin's pronouncements on the zoo and Huxley's socially-committed science it is clear that there is more than just polemical irony in this article. The two photographs were theoretically and functionally connected as parts of the same debate – on nature/culture relationships and on the successful nurture of living forms. To my mind, therefore, this successfully connected Lubetkin's London Zoo buildings to academic debates of the kind raised by Anderson (1995). Beyond that, the buildings seemed to offer a contribution to other debates on the nature of twentieth-century modernism, and particularly to those suggesting that the organic and natural aspects of modernism had been neglected by historians in favour of stressing the technical and rational (Rabinow, 1996).

Conclusion

The danger in attempting to grasp and characterise the immediacy of architecture and the built environment is, perhaps, that the narrative or story-telling element of describing how something came to be where it is can take over from the more analytical or theoretical aims of academic research. When a building is dramatic, eccentric or out of place then the urge to tell its story can be overwhelming. As Baker (1997) notes, it is part of our job as geographers to reconstruct what happened, and if the story has twists and turns, arguments between architect and client, a hostile or rapturous public reception then so much the better! But telling the story is only part of the job; we need also to give a convincing account of what happened and to explain why it matters. Sometimes this part of the job is much harder. I've recently been struggling with a piece of research on the intrigue surrounding the building of a huge holiday camp in a quiet part of rural Wales the 1940s in which the narrative is hugely entertaining (to my mind, at least!), given that it involves alleged bribery, knobbly knees contests, and moral outrage from part of the local and national population. Working out what really matters about that is a different challenge though, and it is that which distinguishes an entertaining from an important piece of work.

At times, it might seem that the broader, theoretical concerns come after the fact; that is, they come almost by way of a reason to tell the story that has already been written. Perhaps there was an element of that in my relationship to Portmeirion; the place and its creator were so eccentric that they tended to dominate until late on in my thinking. In truth, the relationship between empirical research and theoretical or speculative thinking is much more complex and cyclical than this. Few people go out into the 'field' with their ideas already formed, and few people, equally, collect information without any sense of why or what to do with it. The trick, as Stephen Daniels (1993) notes, is not to smash the aesthetic surface of, in this case, the built environment but to write in ways that conveys those aesthetics and amplifies and clarifies their meanings.

Further reading

On architecture in general see, for example:
- Borden, I. et al. (1996) *Strangely Familiar: Narratives of Architecture in the City*. London, Routledge.
- Dovey, K. (1999) *Framing Places: Mediating Power in Built Form*. London, Spon Press.
- Worpole, K. (2000) *Here Comes the Sun: Architecture and Public Space in 20th Century European Culture*. London, Reaktion.
- Zukin, S. (1991) *Landscapes of Power: From Detroit to Disney World*. Berkeley, University of California Press.

On model villages like Portmeirion see:
- Darley, G. (1975) *Villages of Vision*. London, Architectural Press.
- Hardy, D. (1979) *Alternative Communities in Nineteenth Century England*. London, Longman.

For a reading of an 'everyday' landscape, see
- Jakle, J.A. et al. (1997) *The Motel in America: the Road in American Culture*. Baltimore, Johns Hopkins University Press.

A TALE OF RESEARCH

Gender and bodily performance in the department store

Akile Ahmet

I started thinking about possible ideas for my dissertation in September 2002. One day during a social geography lecture I heard the body being mentioned as a research area in geography. It made me think. What has the body got to do with geography? I looked up the word 'body' in *Dictionary of Human Geography* (Johnston et al., 2000), where I found some references, and continued reading from there. What particularly intrigued me was the role of the body in the world of work and consumption (as in Crang, 1994 and McDowell, 1997). It seemed to me that the body itself has become a commodity or a 'front' for employers to use to sell other goods.

Reading about the body and performativity also made me think about what I was experiencing in my part-time job. I started working as a sales assistant in a department store in London in June 2001 and my own experiences of being looked at, of feeling like an embodied female, and particular requirements about my uniform, appearance and performance, all related directly to Judith Butler's work on embodied performativity (1990). My dissertation research was based in the department store where I work, and examined how this site of consumption socially, sexually and racially constructs the body of both male and female workers. The main methods that I used in my research were six interviews and participant observation over a period of four months. I found that doing the research where I worked – and particularly the covert nature of my participant observation – raised many ethical questions and practical difficulties.

I knew that it would be difficult to recruit interviewees, particularly men. As I didn't want many people to find out about my research, I could only ask a limited number of people whom I trusted. The following is an extract from my research diary:

> *I was really dreading today, actually having to ask someone whether they would be willing to do an interview with me. One of the guys from … (another department) … seems to be pretty friendly with me. … So I asked him, his initial reaction was 'I don't get what it is you are researching?' I explained it more simply to him, and his answer was 'Well, if you go out with me for a drink tonight I might think about [it] and I might even say yes'. I just thought forget it. Next was Steve. I like the guy and he likes me in a 'friend' way, he wouldn't dare ask me out. Thankfully he did agree, but under one condition – no tape recorder. I tried to assure him that no one but me would hear it, but he wasn't going to agree to a recorded interview.*

I only managed to interview two men, and I felt that they didn't want to take me seriously whatsoever. The fact that these two male respondents knew me personally and the fact that I was female made the interview dynamics very difficult, particularly for me. For example:

Respondent:	Carry on, I'm fascinated by you now (laughs).
Interviewer:	Stop flirting, this is an interview.
Respondent:	Do you think I'm a flirt?
Interviewer:	Well, that depends on what you call flirting.
Respondent:	Why do you need to complicate questions?
Interviewer:	I'm not complicating the question.
Respondent:	But flirting, it's all part of the job.
Interviewer:	Anyway, your perception on the staff male and female.
Respondent:	Ask away woman.
Interviewer:	Stop it, I think I'm aware that I'm a woman.
Respondent:	And so are the rest of the guys that work in [the store].
Interviewer:	What's that suppose to mean?
Respondent:	Well … When … Can I say?
Interviewer:	Go ahead.
Respondent:	When you came back to work everyone wanted to know who you were, for us you were the new girl.
Interviewer:	And so that makes me the new booty, as you guys would say?
Respondent:	Something like that woman.

According to Valentine (2002) the interview process is a game of positionalities. As much as I tried to perform the role of the detached, disembodied interviewer, I found it impossible to do so. I had fewer difficulties in recruiting female respondents and management, mainly because I had known them for a long time and we had become friends. Despite my initial fears about power relations, my interviews with managers were very relaxed. If I had been an outsider I think that the interview dynamics would have been very different.

The second research method which I used was participant observation. Rather than asking people about their views and feelings, you watch what they do and listen to what they say. This directness provided me with a degree of validity that the interviews didn't, particularly due to the problems I had with the male respondents. I recorded information in the form of a research diary that I wrote each day that I worked. During the day I would write down basic things such as place, time, date, who was there, actions and what was said. Once I got home I completed what Kitchin and Tate (2000) call the narrative part of a research diary in which I used what I had written during the day to construct the story and to explain what was being observed. Participant observation became the main research method that I used to analyse performativity, and also raised new questions that I hadn't initially considered. For example, the following extract from my research diary describes a conversation that made me think about workers as racially embodied, and not just embodied in terms of gender and sexuality:

Saturday, 7th September 2002

What were you thinking when you hired the weekday staff?' said Leila. Kevin and everyone else looked at her, 'What's wrong with them?' he asked. 'Come on, they are all Chinese' she said. I was so shocked at what she had said, I mean how stupid can you be to think like that. 'Yeah, and they work a lot harder than you do. You should

> know by now Leila that I do not discriminate against race or anything else' said Kevin. 'Yeah, I know that, but you need some sort of attractions for the weekdays, it's getting really bad in here, nearly as bad as [another store] the girls there are so ugly, you know those black girls' she said. 'It's always the more attractive ones that don't do any work, and stand around talking to men and not do any work' said Kevin. 'I hope you are not referring to me' she said. 'Come on Kevin, I've heard you say stuff, when someone has come in to drop off their CV and you've said something about their appearance' she said. 'It's not their appearance that I haven't liked it's the way that they have asked for a job' he said. 'You mean to say that if a really fit gay guy wanted to work here you wouldn't hire him straight away?' she asked. 'Leila, I'm 36 years old'. The conversation ended there.

Reading through my diary entries made me think 'what does all of this mean', and probably to other people they would read simply as a story about my summer. However, these stories – the little details about my days at work – produced a vast amount of material, particularly when I read my diary 'between the lines.' It was important that I recorded even the most minor details, such as what people were wearing or the way they spoke to each other.

My participant observation was covert and raised many difficult ethical questions. As Kitchin and Tate (2000: 36) put it:

> Some would argue that covert participant observation is a legitimate and valid research strategy, especially in public or open settings and where anonymity of the person(s) observed is maintained. Observation in closed systems where the researcher is deceiving a particular participant however raises more difficult ethical questions. In this situation [as I was in], some would argue that the act of deception is ethically unsound and should not be practised.

Initially my feeling about becoming a covert participant observer was that it wouldn't be a problem. But after the first week, I began to feel dishonest and that I was treating people as objects – research objects. I was listening to other people's conversations and then writing about what they had said. Details about their personal lives were becoming part of my research. These people were not only my work colleagues but also my friends and most of them knew nothing about what I was doing. But if I was to expose what I was doing I would have risked not only losing my job but staff would have become more conscious around me and not done or said certain things as a result.

My research was both a positive and a negative experience. I soon realised that an objective, impartial and neutral researcher doesn't exist. Researchers are human beings with feelings and emotions, and are not disembodied machines. It is important to think about reflexivity rather than objectivity. For England (1994) and Valentine (2002) the researcher needs to be reflexive in order to place themselves into the research.

The body and performativity have become important areas of research in cultural geography. In my dissertation I argued that men as well as women are constructed as embodied workers, and that race – as well as gender and sexuality – is important in understanding embodied performativity. Turning my part-time job into the basis for my dissertation enabled me to gain a real insight into embodied performativity as I was personally experiencing the things that I was writing about.

I am in my final year of a BA in Geography at Queen Mary, University of London. I finished my dissertation in January 2003 and enjoyed doing the research so much that I want to carry on as a postgraduate student. I am applying to study for an MA (and hopefully then a PhD) so that I can do further research on race and the body.

16
On display
The poetics, politics and interpretation of exhibitions

Mike Crang

This chapter moves through some geographical approaches to and issues about exhibitions, principally museum displays. In the opening part of the chapter I outline some reasons why we might be interested in museums, before considering two different approaches to the study of museums. The first of these approaches consists of two parts. First, picking up on some of the issues raised in Chapter 1, I consider the way in which exhibitions can be thought of as 'disciplining' knowledge. Second, I look at different ways of 'reading' an exhibition, considering both a **semiotic** approach and then, attending more closely to the poetics of display, a narrative approach. Both of these approaches suggest that exhibitions can be treated like texts and this is useful when we want to unpack the politics that is bound up in the display of objects. But I also suggest that there are some limits to these approaches since they tend to 'passify' the audience and participants of displays. The audience and participants are left as silent subjects, either through the assumption that they are controlled by the displays and simply absorb their meaning, or through being spoken for by the clever academic interpreter who sees what is really going on. In response to these limitations, in the second part of the chapter I therefore move on to consider ways in which we can consider displays in terms of **performances** by both creators and consumers, in an approach that looks at interpretation as a co-construction by the different parties involved.

In working through these approaches I will be drawing upon a range of theoretical traditions and, it has to be said, disputes. I will be using the tools of structuralist and post-structuralist linguistics and textual analysis. Both of these offer ways of reading exhibits – and, as you may have guessed, the latter is quite critical of the former. To study performance, I will be drawing upon anthropological and folklore traditions, whilst to examine audience interpretation I will be turning to a literature from media studies. In setting the chapter out in this order, I am aware that it risks being read as having later approaches 'trumping' earlier ones, which is not entirely what I intend. Instead, I want to show how I have used all of them to look at different aspects of the work that exhibits do. This is perhaps the common thread here: all these approaches look at exhibits not simply as displaying things but as *creating* meanings. In other words, I am focusing upon meaning as performed, both by institutions and exhibits, and by the people viewing them.

Methodologically, then, I am going to draw upon a range of techniques and ideas. There is a certain amount of formal textual analysis, certainly close and critical reading of exhibits, but also issues of how to study the practices of performers and users of exhibitions. So we shall be thinking through different forms of observation as well as some conventional social science approaches to working with people. However, I shall also be trying to suggest that in this active perspective on creating meanings we are not just dealing with **representations** but what Allan Pred (1995) called 'repress-entations' where some elements are actively silenced.

Spaces of ethnomimesis and social memory

It is worth a brief word about why we might be studying museums, or rather the angle I am taking here, since it informs the types of approaches used. I am interested in how exhibitions (and, for the sake of clarity and length in this chapter, I shall restrict this to museums) tell us about the world. That is they exhibit the world to us, and thus shape people's knowledge about different aspects of it. I am particularly interested in the stories museums tell us about who we are, who other people are and how we came to be in the situation we are now. Museums have tended to be set up to preserve the 'heritage' of a people and display it to them, so those people can learn from their past. Museums are thus stories we tell ourselves about who we are – at least in the sense that it is our past that made us what we are today. They are part of our social memory. Thus definitions of **identity** typically stress **difference** from others and self-consistency over time: the idea that a group persists. Now, I should add that museums when interpreted critically tend to show that groups do not simply persist over time. Rather they are **reflexively** and more or less consciously refashioned, reinterpreted, reinscribed and reiterated over time as they tell themselves stories about who they are. To do this telling and re-telling they invent and use a variety of institutions at a variety of scales – museums being one, school history being another, films another, oral story telling of folk tales another – that portray a 'publicly imagined past' (Blatti, 1987: 7). All of these are examples of what we might call 'ethnomimesis' – performing our group identity to an audience (Cantwell, 1993).

These different performances use different approaches and involve different ways of communicating. I want to use museums to suggest that we need to think about how these different methods impact upon what is communicated. So I want to look at the relationship of different cultural forms to the stories that are told, that is the poetics of how meanings are put together. Now, so far we have been using collective nouns pretty freely, suggesting groups tell themselves their stories. One of the normal insights of cultural geography is that these forms of representation tend also to be arenas of domination, contestation and resistance between different groups and elements of a society. Thus museums start to give us an insight into whose version of history gets told. In other words, we might see museums as telling a 'dominant memory', which tends to favour the view of powerful groups who control these institutions. Historians have suggested that these dominant groups have used their control over our notions of the past to justify and underline their **power** in the present (Johnson et al., 1982; Hobsbawm and Ranger, 1989; Porter, 1992; Norkunas, 1993). Museums are thus part of hegemonic strategies whereby a particular group in society sustains its powerful position by persuading others to consent to it, by making it appear natural, inevitable or justifiable.

One level of analysis is thus to unpack the interests behind different stories, to untangle institutional histories and so on. Here I am going to focus upon looking at the actual stories told and how they are expressed. In other words, to understand how a geography of group identity is sustained I am going to look at the micro-geographies *within* exhibitions. I am going to try and see how these places persuade us about their version of the world, and what makes them credible. I also want to flag up an issue about this approach. The focus upon the institutional powers and interests behind exhibitions can slip into an approach that criticises an exhibit as a 'distorting mirror', which presents a skewed version of the 'true' past. What I am trying to suggest is that there are in fact multiple, competing versions of the past, all of which use poetics and rhetoric in different ways.

Reading exhibits

Exhibitionary complex: disciplining knowledge

We might begin though with some sense of the formal emergence of the museum. When we think about it, the museum is using the organisation of objects in specially designed spaces to try and communicate messages. It uses spatial configuration as part of a way of shaping knowledge. In terms of its emergence, it has been linked with other practices that sought to categorise, define and regulate knowledge about the world, so in one sense we can see it as like an archive (see Chapter 1). Objects are taken from the world, classified and redisplayed according to those classifications. In other words the authority and classification tends to work by establishing an abstract system of authority and using that to create order and significance among the objects on display. Thus, the folklorist Barbara Kirshenblatt-Gimblett argues that in anthropological museums:

> *Ethnographic artefacts are objects of ethnography. They are artefacts created by ethnographers. Objects become ethnographic by virtue of being defined, segmented, detached and carried away by ethnographers. Such objects are ethnographic not because they were found in a Hungarian peasant household, Kwakiutl village, or Rajasthani market rather than in Buckingham Palace or Michelangelo's studio, but by virtue of the manner in which they have been detached, for disciplines make their objects and in the process make themselves.*
>
> (Kirshenblatt-Gimblett, 1991: 387)

Looking at the emergence of the public museum in the nineteenth century, we can see them as an enterprise producing a vast and expanding network of new classifications as they systematised knowledge about the world. But the classificatory mechanisms are not put on display. They remain hidden in the back regions of these institutions where new professions developed rules that were rarely made apparent to the viewing public. Hooper-Greenhill (1989, 1992) points out that the public/private division of knowledge was hardening in the nineteenth century, with a new role emerging for the state operating in the silent 'back' regions, such as archives, of the museum in order to produce knowledge that is then pedagogically presented in the front to consumers. This stresses a conception of a passive public who are meant to absorb knowledge created elsewhere. What this means is that artefacts, which I have suggested are as much artefacts of classification as the cultures from where they originated, get presented as facts. The authority of objects is in turn mobilised as providing indisputable evidence. This apparent facticity, or evidential quality for displays, means the conceptual work of shaping knowledge about cultures and places is hidden in the back regions of institutions. This means that the political and ideological decisions tend to be screened and it allows the 'authors' of these representations, often the state and its institutions, to 'exnominate' themselves, to leave the version unsigned as it were. Thus museums tended to produce an authoritative **discourse** by hiding the marks of its production (Shelton, 1990). The classifications and rules through which exhibits are interpreted and categorised are written into the spatial ordering of objects, determining which specimens appear alongside which others, in notebooks, archives and exhibit cases. Thus, a neutrally scientific discourse is produced that is expressed at the capillary level of power in the seriated spaces that divide, classify and specify objects of knowledge and produce 'files of objects ordered by the military formations of the fields of knowledge'

(Shelton, 1990: 98). The museum display thus produces artefacts that serve to act reciprocally as evidence for the regime of knowledge that gave rise to them where objects offer not 'authenticity' or knowledge but rather offer authority to the agreed, or always-already, rules of knowledge without which objects are silent texts *in potentia* (Taborsky, 1990: 64; Crew and Sims, 1991: 163). That is, objects only acquire meaning and only communicate to an audience through being taken up and mobilised in an interpretative framework. This organisation of space to allocate significance to objects is typical of a disciplinary knowledge whose 'object is to fix, it is an anti-nomadic force ... [which] uses procedures of partitioning and cellularity' (Foucault, 1977: 218–19).

The mention of Michel Foucault's theorisation of the disciplinary matrix of the carcereal archipelago of prisons, medical institutions and archives accumulating knowledge raises the question as to whether it is not suspicious that, just at the moment when Bentham produces his planned panopticon of enclosed surveillance, a few miles away the Crystal Palace is being built, and a few years later the 'Albertopolis' of museums and exhibitionary institutions in Kensington (the Natural History Museum, The Museum of Mankind, the Victoria and Albert Museum, the Royal Geographical Society and the Albert Hall) all appear. Tony Bennett thus suggests that we need to think about the emergence of an 'exhibitionary complex' that moves objects into progressively more public display in order to broadcast other messages of power (Bennett, 1988: 74). Or, as Derek Gregory puts it, museums and world fairs need to be considered as part of the 'wider constellation in which they are set: a spectacular geography in which the world itself appeared as an exhibition' (1994: 38). Just as Foucault pointed out the sophisticated, incessant 'capillary' scale of power in disciplinary institutions acting through specific spatial configurations, we might apply the same analysis to museums. Here too we have the exercise of an inherently spatial reorganisation where the objects are first removed from their original cultural and communicative context, then recontextualised in the spaces of the museum according to an externally generated syntax. The possible combinations of objects become a chance to play spatially with different sequences of remembering and time. As Hooper-Greenhill suggests, we can see an attempt to 'spatialise material knowledge ... by the way in which words and texts were linked together and arranged in space' (1992: 90). I want to think about the specific ways of linking words and things in the next section.

Exhibition semiotics

Within museums, then, we might have to think about the rules that make objects tell stories. Such a process requires objects to be inserted into a discursive order for them to be legible and intelligible:

> *The problem with things is that they are dumb. They are not eloquent, as some thinkers in art museums claim. They are dumb. And if by some ventriloquism they seem to speak, they lie ... once removed from the continuity of everyday uses in time and space and made exquisite on display, stabilized and conserved, objects are transformed in the meanings they may be said to carry.*
>
> (Crew and Sims, 1991: 159).

In other words, when we take an object as evidence this is often done by selecting what it represents and silencing other possible meanings. This raises issues of authority and credibility – that is why we believe the stories we are told. Now at one level we can look at the public **iconography** of museums, which frequently use classical facades, and often large solid stone fronts engraved with scientific motifs that aim to appear as shrines or temples to secular, universal truths (Shelton, 1990; Duncan, 1991). So we might start to ask questions of museums about how they cast us as the (ignorant) audience and themselves as sources of authoritative knowledge.

Let me take an example of one museum I have studied (see Crang, 1999, 2000) – Skansen, established in Stockholm in 1891 – and unpack how it shaped a message in its displays. What I want to do is illustrate how specific arrangements of artefacts can be used to support a specific version of history, in this case a nationalising project. The first thing to do here is think about the context for the museum. In the nineteenth century Sweden witnessed the rapid industrialisation of its cities and the mass emigration of its rural population – up to 20 per cent – to places like the USA. So we need to understand the museum in a context of rapid social change and instability. In the midst of this Skansen appears as an institution dedicated to telling a story to, principally, urban Stockholmers about the rural peasant types of Sweden. The first open air museum in the world, Skansen was founded, along with the more conventionally ethnological Nordic Museum, by Artur Hazelius to bring together surviving remnants of folk culture throughout Sweden. This is what would now be termed 'salvage anthropology'. Skansen opened in 1891 and now has over 50 significant groups of buildings representing rural life (and others representing Stockholm's urban development) covering some 75 acres. The buildings were purchased from around the country and brought to the park, assembled into clusters not via some abstract typology but in terms of the cultures from which they came. Thus a Danish influenced farmhouse from Skåne stands with its own barn and so forth, and a northern Same camp has its own stores, dwellings and animals. This is in contrast to a thematic display in a classical museum, which might arrange all farmhouses or all barns together so to illustrate typologies of development, for example. 'Against the idea of distributing the nation's cultural heritage without attention to regional specificity – the idea of the classical museum – the ecomuseum pits its own concept of the refraction of museum culture in discrete environments', and instead of presenting them as fragments illustrating the museum's categories, it represents an organic integrity (Poulot, 1994: 73). In other words, its mode of display means that instead of illustrating say technological shifts and progress in specific areas of industry, agriculture or whatever, it illustrates regional types. It set about presenting Sweden in miniature, a Sweden conceived of as a mosaic of local cultures, each thought of as a more or less organic whole. It created a mythic space where in the space of an afternoon the diversity of Swedish culture could be encompassed.

Thinking through the formal structure of the museum led me to think through the implications of this for the sense of Sweden that was conveyed. We might say that contrary to what museums often portray – historical progression – this was a 'musée de l'espace' rather than a 'musée du temps' (Poulot, 1994: 66). This entailed presenting a series of holistic portrayals of organic, unified regional cultures. Put together this tends to stress the unity of local cultures (as opposed, say, to their fracturing by class and gender) and also to present them as static cameos, as cultures that do not evolve – and in this case as rapidly disappearing. So it offers a glimpse of a static disappearing past, one where the 'folk' are rarely named actors but homogenized as types and cultures, and where change is portrayed as threat to or erosion of genuine folk culture. This is wrapped around notions of defining an authentic Swedishness, which we might find represented in one building.

I only began to think about this building when I was standing in front of it and I could not find it in my exhibition catalogue that linked each place to a map of Sweden. Not only that, but as I was taking notes on each building in a notebook it seemed to me that this 'loftharbre' (storehouse) dated from the fourteenth century, making it by my reckoning the second oldest building in Skansen. Looking at the plaque, which was discrete but certainly there, it became clear it also hailed from Telemark in Norway. This made no sense to me, until reading through secondary sources it became clear that the idea behind the museum and its collection emerged over time (obvious enough if I had thought about it that way before) and this building came from a time when Hazelius envisioned a pan-scandic collection. Indeed, Sweden had promoted pan-Scandinavianism through most of the nineteenth century. The secession of Norway from the Royal Union with Sweden in 1904 pushed the nationalisation of the folk culture forward and made displaying specifically Swedish folk types a more important pedagogic element of defining a national consciousness. This emphasis was reinforced as I wandered across the road to the Nordisk Museet, a more classical ethnological collection, to be greeted in the atrium by a statue of the sixteenth-century Swedish king Gustav Vasa, often associated with a high point in Sweden's political fortunes, sternly declaring 'Warer Swenske' (Be Ye Swedish). Formally – and this is a **deconstructive** reading – my interpretation involved looking at the ways in which Skansen articulates a myth about Swedish identity, tracking the ways it produces that through specific exclusions and symbolic techniques.

If we think about museums that recreate the past through living history displays or photodioramas they not only tend to frame a specific moment from the past, but also to create a powerful effect of realism. By using photographs or recreated environments to produce dioramas or whole museums depicting 'the way things were' this realism lends authority. It is very hard to argue with photographs that seem so factual (Porter, 1989; see Chapter 10). Of course they can be selected, they frame things and they tend to be used as backdrops for rather more theoretical and interpretative dioramas of how we think things might have been. Likewise, recreating an entire farmstead tends to replace verification with verisimilitude as a criterion to judge authenticity: does it look like it should? Especially in first person interpretations that try to convey the immediacy of events by having actors play the part of historical figures, they also cannot show ignorance. It may well be there are two or three theories of how something was done, but they will have to do it using one, and all interpretative doubt disappears under recreated solidity. So we need to think about how even with the best of intentions, displays enable and disable specific interpretations.

Poetics and display

The discussion of Skansen should thus indicate that museums work by manipulating symbols, or making objects into symbols of larger cultural processes. That is, the artefacts become 'metonyms' – where one item is taken to stand for the larger class of which it is a part. The other point to note is that this is less about individual items than the combination of them. It is also important to note that this is about the combination and disposition of objects in space:

> The relationship of objects in time are transposed into a spatial context, and that regrouping is imprinted in the memory of the visitors. This transformative capacity of museums, their ability to function as machines for turning time into space, enables them to be used as a system of social memory.
>
> (Yamaguchi, 1991: 61)

This then is not just a semiotic relationship between signs, symbols and the like. It is about the poetics of putting artefacts and exhibits together in particular configurations. So in Skansen we saw the creation of a museum portraying regional cultures as holistic, relatively static entities. We might look for an alternative in the classic 'Universal Survey Museum' (Duncan and Wallach, 1980). This sort of museum attempts to lay out a grand narrative of development in a field. For example, the Louvre in Paris takes art history and classifies it by epochs, defining developmental progress and significance. Its layout moves from Greek, to Roman, to Renaissance Italy, to sixteenth-century Dutch and so on until it finishes with nineteenth-century France. In other words, its categorisation of art history, while claiming to be a neutral depiction, tells a story that happens to lead up to nineteenth-century France as the pinnacle of artistic endeavour. Duncan and Wallach (1978) point out that the layout thus forms the 'script' for a visit, implying that spatial arrangement can place exhibits in a story. In an analysis of the Museum of Modern Art in New York they illustrate how the route 'progresses' from a shared, realistic portrayal of the world to art that grows increasingly abstract and subjective. This is a portrayal where each work of art becomes 'so many moments in a historical scheme', with the exhibits and rooms linked together as if in a chain. As a result, Picasso's *Guernica* ceases to represent the horror of aerial bombing and instead symbolises a shift from Cubism to Surrealism. The effect of these museums is also to locate the spectator at a privileged viewpoint from where they can see the 'whole history', in what might be seen as a totalising gesture.

The narrative museum layout, where the path of the visitor is managed to follow the path of a story, has become much more popular in recent museum exhibits. Thus visiting the British Waterways museum in Gloucester it becomes clear that it tells a story that naturalises industrial change, showing the rise and decline of the canal system, with a slightly upbeat twist at the end that reflects its ownership by the owner of the national canal system (Crang, 1994). Notable in this story is the absence of struggle and conflict. To borrow from a description of Ironbridge Gorge museum, and thinking about absences, this is a depiction of the industrial revolution – without the revolution (West, 1988). As visitors we are guided through a series of stages and developments in much the same we would be as if it were a story in a book. There are few opportunities to skip a few pages ahead since the route is physically prescribed. Indeed, in more prescriptive versions there is a narrator – my favourite being the talking cat (in a codpiece) who leads one through the Timewalk exhibit in Weymouth. Each diorama is lit in turn with a spotlight highlighting the cat mannequin who, in one of his conveniently spaced nine lives, is on hand to explain what is happening. If we think about that literally absurd device, it is clearly an attempt to personify the universal survey museum's 'God-trick' – the all knowing view, omniscient and omnipresent. The designers were clearly trying to take out some of the starched rhetoric from this with a more accessible character, but one that could perform the same function. What it does is reveal fairly starkly the claims lurking in the impersonal, unauthored and apparently neutral voiceless museum that lets its spaces speak for it. I want to return to the sense of narrating the past at the end. But for a moment I want to pick out something else that went on as we followed our cat: the vague sniggers of the audience, the stifled groan at the period costumes the cat wore, and the vague sense of how naff it all was that pervaded the group of spectators with whom I happened to be walking.

Doing displays

In the second main part of this chapter I want to outline some limits to what has been said so far. All the talk of textual readings and semiotics leads Meaghan Morris (1988) to point out that the reader of all these texts seems to be a 'cruising grammarian'. I have cited my own work so far to make clear that I have some sympathy with the effectiveness of these readings, but I am also aware that as I talk of the texts producing certain effects I am speaking for the audience. I am giving you my reading of the implied reader that the museum apparently wants. This ideal reader is one that 'gets' the message, believes it and learns it. I have been outlining how, for instance, conflict and social divisions might be glossed over in the interests of powerful groups in society. This risks suggesting a situation where people visiting museums automatically imbibe this message.

> *The only problem with this wretched scenario is that it has been devised by people who are compulsive readers*
> *of texts. They pay close attention to their semiotic surroundings and believe that others do too.*
>
> (Mellor, 1991: 114)

In other words, although we can be clear that the museum may organise its interpretations in particular ways, that is not the same as saying its visitors come out agreeing or following them. Indeed, Handler and Gable go so far as to suggest that semiotic readings of such representations, catalogues and exhibitions miss the sociality of the process, such that 'most research on museums has proceeded by ignoring what happens in them … very little of it focuses on the museum as a social arena in which many people of differing backgrounds continuously and routinely interact to produce, exchange and consume messages' (1997: 9). Similarly, a museum researcher offered the opinion that:

> *Most analysis has taken the form of critical reviews of the messages inherent in contemporary museum*
> *presentations, with little concern being demonstrated for the experience of those who actually visit them. We*
> *do not therefore know how people use museums and whether they assimilate the messages, intended or*
> *unintended, that museums give out.*
>
> (Merriman, 1989: 149)

So I want to spend a little time pointing to some of the social activities going on in museums and how we might wish to engage with these. I will begin with thinking about visitors, then thinking about people inside museums.

Making sense

One of the principal problems in terms of working out where to start thinking about visitors is the sense that we may be asking the wrong question. In the museum business there is the paradox of, on the one hand, endless visitor surveys showing that visitors really quite like the place, and on the other hand declining markets. The answer, of course, is that if you talk to people who visit you are only getting one subsection of the public, and study after study shows it to be a more well-to-do and educated fraction. But let us suppose we are limiting ourselves to those who visit and what they make of the displays. One simple solution is to ask them. I say 'simple' provided two things work: first, that someone will give you permission to, second, butt in on people's leisure time and ruin their visit with endless questions. It is notoriously difficult to get any in-depth commentary from people in these sorts of environments. So it may be we must think of arranging focus groups or interviews elsewhere. The problem then is that you get a retrospective account of what they remember. Or, even more particularly, what they think you think they should have remembered.

Let us go back to Swedish open air museums, but move away from Stockholm into the rural provinces where hundreds of small institutions preserve the typical buildings of their regions, indeed their parish. Talking to visitors and observing them reveals that in many ways the exhibits here are secondary – to taking a picnic, to playing, to going to a folk concert. The comments in visitor books– a fairly unrepresentative source, of course – can be helpful, but quite often there is a pattern of a few Swedish addresses and one from the United States. Talking to some colleagues, they said that when relatives visited from abroad one of the staple options was to take them to the local museum. So the museum becomes incorporated into personal and familial narratives, and connects them with narratives of local identity and culture. The meaning of the museum begins to shift as its context of use changes.

More formally, we might think about what I was doing wandering around these museums. Or more particularly just how rare I was – a solitary visitor, with a notebook, assiduously studying each exhibit, pondering its significance. You soon realise how odd this is when it is clear that people are staring at you because you are the only one taking things this seriously. The vast majority of visitors are in groups. Even if we discount school groups and the like (although why should we?), then still the bulk of people are in families, couples or organised coach tours. Some of these may have guides who may give things specific ideological slants (Katriel, 1993). But even if there is no tour guide, then there is often an informal expert. How often have we all heard a child ask a parent, who is equally confused, what an exhibit is about? Groups pool expertise, and misinformation, they converse and in this way large and small-scale narratives intertwine (Rowe et al., 2002). Thus studies indicate that a great deal of what we do at exhibits is talk with our fellow visitors, and this is a major factor in how we recall and take on board the visit (McManus, 1987, 1988, 1989, 1993). As a result we may remember rather more about these social events than about the exhibit, and the way we interpret the exhibit may well be framed by our social experience.

Beyond this sense of visitor activity, there are other ways that audiences engage with exhibits. As I loitered and made notes at various museums, I kept having to step out of the way of the steady stream of people. And gradually it dawned upon me that we need to be aware of the steadiness of that stream. Once again observation studies indicate that after about 30 minutes most visitors simply start walking along, looking but rarely lingering (Falk and Dierking, 1992). In other words, the ordering of exhibits also distributes the amount and kind of attention they are likely to get. Now this is not to say that all visitors are inattentive or do not gain things that displays try to tell them. But it is a note of caution about assumptions that museums encode meanings and simply transmit them to audiences. In fact, in some exhibitions we see the opposite flow of interpretative actions and communication. One local museum in Sweden, for example, had an archive of old photographs on display with an invitation to visitors to provide details – clearly speaking to a local audience with its local expertise, asking visitors to contribute to historical interpretation through their personal knowledge.

I do not want to celebrate here some kind of resistance to hegemonic narratives. Sometimes museum directors make clear that they are struggling to get across the basics of chronology, sometimes visitors clearly uncritically take on board the intended message. But you cannot with certainty say that the promoted interpretation will simply be transmitted. The action of personal, group and incidental knowledges might be thought of as an 'anti-discipline' to knowledge, not necessarily good or bad but rather less certain and predictable. The plurality of possible readings then is something that needs to be stressed. It is important to think through how our approaches can respect and reflect these diverse practices.

Enacting exhibits

Earlier I mentioned actors or interpreters recreating past environments. This has become quite popular as a way of getting across the personal and active elements of the past. And, of course, if it uses the first person – with actors pretending to be figures from history, be they famous or 'ideal typical figures' – this lends a fragile but effective authority to the interpretation. They speak as if they know from first hand. I say fragile since it is still not always 'credible' or believed. But in these cases the interaction of visitor and performer may well be crucial. Moreover, some of the claims about these performances are that they have a certain interpretative truth to them because they are fully worked through **embodied** performances. Thus, actors get hot in period clothes, corsets stop people running, and in some institutions long run experiments with agricultural styles of work may go on. What is more, this performance, this ethnomimesis, begins to call into question the viewpoint from which we interpret and criticise what is going on. Representationally these create not holistic islands of regional culture but of time:

> They are all places out of time – anyway, out of this time. They are visits to times past. They allow, encourage, us to play, for a time. In order to do this some of them, rather worryingly to some of us, play with time. Death and decay are, it seems, denied. Strangely and paradoxically in the context of institutions nominally preoccupied with the passage of time, these phenomena are not allowed to occur. This denial of the realities of time, this artificial omission of any interval between then and now leads to the ready assumption, indeed the implication that then and now are very similar, and that we and they are, except for a few superficial differences, similar also.
>
> (Saumerez-Smith, 1989: 65)

Concept Box

Embodiment

As John Fiske has recognised: 'the body is the primary site of social experience ... where social life is turned in to lived experience' (1993: 57). Yet it is only recently that the body has received much attention from cultural geographers. That questions of embodiment are finally on the agenda can perhaps be put down to two developments. On the one hand, the body is gaining more and more prominence in modern western society generally. Hence, whilst the shift to a service economy has increased the emphasis on bodily **performance** within the workplace (with more and more employers now demanding a healthy body and attractive smile) developments in bio-technology and plastic surgery have made it easier to change the shape of our bodies but also blurred the boundaries of the human body itself. On the other hand, the body has also assumed increased prominence with recent developments in social theory. Such developments have come to cultural geography via three main routes: the work of Henri Lefebvre, for whom the body remains the locus of an 'authentic' experience of space and place; Michel Foucault, whose notions of **power** deal with the body as a site for the exercise of power both in terms of the 'disciplining' of individual bodies and the health of the population at large (captured in his notion of 'bio-power'); and psychoanalysis, within which **identity** comes through the recognition of bodily (sexual) differences and of the boundaries of the body itself. Notwithstanding these diverse perspectives, approaches to the study of the body tend to polarise around two basic positions. For some the very physicality (or corporeality) of the body renders it 'pre-discursive': existing beyond the world of ideas. For others, the body is better understood as itself discursively constructed, with ideas about what constitutes a 'healthy' or 'attractive' body, for example, liable to considerable variation both between different social groups and over time (see **social construction**). Not surprisingly, perhaps, very similar divisions are evident in debates around **performativity**, and an analysis of the ways in which different spaces give shape to or demand different bodily performances has proved a fruitful line of enquiry for cultural geographers interested in these issues. For example, Linda McDowell (1995) has examined the bodily performances of women working in merchant banking, and Phil Crang (1994) those of workers in the catering trade. The focus on the body has encouraged work in other areas too – most notably, perhaps, an increased awareness of the geographies of disability – whilst providing an impetus to re-think some traditional yardsticks of social theory: for example, the familiar distinction between sex and gender.

Key reading
- Crang, P. (1994) 'It's showtime! On the workplace geographies of display in a restaurant in Southeast England.', *Environment and Planning D: Society and Space* 12: 675–704.
- Featherstone, M. *et al.* (eds) (1991) *The Body: Social Process and Cultural Theory*. London, Sage.
- McDowell, L. (1995) 'Body work: hetereosexual gender performances in City workplaces', in Bell, D. and Valentine, G. (eds) *Mapping Desire*. London, Routledge.
- McDowell, L. (1999) 'In and out of place: bodies and embodiment', in McDowell, L. *Gender, Identity and Place: Understanding Feminist Geographies*. Cambridge, Polity Press.

In other words, these performances by actors are quite good at intimate vignettes but poor at linking them in to wider trends and long run historical processes. Thus, looking at a small group of southern English historical re-enactors, I decided to use participant observation as a method through which to gain an understanding of what they were doing. I wanted to see the performances, see the interactions with visitors, and experience the supposed historical connections and the strains and stresses of performing the past. I was interested in issues about realism, about hegemony and how English history and identity were negotiated in the portrait of an Elizabethan manor house. But what I rapidly discovered was that I was not the only one interested in these issues. The other re-enactors were also very keen on them. I was interested in looking at how myths developed, instances where first person interpreters gave out poor information and how this developed into an orthodoxy within that institution. I found seven such instances easily enough: they were listed on the back of the coffee room door as things to avoid perpetuating. Meanwhile, just as I was attempting to make an ethnographic account that would work out the norms and customs of a community of re-enactors, I began to discover that the best analogy for what they were doing was being ethnographers of a community that had never existed. As fast as I read books on re-enacting to inform my performance, they were reading books on period customs. As fast as I attended seminars on playing roles within groups, they were going to workshops on Tudor roles to play. To make the life of the researcher harder, I was having to do both of these sets of training (for a more detailed account see Crang, 2000). My days were spent playing a Tudor, before trying at night and during breaks to pour my observations into a tape recorder. And if there is an easy way to feel self-conscious it is taping your thoughts. Because of the costumes, one of the limitations of participant observation was that I could not drop out of character and make notes during the day, and at night in a tent it was too dark to write. So taping it was. In this exercise of ordering my thoughts from sections of the day, then dictating them to myself, I began to think through the parallels of what I was doing and what was being done by the re-enactors. Both of us were trying to interpret a culture to an audience and both of us were doing it through learning embodied performances. Notice I emphasise *trying*, in that I would not claim authoritatively to have become an 'insider'. That tends to overstate both my access and authority, and risks suggesting there was some homogeneous culture of re-enactors I accessed. Likewise they were trying to act like Tudors, knowing that they would make mistakes and that they could never actually succeed.

Figure 16.1 *Playing a role of a re-enactor, playing a role of pedlar: reflexivity, positionality and knowledge. Author's photograph.*

Figure 16.2 *Getting into the fabric of daily life: making costumes for participant observation of living histories, which involved learning skills of research and learning skills of re-enacting, as well as learning about the period staged. Author's photograph.*

The issue I am approaching here is one of reflexivity. Basically I had to position myself in relation to the people I was working with and ask what ability I had to claim the authority to interpret what they were doing, just as they themselves were quite scrupulous about what authority and ability they had to interpret Tudor life. This was especially challenging as re-enactors in general had been the subject of a lot of fairly hostile academic commentary. Much of this seemed to conflate worries over the effects of the form, in terms of downplaying long run narrative and critical debate in favour of small scale immediacy, with a social distaste for it as a hobby and a form of learning. 'Legitimate' education in universities seemed to be judging informal educational approaches and saying they were found wanting. But found wanting against the criteria of the academy, of course. Re-enactors were quite able to turn the judgement around and question the effectiveness of wearisome lectures that pointed to tedious books written in impenetrably cautious language and propped up on obscure and conflicting footnotes. The issue that became clear for me, then, was that there was no neutral point to judge these different criteria. They had to be seen as part of sets of social values that were in competition. It was a situation that needed rather more than a critical reading from an outsider, but a negotiation of how values conflicted and of the different messages coming through displays.

Conclusions and further research

Perhaps unsurprisingly, then, I have tried to suggest a range of approaches might reveal different significances in exhibitions. I outlined how a close critical reading can often suggest the ways in which displays shape their stories and frame arguments in particular ways. Evidence such as objects and artefacts are not independent of these shapings, but rather the stories create their own evidence. This effort to unpack the production of knowledge relies heavily on a textual metaphor, where we treat space as though it were a way of writing the world. The use here has been in part to look at how political and ideological assumptions get written into the fabric of displays, as their underpinning assumptions, which are thus hard to contest or dispute. I have also tried to suggest that sometimes this reading practice can be too seductive, that it offers us the vision of the clever academic telling the world what is really going on. Instead, I have tried to emphasise that this critical approach needs some modesty to accept the plurality of practices and its own **situatedness**. In other words, we can point to a truth but by no means the only one. There are a plurality of readings, or even of ways of reading exhibits, that mean displays are polysemic – they have multiple meanings. I have tried to suggest that we need to think of the range of ways people might interact with and interpret exhibitions, including physical motion, social interactions, inattention as well as attention. The Italian semiotician Umberto Eco once called these 'aberrant readings', but I prefer to see them as engagements in different ways. And these different ways of engaging may challenge the way academics tend to interpret things by stressing different ways of 'apprehending' or grasping the world and thus making different interpretations of it.

I have concentrated on museums to make this discussion manageable. There are some specific histories and issues with museums such as the changing role of the state, of scientific and academic knowledge, of the enclosure and control of space. But there are related spaces that might be approached in the same way. Thus we might think of other exhibitionary spaces such as World Fairs and Expos that we might think about through this lens. Other sorts of exhibitionary spaces might be less spectacular, but things like the Ideal Home Exhibition, agricultural shows or, if we push this more widely, shops or shopping malls, also enable us to consider the placement of items, the surrounding environments and how the poetics of display tries to create certain values and meanings for consumers.

We might also try to connect these to wider theories about why specific forms emerge at specific places and times: an historical geography of exhibitions. Thus I have suggested the technology of the Victorian museum might be linked with other forms of knowledge and power that emerged at the same time. We might ask whether the shift to less serious, or less portentous, more entertainment driven spaces in the last twenty years now speaks to a different constellation of knowledge and power being prevalent in society. We might ask about the continuities and shifts in who gets exhibited to whom: who gets put inside the glass case as it were, made into an object of scrutiny for whom, who gets to classify whom, and how identities are thus shaped in a changing world. And of course in the current world we also need to factor in other technologies of display – ones such as various forms of media – to ask how they interact with, reinforce or conflict with each other. The dusty world of displays and exhibitions, then, can be used to address some key questions in contemporary cultural geography.

Further reading

For a good discussion of museums as institutions disciplining and shaping knowledge, using a Foucauldian approach to interpret different epistemes and knowledge formations, see:
* Hooper-Greenhill, E. (1992) *Museums and the Shaping of Knowledge*. London, Routledge.

For an examination of how museum displays shape the representation of knowledge and the political consequences of this, a good collection of essays can be found in:
* Karp, I. and Lavine, S. (eds) (1991) *Exhibiting Cultures: The Politics and Poetics of Museum Display*. Washington, DC, Smithsonian Press. See specially essays by Kirshenblatt-Gimblett, Alpers and Duncan.

A similar approach, though based on more historical examples, can be found in the following collection that seeks to insert museums in wider notions of exhibition and urban culture:
* Sherman, D. and Rogoff, I. (eds) (1994) *Museum Culture: Histories, Discourses, Spectacles*. London, Routledge.

For a more structuralist interpetation of museums as signifying arenas, see:
* Pearce, S. (ed.) (1990) *Objects of Knowledge*. London, Athlone Press.

An extensive study of the social composition and interests of visitors, and non-visitors, to museums in the UK is:
* Merriman, N. (1991) *Beyond the Glass Case: The Past, the Heritage and the Public in Britain*. Leicester, Leicester University Press.

On the politics and actions of interpretation in specific museums, especially those that recreate environments, exemplary studies are:
* Handler, R. and Gable, E. (1997) *The New History in an Old Museum: Creating the Past at Colonial Williamsburg*. Durham, NC, Duke University Press.
* Snow, S. (1993) *Performing the Pilgrims: A Study of Ethnohistorical Role-playing at Plimoth Plantation*. Jackson, University Press of Mississippi.

A TALE OF RESEARCH

Children's consumption of music lyrics

The Eminen phenomenon

Helen Griffiths

When I chose to do a BA geography degree at the University of Birmingham I was aware that this would include writing a 10,000 word dissertation, but as an eager student fresh out of college this daunting prospect was somewhat overshadowed by alcohol-induced renditions of Rod Stewart's 'Do you think I'm sexy?' and countless attempts to convince my peers that the measly eight hours of lectures I had each week were not spent colouring in pretty pictures.

Sixteen months on, in the January of my second year, I was duly informed that in 21 days, I would need to submit a title and abstract outlining my proposals for a topic that I would be able to write 10,000 words about and one that would motivate me for the best part of a year. Initially, panic set in and I spent the first week trawling through geographical journal after journal in the slim hope of finding an issue that would motivate and stimulate my short attention span for the next 12 months. Realising that I was not getting anywhere fast I changed my course of action.

I came to the conclusion that if reading yet another investigation into the environmental impact of a new shopping centre did not fill me with enthusiasm or tell me something I didn't really already know, then it was unlikely that a examiner would be enthralled at a similar prospect. Rather, I began thinking about issues that mattered to me and stopped thinking about what a 'proper' geography dissertation should involve. After all it was me, not the examiner, who would be spending a significant proportion of their next year researching an issue that would eventually represent 25 per cent of my final degree. I also felt it important to do something that was relevant and on the 'cutting edge' of geography; I did not want to cover well-trodden ground.

The idea of researching children's consumption of Eminem song lyrics sprang to mind whilst reading the newspaper one day. I felt that anyone who George W. Bush described as 'The most dangerous threat to American children since polio' was worth investigating further. The impact of music lyrics on children has saturated the media in recent years, with the controversial rapper Eminem being only the most recent act creating a moral panic amongst parents with his homophobic and misogynistic lyrics such as 'I'll knock you fuckin' faggots the fuck out'. However, because the journalists and adults criticising Eminem are not the chief consumers of his music, I felt that their perceptions could be misplaced.

I discovered, through extensive reading of existing literature, that while research had been carried out into the geography of music, its audiences' own experiences and consumption of such music was overlooked. Similarly, many studies relied on adultist assumptions and interpretations, with children's *own* perspectives neglected.

My aim was to investigate the wider themes of children, their music consumption and how music is part of their daily lives, by focusing on a single artist, Eminem, and the supposed 'negative effect' his lyrics are having on children. Above all, I wanted to examine whether his adolescent fans passively absorb what they hear in the media in a pigeon-fed manner and whether they actually listened to, understood or analysed his lyrics. I wanted to give children the opportunity to have their voices heard and open up adults' minds to different ways of seeing and interpreting the world.

In order to maintain a geographical perspective on the issue I used a multi-method, multi-locale approach to highlight the impact that *context* had on children's responses. My research was carried out with a group of sixteen 15- and 16-year-old music pupils in four different 'contexts', using four different ethnographic techniques. First, I acted as a classroom assistant at my local secondary school, using participant observation to study teenagers' music consumption with their peers and teacher in a formal, classroom situation. Second, I split the class in half and carried out focus groups at lunchtimes and after school to study the way pupils discussed music amongst their peers in an informal situation i.e. replicating the 'playground'. To examine how children talked about music independently, I thought I should talk to them in the place where they *actually* listened to music, the place where their CDs were stored and magazines were read. Thus, third I interviewed them individually at home, usually in their bedroom. Finally, I carried out group interviews with children and their parents. Such an approach enabled me not to study the way children's consumption of music varied according to the geographical context it was experienced in and/or the people it was experienced with.

I used the initial two stages to introduce myself and to obtain information about the children's consumption of music, which could subsequently be used to structure individual interview questions. I frequently emphasised that there were not any right or wrong answers, that I was not here to teach them, but to learn *from them* and I wanted as many different viewpoints as possible. To achieve this I tried to keep my role as moderator limited, allowing them to voice their own opinions and to discuss issues that were important to them. Nevertheless, this did not mean they were given a free rein and I would interrupt, asking them to develop previous points or directing questions towards relevant issues. The main advantages of conducting focus groups were that issues I had failed to foresee were raised and, by letting teenagers interact with each other, emphasis was taken away from me as a researcher. This allowed me to gain *their* perspectives on events, observe *their* responses to, and relationships with, each other and made *them* feel as if their views 'mattered'. I used the knowledge gained from the first two stages to structure individual interviews. However, I tried to make these more like informal chats to encourage them to speak as freely as possible.

I based my questions within each context around five key areas. First the teenagers were asked about *how* they encountered music; whether they played musical instruments, listened to CDs, or listened to music when they were out at a nightclub. Next, they discussed *where* they listened to music. They then told me *why* they liked certain music, describing their favourite songs as being catchy, having a decent beat or good lyrics. After that I questioned the significance of a song's actual lyrics, asking whether they listened to the lyrics, understood them or could even hear them! Finally, we talked about the issue of censoring or banning music and the degree to which they felt that being exposed to controversial lyrics affected them.

After in depth analysis, I concluded that the context music is experienced in is imperative and different types of music are listened to and associated with individual environments. The way music is consumed also varies depending on who is listening to it, with teenagers most interested in music listening to the melody and those dancing to it preferring strong beats. Ultimately, it was asserted that lyrics could not influence someone's behaviour, with one of my interviewees revealing why children are not affected by lyrics:

> *I wouldn't have picked up on any of the raunchy, passionate stuff in Romeo and Juliet unless you really looked into it, and I still had to get the teacher to interpret things for me! It's the same with Eminem and I think that everyone looks into him way too deeply … Unless they [adults] jumped into my skin and experienced a day in my life, how can they possibly know what music means to me? Adults look into his [Eminem] music far too much. They actually listen to it and analyse the words and say 'that's bad' and 'that's going to have such and such effect on them', when kids might just listen to it because they like it!*

Adults and the media alike were blamed for making an overly causal link between children's behaviour and music. However, their arguments did not replace the 'moral panic' I started with but displaced it. Just as they accused the media of transferring the blame onto someone else, so they all-too quickly over speculated by concluding that *they* would never be affected, but *other* people could be.

My dissertation was the first opportunity I had had in 15 years of studying to actually have my own voice and raise the issues that I felt needed raising. Doing research in cultural geography made me realise that what is written in text books is not set in stone and that a 'one size fits all' methodology cannot exist. Furthermore, I became aware that in order to write about a particular group of people, you have to go 'out there' and immerse yourself into that group, become 'one of them'. While I actually put pen to paper and wrote my dissertation, mine was not the only voice talking.

The research was conducted during my 2nd and 3rd years (2001–2002) at The University of Birmingham, where I was studying for a BA geography degree. I graduated with 1st class honours in June 2002 and my dissertation was awarded a prize for the best piece of human geography research in the department. I am currently working in Peru for TAPA (Teaching and Projects abroad), a gap year/voluntary company, where I am restoring Inca terraces for three months, before travelling around the rest of South America with my boyfriend for four months. I am planning to continue my studies when I get back and am anticipating to do a Masters in 'Research in Human Geography' at The University of Birmingham, starting in September 2003.

17
Deep listening
Researching music and the cartographies of sound

Les Back

'Living with music': music, landscape and time

Ralph Ellison, the renowned African-American writer and one-time musician, stated the choice starkly. In his early days as a writer he lived in a black neighbourhood surrounded by a cacophony of sounds from assorted drunks in the street to the flat melodies of an aspiring singer who lived in the apartment above. The streets of sound unsettled him and he struggled in vain to write sentences that would sing or even find his own voice. One day he turned on the radio to hear Kathleen Ferrier singing Handel's *Rodelinda*, she reached out to him from the speaker: *Art thou troubled? Music will calm thee* … From then on Ellison resolved to block out the metropolitan clamour. He acquired and assembled audio equipment and filled his room with the melodies of Mozart and Duke Ellington and waged war with noisy neighbours through the Hi-Fi volume control. Remembering this hostile aural terrain and the refuge he found in music, he wrote in 1955: 'In those days it was either live with music or die with noise, and we chose rather desperately to live' (Ellison, 1972: 187).

I want to extract a number of points from this parable as a means to introduce the discussion of methodology and scholarship within cultural geography in relation to music and sound. We live in an intellectual culture profoundly dominated by The Visual. Metaphors of sight predominate our thinking where knowledge is 'illuminated' and recognition a matter of being 'seen'. The result is that too often we think with our eyes while paying cursory attention to our other senses. Yet, our sense of being in the social world involves a profound interplay of our senses, or what is referred to in cultural theory as *corporeality* (see **embodiment**). Think about the way in which hearing a particular piece of music can invoke a vivid memory, or where a record collection acts as a kind of jukebox of remembrance, each piece of music associated with a particular time and place. Joachim-Ernst Berendt in his extraordinary book *The Third Ear* argues that the primacy of visual terms of reference limits our imagination and he suggests that the account of human experience needs to be rendered through what he calls a 'a democracy of the senses' (Berendt, 1985: 32). My purpose here is to extend Ellison's point: it is not just a matter of living with music but also of making a case for the advantage of thinking with our ears. My contention is that the world seems different when we subject it to deep listening, rather than merely looking at it.

Ralph Ellison's parable alerts us to think about his neighbourhood as an acoustic landscape. In this sense he anticipated what Murray Shaffer calls a *soundscape*, or the auditory terrain in its entirety of overlapping noises, sounds and human melodies (Shaffer, 1977). Susan J. Smith has pointed out the usefulness of examining cultures of sound and music as a means to move beyond geography's concern with visible worlds (Smith, 1994, 1997, 2000). Indeed if we listen to it the landscape is not so much a static topography that can be mapped and drawn, rather it becomes a fluid and changing surface that is transformed as it is enveloped by different sounds. Indeed, thinking with our ears directs us to the temporal aspect of social life. Ellison reached the same conclusion close to half a century ago: 'Perhaps in the swift change of American society in which the meanings of one's origin are so quickly lost, one of the chief values of living with music lies in its power to give us an orientation in time' (Ellison, 1972: 198).

Paul Gilroy has written extensively about the relationship between music, space and time. His book *There Ain't No Black in the Union Jack*, published in 1987, included an extended discussion of black music as containing opposition frameworks, a critique of capitalism and registers of memory. The traces of the past and present of the African diaspora is rendered and recovered through the analysis of music ranging from Bobby Womack to Jah Shaka. The relationship between the aesthetics and form of the music and the contexts of its consumption and where it is enjoyed is central to Gilroy's analysis. Particularly important here is the role that the technology of sound reproduction plays in giving the music a unique quality in the dancehall. Played through massive purpose built sound systems reggae records take on a new sonic quality. Gilroy argues that the bass registers of the sound systems transform the inhospitable concrete metropolitan architecture in which they find an itinerant home.

> *The town halls and municipal buildings of the inner-city in which dances are sometimes held are transformed by the power of these musics to disperse and suspend the temporal and spatial order of the dominant culture. As the sound system wires are strung up and the lights go down, dancers could be transported anywhere in the diaspora without altering the quality of their pleasures.*
>
> (Gilroy, 2002: 284)

Through this process, Kingston, Jamaica is transported and furnishes Lambeth Town Hall, London, and *outernational* forms of culture, music and expression flourish despite the inhospitalities of racism. Comparable insight might be made about the way in which the urban (and sometimes suburban and rural) landscapes are transformed albeit in different ways by a host of dance music cultures including soul and funk warehouse parties to unofficial raves of the 1980s and including the kaleidoscopic cultures of dance found in contemporary club culture. In each case a subterranean cartography is drawn through sound and the nighttime consumption of music. More than this, each of these scenes – be it R&B or Techno – have deeper connections with the cognates elsewhere in New York or Berlin than they do with the next club night and the music brings local space and its physical structure to life in a new way (Straw, 1997).

David Hesmondhalgh and Keith Negus suggest that within the studies of popular music there has been:

> *a move from the nation as the prime focus for understanding the relationship of popular music to places, and a growing emphasis on the minutiae of locality, and on international musical movements. This has been accompanied by a growing realisation that popular music forms are no longer integrally tied to specific ethnic groups (assumptions that link white American males to rock music, Latin identities to salsa and African-Americans to rhythm and blues). Instead, musical forms are increasingly being theorised as the result of a series of transforming stylistic practices and transnational human musical interactions.*
>
> (Hesmondhalgh and Negus, 2002: 8)

The simple point that I want to make here is that all these issues – as well as many others – are interesting for cultural geographers, and thinking with music offers new opportunities to address issues of globalization, place, **identity**, belonging, history and memory.

The kind of listening I want to argue for is not something that can be simply assumed, it is not self-evident or straightforward. Rather, we have to work toward what might be called agile listening and this involves attuning our ears to listen again. More than this, *deep listening* involves practices of dialogue and procedures for investigation, transposition and interpretation. The approach to musical cultures that I argue for consists of three main elements. First, is the commitment to taking musical and sound form seriously, to search for ways to represent and transpose sound and music. Second, the kind of approach I am proposing involves engaging in dialogue with the people who produce and create music as well as those who consume it. This is not a matter of just listening to people tell one how it 'really is'. Rather, it involves a critical and reflective dialogue that examines the status of each account as well as the terms and frameworks of interpretation. Finally, deep listening also involves participation in the spaces where music is made, felt and enjoyed.

In what follows I want to reflect upon these issues methodologically and give an account of what this might sound like while drawing on some examples from my own experience of researching music and musical cultures. My aim here is to provide a series of pointers and recommend some general maxims for researching cultures of music and sound while also being alert to some common pitfalls.

'Cheerleader fans' and the Adornian yoke

Since 1988 I have been writing about music and musical culture as both an academic and a journalist. The lines of my interests have largely been along two axes. First, and picking up from Ralph Ellison's point, I've been interested in how communities on the sharp end of racism live with music as a means to write their own histories and fashion a sense of being through time. Second, I have been concerned with the ways in which black music crossed into the lives and worlds of whites both in the New World and in Europe. The music of the African diaspora is not a recent import to Europe, rather it is and has been an integral part of soundscapes of European societies since the eighteenth century. These sounds were carried here through the hands and voices of slave musicians, Jubilee singers, jazz orchestras, reggae sound system operators and hip hop DJs. It is impossible to think about the social history of Europe without understanding the place of black music within it.

Karl Marx, who lived in London for over thirty years, would render 'German folk-songs and Negro spirituals' while walking with his daughters in Highgate (Wheen, 1999: 221). While Marx may have cheerfully lent his voice to spiritual melodies, the reaction by twentieth-century Marxists to black music was often less than positive. Theodor Adorno is perhaps the best known critic, particularly for his denunciation of jazz and recorded music. Adorno's argument is easily misrepresented, in large part due to his own rhetorical excesses (for example, in one article entitled *Über Jazz* he wrote that jazz most closely resembled 'the spontaneous singing of servant girls' [Adorno, 1990: 53]). Fundamentally, he opposed jazz not because it was archaic or 'primitive', but rather because it provided the ultimate theme tune for modern capitalism. Part of his objection was that the commercialisation of jazz reinforced stereotypes. This is, at least in part, affected by his own experience of studying at Oxford in the 1930s where he encountered the ways in which jazz was assimilated within the elite circle of the English aristocracy (Wilcock, 1997). He argued that modern capitalism exploited blackness: 'like commodity consumption itself, the manufacture (*Herstellung*) of jazz is also an urban phenomenon, and the skin of the black man functions as much as a colouristic effect as does the silver of the saxophone' (Adorno, 1990: 53). Adorno's point is that this results in little more than a parody of colonial imperialism. Nothing that is vital or sensuous is embodied in what he referred to as 'bright musical commodities'. Adorno's work points to the importance of understanding popular music within the context of the culture industries that profit from it. Does the status of music as a commodity change its aesthetic nature? How do the markets for music work within capitalist productive relationships? Are there alternative markets within 'underground' or non-mainstream musical cultures? These are just some of the questions that emerge once we start thinking about music as a commodity form.

The reason why I invoke Adorno here is that he provided an important insight to the ways in which the commercialisation of music was packaged through racial fetish. This line of critique has been picked up recently in the work of Paul Gilroy who argues that similar processes of commercial exploitation have reinforced racist ideologies and reduced black music to posturing or what he calls the 'marketing of hollow defiance' (Gilroy, 2000: 206). Yet paradoxically, the mechanical reproduction of music through records also enabled it to travel in ways that were previously unthinkable. The sounds of black music could be circulated within the African diaspora and enabled connections between dispersed peoples through place and time (Gilroy, 2002). Also, black music entered and was embraced and practised in new worlds. One of my central interests has been to try and recover and make sense of the consequences of this process and what has been referred to as the 'black through white syndrome' (Hewitt, 1983).

I have always been attracted to C. Wright Mills' invitation to make 'personal troubles' a matter of 'public issues' (Mills, 1959: 8). For him, the function of the sociological imagination was to think differently about the things that confine and by extension inspire us in the social world. This is exactly what I did in the context of writing the book *Out of Whiteness: Color, Politics and Culture* (2002) with my friend Vron Ware. Large sections of the book are dedicated to the discussion of a variety of examples of trans-racial dialogue in musical cultures in different times and places. What I did was turn some of my musical passions into the key concerns of the book, including chapters on jazz subcultures in Germany and the United Kingdom during World War Two, and a study of the part played by white session musicians in the creation of the music of the civil rights era in the United States.

In 1996 I visited Alabama and Tennessee in search of the musicians, studio owners and recording engineers who had been involved in the creation of southern soul. It was the culmination of a long sequence of events that started with the intense scrutiny I'd paid to the sleeves and labels of my favourite records. Since my youth I had been a fan of 1960s soul, initially associated with the Mod movement in Britain. Like other soul fans I consumed every scrap of information on the records themselves including song-writing and production credits, the label, catalogue numbers, musician credits. It was through this vinyl archaeology that I first heard of the musicians and songwriters about whom I am going to talk in this chapter.

As a musician I had laboured over the guitar parts found on these records, in an often vain attempt to replicate their extraordinary sound and feel. The contribution of these musicians was hidden by the acclaim given to artists like Aretha Franklin, the Staples Singers, Wilson Pickett and Percy Sledge. Record labels like Fame, Stax, Atlantic, Bell, Goldwax and American Group Productions (AGP) were synonymous with the music that in many respects provided the sound track for the civil rights movement. As I learned about where and how these records were made, it was clear that a small number of white musicians and songwriters had been crucially involved in the making of this music.

Figure 17.1 *Fame Recording Studios, Muscle Shoals, Alabama.*
Photograph by the author.

Their story was not widely known. Over a period of five years, I contacted session players as they passed through London on tours or on recording visits. I went to Alabama to find out more about the racially integrated studios where soul music was made in the shadow of racism. As well as being an academic, I was also working as a music journalist. This could serve as an advantage in terms of access. Being included in a dusty academic tome would not have carried the same value from their point of view. I will return to this issue later, but the important thing to say here is that from the beginning I aimed to reach different kinds of audiences through writing in both academic and popular genres. Some participants were certainly willing to be interviewed because they were attracted to the idea of being featured in a newspaper or magazine article.

My initial starting point was that reducing the identifications of white people with black music to either racial envy or a desire for the exotic was limiting (Lott, 1993; Rubio, 1996). There is a strain of this logic in Brian Ward's otherwise fascinating history of the politics of rhythm and blues, *Just My Soul Responding*. He argued that the constructions of blackness with which whites were identifying harbored a dangerous racial essentialism: 'For many whites, blacks embodied the sensual, spontaneous, creative and sharing side of human nature with which they themselves were rapidly losing contact' (Ward, 1998: 240). The white preoccupation with black authenticity meant 'that many white Rhythm and Blues fans missed, ignored, or dismissed as inauthentic, a whole range of black moods and preoccupations, styles and sensibilities, which did not appear, or were but faintly inscribed, on the ancient mental map by which whites habitually navigated black culture' (ibid.: 243). This observation undoubtedly carries more than a grain of significance, but the bold confidence with which it is asserted both fixes and ossifies white orientations towards black culture without any attempt at qualification or sociological support.

I have mentioned that my impulse to write about soul music was initially driven by a deep love of the music. I was – in short – a fan, and I think this brings perils as a well as advantages. Fandom can be blinding and academic accounts of popular music can read like the uncritical homage of an over-zealous believer. I know that I have been guilty of this in my time and I recognise it in students when their passion for the music overwhelms their critical judgment. Ian Maxwell has called this syndrome the 'curse of fandom' (Maxwell, 2002). The opposite danger is that through writing about music we kill its precious, vibrant and stirring properties. This is particularly true of the writing inspired by Adorno's lead, which understands music as an exotic commodity manipulated through culture industries. Paradoxically, this line of critique – often found in Marxist inspired analysis – is so locked in the logic of capitalism in which everything is fetish, that there is no conception of other regimes of value that are not governed by what is wrapped, bought or sold. The challenge is, perhaps, to produce accounts that move beyond the banal outpourings of dedicated, or for that matter, cynical fans while at the same time not letting the value of popular music be crushed under the yoke of Adornian pessimism.

Notes that are not in the cash register

The late and great sound engineer Tom Dowd once said that the problem with the people who run the music industry is that the only notes they recognise are those found in the cash register! Dowd was Atlantic Records' technical wizard through the heyday of soul music and presided over an incredible range of recording sessions including Otis Redding, Ray Charles and Aretha Franklin. There is something in Dowd's charge against the music industry that is relevant to contemporary writing about music. While I think it is crucial to understand the nature of music as a cultural commodity we have to take the music itself seriously, listen to the people who create it and understand the social contexts from which it emerges.

Roland Barthes pointed out the written language is the only **semiotic** system capable of interpreting another semiotic system. He asked, 'How, then, does language manage when it has to interpret music? Alas, it seems very badly' (Barthes, 1977: 179). Confronted with music there is a poverty of language, we simply don't have the words to transpose the alchemy of sound. Barthes concluded that in describing music we have to rely on 'the poorest of linguistic categories: the adjective' (ibid.). The best one can hope for in writing about music is better kinds of failure: the least that should be insisted on is to avoid prose that strangles the life in music.

The main thing I want to stress is the importance of an attention to form in the types of deep listening proposed here and this may involve adopting forms of representations – in this case musical notation – that are beyond The Word. This, in many respects, is the territory of musicologists and there are dangers inherent within this approach, i.e. viewing musical form as a closed system. As Sebastian Chan warns, 'Musicological analysis [can] reduce vibrant musics to lifeless corpses fit for autopsy' (Chan, 1998: 93). The dangers identified by Chan are important but equally it is important to reach for a way of representing the qualities of sound without merely resorting to adjectives following Roland Barthes' warning. David Brackett's analysis of the music of James Brown is the kind of 'brilliant failure' I'd like to recommend (Brackett, 1995). In this study Brackett develops an aural inventory of Brown's tune 'Superbad', identifying its 'double voiced' quality and notating meticulously the singer's screams and vocal timbre. In the end he fails, but the result is a better kind of failure because Brackett takes the form of the music seriously and offers a way to name some of its elements and structures.

While I want to make a case for the importance of listening to music for its aural qualities and structure, it is equally important to engage with the social context of its production. This in large part was why I sought out the people involved in soul music's recording culture in places like Muscle Shoals, Alabama, and Memphis, Tennessee. The thing that fascinated me was that, even during the period of formal racial segregation in The South, the recording studios were integrated and black and white musicians collaborated – for the most part harmoniously – in the creation of the music. The question of how this was achieved was what I went to Alabama to try and answer.

But prior to the visit I subjected the music itself to a close listening in terms of its structure, form and the recording techniques used in it production. In most cases records like The Staples Singers' 'If You Ready Come Go With Me' or Aretha Franklin's 'I Never Loved a Man the Way I Love You' were recorded live with the rhythm section playing together in real time, unlike today where multi-track recording has made it possible to add one element of sound at a time. Something about the 'slice of time' quality of the recording process fascinated me. One song in particular stuck out, James Carr's 'Dark End of the Street' (Goldwax 317), written by Dan Penn and Chips Moman and released in 1967. The song tells of two illicit lovers who are condemned to meet under the cover of darkness at the end of the street. From the vantage point of my record player this tune always seemed like a metaphor for southern soul itself: music made despite racial segregation, where black and white musicians came together in the recording studio to indulge their love of music secretly.

In late June 1996 I visited Dan Penn – the writer of 'Dark End of the Street' – at his home in Nashville, Tennessee. Penn, a white songwriter and singer, is something of a seminal figure in the soul music recording scenes. Sitting on the couch of his Nashville home in overalls and chewing a toothpick he reflects on his life in music in listless Southern tones. Penn was raised in the tiny rural town of Vernon, Alabama about an hour's drive from the Shoals. Black music reached this community through the high powered radio stations like WLAC in Nashville and in particular the white DJ John R. (Richbourg) who broadcast rhythm and blues to a youthful audience, both black and white, all over the South. By the time Penn entered the emerging recording scene in Muscle Shoals, Alabama he knew as much about contemporary black music as any of his peers. While there were very few black people in Vernon, like many rural communities it harboured a culturally diverse heritage and Penn's own family included native American Indians: on his mother's side of the family these included Creek Indian relatives while on his father's side Cherokee. The Memphis guitarist Reggie Young, who played many sessions in Muscle Shoals, described him to me as 'the most soulful white man I ever met. The thing about Dan Penn is that there's not a fake bone in his body – he is the real thing'. By the time he wrote 'Dark End of the Street' in 1967 Dan Penn had established himself as a songwriter and performer of some note.

I spent the whole day with Dan and we talked for close to four hours in his home studio amidst a string of audio wires and sound equipment. As I folded up my microphone lead and put the tape recorder in my bag, I turned to him to ask a last question: 'You know Dan, I've always wondered about

Figure 17.2 *Dan Penn (on the left) with the author, Nashville, Tennessee. Photograph by the author.*

'Dark End of the Street'. I suppose the studio was a place where black artists and white songwriters and musicians came together in a time when it wasn't easy to integrate with segregation laws. Is 'Dark End of the Street' about that too, you know, not just about forbidden love but also about integration that was also forbidden?' As I kept talking I could feel myself falling ever deeper into a hole I was digging myself syllable by syllable. Dan looked back at me half perplexed, half annoyed. 'Nop. It's a cheatin song – nothing else to it' he said, subject closed. It made me realise that if there was anything political in the way that these musicians related to each other across the colour line, it was a sense of coming together that was lived and practiced in actions and not announced in slogans and fine words.

I offer this fieldwork tale as a caution against over reading, or the import of significance that is not there. I may, or may not, have been right about 'Dark End of the Street' but there is a danger of just reading off meaning from music without trying to corroborate interpretation or check its veracity. This brings us to an important and crucial methodological problem, that is how to assess, interpret and validate the accounts of others? I will discuss this in the following section but here I want to stress the importance of entering into dialogue with those involved in musical culture and participating in the spaces where music is felt and heard. These two things – dialogue and participation – are central to the type of deep listening that I want to propound.

Participation and reflective dialogue

When interviewing musicians and singers there comes a point when they stop talking or telling you about what they do and they simply start singing or take you over to the piano and *show you* what they mean. This is a common experience shared by journalists and researchers. It illustrates the point discussed previously about the limits of language. It also raises questions about the nature of sociological dialogue and the terms on which we expect 'informants' to render their view or account. In this sense the 'interview' is a very particular form of communication with its own conventions and limits (see Chapters 5 and 7). In conducting interviews it is necessary to think through the status that we give the account that is offered. Otherwise, there is a danger of naïvely assuming that what people say corresponds to 'the truth' in a simplistic way. This is particularly the case when one is researching events that have taken place in the past.

In my case this was further complicated by the fact that session musicians would not always know at the time they left through the studio door that they had been involved in a historic or hit making session, they would simply move on to the next gig. Marvel Thomas, keyboard player and session musician at the famous Stax Studio in Memphis, underlined this point during an interview.

> 'Can you tell me what you was doing at 3.00 on January the 12th last year [1995],' Marvell said with a playful smile.
> 'No,' I replied.
> 'Well how in the hell do you expect me to remember a session I did close to thirty years ago. I am a musician – I have done thousands of recording sessions.'

There is more at stake here than a matter of recollection. Walter Benjamin wrote: 'For an experienced event is finite – at any rate, confined to one sphere of experience; a remembered event is infinite, because it is only a key to everything that happened before it and after it' (Benjamin, 1973: 198). What

Benjamin captures is the degree to which the past is narrated through memory and telling. The question here is how history is told? What are the patterns within the narration of the event? This kind of narrative approach is developed in the work of social historian Alessandro Portelli (1991, 1997). The issue that Portelli foregrounds is that the search for the true meaning of an event is not as interesting as the values that are revealed in the telling and shaping of the story.

In my case the situation was complicated by the fact that there had been popular books on soul music published, in particular Peter Guralnick's wonderful book *Sweet Soul Music*, which had been read by the participants (see Guralnick, 1986). On at least three occasions the account given in interviews with musicians followed Peter Guralnick's version of events even when the individual experience and history of the musicians being interviewed contradicted this version. It follows then that as researchers we need to develop a critical interpretation that reflects on the status of the account being offered as well as the discursive pattern and webs of meaning contained within it.

A subsidiary question is how does what respondents say in interviews differ from accounts that might be offered in other contexts? It is here that a commitment to participative research can yield alternative insights and sometimes this can be disturbing. In early July 1996 I arranged to meet a well known white session musician at a restaurant in Memphis. On arriving at the restaurant my interviewee told me that he had been booked for a session and we would have some time to talk if I agreed to drive him to the session. 'I may as well earn $500 as soon as sit on my ass all day talking to you,' he said and got into the car. Yet, he didn't want to pass up the opportunity to be featured in a magazine or newspaper article even if it was with a English journalist. Had I not introduced myself as a music journalist and academic I am pretty sure he would have cancelled the meeting outright.

Figure 17.3 *'Musician's Choice' – the Southland restaurant in Sheffield, Alabama. Photograph by the author.*

The musician was raised in West Memphis across the Mississippi in rural Arkansas and his father was an insurance salesman. He grew up in a house that bordered on a cotton patch. Proud of his rural attitudes and the work ethic he commented, 'I never did have much of a big city attitude' as we drove through Memphis. In his youth he was drawn into a culture of music making, bar bands and nightclubs. He had his first hit rhythm and blues record when he was seventeen years old. As a musician he was an integral part of the Memphis soul and rhythm and blues scene and played on literally hundreds of hits. Sensing I wasn't ever going to get an opportunity to sit down and talk to him I put the tape recorder on the back seat and kept it rolling. What followed I hadn't anticipated.

As we drove through the Midtown district I asked him about the history of the city and touched on issues of race and the impact of Martin Luther King's assassination on Memphis in 1968. 'Memphis Tennessee is a very racially polarised city,' he told me as he looked out of the window. Pointing down the street that led to a black district he warned, 'You'll get your ass killed down that street little white boy and don't you forget it. You get your ass off where your not supposed to be and they're gonna kill your ass.' I couldn't quite believe what he was saying. He continued the lecture laced with racist stereotypes. As we drove towards the Arkansas bridge he disparaged the black poor for being work shy, irresponsible parents, and for 'black on white' racially motivated crime. 'Let's call 'em what they are … Niggers,' he said.

A few innocuous questions had unleashed a tirade of racist outpouring. Yet, I was driving him to a 3.00pm session where he was due to play with his black musical partner of thirty-five years standing. How could he talk so freely of 'niggers' and just a few hours later go to work with a lifetime friend and colleague who is African–American? We stopped off at a BBQ place in Arkansas close to where he grew up to catch a bite to eat before the session. 'We can do the interview over lunch. Do you like BBQ – it is the fish and chips of The South.' I told him I liked BBQ and we sat down to eat. He became suddenly nervous about what he'd said in the car. 'I am just talking to you like I've known you all my life – running my mouth. I hope that you don't put this in [the article] and represent me in this way.' I promised that I wouldn't write about our conversation. I clicked the tape recorder on again and the first words he said: 'I am not going to talk about more of the political stuff …'. The interview lasted fifteen minutes.

That afternoon I watched two soul veterans – one white the other black – go to work in the studio. It was awe-inspiring to watch them, even on this meager $500 session with a young Memphis group without a record deal. The horn parts they overdubbed on this session were full of musical allusions to

Figure 17.4 *Midtown, Memphis. Photograph by the author.*

Figure 17.5 *The Lamar Theatre, South Memphis.*
Photograph by the author.

their previous hit recordings with Al Green, Otis Redding, Wilson Pickett and Aretha Franklin. The melodies were created in 'head arrangements' and written passage by passage. Even in the context of this frankly substandard music they conveyed their unique sonic signatures. As they played their instruments – trumpet and saxophone – they found an intuitive harmony and the combined harmonic effect of them playing together made it seem as if there was a ghostly third horn present. I pointed this out to them and the white musician joked through the talk-back, 'Yeah, lots of people say that… even when we speak we talk in harmony.' Yet, just a few hours prior the white musician had been expressing stereotype after stereotype about the black poor.

The effect of this encounter was very disturbing and depressing. Yet, it also challenged me to re-think the way white people like this musician carried racism despite long histories of inter-racial dialogue. As Marvel Thomas put it later when I asked him about this phenomenon: 'Sometimes white players leave their racism at the studio door as they walk into the session and then they pick it right up again on the way out.' This challenged many of the assumptions I had carried into the research and also made me re-think the way I was interpreting my interview data. I was left with the ethical dilemma of what to do with the tape full of explosive material that had been recorded illicitly. I decided in the end that I couldn't use it but at the same time tried to integrate the insight gained from it within the book as a whole. In recounting it here I have broken that promise. My purpose is to illustrate a larger point, that opening up a space of dialogue can produce unsettling results where the researcher becomes the custodian of information that may be damaging for the participant. This situation is rife with ethical tensions and the example offered here is an extreme case. Should I have exposed this musician for his racism?

Figure 17.6 *A southern home, Sheffield, Alabama. Photograph by the author.*

Some might conclude that proximity to research participants and empirical dialogue always runs the risk of the researcher's judgement being clouded and duped through over-familiarity. Part of the politics of doing the work I've discussed in this chapter is to subject odious and pernicious views to critical evaluation, **deconstruction** and analysis: it is not merely a matter of reproducing them. I would suggest that familiarity, rather than militating against criticism, involves the deepening of critical judgment. There are gains to be had from getting close in ethnographic terms to the thing one is trying to describe and understand. This encounter not only involves confronting unsettling voices, it may produce a disruption in the language and categories of our understanding and interpretation. In the end I resolved to keep the promise I made to this white musician but also to remain loyal to the truth I had learned from him. White involvement in soul music was complex and contradictory. While for many white musicians the recording studio offered an alternative space for black and white collaboration beyond racism's reach. Yet for some a rejection of racism – even in its extreme form – did not automatically follow from inter-racial musical collaboration.

Crossing places and cultures of sound

It is significant that it is in sound that the most profound forms of dialogue and transcultural production are to be found. Music offers what Berendt calls a kind of 'crossing place'. Put simply, you can't segregate the airwaves – sounds move, they escape, they carry. Thinking with sound and music may offer the opportunity for thinking through issues of inclusion, coexistence and multiculture in a more humane way and allow us to imagine what a multicultural landscape might sound like in the age of information and global interdependency.

On 11 September 2002 I attended a Metropolis event in Oslo, Norway. It was a year on from the fateful attacks on New York and the event was intended to reflect on issues of racism, migration and memory since this benchmark in time. The organisers had the good sense to programme some musical performances between the plenary lectures. During one of these interludes two young Norwegians took the stage: Andes, a violinist, and Alion, a kora player. The music they created defied description, combining melodic figures and rhythmic shifts, traces of the past musical traditions and distinct individual voices being heard for the first time. They were living with music and the room was filled with the vitality of aural animation, a sense of inter-being that blurred the distinction between discrete bodies. It made me think about how different the world is when we listen to it, rather than fix it within the visual grammars of race and cultural difference. Neither Andes nor Alion were the bearers of a 'discrete ethnic culture' or 'folk music' that – through the alchemy of mixing – produced something new. In each of the player's distinctive styles could be heard the grain of the past. Yet, at the same time, the music they played was orientated to the present and future: two sounds co-existing with equal measure, definition, touch and clarity.

The verity of multiculture brings no guarantees, as is demonstrated by the case of the racism of the white soul musician discussed above. Inter-racial dialogue and pernicious racism can co-exist in the same individuals without seeming contradiction. But I want to value the everyday kinds of negotiations that are made in banal and often undramatic forms of co-existence, what might be called the 'fact of hybridity' modifying Frantz Fanon's famous formulation concerning the 'fact of blackness' (Fanon, 1986). These moments of critical opening cannot be reduced to a political manifesto, or some didactic call to arms of the sort that tenured revolutionaries yearn for. They are by their very nature unstable, fleeting and paradoxical. They point to quiet transformations and moments in which living with and through **difference** are realised in music, like Andes violin and Alion's kora – it is about co-existence with equal measure while acknowledging individual feel and fidelity. I want to end by returning to where I started with Ralph Ellison, who concluded in 1955:

> *Those who know their native culture and love it unchauvinistically are never lost when encountering the unfamiliar. Living with music today we find Mozart and Ellington, Kirsten Flagstad and Chippie Hill, William L. Dawson and Carl Orff all forming part of our regular fare; all add to its significance […] In so doing, it gives significance to all those indefinable aspects of experience which nevertheless help to make us what we are. In the swift whirl of time music is a constant, reminding us of what we were and of that toward which we aspired. Are thou troubled? Music will not only calm, it will ennoble thee.*
>
> (Ellison, 1972: 198)

It is not only a matter of choosing to 'live with music' but also embracing the invitation to listen to the social world actively with depth and humility.

Acknowledgement
Special thanks Caspar Melville for the wise counsel he offered me in writing this paper.

Further reading
An important statement of the ways in which an appreciation of sound can augment the understanding of cultural geography is:

- Smith, S. J. (1994) 'Soundscape,' *Area*, 26: 232–40.

For a good overview of the debates on spatiality and music, along with an excellent collection of empirical studies of musical culture within a geographical frame of reference, see:

- Leyshon, A., Matless, D. and Revill, G. (eds) (1996) *The Place of Music*. New York, The Guilford Press.

A ground-breaking study of the place of music within the African diaspora along with a sophisticated theorization of the relationship between culture, 'race' and politics is:

- Gilroy, Paul (2002) *There Ain't No Black in the Union Jack: The Cultural Politics of Race and Nation.* Routledge Classics Edition. London, Routledge.

For an exhaustive collection of readings on the concept of subculture that includes extracts from all of the important writers in the field, see:

- Gelder, K. and Thornton, S. (eds) (1997) *The Subcultures Reader.* London, Routledge.

For a good recent overview of the state of popular music studies, including interesting case studies on particular musical genres, see:

- Hesmondhalgh, D. and Negus, K. (eds) (2002) *Popular Music Studies.* London, Arnold.

Bibliography

Adler, S. and Brenner, J. (1992) 'Gender and space: Lesbians and gay men in the city', *International Journal of Urban and Regional Research* 16 (1): 24–34.

Adorno, T. W. (1990) 'On jazz'. *Discourse* (Fall/Winter): 45–69.

Agre, P. (1993) 'Landscape and Identity: A note on the history of the suburbs', *Wide Angle* 15 (4): 22–30.

Aitken, S. (1997) 'Analysis of texts: armchair theory and couch-potato geography', in Flowerdew, R. and Martin, D. (eds) *Methods in Human Geography: A Guide For Students Doing a Research Project.* Harlow, Longman: 197–212.

Aitken, S. (2002) 'Tuning the self: city space and SF horror movies', in Kitchin, R. and Kneale, J. (eds) *Lost in Space: Geographies of Science Fiction.* London and New York, Continuum: 104–22.

Aitken, S. C. and Zonn, L. E. (eds) (1994) *Place, Power, Situation and Spectacle: A Geography of Film.* Lanham, Rowman and Littlefield Publishers.

Akrich, M. and Latour, B. (1992) 'A summary of a convenient vocabulary for the semiotics of human and nonhuman assemblages', in Bjiker, W. and Law, L. (eds) *Shaping Technology/Building Society: Studies in Socio-Technical Change.* Cambridge MA, MIT Press: 259–64.

Allan, J. (1987) 'A song of summer: the restoration of the Penguin Pool' Manuscript in Lubetkin Papers [LUB1/10] RIBA, London.

Allan, J. (1992) *Berthold Lubetkin: Architecture and the Tradition of Progress,* London, RIBA Publications.

Allan, S. (1999) *News Culture.* Buckingham, Open University Press.

Allen, J. (1999) 'Spatial assemblages of power: from domination to empowerment', in D. Massey, J. Allen and P. Sarre (eds) *Human Geography Today.* Cambridge, Polity Press: 194–218.

Anderson, B. (1991) *Imagined Communities: Reflections on the Origin and Spread of Nationalism.* New York and London, Verso.

Anderson, K. (1995) 'Culture and nature at the Adelaide Zoo: at the frontiers of 'human' geography' *Transactions of the Institute of British Geographers* 20:3, 275–94.

Anderson, K. and Gale, F. (eds) (1999) *Cultural Geographies.* Second edition. London, Longman.

Anderson, K., Domosh, M., Pile, S. and Thrift, N. (eds) (2002) *Handbook of Cultural Geography.* London, Sage.

Andrew, D. (1984) *Concepts in Film Theory.* Oxford, Oxford University Press.

Andrews, J.H. (2001) 'Introduction: meaning, knowledge and power in the map philosophy of J.B. Harley', in J.B. Harley, *The New Nature of Maps: Essays in the History of Cartography.* Baltimore, The Johns Hopkins University Press: 1–32.

Architects' Journal (1933) 'Special issue on slum housing', 77, 22nd June: 833–4.

Architects' Journal (1934) 'Penguin Pool, Zoological Gardens: Lubetkin, Drake and Tecton', 79, 14th June: 856–8.

Architectural Design and Construction (1933) 'New gorilla house for the London Zoological Society' 3(8): 316–18.

Armitt, L. (1996) *Theorising the Fantastic*. London, Arnold.

Armitt, L. (2000) *Contemporary Women's Fiction and the Fantastic*. Basingstoke, Palgrave.

Ashforth, A. (1990) 'Reckoning schemes of legitimation: on commissions of inquiry as power/knowledge forms', *Journal of Historical Sociology* 3: 1–22.

Ashley, B. (ed.) (1997) *Reading Popular Narrative: A Source Book*. London and Washington, Leicester University Press.

Atkinson, S. and Laurier, E. (1998) 'A sanitised city? social exclusion at Bristol's 1996 Festival of the Sea', *Geoforum* 29(2): 199–206.

Azaryahu, M. (1996) 'The spontaneous formation of memorial space: the case of Kikar Rabin, Tel Aviv', *Area* 28(4): 501–13.

Back, L. (1998) 'Inside out: racism, class and masculinity in the 'inner city' and the English suburbs', *New Formations* 33: 55–76.

Back, L. and Ware, V. (2001) *Out of Whiteness: Color, Politics, and Culture*. Chicago, Chicago University Press.

Baer, E. (ed.) (1997) *Shadows on my Heart: the Civil War Diary of Lucy Rebecca Buck of Virginia*. Athens, GA, The University of Georgia Press.

Baker, A.R.H. (1997) '"The dead don't answer questionnaires": research and writing historical geography' *Journal of Geography in Higher Education* 21(2): 231–43.

Baker, B. (1992) 'Being part of the process'. *Artists Newsletter* September: 38.

Barber, L.G. (2002) *Marching on Washington: The Forging of an American Political Tradition*. Berkeley, University of California Press.

Barber, P. and Carlucci, A. (eds) (2002) *The Lie of the Land: The Secret Life of Maps*. London, British Library Publishing.

Barnes, T. (1994) 'Probable writing: Derrida, deconstruction and the quantitative revolution in human geography'. *Environment and Planning A* 26: 1021–40.

Barnes, T. (2000) 'Social construction', in Johnston, R.J., Gregory, D., Pratt, G. and Watts, M. (eds) *The Dictionary of Human Geography*. 4th edition. Oxford, Blackwell: 747–48.

Barnes, T. (2002) '"Never mind the economy. Here's culture": economic geography goes punk', in Anderson, K., Domosh, M., Pile, S. and Thrift, N. (eds) *Handbook of Cultural Geography*. London, Sage.

Barnes, T. and Duncan, J. (1992a) 'Introduction: writing worlds', in Barnes, T. and Duncan, J. (eds) *Writing Worlds: Discourse, Text and Metaphor in the Representation of Landscape*. London, Routledge: 1–17.

Barnes, T. and Duncan, J. (eds) (1992b) *Writing Worlds: Discourse, Text and Metaphor in the Representation of Landscape*. London, Routledge.

Barnes, T. and Gregory, D. (eds) (1997) 'Worlding geography: geography as situated knowledge'. In T. Barnes and D. Gregory (eds) *Reading Human Geography*. London, Arnold: 14–25.

Barnett, C. (1998) 'The cultural turn: fashion or progress in human geography', *Antipode* 30: 379–97.

Barrat, D. and Cole, T. (1991) *Sociology Projects: A Student's Guide*. London, Routledge.

Barthes, R. (1973) *Mythologies*. Trans. A. Lavers. London, Paladin.

Barthes, R. (1977) 'The grain of the voice', in *Image Music Text*. London, Fontana.

Barthes, R. (1990) *S/Z*. Translated by Richard Miller. Oxford, Blackwell.

Bartrum, K. (1858) *A Widow's Reminiscences of the Siege of Lucknow*. London, James Nesbit.

Bederman, G. (1995) *Manliness and Civilization: A Cultural History of Gender and Race in the United States, 1880–1917*. Chicago, University of Chicago Press.

Bedford, T. and Burgess, J (2001) 'The focus group experience', in Limb, M. and Dwyer, C. (eds), *Qualitative Methodologies for Geographers*. London, Arnold: 121–35.

Bell, D. and Valentine, G. (1995) 'Introductions: Orientations'. In Bell, D. and Valentine, G. (eds) *Mapping Desire: Geographies of Sexualities*. London, Routledge: 1–27.

Bell, D. and Valentine, G. (1995) *Mapping Desire: Geographies of Sexualities*. London, Routledge.

Bell, D., Binnie, J., Cream, J and Valentine, G. (1994) 'All hyped up and no place to go', *Gender, Place and Culture* 1: 31–47.

Bell, M., Butlin, R.A., and Heffernan, M.J. (eds) (1995) *Geography and Imperialism, 1820–1940*. Manchester, Manchester University Press.

Bender, B. (ed.) (1993) *Landscape, Politics and Perspectives*. Oxford, Berg.

Benjamin, W. (1973) 'The image of Proust', in *Illuminations*. London, Fontana: 197–210.

Bennett, T. (1988) 'The Exhibitionary Complex'. *New Formations* 4: 73–102.

Berendt, J.-E. (1985) *The Third Ear: On Listening to the World*. New York, Henry Holt.

Beresford, P. (1979) 'The public presentation of vagrancy', in Cook, T. (ed.) *Vagrancy: Some New Perspectives*. London, Academic Press: 141–66

Billig, M. (1995) *Banal Nationalism*. London, Sage Publications.

Bingham, N. (1996) 'Object-ions: From technological determinism towards geographies of relations', *Environment and Planning D-Society and Space* 14(6): 635–57.

Binnie, J. (1995a) 'Trading places: Consumption, sexuality and the production of queer space'. In Bell, D. and Valentine, G. (eds) *Mapping Desire: Geographies of Sexualities*. London, Routledge: 182–99.

Binnie, J. (1995b) 'The trouble with camp', *Transgressions: A Journal of Urban Exploration* 1: 51–8.

Binnie, J. and Valentine, G. (1999) 'Geographies of sexuality – a review of progress', *Progress in Human Geography*, 23: 175–87.

Black, I.S. (1995) 'Money, information and space: banking in early-nineteenth-century England and Wales', *Journal of Historical Geography* 21: 398–412.

Black, I.S. (2000) 'Spaces of capital: bank office building in the City of London, 1830–1870', *Journal of Historical Geography* 26:3, 351–75

Blatti, J. (ed.) (1987) *Past Meets Present: Interpretation and Public Audiences*. Washington, DC, Smithsonian Institute Press.

Blodgett, H. (ed.) (1991) *'Capacious Hold-All': An Anthology of Englishwomen's Diary Writings*. Charlottesville, University of Virginia Press.

Blomley, N.K. (1994) *Law, Space, and the Geographies of Power*. New York, Guilford Press.

Blomley, N.K., Delaney, D. and Ford, R.T. (eds) (2001) *The Legal Geographies Reader: Law, Power, and Space*. Oxford, Blackwell.

Blunt, A. (1999) 'Imperial geographies of home: British domesticity in India, 1886–1925', *Transactions of the Institute of British Geographers NS* 24: 421–40.

Blunt, A. (2000a) 'Spatial stories under siege: British women writing from Lucknow in 1857,' *Gender, Place and Culture* 7: 229–46.

Blunt, A. (2000b) 'Embodying war: British women and domestic defilement in the Indian 'Mutiny,' 1857–8', *Journal of Historical Geography* 26: 403–28.

Blunt, A. (2002) ' 'Land of our mothers': home, identity, and nationality for Anglo-Indians in British India, 1919–1947', *History Workshop Journal* 54: 49–72.

Blunt, A. (2003a) 'Home and empire: photographs of British families in the Lucknow Album, 1856–7'. In Schwartz, J. and Ryan, J. (eds) (2003) *Picturing Place: Photography and the Geographical Imagination*. London, IB Tauris: 243–60.

Blunt, A. (in press a) 'Collective memory and productive nostalgia: Anglo-Indian home-making at McCluskieganj'. *Environment and Planning D: Society and Space.*

Blunt, A. (in press b) 'Geographies of diaspora and mixed descent: Anglo-Indians in India and Britain'. *International Journal of Population Geography.*

Blunt, A. and Wills, J. (2000) *Dissident Geographies: An Introduction to Radical Ideas and Practice*. Harlow, Prentice Hall.

Bonnett, A. (1992) 'Art, ideology and everyday space: subversive tendencies from Dada to postmodernism'. *Environment and Planning D: Society and Space* 10: 69–86.

Borden, I., Kerr, J., Pivaro, A. and Rendell, J. (1996) *Strangely Familiar: Narratives of Architecture in the City*. London, Routledge.

Bourgue, L. B. and Clark, V. A. (1992) *Processing Data: The Survey Example*. Sage University Papers Series on Quantitative Applications in the Social Sciences 07–085. Newbury Park, CA, Sage.

Boyle, P. and Halfacree, K. (eds) (1999) *Migration and Gender in the Developed World*. London, Routledge.

Brackett, D. (1995) *Interpreting Popular Music*. Cambridge, Cambridge University Press.

Braddick, M.J. (2000) *State Formation in Early Modern England, c.1550–1700*. Cambridge, Cambridge University Press.

Branston, G. and Stafford, R. (1996) *The Media Student's Book*. London, Routledge.

Braun, B. (2002) *The Intemperate Rainforest: Nature, Culture, and Power on Canada's West Coast*. Minneapolis, University of Minnesota Press.

Brewer, J. (1989) *The Sinews of Power: War, Money and the English State*. London, Allen and Unwin.

Brosseau, M. (1994) 'Geography's literature', *Progress in Human Geography* 18 (3): 333–53.

Brosseau, M. (1995) 'The city in textual form: *Manhattan Transfer*'s New York', *Ecumene* 2: 89–114.

Brown, L. (1951) *The Story of Maps*. London, Cresset Press.

Bruno, G. (1987) 'Ramble city: postmodernism and Blade Runner', *October* 41: 61–74.

Bruno, G. (1997) 'City views: the voyage of film images', in Clarke, D. (ed.) *The Cinematic City*. London, Routledge: 46–58.

Brydon, C. (1978) *The Lucknow Siege Diary of Mrs C. M. Brydon* (edited and published by C. de L. W. fforde).

Buck, P. (1977) 'Seventeenth-century political arithmetic: civil strife and vital statistics', *Isis* 68: 67–84.

Buck, P. (1982) 'People who counted: political arithmetic in the eighteenth century', *Isis* 73: 28–45.

Bulbeck, C. (1998) *Re-orienting Western Feminisms; Women's Diversity in a Post-colonial World*. Cambridge, Cambridge University Press.

Bunge, W. (1988) *The Nuclear War Atlas*. Oxford, Blackwell.

Bunis, W., Yancik, A. and Snow, D. (1996) 'The cultural patterning of sympathy toward the homeless and other victims of misfortune', *Social Problems* 43 (4): 387–402

Burawoy, M. (1991) *Ethnography Unbound: Power and Resistance in the Modern Metropolis*. Berkeley, University of California Press.

Burgess, J. (1985) 'News from nowhere: the press, the riots and the myth of the inner city', in Burgess, J. and Gold, J. (eds) *Geography, the Media and Popular Culture*. London, Croom Helm.

Burgess, J. (1990) 'The production and consumption of environmental meanings in the mass media: a research agenda for the 1990s'. *Transactions of the Institute of British Geographers* NS 15: 139–62.

Burgess, J. and Gold, J.R. (1985a) 'Place, the media and popular culture', in Burgess, J. and Gold, J. R. (eds) *Geography, the Media, and Popular Culture*, London, Croom Helm: 1–52.

Burgess, J. and Gold, J.R. (eds) (1985b) *Geography, the Media and Popular Culture*. London, Croom Helm Ltd.

Burgess, J., Clark, J. and Harrison, C. M. (2000) 'Knowledges in action: an actor network analysis of a wetland agri-environment scheme', *Ecological Economics*, 35: 119–32.

Burgess, J., Harrison, C. and Limb, M. (1988) 'People, parks and the urban green: a study of popular meanings and values for open spaces in the city'. *Urban Studies* 25: 455–73.

Burke, T. (1996) *Lifebuoy Men, Lux Women: Commodification, Consumption, and Cleanliness in Modern Zimbabwe*. Durham, NC, Duke University Press.

Burrows, R., Pleace, N. and Quilgars, D. (eds) (1997) *Homelessness and Social Policy*. London, Routledge.

Butler, J. (1990) *Gender Trouble: Feminism and the Subversion of Identity*. London, Routledge.

Butler, J. (1993) *Bodies that Matter: On the Discursive Limits of 'Sex'*. London, Routledge.

Butler, J. (1993) 'Imitation and gender subordination'. In Abelove, H., Barale, M. and Halperin, D. (eds) *The Lesbian and Gay Studies Reader*. London, Routledge: 307–20.

Butler, J. (1997) *Excitable Speech*. London, Routledge.

Butler, R. and Parr, H. (eds) (1999) *Mind and Body Spaces: Geographies of illness, impairment and disability*. London, Routledge.

Callon, M. (1986) 'Some elements of a sociology of translation: domestication of the scallops and fishermen of St Brieuc Bay', in J. Law (ed.) *Power, Action and Belief: a New Sociology of Knowledge?* London, Routledge and Kegan Paul: 196–233.

Cantwell, R. (1993) *Ethnomimesis: Folklife and the Representation of Culture*. Chapel Hill, University of North Carolina Press.

Case, A. (1858) *Day by Day at Lucknow: a Journal of the Siege of Lucknow*. London, Richard Bentley.

Castells, M. (1983) *The City and the Grassroots*. Berkeley, University of California Press.

Castree, N. and Braun, B. (eds) (2001) *Social Nature: Theory, Practice and Politics*. Oxford, Blackwell.

Castree, N. and Macmillan, T. (2001) 'Dissolving dualisms: actor-networks and the reimagination of nature', in N. Castree and B. Braun (eds) *Social Nature: Theory, Practice and Politics*. Oxford, Blackwell: 208–24.

Chabot, H. T. (1996) *Kinship, Status and Gender in South Celebes*. Leiden, the Netherlands, KITLV Uitgeverij.

Chakrabarty, D. (2000) *Provincializing Europe: Postcolonial Thought and Historical Difference*. Princeton, Princeton University Press.

Chalita, P. (1990) *'Meditacion en el Umbral': The Woman-headed Household in Urban Latin America as Possibility and Constraint*. Unpublished MA thesis, Geography, University of Washington, Seattle.

Chan, S. (1998) 'Music(ology) needs context – reinterpreting Goa Trance'. *Perfect Beat* 3: 93–7.

Chant, S. (ed.) (1992) *Gender and Migration in Developing Countries*. London, Belhaven.

Chapman, T. and Hockey, J. (eds) (1999) *Ideal Homes: Social Change and Domestic Life*. London, Routledge.

Chatterjee, P. (1993) *The Nation and its Fragments: Colonial and Postcolonial Histories*. New Delhi, Oxford University Press.

Chombart de Lauwe, P.-H. (1952) *Paris et L'agglomération Parisienne*, 2 volumes. Paris, Presses Universitaires de France.

Cieraad, I. (ed.) (1999) *At Home: An Anthropology of Domestic Space*. Syracuse, Syracuse University Press.

Clanchy, M.T. (1979) *From Memory to Written Record: England 1066–1307*. London, Edward Arnold.

Clark, G. and Dear, M. (1984) *State Apparatus: Structures and Languages of Legitimacy*. London, Allen and Unwin.

Clark, J. and Murdoch, J. (1997) 'Local knowledge and the precarious extension of scientific networks: a reflection on three case studies', *Sociologia Ruralis* 37: 38–60.

Clarke, D. (ed.) (1997) *The Cinematic City*. London, Routledge.

Clayton, D.W. (2000) *Islands of Truth: The Imperial Fashioning of Vancouver Island*. Vancouver, UBC Press.

Clifford, N. and Valentine, G. (eds) (2003) *Research Methods in Human and Physical Geography*. London, Sage.

Cloke, P. and Milbourne, P. (1992) 'Deprivation and lifestyles in rural Wales II: rurality and the cultural dimension', *Journal of Rural Studies* 8: 359–72.

Cloke, P., Johnson, S. and May, J. (2002) *A National Survey of Direct Access Hostel and Night Shelter Provision outside of London: summary of findings*. Department of Geography, Queen Mary, University of London.

Cloke, P., Milbourne, P. and Widdowfield, R. (2000a) 'Homelessness and rurality: 'out of place' in purified space?' *Environment and Planning D: Society and Space* 18 (6): 715–36.

Cloke, P., Milbourne, P., and Widdowfield, R. (2000b) 'The hidden and emerging spaces of rural homelessness', *Environment and Planning A* 32: 77–90

Coelho, D. (1986) *Orchids and Algebra: The Story of Dow Hill School*. Hornchurch, K. B. Mainstone Publications.

Cohen, S. and Young, J. (eds) (1981) *The Manufacture of News: Social Problems, Deviance and the Mass Media*. London, Constable.

Collins, J., Radner, H. and Collins, A. P. (eds) (1993) *Film Theory Goes to the Movies*. London, Routledge.

Collins, P. H. (1990) *Black Feminist Thought: Knowledge, Consciousness, and the Politics of Empowerment*. Boston, Unwin Hyman.

Cook, I., Crouch, D., Naylor, S. and Ryan, J. (eds) (2000) *Cultural Turns/Geographical Turns: Perspectives on Cultural Geography*. Harlow, Prentice Hall.

Corrigan, P. and Sayer, D. (1985) *The Great Arch: English State Formation as Cultural Revolution*. Oxford, Basil Blackwell.

Cosgrove, D. (1984) *Social Formation and Symbolic Landscape*. London, Croom Helm.

Cosgrove, D. (1993) 'Commentary on 'The reinvention of cultural geography' by Price and Lewis' *Annals of the Association of American Geographers* 83: 515–17.

Cosgrove, D. (1998) *Social Formation and Symbolic Landscape, with a new introduction*. Madison, University of Wisconsin Press.

Cosgrove, D. (ed.) (1999) *Mappings*. London, Reaktion Books.

Cosgrove, D. and Daniels, S. (eds) (1988) *The Iconography of Landscape*. Cambridge, Cambridge University Press.

Craig, H. I. (1996) *Under the Old School Topee*. Rickmansworth, Hazel Innes Craig.

Crampton, J. (1994) 'Cartography's defining moment: the Peters projection controversy 1974–1990'. *Cartographica* 31(4): 16–32.

Crampton, J. (2001) 'Maps as social constructions: power, communication and visualization'. *Progress in Human Geography* 25(2): 235–52.

Crang, M. (1994) 'Spacing time, timing spaces and narrating the past'. *Time & Society* 3(1): 29–45.

Crang, M. (1997) 'Analyzing qualitative material', in Flowerdew, R. and Martin, D. (eds) *Methods in Human Geography*. London, Longman.

Crang, M. (1998) *Cultural Geography*. London, Routledge.

Crang, M. (1999) 'Nation, region and homeland: history and tradition in Dalarna Sweden'. *Ecumene* 6(4): 447–70.

Crang, M. (2000a) 'Between academy and popular geographies: cartographic imaginations and the cultural landscape of Sweden', in Cook, I., Crouch, D., Naylor, S. and Ryan, J. (eds) *Cultural Turns/Geographical Turns: Perspectives on Cultural Geography*. London, Prentice Hall: 88–108.

Crang, M. (2000b) 'Playing nymphs and swains in a pastoral myth?', in Hughes, A., Morris, C. and Seymour, S. (eds) *Ethnography and Rural Research*, Cheltenham, Countryside and Community Press: 158–78.

Crang, M., Hudson, A., Reimer, S. and Hinchcliffe, S. (1997) 'Software for qualitative research', *Environment and Planning A* 29: 771–787.

Crang, P. (1994) 'It's showtime: on the workplace geographies of display in a restaurant in Southeast England', *Environment and Planning D: Society and Space* 12: 675–704.

Crang, P. (1997) 'Cultural turns and the (re)constitution of economic geography', in Lee, R. and Wills, J. (eds) *Geographies of Economies*. London, Arnold: 3–15.

Cream, J. (1995) 'Re-solving riddles: the sexed body' in Bell, D. and Valentine, D. (eds) *Mapping Desire: Geographies of Sexualities*. London, Routledge: 31–40.

Cresswell, T. (1993) 'Mobility as resistance: a geographical reading of Kerouac's *On the Road*'. *Transactions of the Institute of British Geographers* 18: 249–62.

Cresswell, T. (1994) 'Putting women in their place: the carnival at Greenham Common', *Antipode* 26: 35–58.

Cresswell, T. (1996) *In Place/Out of Place: Geography, Ideology and Transgression*. Minneapolis, University of Minnesota Press.

Cresswell, T. (1997) 'Weeds, plagues and bodily secretions: geographical interpretations of metaphors of displacement', *Annals of the Association of American Geographers* 87(2): 330–45.

Cresswell, T. (2001) *The Tramp in America*. London, Reaktion Books.

Crew, S. and Sims, J. (1991) 'Locating authenticity: fragments of a dialogue', in Karp, I. and Lavine, S. (eds) *Exhibiting Cultures: The Politics and Poetics of Museum Display*. Washington DC, Smithsonian Press: 159–75.

Crouch, D. and Matless, D. (1996) 'Refiguring geography: Parish Maps of Common Ground'. *Transactions of the Institute of British Geographers* 21: 236–55.

Crowther, B. (1997) 'Viewing what comes naturally: A feminist approach to television natural history' *Womens Studies International Forum* 20: 289–300.

Crowther, M. (1992) 'The tramp', in Porter, R. (ed.) *Myths of the English*. Cambridge, Polity: 91–113.

Crush, J. (ed.) (1995) *Power of Development*. London, Routledge.

Curry, P. (1998) *Defending Middle-Earth: Tolkien, Myth and Modernity*. London, HarperCollins.

Da Costa, M. H. B. V. (2000) *Cities in Motion: Towards an Understanding of the Cinematic City*. Unpublished DPhil Thesis. Media Studies Division: Sussex University.

Dahlgren, P. and Sparks, C. (eds) (1992) *Journalism and Popular Culture*. London, Sage.

Daily Express (1994) 'Beggar Army lays siege to our City', Express Newspapers 22/06/94.

Daily Express (1994) 'Where subway nasties lurk', Express Newspapers 22/06/94.

Daily Star (1993) 'Junkie Beggars Who Hold our City to Ransom', Star Newspapers 30/08/93.

Daily Star (1994) 'Beggar Off!' Star Newspapers 01/06/94.

Daily Star (1995) 'Hobo's House: tramp's EIGHT years in bus shelter', Star Newspapers 15/09/95.

Daniels, S. (1993) *Fields of Vision: Landscape Imagery and National Identity in England and the United States*. Cambridge, Polity Press.

Daniels, S. (1999) *Humphry Repton: Landscape Gardening and the Geography of Georgian England*. New Haven, Yale University Press.

Daniels, S. and Rycroft, S. (1993) 'Mapping the modern city: Alan Sillitoe's Nottingham novels'. *Transactions of the Institute of British Geographers* 18: 460–80.

Darby, H.C. (1977) *Domesday England*. Cambridge, Cambridge University Press.

Darley, G. (1975) *Villages of Vision*. London, Architectural Press.

Darnton, R. (2000) *The Great Cat Massacre … and Other Episodes in French Cultural History*. New York, Basic Books.

Davenant, C. (1771) *The Political and Commercial Works of the Celebrated Writer Charles Davenant … Collected and Revised by Sir Charles Whitworth*. Volume I, London.

Davies, G. (1999) 'Exploiting the archive: and the animals came in two by two, 16mm, CD-ROM and BetaSp'. *Area*, 31(1): 49–58.

Davies, G. (2000a) 'Narrating the Natural History Unit: institutional orderings and spatial strategies', *Geoforum* 31: 539–51.

Davies, G. (2000b) 'Science, observation and entertainment: competing visions of postwar British natural history television, 1946–1967', *Ecumene* 7(4): 432–60.

Davies, G. (2000c) 'Virtual animals in electronic zoos: the changing geographies of animal capture and display', in C. Philo and C. Wilbert (eds) *Animal Spaces, Beastly Places: New Geographies of Human-Animal Relationships*. London: Routledge: 243–67.

Davis, M. (1990) *City of Quartz*. London, Verso.

Davis, M. (1992) *Beyond Blade Runner: Urban Control, the Ecology of Fear*. New Jersey, Open Magazine Pamphlet Series, No. 23.

Davis, M. (2000) *Magical Urbanism: Latinos Reinvent the US Big City*. London, Verso.

Dean, H. (ed.) (1999) *Begging Questions: Street Level Economic Activity and Social Policy Failure*. Bristol, Policy Press.

Debord, G. (1981) [1956] 'Theory of the dérive'. Trans. K. Knabb. In Knabb, K. (ed.) *Situationist International Anthology*. Berkeley, Bureau of Public Secrets: 50–4.

Dennis, R. (2002) 'Morley Callaghan and the moral geography of Toronto'. *British Institute of Canadian Studies* 14: 35–52.

Denzin, N. K. (1991) *Images of Postmodern Society: Social Theory and Contemporary Cinema*. London, Sage.

Department Transport Local Government and the Regions (2002) *More Than a Roof: A Report in to tackling homelessness*. London, HMSO.

Dery, M. (1992) 'Cyberculture', *South Atlantic Quarterly* 91: 501–23.

Deutsche, R. (1991a) 'Alternative space', in Wallis, B. (ed.) *If You Lived Here*. Seattle, Washington, Bay Press: 45–66.

Deutsche, R. (1991b) 'Uneven development: public art in New York City', in Ghirardo, D. (ed.) *Out of Site*. Seattle, Washingston, Bay Press: 157–219.

Dodds, K. (1998) 'Enframing the Falklands: identity, landscape, and the 1982 South Atlantic War', *Environment and Planning D: Society and Space* 16: 733–56.

Dodge, M. and Kitchin, R. (2001) *Mapping Cyberspace*. London and New York, Routledge.

Doel, M. (1999) *Poststructuralist Geographies: The Diabolical Art of Spatial Science*. Edinburgh, Edinburgh University Press.

Domosh, M. (1989) 'A method for interpreting landscape: a case study of the New York World Building' *Area* 21: 347–55.

Dorling, D. and Fairbairn, D. (1997) *Mapping: Ways of Representing the World*. Harlow, Longman.

Dorn, M. and Laws, G. (1994) 'Social theory, body politics and medical geography', *Professional Geographer* 46: 106–10.

Dovey, K. (1999) *Framing Places: Mediating Power in Built Form*. London, Spon.

Doyle, L. (1999) 'The Big Issue: empowering homeless women through academic research?' *Area* 31 (3): 239–46

Driver, F. (1988) 'Moral geographies: social science and the urban environment in mid-nineteenth-century England', *Transactions of the Institute of British Geographers* 13: 275–87

Driver, F. (1991) 'Political geography and state formation: disputed territory', *Progress in Human Geography* 15: 268–80.

Driver, F. (1993) *Power and Pauperism: The Workhouse System, 1834–1884*. Cambridge, Cambridge University Press.

Driver, F. (2001) *Geography Militant: Cultures of Exploration and Empire*. Oxford, Blackwell.

Driver, F. and Gilbert, D. (1998) 'Heart of Empire? Landscape, space and performance in imperial London', *Environment and Planning D: Society and Space,* 16: 11–28.

Driver, F. and Gilbert, D. (eds) (1999) *Imperial Cities: Landscape, Display and Identity*. Manchester, Manchester University Press.

Duncan, C. (1991) 'Art museums and the ritual of citizenship', in Karp, I. and Lavine, S. (eds) *Exhibiting Cultures: The Politics and Poetics of Museum Display*. Washington DC, Smithsonian Press: 88–103.

Duncan, C. and A. Wallach (1978) 'The museum of modern art as late capitalist ritual: an iconographic analysis'. *Marxist Perspectives* 1: 28–51.

Duncan, C. and A. Wallach (1980) 'The universal survey museum'. *Art History* 3: 448–69.

Duncan, J. (1999) 'Complicity and resistance in the colonial archive: some issues of method and theory in historical geography', *Historical Geography* 27: 119–28.

Duncan, J. and Duncan, N. (1992) 'Ideology and bliss: Roland Barthes and the secret histories of landscape', in Barnes, T. and Duncan, J. (eds) *Writing Worlds: Discourse, Text and Metaphor in the Representation of Landscape*. London, Routledge: 18–37.

Duncan, J. and Gregory, D. (1999a) 'Introduction', in Duncan, J. and Gregory, D, (eds) *Writes of Passage: Reading Travel Writing*. London and New York, Routledge: 1–13.

Duncan, J. and Gregory, D. (eds) (1999b) *Writes of Passage: Reading Travel Writing*. London, Routledge.

Duncan, J. and Ley, D. (1993a) 'Introduction: representing the place of culture', in Duncan, J. and Ley, D. (eds) *Place/Culture/Representation*. London and New York, Routledge: 1–21.

Duncan, J. and Ley, D. (eds) (1993b) *Place / Culture / Representation*. London. Routledge.

Duncan, J. (1980) 'The superorganic in American cultural geography' *Annals of the Association of American Geographers* 70, pp. 181–98.

Duncan, J. (1990) *The City as Text: the Politics of Landscape Interpretation in the Kandyan Kingdom*, Cambridge, Cambridge University Press.

Duncan, N. (1996) *BodySpace: Destabilising Geographies of Gender and Sexuality*. London, Routledge.

Duncan, N. (1996) 'Renegotiating gender and sexuality in public and private spaces'. In Duncan, N. (ed.) *BodySpace: Destablising Geographies of Gender and Sexuality*. London, Routledge: 127–45.

Dunlop, J. (1995) 'Beyond decoration'. *Artists Newsletter* (June 26–29).

Dunn, C. and Roberts, B.K. (1997) 'Maps and illustrations', in R. Flowerdew and D. Martin (eds) *Methods in Human Geography: A Guide for Students Doing Research Projects*. Harlow, Longman: 254–74.

Dwelley, T. (2001) *Creative Regeneration: Lessons from Ten Community Arts Projects*. York, Joseph Rowntree Foundation.

Dwyer, C. (1999a) 'Contradictions of community: questions of identity for British Muslim women', *Environment and Planning A* 31: 53–68.

Dwyer, C. (1999b) 'Veiled meanings: British Muslim women and negotiation of differences', *Gender, Place and Culture* 6: 5–26.

Dyck, I. (1995) 'Hidden geographies: the changing lifeworlds of women with disabilities', *Social Science and Medicine* 40: 307–20.

Dyck, I. (1999) 'Body troubles: women, the workplace and negotiations of a disabled identity', in Butler, R. and Parr, H. (eds) *Mind and Body Spaces: Geographies of Illness, Impairment and Disability*. London, Routledge: 119–37.

Eaton, T. (1990) 'Art in the environment', *The Planner* (23 February): 71–7.

Eden, S., Tunstall, S. M. and Tapsell, S. M. (2000) 'Translating nature: river restoration as nature culture', *Environment and Planning D: Society and Space*, 18: 257–73.

Edney, M.H. (1997) *Mapping an Empire: The Geographical Construction of British India, 1765–1843*. Chicago, Chicago University Press.

Edney, M.H. (1999) 'Reconsidering Enlightenment geography and map making: reconnaissance, mapping, archive'. In Livingstone, D. and Withers, C. (eds) *Geography and Enlightenment*. Chicago, Chicago University Press: 165–98.

Edwards, E. (2001) *Raw Histories: Photographs, Anthropology and Museums*. Oxford, Berg.

Edwards, E. (ed.) (1997) *Anthropology and Colonial Endeavour*, theme issue of *History of Photography* 21: 1.

Edwards, M. (1994) *Raymond Mason*. London, Thames and Hudson.

Elder, G. (forthcoming) 'Somewhere, over the rainbow: Cape Town, South Africa, as a "Gay Destination" ', *Social and Cultural Geography*.

Eldridge, J., Kitzinger, J. and Williams, K. (1997) *The Mass Media and Power in Modern Britain*. Oxford, Oxford University Press.

Ellison, R. (1972) 'Living with Music', in *Shadow and Act*. New York, Random House: 187–98.

England, K. (1994) 'Getting personal: reflexivity, positionality and feminist research', *Professional Geographer* 46: 80–9.

Escobar, A. (1995) *Encountering Development: The Making and Unmaking of Third World Development*. Princeton, Princeton University Press.

Escobar, A. (2001) ' "Past", "Post" and "Future" Development', *Development* 43: 1–5.

Ettore, E. (1978) 'Women, urban social movements and the lesbian ghetto', *International Journal of Urban and Regional Research* 2: 499–519.

Evening Standard (1998) 'In the heart of London, a sickening scene of squalor', Standard Newspapers 11/12/98.

Ewen, S. (1976) *Captains of Consciousness: Advertising and the Social Roots of the Consumer Culture*. New York, McGraw-Hill.

Eyles, J. and Peace, W. (1990) 'Signs and symbols in Hamilton: an iconology of Steeltown'. *Geografiska Annaler* 72B: 73–88.

Eyles, J. and Smith, D.M. (eds) (1988) *Qualitative Methods in Human Geography*. Cambridge, Polity Press.

Fairclough, N. (1989) *Language and Power*. Harlow, Addison Wesley Longman.

Falk, J. and Dierking, L. (1992) *The Museum Experience*. Washington, DC, Whalesback Books.

Fanon, F. (1986) *Black Skins, White Masks*. London, Pluto Press.

Farrington, J. and Silber, E. (eds) (1989) *Raymond Mason: Sculptures and Drawings*. London, Lund Humpheries in association with Birmingham Museum and Art Gallery.

Featherstone, M. and Burrows, R. (1995) *Cyberspace, Cyberbodies and Cyberpunk: Cultures of Technological Embodiment*. London, Sage.

Featherstone, M., Hepworth, M. and Turner, B. S. (eds) (1991) *The Body: Social Process and Cultural Theory*. London, Sage

Fincher, R. and Jacobs, J. (eds) (1998) *Cities of Difference*. New York, Guilford Press.

Fiske, J. (1992) 'Popularity and the politics of information', in Dahlgren, P. and Sparks, C. (eds) *Journalism and Popular Culture*. London, Sage.

Fiske, J. (1993) *Power Plays, Power Works*. London, Verso.

Fitzpatrick, S., Kemp, P. and Klinker, S. (2000) *Single Homelessness: An Overview of Research in Britain*. Bristol, Policy Press.

Flowerdew, R. and Martin, D. (eds) (1997) *Methods in Human Geography: A Guide for Students Doing Research Projects*. Harlow, Longman.

Forest, B. (1995) 'West Hollywood as symbol: the significance of place in the construction of gay identity', *Environment and Planning D: Society and Space* 13: 133–57.

Foster, J. and Sheppard, J. (2000) *British Archives: A Guide to Archival Resources in the United Kingdom*. Basingstoke, Macmillan.

Foucault, M. (1973) *The Birth of the Clinic: An Archaeology of Medical Perception*. London, Tavistock Publications.

Foucault, M. (1977) *Discipline and Punish*. London, Allen Lane.

Foucault, M. (1980) *Power/Knowledge: Selected Interviews and Other Writings, 1972–1977*. Brighton, Harvester Press.

Foucault, M. (1986) 'Of other spaces', *Diacritics* 16: 22–7.

Frank, A. (1967) *The Diary of a Young Girl*. New York, Doubleday.

Frankfort-Nachmias, C. and Nachmias, D. (1996) *Research Methods in the Social Sciences*, London, Edward Arnold.

Franklin, B and Murphy, D. (1991) *What News? The Market, Politics and the Local Press*. London, Routledge.

Galtung, J. and Ruge, M. (1981) 'Structuring and selecting news', in Cohen, S. and Young, J. (eds) *The Manufacture of News: Social Problems, Deviance and the Mass Media*. London, Constable.

Geertz, C. (1973) 'Thick description: toward an interpretative theory of culture' in C. Geertz (ed.) *The Interpretation of Cultures*. New York, Basic Books.

Gelder, K. and Thornton, S. (eds) (1997) *The Subculture Reader*. London, Routledge.

George, R. M. (1996) *The Politics of Home: Postcolonial Relocations and Twentieth-Century Fiction*. Cambridge, Cambridge University Press.

George, R. M. (ed.) (1998) *Burning Down the House: Recycling Domesticity*. Boulder, Westview Press.

Germon, M. (Edwardes, M. ed.) (1957) *Journal of the Siege of Lucknow: An Episode of the Indian Mutiny*. London, Constable.

Gibson, K., Law, L. and McKay, D. (2002) 'Beyond heroes and victims: Filipina contract migrants, economic activism and class transformations', *International Feminist Journal of Politics* 3: 365–86.

Gibson, W. (1984) *Neuromancer*. London, HarperCollins.

Gibson, W. (1986) *Count Zero*. London, Grafton.

Gibson, W. (1988) *Mona Lisa Overdrive*. London, Grafton.

Gillespie, M. (1995) *Television, Ethnicity and Cultural Change*. London, Routledge.

Gilman, S. (1988) *Health and Illness: Images of Difference*. London, Reaktion.

Gilroy, P. (1993) *The Black Atlantic: Modernity and Double Consciousness*. London, Verso.

Gilroy, P. (2000) *Between Camps: Nations, Cultures and the Allure of Race*. London, Allen Lane Penguin Press.

Gilroy, P. (2002) [1987] *There Ain't No Black in the Union Jack: The Cultural Politics of Race and Nation*. Routledge Classics Edition. London, Routledge.

Girgus, S. B. (1993) *The Films of Woody Allen*. Cambridge, Cambridge University Press.

Glasscock, R.E. (1973) 'England *circa* 1334', in H.C. Darby (ed.) *A New Historical Geography of England and Wales*. Cambridge, Cambridge University Press: 136–85.

Gleeson, B. (2001) 'Domestic space and disability in nineteenth-century Melbourne, Australia', *Journal of Historical Geography* 27: 223–40.

Gluck, S. B. and Patai, D. (eds) (1991) *Women's Words: The Feminist Practice of Oral History*. New York, Routledge.

Godlewska, A. and Smith, N. (eds) (1994) *Geography and Empire*. Oxford, Blackwell.

Goetzmann, W.H. (1966) *Exploration and Empire: The Role of the Explorer and Scientist in the Winning of the American West, 1800–1900*. New York, Alfred A. Knopf.

Goffman, E. (1967) *Interaction Ritual: Essays on Face-to-Face Behaviour*. New York, Doubleday.

Gogol, N. (1992) 'The Nose', in *The Overcoat and Other Stories*. Trans. G. and M. Struve. New York, Dover: 58–78.

Gold, J. (1985) 'From '*Metropolis*' to '*The City*': film visions of the future city, 1919–39', in Burgess, J. and Gold, J. (eds) *Geography, The Media, and Popular Culture*. London and Sydney, Croom Helm: 123–43.

Gold, J. (1987) 'Blueprints, false utopias and the siren's song: *Equinox* and the future city', *Landscape Research* 12: 26–30.

Gold, J. (1997) *The Experience of Modernism: modern architects and the future city, 1928–53*. London, Spon Press.

Gold, J. (2001) 'Under darkened skies: the city in science-fiction film', *Geography* 86: 337–45.

Goodey, B. (1994) 'Art-ful places: public art to sell public spaces?' in Gold, J. and Ward, S, (eds) *Place Promotion: The Use of Publicity and Marketing to Sell Towns and Regions*. Chichester, John Wiley: 153–79.

Gottdiener, M. (1986) 'Recapturing the center: a semiotic analysis of shopping malls', in Gottdiener, M. and Lagopoulos, A. P. (eds) *The City and the Sign: An Introduction to Urban Semiotics*. New York, Columbia University Press: 288–302

Gottdiener, M. (1995) *Postmodern Semiotics: Material Culture and the Forms of Postmodern Life*. Oxford, Blackwell.

Gowans, G. (2001) 'Gender, imperialism and domesticity: British women repatriated from India, 1940–47', *Gender, Place and Culture* 8: 255–69.

Graham, E. (1999) 'Breaking out: the opportunities and challenges of multi-method research in geography', *Professional Geographer* 51: 76–89.

Graham, K. (1997) *Personal History*. New York, Vintage Books.

Granovetter, M. (1974) *Getting a Job: A Study of Contacts and Careers*. Cambridge, Harvard University Press.

Greenhalgh, P. (1988) *Ephemeral Vistas: the Expositions Universelles, Great Exhibitions and World's Fairs, 1851–1939*. Manchester, Manchester University Press.

Gregory, D. (1994) *Geographical Imaginations*. Oxford, Blackwell.

Gregson, N. and Rose, G. (2000) 'Taking Butler elsewhere: performativities, spatialities and subjectivities', *Environment and Planning D: Society and Space* 18: 433–52.

Gruffudd, P. (1994) ''Back to the land: historiography, rurality and the nation in interwar Wales', *Transactions of the Institute of British Geographers* 19: 61–77.

Gruffudd, P. (1995) ' "Propaganda for seemliness"' Clough Williams-Ellis and Portmeirion, 1918–1950' *Ecumene* 2: 399–422.

Gruffudd, P. (1995b) 'Remaking Wales: nation-building and the geographical imagination, 1925–50', *Political Geography* 14: 219–39.

Gruffudd, P. (2000) 'Biological cultivation: Lubetkin's modernism at London Zoo in the 1930s' in C. Philo and C. Wilbert (eds) *Animal Spaces, Beastly Places: New Geographies of Human-Animal Relations*. London, Routledge: 222–42.

Gruffudd, P. (2001) 'Science and the stuff of life': modernist health centres in 1930s London' *Journal of Historical Geography* 27(3): 395–416.

Guardian (1991) 'The other side of the pier', Guardian Newspapers 25/5/91.

Guralnick, P. (1986) *Sweet Soul Music: Rhythm and Blues and the Southern Dream of Freedom*. London, Penguin Books.

Hage, G. (1998) *White Nation: Fantasies of White Supremacy in a Multicultural Society*. Sydney, Pluto Press Australia.

Halfacree, K.H. (1996) 'Out of place in the country: travellers and the 'rural idyll'', *Antipode* 28: 42–72.

Halfacree, K. and Boyle, P. (1993) 'The challenge facing migration research: the case for a biographical approach', *Progress in Human Geography* 17: 333–48.

Hall, E. (2000) 'Blood, brains and bones': taking the body seriously in the geography of health and impairment', *Area* 32: 21–30.

Hall, S., Critcher, C., Jefferson, T., Clarke, J. and Roberts, B. (1978) *Policing the Crisis: Mugging, the State and Law and Order*. London, Macmillan.

Hall, T. (1995a) 'Public art, urban image'. *Town and Country Planning* 64: 122–3.

Hall, T. (1995b) ' "The second industrial revolution": cultural reconstructions of industrial regions'. *Landscape Research* 20: 112–23.

Hall, T. (1997a) 'Images of industry in the post-industrial city: Raymond Mason and Birmingham', *Ecumene* 4 (1): 46–68.

Hall, T. (1997b) '(Re)placing the city: cultural relocation and the city as centre', in Westwood, S. and Williams, J. (eds) *Imagining Cities: Scripts, Signs and Memories*. London, Routledge: 202–18.

Hall, T. and Robertson, I. (2001) 'Public art and urban regeneration: advocacy, claims and critical debates'. *Landscape Research* 26 (1): 5–26.

Hammersley, M. and Atkinson, P. (1983) *Ethnography: Principles in Practice*. London, Tavistock.

Handler, R. and Gable, E. (1997) *The New History in an Old Museum: Creating the Past at Colonial Williamsburg*. Durham, NC, Duke University Press.

Hannah, M.G. (2001) *Governmentality and the Mastery of Territory in Nineteenth-Century America*. Cambridge, Cambridge University Press.

Hanson, S. (2002) 'It was an accident! Entrepreneurship as serendipity'. Mimeo.

Hanson, S. and Pratt, G. (1991) 'Job search and the occupational segregation of women', *Annals of the Association of American Geographers* 81: 229–53.

Hanson, S. and Pratt, G. (1995) *Gender, Work, and Space*. New York and London, Routledge.

Haraway, D. (1988) 'Situated knowledges: the science question in feminism and the privilege of partial perspective', *Feminist Studies* 14(3): 575–599.

Haraway, D. (1991) *Simians, Cyborgs and Women: The Reinvention of Nature*. London, Free Association Books.

Harding, S. (1991) *Whose Science? Whose Knowledge? Thinking from Women's Lives*. Ithaca, Cornell University Press and Milton Keynes, Open University Press.

Hardy, D. (1979) *Alternatve Communities in Nineteenth-Century England*. London, Longman.

Harley, J.B. (1988) 'Maps, knowledge, and power'. In Cosgrove, D. and Daniels, S. (eds) *The Iconography of Landscape*. Cambridge, Cambridge University Press: 277–312.

Harley, J.B. (1989) 'Historical geography and the cartographic illusion'. *Journal of Historical Geography* 15: 80–91.

Harley, J.B. (1991) 'Can there be a cartographic ethics?' *Cartographic Perspectives* 10: 9–16.

Harley, J.B. (1992a) 'Deconstructing the map'. In Barnes, T. and Duncan, J. (eds) *Writing Worlds: Discourse, Text and Metaphor in the Representation of Landscape*. London, Routledge: 231–47.

Harley, J.B. (1992b) 'Rereading the maps of the Columbian Encounter', *Annals of the Association of American Geographers* 82: 522–42.

Harley, J.B. (2001) *The New Nature of Maps: Essays in the History of Cartography*. Baltimore, The Johns Hopkins University Press.

Harris, K. (1858) *A Lady's Diary of the Siege of Lucknow*. London, John Murray.

Harrison, M. (1988) 'Symbolism, "ritualism" and the location of crowds in early nineteenth-century English towns' in D. Cosgrove and S. Daniels (eds) *The Iconography of Landscape: Essays on the Symbolic Representation, Design and Use of Past Environments*. Cambridge, Cambridge University Press: 194–213.

Harvey, D. (1979) 'Monument and myth', *Annals of the Association of American Geographers* 69(3): 362–81.

Harvey, D. (1987) 'Flexible accumulation through urbanisation: reflections on "post-modernism" in the American city'. *Antipode* 19: 260–86.

Harvey, D. (1989a) *The Condition of Postmodernity: An Enquiry into the Origins of Cultural Change*. Oxford, Blackwell.

Harvey, D. (1989b) 'From managerialism to entrepreneurialism: the transformation of urban governance in late capitalism', *Geografiska Annaler* 71B: 1–17.

Harvey, D. (2001) 'Cartographic identities: geographical knowledges under globalization', in *Spaces of Capital: Towards a Critical Geography*. Edinburgh, Edinburgh University Press: 208–33.

Harvey, D.C. (2000) 'Landscape organisation, identity and change; territoriality and hagiography in medieval west Cornwall', *Landscape Research* 25: 201–12.

Hassam, A. (1990) 'As I write': narrative occasions and the quest for self-presence in the travel diary', *Ariel* 21: 33–47.

Hay, I. (ed.) (2000) *Qualitative Research Methods in Human Geography*. Melbourne, Oxford University Press.

Haylett, C. (2001) 'Illegitimate subjects?: abject whites, neoliberal modernisation, and middle-class multiculturalism', *Environment and Planning D: Society and Space* 19: 351–70.

Headrick, D. (1981) *Tools of Empire: Technology and European Imperialism in the Nineteenth Century*. New York, Oxford University Press.

Heffernan, M. (1994) 'The science of empire: the French geographical movement and the forms of French imperialism, 1870–1920', in Godlewska, A. and Smith, N. (eds) *Geography and Empire*. Oxford, Blackwell: 92–114.

Heffernan, M. (1995) 'For ever England: the Western Front and the politics of remembrance in Britain', *Ecumene* 2: 293–324.

Heilbrun, C. (1979) *Reinventing Womanhood*. New York, W. W. Norton.

Herbert, S. (2000) 'For Ethnography', *Progress in Human Geography* 24: 550–68.

Herman, E. S. and Chomsky, N. (1988) *Manufacturing Consent: The Political Economy of the Mass Media*. New York, Pantheon.

Hesmondhalgh, D. and Negus, K. (eds) (2002) *Popular Music Studies*. London, Arnold.

Hetherington, K. (1997) *The Badlands of Modernity*. London and New York, Routledge.

Hetherington, K. and Law, J. (2000) 'After networks', *Environment and Planning D: Society and Space* 18(2): 127–32.

Hetler, C. (1989) 'The impact of circular migration on a village economy', *Bulletin of Indonesian Economic Studies* 25: 53–75.

Hewitt, R. (1983) 'Black through white: Hoagy Carmichael and the cultural reproduction of racism'. *Popular Music* 3: 33–50.

Hiebert, D. (1991) 'Local geographies of labor market segmentation: Montreal, Toronto and Vancouver', *Economic Geography* 75: 339–69.

Higgs, E. (1996) 'A cuckoo in the nest? The origins of civil registration and the state of medical statistics in England and Wales', *Continuity and Change* 11: 115–34.

Hine, C. (2000) *Virtual Ethnography*. London, Sage.

Hobsbawm, E. and Ranger, T. (eds) (1989) *The Invention of Tradition*. Cambridge, Cambridge University Press.

Hodge, D. (ed.) (1995) 'Should women count? The role of quantitative methodology in feminist geographic research'. *The Professional Geographer* 47: 426–66.

Hoggart, K., Lees, L. and Davies, A. (2002) *Researching Human Geography*. London, Arnold.

Holcomb, B. (1993) 'Revisioning place: de- and re-constructing the image of the industrial city', in Philo, C. and Kearns, G. (eds) *Selling Places: The City as Cultural Capital, Past, Present and Future*. Oxford, Pergamon Press: 133–43.

Holcomb, B. (1994) 'City make-overs: marketing the post-industrial city', in Gold, J. and Ward, S. (eds) *Place Promotion: The Use of Publicity and Marketing to Sell Towns and Regions*. Chichester, John Wiley: 115–31.

Holloway, J. (1998) '"Undercurrent affairs': radical environmentalism and alternative news', *Environment and Planning A* 30: 1197–1217.

Hondagneu-Sotelo, P. (1994) *Gendered Transitions: Mexican Experiences of Immigration*. Berkeley, University of California Press.

Hooper-Greenhill, E. (1989) 'The museum in a disciplinary society', in S. Pearce (ed.) *Museum Studies in Material Culture*. Leicester, Leicester University Press: 110–26.

Hooper-Greenhill, E. (1992) *Museums and the Shaping of Knowledge*. London, Routledge.

Hopkins, J. (1994) 'Mapping cinematic places: icons, ideology, and the power of (mis)representation', in Aitken, S. C. and Zonn, L. E. (eds) *Place, Power, Situation and Spectacle: A Geography of Film*. Lanham, Rowman amd Littlefield Publishers: 47–65.

Hopper, K. (1991) 'A poor apart: the distancing of homeless men in New York's history', *Social Research* 58: 107–32.

Hoppit, J. (1996) 'Political arithmetic in eighteenth-century England', *Economic History Review* XLIX: 3: 516–40.

Houston, D. and Pulido, L. (2002) 'The work of performativity: staging social justice at the University of Southern California', *Environment and Planning D: Society and Space* 20: 401–24.

Hubbard, P. (1996) 'Re-imagining the city: the transformation of Birmingham's urban landscape'. *Cities* 12: 243–51.

Hubbard, P. (2000) 'Desire/disgust: Mapping the moral contours of heterosexuality', *Progress in Human Geography* 24: 191–217.

Huffman, N. (1997) 'Charting the other maps: cartography and visual methods in feminist research', in Jones III, J.P., Nast, H. and Roberts, S. (eds) *Thresholds in Feminist Geography: Difference, Methodology, Representation*. Lanham, Rowman and Littlefield Publishers: 255–83.

Hugo, G. (1992) 'Women on the move: changing patterns of population movement in Indonesia'. In Chant, S. (ed.) *Gender and Migration in Developing Countries*. London, Belhaven Press: 174–96.

Hussey, C. (1930) 'Large ideas for small estates: Portmeirion [sic], Merioneth' *Country Life* 5, April 1930: 502.

Hutson, S. (1992) 'Public images of youth homelessness', in Kennett, P. (ed.) *New Approaches to Homelessness*. Bristol, SAUS.

Huxley, J. (1934) *Scientific Research and Social Needs*. London, Watts & Co.

Huyda, R. J. (1996) 'Photography and the choice of Canada's capital', *History of Photography* 20: 104–7.

Independent (1991) 'Homeless swell ranks of deprived in city of learning' Independent Newspapers 03/01/91.

Independent (1992) 'Charter for homeless attacks vagrancy laws', Independent Newspapers 04/04/92.

Inglis, J. (1892) *The Siege of Lucknow, a Diary*. London, James R. Osgood.

Innes, M. (1895) *Lucknow and Oude in the Mutiny: A Narrative and a Study*. London, A. D. Innes.

Jackson, J.B. (1984) *Discovering the Vernacular Landscape*. New Haven, Yale University Press.

Jackson, P. (1989) *Maps of Meaning: An Introduction to Cultural Geography*. London, Unwin Hyman.

Jackson, R. (1981) *Fantasy: The Literature of Subversion*. London, Routledge.

Jacobs, J. M. (1996) *Edge of Empire: Postcolonialism and the City*. London, Routledge.

Jacobs, J. M. (2002) 'The global domestic: the highrise (once again) reconsidered'. Paper presented in the ESRC Transforming London seminar series, 24 October 2002.

Jacobson, M. F. (2000) *Barbarian Virtues: The United States Encounters Foreign Peoples at Home and Abroad, 1876–1917*. New York, Hill and Wang.

Jakle, J. A., Rogers, J. S. and Sculle, K. A. (1997) *The Motel in America: The Road in American Culture*. Baltimore, Johns Hopkins University Press.

James, D. E. (1999) 'Toward a geo-cinematic hermeneutics: representations of Los Angeles in non-industrial cinema – Killer of Sheep and Water and Power', *Wide Angle*, 20: 23–53.

Jameson, F. (1991) *Postmodernism, Or, The Cultural Logic of Late Capitalism*. London and New York, Verso.

Johnson, N.C. (1994) 'Sculpting heroic histories: celebrating the centenary of the 1798 rebellion in Ireland', *Transactions of the Institute of British Geographers*, 19:1: 78–93.

Johnson, N.C. (1995) 'Cast in stone: monuments, geography and nationalism', *Environment and Planning D: Society and Space* 13: 51–65.

Johnson, R., et al. (eds) (1982) *Making Histories*. London, Hutchinson.

Johnston, L. (1997) 'Queen(s') street or Ponsonby poofters? embodied HERO parade sites', *New Zealand Geographer* 53 (2): 29–33.

Johnston, L. (1998) *Body Tourism in Queered Streets: Geographies of Gay Pride Parades*, Unpublished PhD thesis, University of Waikato.

Johnston, L. (2001) '(Other) bodies and tourism studies', *Annals of Tourism Research: A Social Science Journal* 28: 180–201.

Johnston, L. (2002) 'Borderline bodies at gay pride parades', in Bondi, L., Avis, H., Bingley, A. F., Davidson, J., Duffy, R., Einagel, V. I., Green, A-M., Johnston, L. T., Lilley, S. M., Listerborn, C., Marshy, M., McEwan, S., O'Connor, N., Rose, G. C., Vivat, B. and Wood, N. (eds) *Subjectivities, Knowledges and Feminist Geographies: The Subjects and Ethics of Social Research*, Lanham, MD, Rowman and Littlefield Publishers, 75–89.

Johnston, R., Gregory, D., Pratt, G. and Watts, M. (eds) (2000) *The Dictionary of Human Geography*. 4th edition. Oxford, Blackwell.

Jones, J. P., Nast, H. J. and Roberts, S. M. (eds) (1997) *Thresholds in Feminist Geography: Difference, Methodology, Representation*. Lanham MD, Rowman and Littlefield Publishers.

Jones, R. (1999) 'Mann and men in a medieval state: the geographies of power in the Middle Ages', *Transactions of the Institute of British Geographers* 24: 65–78.

Jones, S. (ed.) (1992) *Art in Public: What, Why and How*. Sunderland, AN Publications.

Jorn, A. (1958) *Pour la Forme: Ébauche d'une Méthodologie des Arts*. Paris, L'Internationale situationniste.

Kaiser, W.L. and Wood, D. (2001) *Seeing Through Maps: The Power of Images to Shape Our World View*. Amherst, Mass., ODT Inc.

Karp, I. and Lavine, S. (eds) (1991) *Exhibiting Cultures: The Politics and Poetics of Museum Display*. Washington, DC, Smithsonian Press.

Karsten, P. and Modell, J. (eds) (1992) *Theory, Method, and Practice in Social and Cultural History*. New York, New York University Press.

Katriel, T. (1993) 'Our future is where our past is: studying heritage museums as ideological performative arenas'. *Communication Monographs* 60: 69–75.

Kearns, R. A. (1993) 'Place and health: toward a reformed medical geography', *Professional Geographer* 45: 139–47.

Kearns, R. A. (2000) 'Being there: research through observing and participating'. In Hay, I. (ed.) *Qualitative Research Methods in Human Geography*. Victoria, Australia, Oxford University Press.

Kendall, G. and Wickham, G. (1998) *Using Foucault's Methods*. London, Sage.

Kenny, J. (1995a) 'Climate, race and imperial authority: the symbolic landscape of the British hill station in India', *Annals of the Association of American Geographers* 85(4): 694–714.

Kenny, J. (1995b) 'Making Milwaukee famous: cultural capital, urban image and the politics of place'. *Urban Geography* 16: 440–58.

Kessler-Harris, A. (2001) *In Pursuit of Equity: Women, Men, and the Quest for Economic Citizenship in Twentieth-Century America*. New York, Oxford University Press.

Khatib, A. (1958) 'Essai de description psychogéographique des Halles', *Internationale situationniste* 2: 13–18.

King, A. (1984) *The Bungalow: The Production of a Global Culture*. London, Routledge and Kegan Paul.

Kirshenblatt-Gimblett, B. (1991) 'Objects of ethnography', in Karp, I. and Lavine, S. (eds) *Exhibiting Cultures: The Poetics and Politics of Museum Displays*. Washington, DC, Smithsonian Press: 386–443.

Kitchin, R. (1998) *Cyberspace: The World in the Wires*. Chichester, Wiley.

Kitchin, R. and Kneale, J. (2001) 'Science fiction or future fact? exploring imaginative geographies of the new millennium', *Progress in Human Geography* 25: 17–33.

Kitchin, R. and Tate, N. (2000) *Conducting Research into Human Geography*. Harlow, Pearson Education Limited.

Kitzinger, J. (1993) 'Understanding AIDS: media messages and what people know about AIDS', in Eldridge, J. (ed.) *Getting the Message*. London, Routledge.

Kitzinger, J. and Hunt, K. (1993) *Evaluation of the Zero Tolerance Campaign*. Edinburgh, Edinburgh District Council Women's Committee.

Knabb, K. (ed.) (1981) *Situationist International Anthology*. Berkeley, Bureau of Public Secrets.

Kneale, J. (1999) 'The virtual realities of technology and fiction: reading William Gibson's cyberspace', in Crang, M., Crang, P. and May, J. (eds) *Virtual Geographies*. London and New York, Routledge: 205–21.

Kneale, J. (2001) 'Working with groups', in Limb, M. and Dwyer, C., (eds) *Qualitative Methodologies for Geographers*. London, Arnold: 136–50.

Kneale, J. and Kitchin, R. (2002a) 'Lost in Space' in Kitchin, R. and Kneale, J. (eds) *Lost in Space: geographies of science fiction*. London and New York, Continuum: 1–16.

Kneale, J. and Kitchin, R. (eds) (2002b) *Lost in Space: Geographies of Science Fiction*. London, Continuum.

Knight, D.B. (1991) *Choosing Canada's Capital: Conflict Resolution in a Parliamentary System*. Ottawa, Carleton University Press.

Knopp, L. (1987) 'Social theory, social movements and public policy: Recent accomplishments of the gay and lesbian movements in Minneapolis', *International Journal of Urban and Regional Research* 11: 243–61.

Knopp, L. (1990a) 'Some theoretical implications of gay involvement in an urban land market', *Political Geography Quarterly* 9: 337–52.

Knopp, L. (1990b) 'Exploiting the rent-gap: the theoretical significance of using illegal appraisal schemes to encourage gentrification in New Orleans', *Urban Geography* 11: 48–64.

Knox, P. (ed.) (1993) *The Restless Urban Landscape*. New Jersey, Prentice Hall.

Kofman, E., Sales, R., Phizucklea, A. and Raghuran, P. (eds) (2000) *Gender and International Migration in Europe*. London, Routledge.

Koltun, L. (1978) 'Pre-Confederation photography in Toronto' *History of Photography* 2: 249–63.

Konvitz, J.W. (eds) (1987) *Cartography in France 1660–1848: Science, Engineering, and Statecraft*. Chicago, Chicago University Press.

Kotányi, A. (1960) 'Gangland et philosophie'. *Internationale situationniste* 4: 33–5.

Krippendorf, K. (1980) *Content Analysis: An Introduction to its methodologies*. London, Sage.

Kruth, P. (1997) 'The Color of New York: places and spaces in the films of Martin Scorsese and Woody Allen', in Penz, F. and Thomas, M. (eds) *Cinema and Architecture*. Méliès, Mallet-Stevens, Multimedia. London: BFI: 70–83.

Krutnik, F. (1991) *In a Lonely Street: Film Noir, Genre, Masculinity*. London, Routledge.

Kumar, K. (1986) *Utopia and anti-Utopia in Modern Times*. Oxford, Blackwell.

Kumar, K. (1991) *Utopianism*. Minneapolis, University of Minnesota Press.

Kurtz, M. (2001) 'Situating practices: the archive and the file cabinet', *Historical Geography* 29: 26–37.

Kwan, M.-P. (2002) 'Feminist visualization: re-envisioning GIS as a method in feminist geographic research', *Annals of the Association of American Geographers* 92: 645–61.

Lacy, S. (1993) 'Mapping the terrain: the new public art'. *Public Art Review* (Fall/Winter): 26–33.

Lacy, S. (ed.) (1995) *Mapping the Terrain: New Genre Public Art*. Seattle, Washington, Bay Press.

Laird, P. W. (1988) *Advertising Progress: American Business and the Rise of Consumer Marketing*. Baltimore, The Johns Hopkins University Press.

Latour, B. (1986) 'Visualization and cognition: thinking with eyes and hands', in *Knowledge and Society: Studies in the Sociology of Culture Past and Present. A Research Annual* 6: 1–40.

Latour, B. (1987) *Science in Action: How to Follow Scientists and Engineers Through Society*. Milton Keynes, Open University Press.

Latour, B. (1988) *The Pasteurization of France*. Cambridge MA, Harvard University Press.

Latour, B. (1993) *We Have Never Been Modern*. London, Harvester Wheatsheaf.

Law, J. (1994) *Organizing Modernity*. Oxford, Blackwell.

Lawson, V. (1998) 'Hierarchical households and gendered migration: a research agenda', *Progress in Human Geography* 22: 32–53.

Lawson, V. (1999) 'Questions of migration and belonging: understandings of migration under neoliberalism in Ecuador', *International Journal of Population Geography* 5: 261–76.

Lawson, V. (2000) 'Arguments within geographies of movement: the theoretical potential of migrants' stories', *Progress in Human Geography* 24:173–89.

Leach, W. (1994) *Land of Desire: Merchants, Power, and the Rise of a New American Culture*. New York, Vintage Books.

Lears, J. (1994) *Fables of Abundance: A Cultural History of Advertising in America*. New York, Basic Books.

Lees, L. (2001) 'Towards a critical geography of architecture: the case of an ersatz colosseum' *Ecumene* 8: 51–86.

Lefebvre, H. (1991) [1974] *The Production of Space*. Trans. D. Nicholson-Smith. Oxford, Blackwell.

Leitner, H. and Kang, P. (1999) 'Contested urban landscapes of nationalism: the case of Taipei', *Ecumene* 6: 214–33.

Lepore, J. (1998) *The Name of War: King Philip's War and the Origins of American Identity*. New York, Vintage.

Letterist International (LI) (1996) *Potlatch (1954–1957)*. Édition augmentée. Paris, Gallimard.

Ley, D. and Mills, C. (1993) 'Can there be a postmodernism of resistance in the urban landscape?', in Knox, P. (ed.) *The Restless Urban Landscape* New Jersey, Prentice Hall, Englewood Cliffs 255–78.

Liddiard, N. and Hutson, S. (1998) 'Youth homelessness, the press and public attitudes', *Youth and Policy* 59: 57–69.

Limb, M. and Dwyer, C. (eds) (2001) *Qualitative Methodologies for Geographers: Issues and Debates*. London, Arnold.

Llewellyn, M. (2001) *Domestic Modernities: The Experience of Architecture, Planning and Home, 1933–1953*, Unpublished PhD thesis, Department of Geography, University of Wales Swansea.

Loftman, P. and Nevin, B. (1998) 'Pro-growth local economic development strategies: civic promotion and local needs in Britain's second city 1981–1996', in Hall, T. and Hubbard, P. (eds) *The Entrepreneurial City: Geographies of Politics, Regime and Representation*. Chichester, Wiley: 129–48.

Longhurst, R. (1996) 'Refocusing groups: pregnant women's geographical experiences of Hamilton, New Zealand/Aotearoa', *Area* 28: 143–9.

Longhurst, R. (1997) '(Dis)embodied geographies', *Progress in Human Geography* 21 (4): 486–501.

Longhurst, R. (2001) *Bodies: Exploring Fluid Boundaries*. London, Routledge.

Lord, P. (1992) *The Aesthetics of Relevance*. Llandysul, Gwasg Gomer.

Lott, E. (1993) *Love and Theft: Blackface Minstrelsy and the American Working-Class*. Oxford, Oxford University Press.

Lovell, V. (1988) *Report by the Public Arts Commissions Agency to the Arts Working Party* (12 January). Unpublished.

Lukes, S. (ed.) (1986) *Power*. Oxford, Blackwell.

Lury, K. and Massey, D. (1999) 'Making connections', *Screen* 40: 229–38.

Lynch, K. (1961) *The Image of the City*. Cambridge, MA., MIT Press.

Mackay, D. (2002) 'Negotiating positionings: exchanging life stories in research interviews', in Moss, P. (ed.) *Feminist Geography in Practice: Research and Methods*. Oxford, Blackwell: 187–99.

Mackenzie, J.M. (ed.) (2001) *The Victorian Vision: Inventing New Britain*. London, V&A Publications.

Macnaghten P. and Urry, J. (1998) *Contested Natures*. London, Sage.

Malbon, B. (1999) *Clubbing: Dancing, Ecstasy and Vitality*. London, Routledge.

Mann, M. (1984) 'The autonomous power of the state: its origins, mechanisms and results', *Archives Européenes de Sociologie* 25: 185–213.

Marchand, R. (1985) *Advertising the American Dream: Making Way for Modernity, 1920–1940*. Berkeley, University of California Press.

Marin, L. (1984) *Utopics: Spatial Play*. Translated by R. A. Vollrath. London, Macmillan.

Marin, L. (1993) 'The frontiers of utopia', in Kumar, K. and Bann, S. (eds) *Utopias and the Millennium*. London, Reaktion Books:7–15.

Massey, D. (1993) 'Power-geometry and a progressive sense of place', in Bird, J., Putnam, T., Robertson, G. and Tickner, L. (eds) *Mapping the Futures*. London, Routledge: 59–69.

Massey, D. (1995) 'Imagining the world', in Allen, J. and Massey, D. (eds) *Geographical Worlds*. Oxford, Oxford University Press: 5–51.

Matarasso, F. (1997) *Use or Ornament? The Social Impact of Participation in the Arts*. Stroud, Comedia.

Matless, D. (1998) *Landscape and Englishness*. London, Reaktion.

Maxwell, I. (2002) 'The curse of fandom: insiders, outsiders and ethnography', in Hesmondhalgh, D. and Negus, K., (eds) (2002) *Popular Music Studies*. London, Arnold: 103–16.

Maxwell, J. (1996) *Qualitative Research Design: An Interactive Approach*. Thousand Oaks, Sage.

May, J. (2000) 'Of nomads and vagrants: single homelessness and meanings of home as place', *Environment and Planning D: Society and Space* 18: 737–59.

May, J. (2002) 'Making news: constructions of homelessness in the (British) newspaper press', Unpublished Paper, Department of Geography, Queen Mary, University of London.

May, J. (2003) 'Local Connection Criteria and single homeless people's geographical mobility: evidence from Brighton and Hove', *Housing Studies* 18: 29–46.

Mayne, J. (1993) *Cinema and Spectatorship*. London, Routledge.

McArthur, C. (1997) 'Chinese boxes and Russian dolls: tracking the elusive cinematic city', in Clarke, D. B. (ed.) *The Cinematic City*. London, Routledge: 19–45.

McCann, G. (1990) *Woody Allen: New Yorker*. Cambridge, Polity Press.

McCannon, J. (1995) 'To storm the Arctic: Soviet polar exploration and public visions of nature in the USSR, 1932–1939', *Ecumene* 2: 15–31.

McClintock, A. (1995) *Imperial Leather: Race, Gender and Sexuality in the Colonial Context*. London, Routledge.

McDonough, T. (2002) 'Situationist space'. In McDonough, T. (ed.) *Guy Debord and the Situationist International*. Cambridge, MA., MIT Press: 241–65.

McDowell, L. (1995) 'Body work: heterosexual gender performances in City workplaces', in Bell, D. and Valentine, G. (eds) *Mapping Desire*. London, Routledge: 75–95.

McDowell, L. (1997) *Capital Culture: Gender at Work in the City*. Oxford, Blackwell.

McDowell, L. (1999) 'In and out of place: bodies and embodiment', in McDowell, L. *Gender, Identity and Place: Understanding Feminist Geographies*. Cambridge, Polity Press.

McHugh, K. E. (2000) 'Inside, outside, upside ddown, backward, forward, round and round: a case for ethnographic studies in migration', *Progress in Human Geography* 24 (1): 71–89.

McKee, L. (1999) 'A little click, a lot of clout', *Guardian G2* 12th January: 6.

McKendrick, J. (1999) 'Multi-method research: an introduction to its application in population geography', *Professional Geographer* 51: 40–50.

McManus, P. (1987) 'It's the company you keep … social determinants of learning related behaviour in a science museum'. *International Journal of Museum Management and Curatorship* 6: 263–70.

McManus, P. (1988) 'Good companions: more on the social determination of learning-related behaviour in a science Museum', *International Journal of Museum Management and Curatorship* 7: 37–44.

McManus, P. (1989) 'What people say and how they think in a science museum', in Uzzell, D. (ed.) *Heritage Interpretation (Vol. 2): The Visitor Experience*. London, Belhaven: 156–65.

McManus, P. (1993) 'Memories as indicators of the impact of museum visits', *International Journal of Museum Management and Curatorship* 12(4): 367–80.

Meinig, D. (ed.) (1979) *The Interpretation of Ordinary Landscapes: Geographical Essays*. New York, Oxford University Press.

Mellor, A. (1991) 'Enterprise and heritage in the Dock', in Corner, J. and Harvey, S. (eds) *Enterprise and Heritage. Crosscurrents in National Culture*. London, Routledge: 93–115.

Merish, L. (2000) *Sentimental Materialism: Gender, Commodity, Culture, and Nineteenth-Century American Literature*. Durham, NC, Duke University Press.

Merriman, N. (1989) 'Museum visiting as a cultural phenomenon', in Vergo, P. (ed.) *The New Museology*. London, Reaktion.

Merriman, N. (1991) *Beyond the Glass Case: The Past, the Heritage and the Public in Britain*. Leicester, Leicester University Press.

Mikkelson, B. (1995) *Methods for Development Work and Research: A Guide for Practioners*. London, Sage.

Miles, M. (1997) *Art, Space and the City*. London, Routledge.

Miles, M. (1998) 'A game of appearance: public art in urban development, complicity or sustainability?', in Hall, T. and Hubbard, P. (eds) *The Entrepreneurial City: Geographies of Politics, Regime and Representation*. Chichester, Wiley: 203–24.

Miles, M. and Huberman, A. M. (1994) *Qualitative Data Analysis: An Expanded Source Book*. Thousand Oaks, CA, Sage.

Millar, S. B. (1983) 'On interpreting gender in Bugis society', *American Ethnologist* 10: 477–93.

Miller, D. (ed.) (2001) *Home Possessions: Material Culture Behind Closed Doors*. Oxford, Berg.

Miller, D. and Slater, D. (2000) *The Internet: An Ethnographic Approach*. Oxford, Berg.

Miller, D., Jackson, P. and Thrift, N. (1998) *Shopping, Place and Identity*. London, Routledge.

Mills, C. W. (1959) *The Sociological Imagination*. Oxford, Oxford University Press.

Mills, M. B. (1997) 'Contesting the margins of modernity: women, migration, and consumption in Thailand', *American Ethnologist* 24: 37–61.

Mills, S. (1997) *Discourse*. London, Routledge.

Mills, S. (1997) 'Pocket tigers: the sad unseen reality behind the wildlife film'. *Times Literary Supplement* (21 February).

Mills, S. (1999) 'Gender and colonial space', *Gender, Place and Culture*, 3: 125–47.

Mitchell, D. (1997) 'The annihilation of space by law: the roots and implications of anti-homeless laws in the United States', *Antipode* 29: 306–36

Mitchell, D. (2000) *Cultural Geography: A Critical Introduction*. Oxford, Blackwell.

Mitman, G. (1999) *Reel Nature*. London, Harvard University Press.

Mohanty, C. T. (ed.) (1991) *Third World Women and the Politics of Feminism*. Bloomington, Indiana University Press.

Mokhtarian, P. (1998) 'A synthetic approach to estimating the impacts of telecommuting on travel'. *Urban Studies* 35: 215–41.

Mol, A. and Mesman, J. (1996) 'Neonatal food and the politics of theory: some questions of method', *Social Studies of Science* 26: 419–44.

Momsen, J. H. (ed.) (1999) *Gender, Migration, and Domestic Service*. London, Routledge.

Monmonier, M. (2001) *How to Lie with Maps*. Second edition. Chicago, Chicago University Press.

Moody, E. (1990) 'Introduction', in Public Art Forum (ed.) *Public Art Report*. London, Public Art Forum: 2–3.

Morales, N. (2000) 'Public ppinion, foreign policy, and overseas Filipino workers'. Unpublished manuscript.

Morin, K. (1998) 'British women travellers and constructions of racial difference across the nineteenth-century American west'. *Transactions of the Institute of British Geographers*, 23(3): 311–29.

Morris, M. (1988) 'Things to do with shopping centres', in Sheridan, S. (ed.) *Grafts: Feminist Cultural Criticism*. London, Verso: 193–224.

Mort, F. (1995) 'Archaeologies of cultural life: Commercial culture, masculinity, and spatial relations in 1980s London', *Environment and Planning D: Society and Space* 13: 573–90.

Moss, P. (1999) 'Autobiographical notes on chronic illness', in Butler, R. and Parr, H. (eds) *Mind and Body Spaces: Geographies of Illness, Impairment and Disability*. London, Routledge: 155–66.

Moss, P. (ed.) (2000) *Placing Autobiography in Geography*. Syracuse, Syracuse University Press.

Moss, P. (ed.) (2002) *Feminist Geography in Practice: Research and Methods*. Oxford, Blackwell.

Moss, P. and Dyck, I. (1999) 'Body, corporeal space, and legitimating chronic illness: women diagnosed with ME', *Antipode* 31: 372–97.

Moyles, R.G., and Owram, D. (1988) *Imperial Dreams and Colonial Realities: British Views of Canada, 1880–1914*. Toronto, University of Toronto Press.

Munt, S. (1995) 'The lesbian flâneur'. In Bell, D. and Valentine, G. (eds) *Mapping Desire: Geographies of Sexualities*. London, Routledge: 114–25.

Murdoch, J. (1997a) 'Inhuman/nonhuman/human: actor-network theory and the prospects for a nondualistic and symmetrical perspective on nature and society', *Environment and Planning D: Society and Space* 15: 731–56.

Murdoch, J. (1997b) 'Towards a geography of heterogeneous associations', *Progress in Human Geography* 21: 321–37.

Nagar, R. (1997) 'Exploring methodological borderlands through oral narratives', in Jones, J. P., Nast, H. J. and Roberts, S. M. (eds) *Thresholds in Feminist Geography: Difference, Methodology, Representation*. Lanham, MD, Rowman and Littlefield: 203–24.

Nash, C. (1993) 'Remapping and renaming: new cartographies of gender, landscape and identity in Ireland'. *Feminist Review* 44: 39–57.

Nash, C. (1996) 'Geo-centric education and anti-imperialism: theosophy, geography and citizenship in the writings of J. H. Cousins', *Journal of Historical Geography* 22: 399–411.

Nash, C. (2000) 'Performativity in practice: some recent work in cultural geography', *Progress in Human Geography*, 24: 653–64.

Natter, W. and Jones III, J.P. (1993) 'Pets or meat: class, ideology and space in *Roger and Me*', *Antipode* 25: 140–58.

Negrine, R. (1994) *Politics and the Mass Media in Britain*. London, Routledge.

Neumann, R.P. (1995) 'Ways of seeing Africa: colonial recasting of African society and landscape in Serengeti National Park', *Ecumene* 2: 14–69.

News of the World (1998) 'Hungry and homeless – our man discovers the hidden hell of living rough on the streets of Britain 1998', *News of the World* 26/07/98.

Norkunas, M. (1993) *The Politics of Public Memory: Tourism, History and Ethnicity in Monterey, California*, New York, SUNY Press.

Norris, C. (2002) *Deconstruction: Theory and Practice*. London, Taylor and Francis.

Ó Tuathail, G. (1996) *Critical Geopolitics*. Minneapolis, Minnesota University Press.

O'Brien, P.K. and Hunt, P. (1993) 'The rise of the fiscal state in England, 1485–1815', *Historical Research* 66: 129–76.

Ogborn, M. (1992) 'Local power and state regulation in nineteenth-century Britain', *Transactions of the Institute of British Geographers* 17: 215–26.

Ogborn, M. (1995) 'Discipline, government and law: separate confinement in the prisons of England and Wales, 1830–1877', *Transactions of the Institute of British Geographers* 20: 295–311.

Ogborn, M. (1998a) 'The capacities of the state: Charles Davenant and the management of the Excise, 1683–1698', *Journal of Historical Geography* 24: 289–312.

Ogborn, M. (1998b) *Spaces of Modernity: London's Geographies, 1680–1780*. New York, Guilford Press.

Ogborn, M. (2003) 'Finding historical data', in N. Clifford and G. Valentine (eds) *Research Methods in Human and Physical Geography*. London, Sage: 101–15.

Ogden, P. E. (2000) 'Weaving demography into society, economy and culture: progress and prospect in population geography', *Progress in Human Geography* 24: 627–40.

Ohmann, R. (1996) *Selling Culture: Magazines, Markets, and Class at the Turn of the Century*. New York and London, Verso.

Ollman, A. (1983) *Samuel Bourne: Images of India*. Carmel, CA, Friends of Photography.

Ong, A. and Peletz, M. (eds) (1995) *Bewitching Women, Pious Men: Gender and Body Politics in Southeast Asia*. Berkeley, University of California Press.

Painter, J. (1995) *Politics, Geography and Political Geography*. London, Edward Arnold.

Panofsky, E. (1955) *Meaning in the Visual Arts*. New York, Doubleday.

Parfitt, J. (1997) 'Questionnaire design and sampling'. In Flowerdew, R. and Martin, D. (eds) *Methods in Human Geography: A Guide for Students doing Research Projects*, Harlow, Longman: 76–109.

Parr, H. (2002) 'New body-geographies: the embodied species of health and medical information on the Internet', *Environment and Planning D: Society and Space* 20(1): 73–95.

Peach, C. (2002) 'Social geography: new religions and ethnoburbs: contrasts with cultural geography', *Progress in Human Geography* 26, 252–60.

Peake, L. (1993) "'Race' and sexuality: challenging the patriarchal structure of urban social space', *Environment and Planning D: Society and Space* 11: 415–32.

Pearce, S. (ed.) (1990) *Objects of Knowledge*. London, Athlone Press.

Penner, M. and Penner, S. (1994) 'Publicising, politicizing, and neutralising homelessness: comic strips', *Communication Research* 21: 766–81.

Pepper, D. (1996) *Modern Environmentalism*. London, Routledge.

Perks, R. and Thomson, A. (eds) (1998) *The Oral History Reader*. London, Routledge.

Petherbridge, D. (1987) *Art for Architecture: A Handbook on Commissioning*. London, Department of the Environment/HMSO.

Pettman, J.J. (1996) *Worlding Women: A Feminist International Politics*. New York, Routledge.

Phillips, P. (1988) 'Out of order: the public art machine', *Artforum* (December): 92–96. Reprinted in Miles, M., Borden, I. and Hall, T. (eds) (2000) *The City Cultures Reader*, London, Routledge: 96–102.

Phillips, R. (2001) 'Politics of reading: cultural politics of homelessness', *Antipode* 32: 429–62.

Philo, C.P. (1989) ' "Enough to drive one mad": the organisation of space in 19th-century lunatic asylums', in Wolch, J. and Dear, M. (eds) *The Power of Geography: How Territory Shapes Social Life*. London, Unwin Hyman: 258–90.

Pickles, J. (1992) 'Text, hermeneutics and propaganda maps'. In Barnes, T. and Duncan, J. (eds) *Writing Worlds: Discourse, Text and Metaphor in the Representation of Landscape*. London, Routledge: 193–230.

Pickles, J. (1995) *Ground Truth: The Social Implications of Geographic Information Systems*. New York, Guilford Press.

Pinder, D. (1996) 'Subverting cartography: the situationists and maps of the city'. *Environment and Planning A* 28: 405–27.

Pinder, D. (1999) 'Utopia, utopian thought, utopian communities', in McDowell, L. and Sharpe, J. P. (eds), *A Feminist Glossary of Human Geography*. London, Edward Arnold: 285–86.

Pinder, D. (2000) ' "Old Paris is no more": geographies of spectacle and anti-spectacle',. *Antipode* 32: 357–86.

Pinder. D. (2001a) 'Utopian transfiguration: the other spaces of New Babylon', in Borden, I. and McCreery, S. (eds) 'New Babylonians'. *Architectural Design* 71: 15–19.

Pinder, D. (2001b) 'Ghostly footsteps: voices, memories and walks in the city', *Ecumene* 8: 1–19.

Pinder, D. (forthcoming) *Visions of the City: Utopianism, Power and Politics in Twentieth-Century Urbanism*. Edinburgh, Edinburgh University Press.

Pink, S. (2001) *Doing Visual Ethnography: Images, Media and Representation in Research*. London, Sage.

Pleace, N. and Quilgars, D. (1997) *Health and Homelessness in London*. London, Kings Fund.

Ploszajska, T. (1994) 'Moral landscapes and manipulated spaces: gender, class and space in Victorian reformatory schools', *Journal of Historical Geography* 20: 413–29.

Pointon, M. (1997) *History of Art: A Students' Handbook*. Fourth Edition. London, Routledge.

Policy Studies Institute (1994) 'The benefits of public art', *Cultural Trends* 23: 37–55.

Poovey, M. (1995) *Making and Social Body: British Cultural Formation, 1830–1864*. Chicago, University of Chicago Press.

Portelli, A (1991) *The Death of Luigi Trastulli and Other Stories: Form and Meaning in Oral History*. Albany, NY, State University of New York Press.

Portelli, A. (1997) *The Battle of Valle Giulia: Oral History and the Art of Dialogue*. Madison, Wisconsin, The University of Wisconsin Press.

Porter, G. (1989) 'The economy of truth: photography in museums'. *Ten.8* 34: 20–33.

Porter, P.W. and Luckermann, F.E. (1976) 'The geography of utopia' in D. Lowenthal and M.J. Bowden (eds) *Geographies of the Mind*. New York, Oxford University Press.

Porter, R., (ed.) (1992) *Myths of the English*. Cambridge, Polity Press.

Porter, T. (1995) *Trust in Numbers: The Pursuit of Objectivity in Science and Public Life*. Princeton, NJ, Princeton University Press.

Potts, A. (1989) ' "Constable Country" between the wars' in R. Samuel (ed.) *Patriotism: the Making and Unmaking of British National Identity, Vol 3*. London, Routledge: 160–86.

Poulot, D. (1994) 'Identity as self-discovery: the ecomuseum in France', in Sherman, D. and Rogoff, I. (eds) *Museum Culture: Histories, Discourses, Spectacles*. London, Routledge: 66–84.

Pratt, G. (1997) 'Stereotypes and ambivalence: the construction of domestic workers in Vancouver, British Columbia', *Gender, Place and Culture* 4: 159–78.

Pratt, G. (1998) 'Geographic metaphors in feminist theory', in Aiken, S. H., Brigham, A., Marston, S. A. and Waterstone, P. (eds) *Making Worlds: Gender, Metaphor, Materiality*. Tucson, University of Arizona Press: 13–30.

Pratt, G. (1999) 'From registered nurse to registered nanny: discursive geographies of Filipina domestic workers in Vancouver, B.C'. *Economic Geography* 75: 215–36.

Pratt, G. (2000). 'Research Performances', *Environment and Planning D: Society and Space* 18(5): 639–51.

Pratt, G. (forthcoming) 'Trouble in suburbia: costs and practices of devaluing childcare in Vancouver Canada', *London Journal of Canadian Studies*.

Pratt, G. and Hanson, S. (1994) 'Geography and the construction of difference', *Gender, Place and Culture* 1: 5–30.

Pratt, M. B. (1984) 'Identity: skin, blood, heart', in Burkin, E., Pratt, M. B., and Smith, B. (eds) *Yours in Struggle: Three Feminist Perspectives on Anti-Semitism and Racism*. New York, Long Haul Press: 9–64.

Pratt, M.L. (1992) *Imperial Eyes: Travel Writing and Transculturation*. London, Routledge.

Pred, A. (1992) 'Languages of everyday practice and resistance: Stockholm at the end of the nineteenth century', in Pred, A. and Watts, M.J. (eds) *Reworking Modernity: Capitalisms and Symbolic Dissent*. New Brunswick, Rutgers University Press: 118–54.

Pred, A. (1995) *Recognizing European Modernities: A Montage of the Present*. London, Routledge.

Price, M. and Lewis, M. (1993) 'The reinvention of cultural geography' *Annals of the Association of American Geographers* 83: 1–17

Public Art Forum (eds) (1990) *Public Art Report*. London, Public Art Forum.

Rabinow, P. (1996) 'On the archaeology of late modernity' in P. Rabinow, *Essays on the Anthropology of Reason*. Princeton: Princeton University Press: 59–79.

Radcliffe, S. (1991) 'The Role of Gender in Peasant Migration: Conceptual Issues from the Peruvian Andes', *Review of Radical Political Economics* 23: 129–47.

Ragin, C. C. (1987) *The Comparative Method: Moving Beyond Qualitative and Quantitative Strategies*. Berkeley, University of California Press.

Ragin, C.C. (1994) *Constructing Social Research*. Thousand Oaks, California, Pine Forge.

Rahnema, M. and Bawtree, V. (eds) (1997) *The Post-Development Reader*. London, Zed.

Ramamurthy, P. (2000) 'Indexing alternatives; feminist development studies and global political economy', *Feminist Theory* 1: 239–256.

Relph, E. (1976) *Place and Placelessness*. London, Pion.

Reynolds, L. J. and Heuter, G. (eds) (2000) *National Imaginaries, American Identities: The Cultural Work of American Iconography*. Princeton, Princeton University Press.

Rheingold, H. (1994) *The Virtual Community: Homesteading on the Electronic Frontier*. New York, Addison-Wesley.

Rice, S. and Valentine, G. (eds) (2003) *Key Concepts in Geography*. London, Sage.

Richards, T. (1993) *The Imperial Archive: Knowledge and the Fantasy of Empire.* London, Verso.

Roberts, M. and Marsh, C. (1995) 'For art's sake: public art, planning policies and the benefits for commercial property'. *Planning Practice and Research* 10: 189–98.

Robertson, I. and Richard, P. (2002) *Studying Landscapes: Cultural and Symbolic Landscapes in the Western European Tradition.* London, Arnold.

Robins, K. (1991) 'Prisoners of the city: whatever could a postmodern city be?'. *New Formations* 15: 1–22.

Robinson, G. (1998) *Methods and Techniques in Human Geography.* Chichester, John Wiley.

Robinson, J. (1990) ' "A perfect system of control"? State power and "native locations" in South Africa', *Environment and Planning D: Society and Space* 8: 135–62.

Robinson, J. (1996) *Angels of Albion: Women of the Indian Mutiny.* London, Viking.

Robson, C. (1993) *Real World Research: A Resource for Social Scientists and Practitioner-Researchers.* Oxford, Blackwell.

Rose, G. (1993) *Feminism and Geography: The Limits of Geographical Knowledge.* Cambridge, Polity.

Rose, G. (1995) 'Place and identity: a sense of place', in Massey, D. and Jess, P. (eds) *A Place in the World?* Oxford, Oxford University Press: 87–132.

Rose, G. (1996) 'Teaching visualised geographies: towards a methodology for the interpretation of visual materials', *Journal of Geography in Higher Education* 20: 281–94.

Rose, G. (1997) 'Positionality, reflexivity and other tactics'. *Progress in Human Geography* 31: 305–20.

Rose, G. (2001) *Visual Methodologies: An Introduction to the Interpretation of Visual Materials.* London, Sage.

Rosenberg, E. S. (1982) *Spreading the Dream: American Economic and Cultural Expansion 1890–1945.* New York, Hill and Wang.

Ross, A. (1991) *Strange Weather: Culture, Science, and Technology in the Age of Limits.* London and New York, Verso.

Rothenberg, T. (1995) ' "And she told two friends": lesbians creating urban social space'. In Bell, D. and Valentine, G. (eds) *Mapping Desire: Geographies of Sexualities.* London, Routledge: 165–81.

Routledge, P. (1997) 'The imagineering of resistance: Pollock Free State and the practice of postmodern politics', *Transactions of the Institute of British Geographers* 22: 359–76.

Rowe, S. M., Wertsch, J.V. and Kosyaeva, T. Y. (2002) 'Linking little narratives to big ones: narrative and public memory in history museums'. *Culture and Psychology* 8: 96–112.

Rubio, P. (1996) 'Crossover dreams: the "exceptional white" in popular culture', in Ignatiev, N. and Garvey, J. (eds) *Race Traitor.* London, Routledge.

Ruddick, S. (1996) *Young and Homeless in Hollywood: Mapping Social Identities.* London, Routledge.

Ryan, B. F. and Joiner, B. L. (1994) *MINITAB Handbook.* Delmont, CA, Duxbury Press.

Ryan, J. R. (1997) *Picturing Empire: Photography and the Visualization of the British Empire.* London, Reaktion and Chicago, University of Chicago Press.

Rydell, R. (1984) *All the World's a Fair: Visions of Empire at American International Expositions, 1876–1916.* Chicago, Chicago University Press.

Sachs, W. (ed.) (1992) *The Development Dictionary: A Guide to Knowledge as Power.* London, Zed.

Sadler, S. (1998) *The Situationist City.* Cambridge, MA., MIT Press.

Said, E. (1978) *Orientalism.* Harmondsworth, Penguin.

Said, E. (1994) *Culture and Imperialism.* New York, Vintage Books.

Said, E. (1999) *Out of Place: a Memoir.* London, Granta.

Sargent, A. (1996) 'More than just the sum of its parts: cultural policy and planning in Birmingham'. *Cultural Policy* 2: 303–25.

Saumerez-Smith, C. (1989) 'Museums, artefacts and meanings', in Vergo, P. (ed.) *The New Museology*. London, Reaktion: Ch.1.

Sayer, A. (1994) 'Cultural studies and "the economy, stupid", *Environment and Planning D: Society and Space* 12: 635–7.

Scherer, J. C. (ed.) (1990) *Picturing Cultures: Historical Photographs in Anthropological Inquiry*, a special issue of *Visual Anthropology* 3: 235–58.

Schlesinger, P. and Tumber, H. (1994) *Reporting Crime: The Media Politics of Criminal Justice*. Oxford, Clarendon.

Schuurman, N. (2000) 'Trouble in the heartland: GIS and its critics in the 1990s'. *Progress in Human Geography* 24: 569–90.

Schwartz, J.M. (1996) 'The Geography Lesson: photographs and the construction of imaginative geographies' *Journal of Historical Geography* 22: 16–45.

Schwartz, J. M. and Ryan, J. R. (eds) (2003) *Picturing Place: Photography and the Geographical Imagination*. London, IB Tauris.

Scott, J.C. (1998) *Seeing Like a State: How Certain Schemes to Improve the Human Condition Have Failed*. New Haven, Yale University Press.

Seager, J. (1997) *The State of Women in the World Atlas*. London, Addison Wesley.

Seamon, D. (1979) *A Geography of the Lifeworld: Movement, Rest and Encounter*. London, Croom Helm.

Segal, L.M. and Sullivan, D. G. (1997) 'The temporary labor force'. *Economic Perspectives, Review from the Federal Reserve Bank of Chicago* 19: 2–19.

Selwood, S. (1995) 'The good, the bad and the public', *Artists Newsletter* (October): 24–7.

Shaffer, R.M. (1977) *Tuning the World*. New York, Alfred A. Knopf.

Sharp, J. (1999) 'Critical geopolitics', in P. Cloke, P. Crang and M. Goodwin (eds) *Introducing Human Geography*. London, Arnold: 181–8.

Sharp, J. (2000) 'Towards a critical analysis of fictive geographies', *Area* 32: 327–34.

Shelton, A. (1990) 'In the lair of the monkey: notes towards a post-modernist museography', in Pearce, S. (ed.) *Objects of Knowledge*. London, Athlone Press: 78–102.

Sherman, D. and Rogoff, I. (eds) (1994) *Museum Culture: Histories, Discourses, Spectacles*. London, Routledge.

Shiel, M. and Fitzmaurice, T. (eds) (2001) *Cinema and the City: Film and Urban Societies in a Global Context*. Oxford, Blackwell.

Shiel, M. and Fitzmaurice, T. (eds) (2003) *Screening the City*. London, Verso

Shields, R. (1991) *Places on the Margin: Alternative Geographies of Modernity* London, Routledge.

Shields, R. (1999) *Lefebvre, Love and Struggle: Spatial Dialectics*. London, Routledge.

Short, B. (1997) *Land and Society in Edwardian Britain*. Cambridge, Cambridge University Press.

Short, J.R. and Kim, Y.-K. (1998) 'Urban crises/urban representations: selling the city in difficult times', in Hall, T. and Hubbard, P. (eds) *The Entrepreneurial City: Geographies of Politics, Regime and Representation*, Chichester, Wiley: 55–76

Shurmer-Smith, P. (ed.) (2002) *Doing Cultural Geography*. London, Sage.

Shurmer-Smith, P. and Hannam, K. (1994) *Worlds of Desire, Realms of Power: A Cultural Geography*. London, Arnold.

Sibley, D. (1995) *Geographies of Exclusion: Society and Difference in the West*. London, Routledge.

Silverman, D. (2001) *Interpreting Qualitative Data: Methods for Analysing Talk, Text and Interaction*. London, Sage.

Silverstone, R. (1986) 'Putting the natural into natural-history', *Journal of Geography in Higher Education* 10: 89–92.

Silvey, R. (2000a) 'Diasporic subjects: gender and mobility in Sulawesi', *Women's Studies International Forum* 23 (4): 501–15.

Silvey, R. (2000b) 'Stigmatized spaces: moral geographies under crisis in south Sulawesi, Indonesia', *Gender, Place and Culture* 7: 143–61.

Silvey, R. and Lawson, V. (1999) 'Placing the migrant', *Annals of the Association of American Geographers* 89: 121–32.

Singleton, V. (1993) *Actor Network Theory: A Useful Tool for Feminists Approaching Science?* Brunel University, Discussion paper prepared for conference on 'Theoretical Perspectives on New Technology: Feminism, Constructivism and Utility'.

Situationist International (SI) (1997) *Internationale Situationniste*. Édition augmentée. Paris, Librarie Arthème Fayard.

Skeldon, R. (1995) 'The challenge facing migration research: a case for greater awareness', *Progress in Human Geography* 19: 91–6.

Slim, H. and Thompson, P. (1993) *Listening for Change: Oral History and Development*. London, Panos.

Smith, D. (1994) *Geography and Social Justice*. Oxford, Blackwell.

Smith, D. (1999) *The State of the World Atlas*. London, Penguin.

Smith, D. (2003) *Atlas of War and Peace*. London, Earthscan.

Smith, N. (1992) 'History and philosophy of geography: real wars, theory wars', *Progress in Human Geography* 16: 257–71.

Smith, N. (1996) *The New Urban Frontier: Gentrification and the Revanchist City*. London, Routledge.

Smith, S.J. (1994) 'Soundscape', *Area* 26: 232–40.

Smith, S.J. (1997) 'Beyond geography's visible worlds: a cultural politics of music', *Progress in Human Geography*, 21: 502–29.

Smith, S.J. (2000) 'Performing the (sound)world', *Environment and Planning D: Society and Space*, 18: 615–37.

Snow, S. (1993) *Performing the Pilgrims: A Study of Ethnohistorical Role-playing at Plimoth Plantation*. Jackson, University Press of Mississippi.

Soja, E. (1989) *Postmodern Geographies: The Reassertion of Space in Critical Social Theory*. London, Verso.

Sollors, W. (1997) *Neither Black nor White yet Both: A Thematic Analysis of Interracial Literature*. New York, Oxford University Press.

Soothill, K. and Walby, S. (1991) *Sex Crime in the News*. London, Routledge.

Sparke, M. (1995) 'Between demythologising and deconstructing the map: Shawnadithit's New-Found-Land and the alienation of Canada'. *Cartographica* 32: 1–21.

Sparke, M. (1998) 'A map that roared and an original atlas: Canada, cartography, and the narration of nation'. *Annals of the Association of American Geographers* 88: 463–95.

Spivak, G. C. (1990) *The Post-Colonial Critic: Interviews, Strategies, Dialogues*. New York, Routledge.

Stam, R. (2000) *Film Theory: An Introduction*. Oxford, Blackwell.

Steedly, M. M. (1999) 'The State of Culture Theory in the Anthropology of Southeast Asia', *Annual Review of Anthropology* 28: 431–54.

Steiger, J. (1992) *Interpreting Films: Studies in the Historical Reception of American Cinema*. New Jersey, Princeton University Press.

Stickler, P.J. (1990) 'Invisible towns: a case study in the cartography of South Africa'. *GeoJournal* 22: 329–33.

Stone, L. (ed.) (1994) *An Imperial State at War: Britain from 1689 to 1815*. London, Routledge.

Storey, J. (1996) *Cultural Studies and the Study of Popular Culture: Theories and Methods*. Edinburgh, Edinburgh University Press.

Straw, W. (1997) [1991] 'Communities and scenes in popular music', in Gelder, K. and Thornton, S. (eds) *The Subcultures Reader*. London, Routledge.

Sumeray, D. (1999) *Discovering London Plaques*. Buckinghamshire, Shire.

Swales, P. (1992) 'Approaches', in Jones, S. (ed.) *Art in Public: What, Why and How*. Sunderland, AN Publications: 63–77.

Szreter, S. (ed.) (1991) 'The General Register Office of England and Wales and the public health movement 1837–1914', Special issue of *Social History of Medicine* 4: 401–537.

Taborsky, E. (1990) 'The discursive object', in Pearce, S. (ed.) *Objects of Knowledge*. London, Athlone Press: 50–77.

Takahashi, L. M. (1996) 'A decade of understanding homelessness in the USA: from characterization to representation', *Progress in Human Geography* 20: 291–310

Tauxe, C.S. (1996) 'Mystics, modernists, and constructions of Brasilia' *Ecumene* 3: 43–61.

Taylor, I. and Taylor, A. (eds) (2000) *The Assassin's Cloak: An Anthology of the World's Greatest Diarists*. Edinburgh, Canongate.

Taylor, J.A. (1990) 'The alphabetic universe: photography and picturesque landscape' in Pugh, S. (ed.) *Reading Landscape: Country-City-Capital*. Manchester, Manchester University Press: 177–96.

Taylor, P.J. (1989) *Political Geography: World-Economy, Nation-state and Locality*. Second edition. London, Longman.

Taylor, R. (1974) *The Word in Stone: The Role of Architecture in National Socialist Ideology*. Berkeley, University of California Press.

Telegraph (1990) 'Homeless and hopeless', Telegraph Newspapers 22/06/90.

Telegraph (1991) 'Vagrancy acts essential to curb beggars, says Earl', Telegraph Newspapers 21/05/91.

Thomas, H. (1994) 'The local press and urban renewal: a South Wales case study'. *International Journal of Urban and Regional Studies* 18(2): 315–33.

Thompson, B. and Tyagi, S. (eds) (1996) *Names we call Home: Autobiography on Racial Identity*. New York, Routledge.

Thompson, P. (2000) *The Voice of the Past: Oral History*, 3rd edition. Oxford, Oxford University Press.

Thrift, N. (1978) 'Landscape and Literature', *Environment and Planning A* 10: 347–9.

Thrift, N. (2000a) 'Non-representational theory', in Johnston, R., Gregory, D., Pratt, G. and Watts, M. (eds) *The Dictionary of Human Geography*, 4th edition. Oxford, Blackwell: 556.

Thrift, N. (2000b) 'Performance', in Johnston, R.J., Gregory, D., Pratt, G. and Watts, M. (eds) *The Dictionary of Human Geography*, 4th edition. Oxford, Blackwell: 577.

Thrift, N. and Dewsbury, J.-D. (2000) 'Dead geographies and how we can make them live', *Environment and Planning D: Society and Space* 18: 411–32.

Thrift, N., Driver, F., and Livingstone, D. (1995) 'Editorial: the geography of truth', *Environment and Planning D: Society and Space*, 13: 1–3.

Times (1993) 'Town gets tough on undeserving poor', Times Newspapers 07/06/93.

Todorov, T. (1973) *The Fantastic: A Structural Approach to a Literary Genre*. Ithaca, NY, Cornell University Press.

Tolkien, J.R.R. (1993 edn, 1999 edn) *The Fellowship of the Ring: Lord of the Rings part I*. London, HarperCollins.

Tuan, Y-F. (1977) *Space and Place: the Perspective of Experience*. London, Edward Arnold.

Tuchman, G. (1978) *Making News: A Study in the Construction of Reality*. New York, The Free Press.

Turnbull, D. (1993) *Maps are Territories: Science is an Atlas*. Chicago, Chicago University Press.

Tuson, R. (1998) 'Mutiny narratives and the imperial feminine: European women's accounts of the rebellion in India in 1857', *Women's Studies International Forum* 21: 291–303.

Urry, J. (1990) *The Tourist Gaze: Leisure and Travel in Contemporary Societies*. London, Sage.

Urry, J. (1992) 'The Tourist Gaze "Revisited" ', *American Behavioural Scientist* 36: 172–86.

Valentine, G (1997) 'Tell me about … :using interviews as a research methodology', in Flowerdew, R. and Martin, D. (eds) *Methods in Human Geography: A Guide for Students Doing Research Projects*. Essex, Longman: 111–26.

Valentine, G. (1993) '(Hetero)sexing space: lesbian perceptions and experiences of everyday spaces'. *Environment and Planning D: Society and Space* 11: 395–413.

Valentine, G. (1993) 'Negotiating and managing multiple sexual identities: lesbian time-space strategies', *Transactions of the Institute of British Geographers* 18: 237–48.

Valentine, G. (1995) 'Creating transgressive space: the music of kd lang', *Transactions of the Institute of British Geographers* 20: 474–85.

Valentine, G. (1996) '(Re)negotiating the 'heterosexual street': lesbian productions of space', In Duncan, N. (ed.) *BodySpace: Destablizing Geographies of Gender and Sexuality*. London, Routledge: pp. 146–55.

Valentine, G. (1998) 'Sticks and stones may break my bones: a personal geography of harassment'. *Antipode* 30: 305–32.

Valentine, G. (1999) 'A corporeal geography of consumption', *Environment and Planning D: Society and Space* 17: 329–51.

Valentine, G. (2002) 'People like us: negotiating sameness and difference in the research process' in Moss. P. (ed.) *Feminist Geography in Practice: Research and Methods*. Oxford, Blackwell: 116–27.

Veijola, S. and Jokinen, E. (1994) 'The body in tourism', *Theory, Culture and Society* 11: 125–51.

Vujakovic, P. (1998) 'Reading between the lines: using news media materials for geography', in *Journal of Geography in Higher Education Study Guide*, London, Carfax.

Wainwright, H. (1997) 'In the neighborhood: a critique of social activist art', *Public Art Review* (Fall/Winter): 16–20.

Wakeford, N. (1999) 'Gender and the landscapes of computing in an internet cafe', in Crang, M. Crang, P. and May, J. (eds) *Virtual Geographies: Bodies, Spaces, Relations*. London, Routledge: 178–201.

Walter, B. (2001) *Outsiders Inside: Whiteness, Place and Irish Women*. London, Routledge.

Ward, B. (1998) *Just My Soul Responding: Rhythm and Blues, Black Consciousness and Race Relations*. London, UCL Press.

Watson, S. (1991) 'Gilding the smokestacks: the new symbolic representations of deindustrialised regions'. *Environment and Planning D: Society and Space* 9: 59–70.

Webster, W. (1998) *Imagining Home: Gender, 'Race' and National Identity, 1945–64*. London, UCL Press.

Weedon, C. (1987) *Feminist Practice and Poststructuralist Theory*. Oxford, Blackwell.

Weedon, C. (1999) *Feminism, Theory and the Politics of Difference*. Oxford, Blackwell.

Weideger, P. (1991) 'Larger than life tribute to Brum's golden age'. *The Independent* (8 June): 14.

Weiner, M. (1997) *A Heritage of Woe: The Civil War Diary of Grace Brown Elmore, 1861–1868*. Athens GA, The University of Georgia Press.

Weinreb, B. and Hibbert, C. (eds) (1983) *The London Encyclopaedia*. London, Macmillan.

West, R. (1988) 'The making of the English working past: a critical view of the Ironbridge Gorge museum', in Lumley, R. (ed.) *The Museum Time Machine: Putting Cultures on Display*. London, Comedia: 36–62.

West, R. C. (1975) 'The Interlace Structure of The Lord of the Rings', in Lobdell, J. *A Tolkien Compass: Including J. R. R. Tolkien's Guide to Names in The Lord of the Rings*. Illinois, Open Court Publishing: 77–94.

Wexler, J. (1993) *Rhythm and the Blues: A Life in American Music*. New York, Alfred A. Knopf.

Wexler, J. (2000) *Tender Violence: Domestic Visions in an Age of US Imperialism*. Chapel Hill, University of North Carolina Press.

WGSG (Women and Geography Study Group) (1997) *Feminist Geographies: Explorations in Diversity and Difference*. Harlow, Longman.

Whatmore, S. (1999a) 'Culture-nature', in Cloke, P., Crang, P. and Goodwin, M. (eds) *Introducing Human Geographies*. London, Arnold: 4–11.

Whatmore, S. (1999b) 'Hybrid geographies', in Massey, D., Allen, J. and Sarre, P. (eds) *Human Geography Today*. Cambridge, Polity: 22–40.

Whatmore, S. and Thorne, L. (2000) 'Elephants on the move: spatial formations of wildlife exchange', *Environment and Planning D-Society and Space* 18: 185–203.

Wheeler, J.T. (1861) *Handbook to the Madras Records*. Madras, Government Press.

Wheen, F. (1999) *Karl Marx*. London, Fourth Estate.

Whelan, Y. (2002) 'The construction and destruction of a colonial landscape: monuments to British monarchs in Dublin before and after independence' *Journal of Historical Geography* 28: 508–33.

Whitlock, G. (2000) *The Intimate Empire: Reading Women's Autobiography*. London, Cassell.

Wiener, M.J. (1981) *English Culture and the Decline of the Industrial Spirit, 1850–1980*. Cambridge, Cambridge University Press.

Wilcock, E. (1997) 'Adorno, jazz and racism: über jazz and the 1934–7 British jazz debate'. *Telos*. 107: 63–80.

Wilkins, M. (1970) *The Emergence of Multinational Enterprise: American Business Abroad from the Colonial Era to 1914*. Cambridge, Harvard University Press.

Williams, R. (1990 [1975]) *Television, Technology and Cultural Form*. London, Routledge.

Williams-Ellis, C. (1928) *England and the Octopus*. London, Geoffrey Bles.

Williams-Ellis, C. (1929a) 'The ruin of the countryside', *Socialist Review* March, 24–5.

Williams-Ellis, C. (1929b) 'England's beauty limited', *The Spectator* 16th November.

Williams-Ellis, C. (1932) 'An owner-developer's creed' in N. Carrington (ed.) *Portmeirion Explained: Essays by Several Hands with Pictures*. Birmingham, Kynoch Press, 11–16.

Williams-Ellis, C. (1976) *Portmeirion: The Place and its Meaning*. Portmeirion, Portmeirion Ltd.

Williams-Ellis, C. (1980) *Architect Errant: The Autobiography of Clough Williams-Ellis*. Portmeirion, Golden Dragon Books.

Williams-Ellis, C. (ed.) (1937) *Britain and the Beast*. London, Dent.

Williams-Ellis, C. and Williams-Ellis, A. (1924) *The Pleasures of Architecture*. London, Jonathan Cape.

Willis, K. and Yeoh, B. (eds) (2000) *Gender and Migration*. Cheltenham, Edward Elgar.

Wilson, C. and Groth, P. (eds) (2003) *Everyday America: Cultural Landscape Studies after J.B. Jackson*. Berkeley, University of California Press.

Winchester, H. and White, P. (1988) 'The location of marginalized groups in the inner city', *Environment and Planning D: Society and Space* 6: 37–54.

Wolf, D. (1992) *Factory Daughters: Gender, Household Dynamics and Rural Industrialization in Java*. Berkeley, University of California Press.

Wolf, D. (ed.) (1996) *Feminist Dilemmas in Fieldwork*. Boulder, CO, Westview Press.

Wood, D. (1993) *The Power of Maps*. London, Routledge.

Wood, D. (1978) 'Introducing the cartography of reality'. In Ley, D. and Samuels, M. (eds) *Humanistic Geography: Prospects and Problems*. London, Croom Helm: 207–19.

Worpole, K. (2000) *Here Comes the Sun: Architecture and Public Space in 20th Century European Culture*. London, Reaktion.

Worswick, C. and Embree, A. (1977) *The Last Empire: Photography in British India, 1855–1911*. New York, Aperture.

Wylie, J (2000) 'New and old worlds: the Tempest and early colonial discourse', *Social and Cultural Geography* 1: 45–63.

Yamaguchi, M. (1991). 'The poetics of exhibition in Japanese culture', in Karp, I. and Lavine, S. (eds) *Exhibiting Cultures: The Politics and Poetics of Museum Display*. Washington, DC, Smithsonian Press: pp. 57–67.

Yeoh, B. S. A. and Huang, S. (2000) ' "Home" and "away": foreign domestic workers and negotiations of diasporic identity in Singapore', *Women's Studies International Forum* 23: 413–29.

Young, I. M. (1990) *Justice and the Politics of Difference*. Princeton, Princeton University Press.

Young, I. M. (1997) 'House and home: feminist variations on a theme'. In I. M. Young, *Intersecting Voices: Dilemmas of Gender*. Princeton, Princeton University Press: 134–64.

Younger, C. (1987) *Anglo-Indians: Neglected Children of the Raj*. New Delhi, BR Publishing Corporation.

Zukin, S. (1991) *Landscapes of Power: From Detroit to Disney World*. Berkeley, University of California Press.

Index

NOTE: Page numbers in *italic type* refer to figures or tables, page numbers in **bold type** refer to concept boxes.

Lightning Source UK Ltd.
Milton Keynes UK
UKOW05f0757240815

257373UK00009B/139/P